Renaissance Europe 1480–1520

Blackwell Classic Histories of Europe

This series comprises new editions of seminal histories of Europe. Written by the leading scholars of their generation, the books represent both major works of historical analysis and interpretation and clear, authoritative overviews of the major periods of European history. All the volumes have been revised for inclusion in the series and include updated material to aid further study. *Blackwell Classic Histories of Europe* provides a forum in which these key works can continue to be enjoyed by scholars, students and general readers alike.

Published

Europe: Hierarchy and Revolt 1320–1480
Second Edition
George Holmes

Renaissance Europe 1480–1520
Second Edition
John Hale

Reformation Europe 1517–1559
Second Edition
G. R. Elton

Europe Divided: 1559–1598
Second Edition
J. H. Elliott

Europe Transformed: 1878–1919
Second Edition
Norman Stone

Forthcoming

Europe in Crisis: 1598–1648
Second Edition
Geoffrey Parker

Europe Unfolding: 1648–1688
Second Edition
John Stoye

Europe: Privilege and Protest 1730–1798
Second Edition
Olwen Hufton

Revolutionary Europe 1783–1815
Second Edition
George Rudé

RENAISSANCE EUROPE
1480–1520
Second Edition

J. R. Hale

*With an Additional Bibliography
by Michael Mallett*

BLACKWELL
Publishers

BLACKWELL PUBLISHING
350 Main Street, Malden, MA 02148-5020, USA
9600 Garsington Road, Oxford OX4 2DQ, UK
550 Swanston Street, Carlton, Victoria 3053, Australia

First published 1971 by Fontana Books
Second edition published 2000 by Blackwell Publishers Ltd

2 2005

Library of Congress Cataloging-in-Publication Data

Hale, J. R. (John Rigby), 1923–
    Renaissance Europe, 1480–1520 / J. R. Hale. — 2nd ed.
        p.   cm. — (Blackwell classic histories of Europe)
    Includes bibliographical references and index.
    ISBN 0-631-21624-3 (alk. paper) — ISBN 0-631-21625-1 (pbk. : alk. paper)
        1. Europe—History—1492–1517. 2. Renaissance. I. Title. II. Series.

D228 H23 2000
940.2′1 — dc21
                                                                    99-089393

ISBN-13: 978-0-631-21624-7 (alk. paper); ISBN-13: 978-0-631-21625-4 (pbk. : alk. paper)

A catalogue record for this title is available from the British Library.

Set in 10.5 on 12 pt, Sabon
by Kolam Information Services Pvt Ltd, Pondicherry, India

For further information on Blackwell Publishing, visit our website:
www.blackwellpublishing.com

Contents

Preface to the Second Edition
by Michael Mallett

I had undertaken the task of revising John Hale's 1971 textbook before his death in August of this year, but already he was unable to contribute significantly to the work of revision because of the serious stroke which he had suffered in 1992. However, his last book, *The Civilisation of Europe in the Renaissance*, published in 1993, was in many ways an extended reworking of the themes already explored in *Renaissance Europe*. The emphases and enthusiasms had changed little in the intervening years; the insistence that the Renaissance was essentially a European movement and not just an Italian one crossing the Alps and the Mediterranean became even more apparent in the later work, as did the emphasis on the half-century before the Reformation as the last moment of a united Christian Europe. Having the *Civilisation* by my side has enabled me to reflect with greater confidence on how John himself would have set about revising his earlier work.

The intention of the publishers in preparing these revised editions of volumes of the Fontana History of Europe has been to leave the original texts largely intact and to focus the process of updating on new prefaces and additional bibliographies. I have, therefore, made very few amendments to the text and have used this preface for a discussion of some of the issues that have emerged in recent research and debate. The bibliography has been substantially expanded and the criteria which I have used for doing that are explained at the appropriate point.

John Hale in his preface wrote of the Renaissance as 'the most glamorous piece of shorthand in historical language'. However, despite a long tradition of enthusiasm for, and writing about, Renaissance Italy, English professional historians have always had difficulty with the idea of a Renaissance historical 'period', something between Middle Ages and Early Modern, between Plantagenet and Lancastrian, and Tudor. Denys Hay once remarked on the difficulties of being a Renaissance historian in Britain where the strong traditions of medieval history and of Tudor and Stuart history left little opportunity for the Renaissance specialist, particularly the Italian Renaissance specialist. Hale never had quite the same problem as his main interests lay firmly in the sixteenth century; his Renaissance was always European as much as Italian. But, nevertheless, his involvement with and passion for Italy led him to look beyond the generation of Erasmus and Thomas More, of Leonardo da Vinci, Raphael, Dürer and Michelangelo, for his encapsulation of Renaissance Europe. The year 1500 was the convenient crossover point in most British textbooks for the transition from Middle Ages to Early Modern Europe. This coincided conveniently with the 'Age of Discovery' and the opening of a wider world to European curiosity and exploitation, but, as Hale pointed out, the initial impact of the voyages of Columbus and Vasco de Gama was almost imperceptible in economic and political terms. It also provided a satisfactory time-frame for getting on with the real business of the Reformation. A quick chapter on humanism and reform, a disparaging glance at the corruption and worldliness of early sixteenth-century Rome, the root of all the trouble, and the traditional textbooks took off into the key issues of the sixteenth century – the religious divisions of Europe and the growth of nation states. Cultural history, in both the narrow and the broader senses of that term, played little part in such surveys.

Hale in *Renaissance Europe* broke significantly with this tradition of British textbook writing. He chose a starting date in the middle of the second half of the fifteenth century and ended with the excommunication of Martin Luther. Here was a chronology which seemed to separate Renaissance from Reformation, in conflict with hallowed North American traditions. But of course it did not; on the contrary it enabled Hale to study the road to Reformation in more detail with all the implications of emerging secularism, the rise of lay piety, religio-political confrontations with secular authorities in the process of consolidation, heightened international tensions and the growing confidence and authoritarianism of a renascent Papacy. It also enabled him to focus on key questions of social change in a rapidly advancing economic environment from the middle of the fifteenth century, and on the recovery of confidence of western European governments in the aftermath of the Hundred Years, War, the communal struggles in Italy, and the *reconquista* in Spain. Above all it enabled him to unfurl a new Burckhardtian banner of European Renaissance; not so much that of the Italians as 'the first-born among the sons of modern Europe' as a Europe relatively united by all sorts of cross-currents and influences in a cultural movement which we associate with the High Renaissance. This was the moment, Hale suggests, when maps began to be common and men were learning to conceptualise the space within which they lived. It was the moment when the words 'Europe' and 'European' began to acquire meaningful significance. It is interesting to note that textbooks spanning the 1500 divide have become more common since the 1970s despite continued doubts in some specialist circles about the validity of the concept of the Renaissance as an historical period (see below).

As Hale admitted in his preface, *Renaissance Europe* is also an unusual type of textbook. It is what he called 'majority history': an attempt to assess the mood, the attitudes, the beliefs, the culture, the state of mind in the broadest sense, of the times, organised into themes rather than chronological sections with their inevitable focus on events, dates and facts. This approach probably makes the book less accessible to the uninitiated, but stimulates and provokes those already familiar with the period. The problem, and for one charged with the task of revising the work the advantage, of this approach is a certain timelessness. Over and over again Hale empha-sises the degree of continuity with the earlier centuries in terms of popular attitudes and ideas, while at the same time he wants to suggest that in certain respects, and particularly in certain strata of society, this was a period of significant change. The blending of tradition and innovation is, of course, now an accepted key to the understanding of the Renaissance; Hale is springing no surprises when he emphasises the continued strength of the scholastic intellect-ual tradition, or the contrast between the conservatism of the Euro-pean countryside and the comparative social mobility and intellectual radicalism apparent in the rapidly expanding cities, or the tensions between an avant-garde classical revival culture and the long stirrings of vernacular cultures in the various parts of western Europe. But, inevitably, recognition of these tensions weakens the messages implied in periodisation.

The method chosen to conduct this enquiry into what it was like to live in Renaissance Europe also has its problems. Extended use of a brilliantly chosen range of quotations from contemporary sources – mostly, inevitably, the utterances of members of elite groups, literate, articulate, men, but also as far as possible reflections of lesser bour-geois and artisan opinions and ideas when these are recoverable, gives an entry to their world, a sense of what it was like to live and think and talk in the Renaissance. But at the same time the purist would argue that opinions, individual points of view, are less certifi-able than facts, than signatures on documents, outcomes of battles, etc. In response to this Hale would have suggested, with some justification, that frequently expressed ideas are just as cogent and verifiable as wills and treaties, which are themselves often subjected to intense historical scrutiny as to what precisely was their intention and effect. The evidence of Hale's continued belief in his approach lies in the extent to which he continued to use it in *Civilisation*, and this confirms a view that Renaissance Europe would not have come out very differently had he written it today.

Much has been written on the Renaissance since 1971 and some of the recent debates will be briefly discussed in these pages. However, the task of revising *Renaissance Europe* has not been a difficult one because of the timelessness of the work. Historical reinterpretation is mostly about the causes and effects of events and human actions. Hale's tapestry may have threads unpicked, or it may be thrown away entire, but the basic design and impact is not going to change. There have, of course, been whole new areas of research and debate opened up but they were on the whole anticipated by Hale. He was, for example, already heavily influenced by the writings of the French *Annales* school in the early 1970s, before Fernand Braudel's *Mediterranean* was translated into English. The emphasis on socio-economic structures and the importance of the *longue-durée* was very apparent in *Renaissance Europe*. Braudel's 'long sixteenth century' overlapping into both the fifteenth and the seventeenth centuries was already a familiar idea, just as was the interest in social history and the 'forgotten classes'. It is worth remembering that John Hale and Edward Thompson were colleagues at the University of Warwick in the late 1960s, and in their very different periods they had many historical interests in common. It is unlikely, therefore, that the flood of writing which was to come in the next two decades on aspects of popular culture and popular belief would have much affected the balance which he achieved in *Renaissance Europe* between the driving force of elite initiatives and the responses of the rest of the population.

Hale was also well aware in 1971 of the emerging debates about the history of women, and he anticipated in his discussion of the topic in this book the thesis of Joan Kelly, published in 1977 ('Did Women have a Renaissance' in Bridenthal and Koonz, cit. in the bibliography), that the Renaissance was actually a low point in terms of women's rights and levels of participation in public life. It is certainly true that the debate has become more nuanced since the 1970s and this book would not accept a decline in the status of women quite so easily if written today (see p. 91).

Another area in which John Hale was able to anticipate a main stream of later writing was that of warfare. Here he has been one of the leaders in an historical movement to re-examine the role of war in history, and his emphasis on the impact of war in this book, not just in terms of mortality and damage, but also in terms of changing institutions and attitudes, remains very influential. The rapid developments in international relations, diplomacy and war during these years round 1500 provide one of the strongest supports for the periodisation, and the term 'Military Revolution', or 'Military

Reformation' as Hale preferred to call it in his later work, which would undoubtedly have appeared in any revised text. The real significance of the expansion of armies and the growing involvement of mass infantry and gunpowder weapons in this period has still to be fully explored, but the paramount importance that Hale attributed to this sector remains undisputed.

In a number of other, less obvious, areas Hale signposted the way that historical interests were going in the early 1970s. His discussion of the interactions of political centralisation and emergent national feeling with regional structures and identities still stands as an effective introduction to what is a major field of research. His emphasis on emerging bureaucracy as both an instrument of political power and as a factor in social mobility appeared again in *Civilisation* as fresh and as caustic as in 1971: 'the non-ministerial bureaucrat pushed aside the medieval arras behind which his shadowy existence had been passed, and strode with confidence down the corridors of power...'. The fact that he put music and theatre ahead of painting, sculpture and architecture in his discussion of the arts also anticipated a growing focus on those areas. By contrast there are certainly sections of this book that would appear a little different if written today; economic growth in the later fifteenth century would be more emphasised, the development of international diplomacy would be described in terms less dependent on Mattingly's *Renaissance Diplomacy*, the growth of consumerism and collecting would figure more largely in the discussion of the arts, and Renaissance science would get a more prominent billing.

These are all, however, matters of nuances and emphases; the crucial question to address concerns the whole intention of the book and Hale's view of the significance and role of the Renaissance. During the period since he wrote, and particularly in the 1990s, American historians of the Renaissance have become involved in heated debates over the use of the term Renaissance. This has been perhaps as much a reaction to the great importance traditionally given to the period and the culture in the popular Western Civilisation courses at American universities as it is one to surviving Burckhardtian ideas. Hale, as we have seen, was much attuned to the ideas of Burckhardt, to the belief in a transformation of cultural ideas and style – in state of mind – sufficiently dramatic to warrant the linking of the term Renaissance to a historical period. *Renaissance Europe* proposes a very limited period, as opposed to the three centuries from 1300 to 1600 favoured by some, and suggests that the relatively brief moment of European cultural unanimity, if that is not too strong a word, was as much due to similar socio-economic and political forces at work in different parts of Europe as it was to

Italian cultural leadership. However, doubters in America, stimulated by William Bouwsma's famous presidential address to the American Historical Association in 1978 ('Renaissance and the Drama of Western History', *American Historical Review*, 84, Feb. 1979) have launched a fierce attack on the coherence of the Renaissance as an historical period and to a lesser extent on the value of studying it at all. Bouwsma lamented that 'the venerable Renaissance label has become little more than an administrative convenience, a kind of blanket under which we huddle together, less out of mutual attraction than because for certain purposes we have nowhere else to go'. This sense of disorientation and pessimism was partly the result of the growing reluctance of many modern historians to accept the birthplace of the modern world in the pre-industrial era, but more importantly of the growth of interest in the history of the lower classes, the underprivileged, the poor, the illiterate, as opposed to the focus on elites which was an essential part of the idea of the Renaissance. A particularly underprivileged group were women and the publication of Joan Kelly's essay in 1977 (see above) with its implications of a decline in the status of women in the fifteenth and sixteenth centuries added another strand to the argument.

It has to be said that Hale seems to have had little time for these worries and criticisms; neither the Bouwsma address nor the Kelly article appear in the bibliography of *Civilisation*. Indeed, as has already been suggested, his 1971 synthesis is filled with references to the roles and attitudes of the underprivileged classes, in so far as it remains possible to perceive them in this period, and he has a section on gender in which the ideas of Kelly were anticipated. It also has to be said that since *Civilisation* was published in 1993 the tide of the debate has somewhat turned. Renaissance scholars other than the historians have closed ranks behind the banner of interdisciplinary methodologies and cultural history to give new life to the idea of a widely accepted culture having a genuinely transformative influence on broader ideas and attitudes. A new emphasis on humanism as an attempt to recover the spirit and culture of the past and to utilise it to revitalise and redirect contemporary culture, and on demand and consumerism as essential factors in the artistic innovations of the Renaissance, are positive results of this debate (see 'The AHR. Forum', *American Historical Review*, 103, 1998, pp. 57–124). Perhaps it is sufficient to say that the Renaissance remains *a* defining moment in the history of Europe, and indeed in world history, rather than *the* defining moment which enthusiasts have sometimes claimed.

Michael Mallett
Cumbria, October 1999

Preface to the First Edition

This book is planned on somewhat different lines from its companions in the Fontana History of Europe. While not ignoring the events on which a sense of chronology depends, it aims chiefly at providing a means of understanding the quality of the lives of as many people as the nature of the surviving evidence and the limitations of my own knowledge make possible. It is concerned with material circumstance but also with states of mind, not only to record what happened in the forty years from 1480 to 1520 but, and with greater emphasis, to suggest what it was like to have lived then.

Each chapter is designed to provide information about a specific field of inquiry and at the same time to offer an answer to certain basic questions that must be asked in order to understand men of any period. What were their feelings about the passage of time and about their environment? What sort of polity did they live within and what sense of relationship did they have with it and with other communities ranging in size all the way from the family to Christendom? Within what general economic framework and in what ways did they earn a living? How did they regard themselves and others in terms of status, occupation and living standards? What part did religion play in their lives, and what cultural and intellectual satisfactions were open to them?

I hope I am sufficiently aware of the danger of pretension which hangs over such an approach. But there are other hazards to which the reader should be alert. The evidence from which 'states of mind' at this period can be reconstructed is patchy and extremely difficult to assess; decisions about what evidence to use as well as what areas of experience to explore are ominously subjective. The desire to appraise the feelings of majorities means blurring the inexhaustible variety of individual reactions. Finally, this approach reduces the interest that comes to the reader of history from continuous narrative, full-scale portraiture and realistic close-ups of the intricacies of public affairs.

Much is lost, in fact, and much put at risk. But personal bias apart, I think that the gains of this approach (which, of course, is in no way

original) as an introduction to a period can out-weigh the losses.
'Renaissance' is the most glamorous piece of shorthand in historical
language, and these years – with America brought enduringly into
contact with Europe, with Borgia, della Rovere and Medici popes,
with thinkers and artists of the calibre of Machiavelli and Erasmus,
Leonardo, Michelangelo and Dürer – are the most glamorous of the
Renaissance. Their historian has a special responsibility to deepen his
focus to include processes and personalities other than those which in
the long course of historiographical inquiry have become almost self-
selecting. Majority history also helps to correct the latent Whiggish-
ness of popular tradition by relating 'events' to their contemporary
audience. The discovery of America for instance was of interest only
to a tiny minority in this period;* Machiavelli was not a name to
conjure with because his political works, though written, were not
published; the role of papal nepotism, militancy and cultural extravagance in undermining respect for the authority of Rome must be
measured in terms of who could have known about it and to what
extent they would have cared.

Finally, the demand for 'relevance' in what is studied has its lazy,
philistine and intolerant sides. But relevance has always been sought
by readers if not (for good reasons) by writers of history, for without
a knowledge of his links to the past man is a social amnesiac,
intellectually and therefore to some extent emotionally rootless.
And for many the sort of relevance that encourages the pursuit of
this knowledge is not so much to be found in looking to the past for
situations analogous to our own or, still less, for solutions to present
problems, as in making it possible to compare our own attitudes to
questions of basic concern (social justice, say, or love, or the response
to works of art) with those of past ages, and, vice versa, to review
past attitudes in order to wonder afresh about our own.

This, at least, has been my experience as a teacher of Renaissance
history here and in the United States, and my first acknowledgement
of indebtedness is to my students at Warwick and Berkeley. I also owe
a great deal to the encouragement of Professor G. R. Potter, who read
the hideous bulk of the first draft as well as the proofs, to the firm
and sympathetic guidance I received from Professor J. H. Plumb and
to the detailed advice as well as the exemplary patience of Mr.
Richard Ollard.

---

* See J. H. Elliott, *The old world and the new* (Cambridge, 1969) esp. ch. 1.

I

Time and Space

Calendar, Clock and Life Span

'O slow-moving clock', exclaimed the infatuated hero of Fernando de Rojas's romance *La Celestina*, 'would I could see you burned with the sharp fires of love! If you expected the same joys as I at midnight, you would cease to obey the will of the craftsman who made you... But what am I demanding?... There is a fixed period for the secret revolutions of the celestial firmament, the planets and the north star, and for the monthly waxing and waning of the moon... What would it profit me that my iron clock struck twelve, if the heavenly clock did not agree?'*

This comparison of clock time with natural time was no mere trope. Though clocks had long ceased to be a novelty, for most men time meant the length of a task within the context of sunlight and season. Nature set the alarm and measured the day. 'At dawn', 'about noon', 'towards sunset': these were still the commonest references to time. The month was seen in terms of its characteristic rural activity within a calendar of survival. Emotionally, the year began with the first flowers, the lengthening of the day, the first judgement on the fortune of the winter-sown grain. Only those concerned with legal or diplomatic documents thought of the year as beginning on an official rather than a seasonal date, and even here there was no uniformity, the date on which a new year started varying, country by country, from December 25th to January 1st, March 1st, March 25th and September 1st. It could vary in this way from city to city and even for different types of documents within one city: in Rome bulls were dated according to a year that began on March 25th, papal letters according to a year starting on December 25TH.

The most commonly used New Year's days corresponded with church festivals: the Annunciation, the Nativity and, in parts of France, the beginning of Easter. The church's calendar, in fact, played

---

* Here, as elsewhere, I quote from the translation by C. M. Cohen, *The Spanish Bawd* (London, 1964).

a part second only to that of nature in determining the notion of time, from the division of the day into observances to the spacing of the major festivals throughout the year. Rents were paid not from September 29th but from St. Michael's day, the Sorbonne commenced not on November 12th but on 'the day after the feast of St. Martin'. Though chronicles came increasingly to use dates the two ways of reckoning continued to exist side by side. According to *The Great Chronicle of London* the Anglo-Scottish peace of 1499 was proclaimed 'upon Saint Nicholas day, or the VIth day of December', and the outbreak of fire at Sheen, where the king was holding his Christmas court, took place 'upon the night following Saint Thomas' day the martyr'. And more meaningful than the division of the day into hours was its division into meals. Season, church service and stomach, these spaced the routines of the rural year. With night-time perilous and illumination expensive, these routines were restricted as much as possible to daylight, pressed together in winter and spaced out again in summer. Churches and monasteries kept the canonical hours for their services, but these 'hours' were compressed in winter to get twelve into the day, however short.

This attitude to time, however, did not suffice the commercial towns, where the hour could be a measure of production and a day could mean the difference between one exchange rate and another. Time was accordingly measured in equal hours and by clocks. In the country schoolboys assembled for their lessons an hour after dawn. In the town, as one of Erasmus' *Colloquies* shows, matters were more precisely ordered.

> Unless I'm there before roll's called I'll get a hiding. Not the slightest danger on that score. It's just half past five. Look at the clock: the hand hasn't yet touched the half-hour point.

After their slow introduction from the fourteenth century, clocks were striking the hours in towns all over Europe. The system of counting them, however, differed. In Italy clocks struck from 1 to 24 starting at sunset, in Germany from 1 to 24 starting at sunrise, in England and Flanders from 1 to 12 starting at midday and midnight. Every town had its own time based on the moment when the sun dipped behind, or rose above its own particular local horizon. Though many clocks struck the hour, fewer had a minute hand, very few indeed struck the quarters. And all were inaccurate and required frequent resetting. Though the clock with its equal hours did help to introduce a different concept of time, we must not see the contrast in terms of the conflict between the times of the sun and of the machine, the 'natural' tempo of the countryside and the

'unnatural' one of the town, that characterised the Industrial Revolution. Many small villages in France and the Low Countries possessed
public clocks. A petition of 1481 urging the town council of Lyons to
install 'a great clock whose strokes could be heard by all citizens in
all parts of the town', pointed out that 'if such a clock were to be
made, more merchants would come to the fair', but other reasons too
were offered: 'the citizens would be very consoled, cheerful and
happy and would live a more orderly life and the town would gain
in decoration'. Moreover, certain routines, like the changing of the
watch in garrison towns, the closing of city gates for the night and the
establishment of a curfew hour after which crimes were punished by
a double or even a quadruple penalty, called for accurate time-
keeping. In the towns men made appointments and attended
meetings: clocks expressed the social convenience of a common and
precise vocabulary of time as well as an attitude to the spacing of the
day in the interest of profit. The large public sundial set on the façade
of a medieval church or city hall and the pocket dial: these had told
the time almost as effectively, if with less insistence. The multiplying
of clocks and the introduction at this time of portable clocks and
spring-driven watches (even more inaccurate than town clocks)
reflected fashion as well as need. Antonio de Beatis, who accompanied the cardinal of Aragon on a European tour in 1517–18, noted
that he ordered watches and other complicated gadgets in metal work
at Nuremberg to serve as presents for non-capitalist dignitaries. The
consciousness of the pace of a working day may indeed have been
enhanced by all these reminders that time was passing, but the cult of
work and the scourging of sloth had been features of the early middle
ages, and *nulla dies sine linea* antedates the invention of double-entry
bookkeeping. It could even be urged that clock time, far from being a
symbol of capitalism, actually protected the artisan by making his
statutory working times more precise. The lunch break of the fullers
of Orleans was newly spelled out, for instance, as one full hour
before and one full hour after noon. Nor is there evidence that
working hours increased because employers had clocks in their
shops and homes. In Paris, as well-equipped with clocks as any
European city, when the statutes governing the working conditions
of the leather softeners were revised, the pre-clock wording was
reproduced intact: they were to work from dawn to dusk 'at such
time that one can only just distinguish the coins of Tours from those
of Paris'. Nor were holidays cut short by an invasion of clock into
church time. Though the two-day working week on their island
dependency of Skyros was a scandal to the Venetians, who kept
250 working days in the year, holiday on Sundays and saints' days
(with a half-holiday before them for confession) continued to keep

the average working year in Europe to some 200 days, and though there was possibly some increase in nightwork, particularly among the more recent trades like printing, for most men work still stopped when the sun went down.

Just as there was a natural rhythm for the day and an artificial one spaced by the town clock, and a seasonal as well as an official year, so there was both a natural and an official time span for a man's life. Apart from some of the Italian cities, births were seldom recorded with any regularity (the chief reason why demographic work on this period is so inexact) and most men were uncertain of their own age. Entirely typical is this list of witnesses to an assault made on a party of travelling merchants south of Paris: 'Jehan Gefroy, labourer, age about 40 years... Queriot Nichalet, butcher, age about 60... Pernet Callet, labourer, age about 27, Colin Byson, householder, age about 80,' Yet for organisational purposes governments had to assume a precision that did not exist. When an army had to be raised, the ages for enlistment were carefully spelled out. The upper limit at which men were assumed to be fit for military service was commonly 60, the lower limit varied with the urgency of the situation from 20 to 15. For taxation purposes the lowest chargeable age was also spelled out, commonly as low as 15.

In Florence a man came politically of age at 14: at that age he could be summoned to attend a *parlamento*. There, as elsewhere, minimum age limits were set to appointments to the various organs of government, and to the period of reduced penalties 'propter aetatis imbecillitatem' in the administration of criminal law. Manuals for confessors named 14 as the age when a knowledge of the nature of mortal sin might be assumed. During the controversy about the forcible baptism of Jewish children, 12 was named as the minimum age at which this might be permitted. Legal majority differed from place to place but was always clearly defined, so was the age at which a young prince could dispense with a regency or at which a feudal dependant had to pay homage or a ward could resume his inheritance.

Yet even at these upper reaches of society uncertainty about age was common, especially outside Italy. One of the seamiest lawsuits of the age was the attempt of Charles VIII's successor, Louis XII of France, to obtain an annulment of his marriage so that he could marry Charles' widow Anne instead, thereby preventing her from withdrawing her duchy of Brittany from the jurisdiction of the French crown. Louis claimed, with the wealth of physical detail required to sustain his accusation of malformation, that he had been unable to have sexual relations with his wife. This was not only an unpleasant, but an uncertain charge. Jeanne was able to produce evidence to the contrary including witnesses who swore that the king had come in one morning saying, 'I have earned, and well earned a drink, for I mounted my wife three or four times during the night.' Louis also pleaded that his own performance had been impeded by witchcraft. In that case, answered Jeanne, how was he able to know what it was like to try to make love to her? The king's case was so weak that if the Pope, Alexander VI, had not been committed to granting the annulment for political purposes, he would have lost it. But he was forced into this dubious territory for one reason: he was, in fact, closely enough related to Jeanne to have obtained an annulment on this ground alone – but he could not prove it. All he could do was produce witnesses to say that 'in their opinion' or 'in their experience, having lived then at the court' the various linking marriages had taken place. Chronicles, too, were invoked, but in vain: there was no documentary proof. And it was the same when Louis thought of pleading that he had been under the age of consent – fourteen – when the union was forced on him. He could not prove it because there was no certainty about when he had been born. He claimed that he had been twelve, but he could name neither his birthday, nor that of his wife. Witnesses varied in their estimates: the king 'must have been' 11, or $11\frac{1}{2}$, or 12 or 13. Others said that 'he must have been' under age because of what they remembered about his height and build. It was because of a clash between subjective and objective time that the king was forced into the muddy waters of his non-consummation suit.

Challenges to precision of this sort were uncommon in a relatively unbureaucratic age. A few tombs, a growing number of portraits gave the age of the defunct now that artists were technically able to produce a likeness fixing the image of a man as he was at a particular time. But this concern was limited to a few of the best educated sections of the community, men who were proud to relate their age to their achievements in business, scholarship or public affairs; the occasion for so precise a temporal perspective did not come the way of many. There was, on the other hand, a lively concern with age in a generalised, subjective sense. Fainter than the time imprint of nature and of worship on the day, but more meaningful for some than the time of the iron clock was physiological time, the succession of moods codified by the ancients into the system of humours and accepted by the medicine of the day: blood dominant from midnight to dawn, choler from dawn to noon, melancholy from noon till dusk and phlegm from dusk to midnight. Literature and sermon gave wide currency to the notion that life was measured less tellingly by years than by such stages as infancy, youth, maturity, old age and senility: stages all the more dramatic because malnutrition and disease compressed them into an average life expectancy of some 30 to 35 years, and among those who lived longer all but the rich began to take on the physical attributes of old age. Erasmus (who lived to be about 70) recorded gloomily that at 35 dried-up old age tires the body's strength. Priests found it difficult to obtain the services of housekeepers who had attained the no longer scandal-provoking age of 40. The Utopian people described in Antonio de Guevara's *Relox de Principes* (*c.* 1518) indeed, killed all their women at 40 and their men at 50 to save them from the weaknesses into which the aged lapsed.

Perhaps 50 per cent of children, and not only those of the poor, died in their first year. No special regard for childhood as a separate, precious state grew from this holocaust of infants. Children were dressed in adult styles and hurried into adult occupations. They were subjected to no special discipline nor were they insulated by nurseries and reticences from the pre-occupations of adults. Schooling was not taken for granted, it did not involve uniform or boarding or a special code of behaviour; at universities students were largely self-governing; no convention, but only circumstance, divided the carefree from the responsible years. The 'five ages' owed their poignancy to the fact that they were not related so closely to different moods and different sorts of activity as to the all-too-short passage of man's body from one form of helplessness to another. Generational time was haunted by the image of decrepit age, the crooked back and toothless grimace of a thousand carvings and caricatures. In painting, engraving and woodcut the legend of the Fountain of Life held out its illusory promise; from all directions greybeards came hobbling to drag themselves over its rim and tumble into its waters – there to be transformed into clean-shaven youths, grinning at the partners they clutch in greed to demonstrate their refound sexuality. The faintly pornographic air that exhales from tombs showing the dead as near skeletons, bellies crawling with worms; the boast with which Henry VIII slapped his thigh and crowed his virility to the Venetian ambassador; the satirical popular prints of old men ogling young brides; the splendour with which art invested taut muscle and firm flesh: all, under cover of morality or myth, or openly, were comments on the body on which time forced so swift a revenge. It was to discover the fountain of life that Ponce de Leon explored Florida. This is not to say that old men were a rarity. In the countryside there were many Queriot Nichalets, 'age about 60', many obscure Colin Bysons, 'age about 80'. Pope Alexander VI at 70 was described as growing 'younger every day; his cares never last the night through; he is always merry and never does anything he does not like'. The Venetian merchant Francesco Balbi kept his grip on affairs until he died at 84. As historiographer royal, Marineo Siculo toured the battlefields where Spanish troops had fought, breaking his arm on one such expedition at the age of 70, and he died, still writing, at 89. Much of Leonardo's anatomical work was based on his dissection of the corpse of a centenarian. It was not without cause that Cicero's *De Senectute* was one of the most frequently reprinted secular works of its day. Certainly old age was not so rare as to evoke a special respect for the lore and experience of the venerable. One of the most frequent exhortations of preachers, moralists and writers on etiquette was that the young should show more respect for the old.

Diet and Health

The consciousness of generational time was bound up with the material determinants of the span of life: diet, health and the incidence of violence. Each had a double effect: violence killed some but affected the outlook of more; bubonic plague, typhus and other diseases like the English sweat, killed many and poisoned the security of all; famines like those of 1502–3 and 1506–7 in Spain could depopulate whole regions whence the survivors, as a contemporary put it, 'wandered down the roads carrying their children, dead of hunger, on their backs'. The physical and nervous tone of life was conditioned by what men could afford to eat.

In many aspects of life, if only for a minority, this period was one of change, but diet constituted a drab and universal continuity with the Middle Ages. It was not only that food supplies were precarious, the possibility of starvation and the probability of a permanently enfeebling malnutrition omnipresent; at its best the diet of the majority was not calculated to build energy or preserve health but to produce the moods of nervy restlessness, the fits of panic that underlay some at least of the political discontent and the religious crazes of the time. Overwhelmingly it was a farinaceous diet: wheat, rye, barley, oats, millet; the commonest meal was bread floating in a thin vegetable soup. Fresh meat was eaten rarely, perhaps a dozen times a year by most families. Because of the concentration on cereals and the difficulty of keeping stock alive during the winter the animal population was small; butchers were only to be found in sizeable towns, their supplies were intermittent and their charges high. Milk and butter and the hard, keeping cheeses were all expensive and the poor townsmen probably never tasted them. Eggs and an occasional fowl provided the main variety in the country. A pig was more likely to be sent to town or the local manor for cash than eaten, because of the high cost of salting it. Game was jealously protected by the large

landowners. Fresh sea fish was of course available only near the coast
and it is doubtful whether salt fish played a part in the ordinary
man's diet; the costs of salting and transport meant that he normally
kept his Fridays and other fast days by not varying his normal
meatless diet. Rivers and lakes were fished – on the town wall of
Constance was a circle showing which fish was best to eat in each
month of the year – but fishing rights were restricted to the big
riparian landlords and much of the catch channelled to market or
to monastic or noble households.

The pattern varied widely. The alert and full-fleshed men and
women who gaze from their portraits did not owe their confidence
to bread and soup. Depending on soil and climate there were differences between one region and another and a much sharper difference
between the great house and the surrounding countryside and
between the country as a whole and the towns. The dependents of
a noble household might have meat every day – twice a day according
to the accounts of the Bavarian count Joachim von Gettingen, the
prosperous bourgeois housewife might use sugar from Sicily not as a
medicine, its normal use, but as a substitute for honey as a sweetener,
monastic gardens, well tended and properly manured, could produce
asparagus and artichokes and melons: but even though the contrast in
diet between rich and poor was extreme, even the most fortunate ate
frugally and monotonously by modern European standards, and the
bouts of indulgence which figure so largely in contemporary records
were given prominence because they contrasted with an abstemious-
ness fostered by high prices and scarcity. The raw glee with which the
aristocratic feast, with its gargantuan catalogue of meats and fowls
and fishes is described is not far in mood from the peasant orgy when
a wedding, a death or the harvest home was seized as an excuse to
take holiday from the workaday margins of existence. Not only
sermons but the stage took advantage of their aftermath of bastards,
broken heads and illnesses. In the play *A Condemnation of Feasting*
by Nicholas de la Chesnaye, a French doctor of civil and canon law,
DINNER, SUPPER and BANQUET invite GOURMAND, EPICURE,
PLEASURE, and GOOD COMPANY to eat. In the midst of their meal
they are attacked by a horde of sinister monsters: APOPLEXY,
PARALYSIS, EPILEPSY, PLEURISY, COLIC, and GOUT among
them. After a violent dance the gourmets expel their unwelcome
guests and repair from DINNER'S house to SUPPER'S where they
at once fall to again. The diseases once more invade their potations
and this time they are the victors. They have brought DAME
EXPERIENCE with them, and when GOOD COMPANY confesses
his fault, she hands him over to her servitors, PILL, ENEMA and
BLEEDING. SUPPER is sentenced never again to approach nearer

than six hours to DINNER and to wear bracelets of lead so that his hands will not fly so readily to his mouth. DINNER escapes with a scolding, but BANQUET, having confessed the grossness of his conduct, is ceremoniously hung by DIET as a warning to the audience.

It was a warning that few needed to take to heart, but it was repeated by inference in the legislation by which governments attempted to limit the number of dishes that might be served at weddings and other occasions of rejoicing; the consumption of the well-to-do must not be such as to excite the jealousy of the poor. The printing of cookery books, of which the English *Boke of Kerving* (1508) is an early example, suggests that among the reasonably wealthy a more sophisticated mean was becoming established between fast and feast; if we wish, however, to understand the sense of time as it is marked off by red-letter days, we must imagine a calendar of widely spaced and memorable excesses at the table.

No topic figured more consistently in royal and municipal legislation than attempts to keep down the price of bread, to prevent the forestalling of grain and to encourage the movement of supplies to areas of dearth. Of all food markets that of grain was most commonly overlooked architecturally, as well as administratively, by the town hall; grain stores, from the heavily barred magazines of the north to the underground silos of the Mediterranean islands, were as important to the preservation of law and order within the city as were its walls to protection from without. The fields yielded poorly, seldom enough to provide plenty for all. The landlord and the church took their portion before distribution could begin; poultry and livestock absorbed another fraction before the grain could move (were a surplus left from local needs) to market and to brewery – for throughout northern Europe, grain for drink competed strongly with grain for food. Of all the food products discovered in the Americas before the later importation of the potato it was maize that was seized on with the greatest avidity; from its introduction *c.* 1500 it began to spread from Spain across France, Italy and the Balkans. That a balanced diet was known to be desirable is shown from the stores taken on voyages of discovery. Da Gama's men had a daily allowance made up as follows: $1\frac{1}{2}$ pounds biscuit, 1 pound salt beef or $\frac{1}{2}$ pound salt pork, $\frac{1}{3}$ gill vinegar, $\frac{1}{6}$ gill olive oil, occasionally beans, lentils, onions or prunes, a daily $2\frac{1}{2}$ pints of water and $1\frac{1}{4}$ pints of wine. There were also large quantities of salt fish. Had such a diet, with the addition of fruit and fresh vegetables, been regularly available all over Europe it could have drastically altered the mental tone, the productivity and the longevity of the population.

As it was, men, women and children were highly vulnerable to disease. Domestic garbage had been tipped casually against the walls of Paris to such a height that they had in places to be dug free against the fear of an English attack in 1512. Erasmus ascribed the plague and sweating-sickness in England to the filth in the streets and the sputum and dogs' urine clogging the rushes strewn on the floors. But it is easy to exaggerate the unhygienic conditions of the towns. Most contained many open spaces, and the infrequency of paned windows meant that houses had a positively inconvenient amount of fresh air. In spite of, perhaps because of, the ineffectiveness of contemporary physicians, urbanised Europe had achieved a reasonably sophisticated standard of preventative medicine. Private charity and municipal commonsense had led to a generous provision of hospitals. Otherwise sweeping in his condemnation of Italy, Luther, during his visit there in 1511, recorded that 'the hospitals are handsomely built and admirably provided with excellent food and drink, careful attendants and learned physicians.' Hospitals probably effected few cures, but their value as isolation wards for the city as a whole was great. It was, indeed, by recognising the importance of isolation and quarantine – and by forbidding old-clothes dealers to sell garments that had been worn by sufferers – that leprosy had almost been conquered; in 1490 Pope Innocent dissolved the Order of Lazarists because the purpose for which they had been founded had come to an end.

Obstacles in the way of achieving personal hygiene were formidable. In Germany and some parts of Switzerland the maintenance of public baths set a high standard, but in countries without this subsidised and tradition-supported ritual the cost and inconvenience of heating water, and the high price of tallow- or olive oil-based soap meant that bodies went dirty to table and to bed. In some places it was the custom to wear a little piece of fur on the person as an encouragement to bugs to congregate there, in others mulberry twigs were put under the bed to divert the fleas: the wealthy Venetian Marco Falier noted in his household accounts in 1509 that he had renewed them at the cost of five *soldi*. Etiquette books reflected a growing concern for domestic hygiene: some were printed in verse to aid the memory, some were set to popular turnes, like the German *Tischzucht im Rosenton*. 'Your nose, your teeth, your nails from picking/Keep at your meat' advised an English work – and don't spit on the table.

When physicians were reduced to saying 'anyone who drinks half a spoonful of brandy every morning will never be ill' and housewives wisely preferred home-brewed elixirs to leech and lancet, it was the city fathers rather than the doctor who saved lives. Great care was taken, for example, that when meat was available it should not spread disease. The statutes (1514) of the butchers' guild of Chevreuse, a small town in the Île de France, specified, among other regulations, that any pig which had been reared on or near the premises of a barber's shop or smithy should be fed in a separate place for nine days (twenty, in the case of a hospital) before being killed. But no regulations were efficacious against plague. Houses were sealed off and identified with daubed crosses, the sale of infected clothing was forbidden, large bonfires were kept burning in every open space, sanitary inspectors searched for undisclosed sufferers, but nothing stopped the appearance of the blueish-black abscess in the arm-pit or the palm of the hand that was the herald of a few days of agony followed, probably in the majority of cases, by death. Venice, forced by constant commerce with the east to adopt the most stringent health regulations in Europe, was helpless before the plague; Titian's early masterpiece, St. Mark Enthroned, was painted as an *ex voto* after the plague of 1510 in which his young contemporary, Giorgione, died. In 1484 a schoolmaster in Deventer wrote to a friend, with revealing casualness: 'You ask how my school is doing. Well, it is full again now; but in summer the numbers rather fell off. The plague, which killed twenty of the boys, drove many others away, and doubtless kept some from coming to us at all.' Doctors debated the miasma theory against that of contagion, corrupt air against corrupt body, but their wisdom boiled down to one piece of advice: 'flee from such persons as be infect.' In was not necessary to read to follow this prescription. In the plague epidemics that struck France in 1493, 1497, 1518 and 1520, whole towns were evacuated, their inhabitants fleeing to forests and heathlands they would normally have shunned. There whole families starved to death and the French chronicler Jean d'Autun described how in yet another outbreak, in 1502, the king and his nobles were forced to organise hunts in order to save weakened refugees from being devoured by wolves.

This spectre was at least a habitual visitant. Syphilis, when it first struck Europe in 1494 (almost certainly brought in a virulent form from the New World) brought with it the terror of novelty. Its passage through Europe was frighteningly swift: from Naples it reached Bologna early in 1495 and crossed the Alps later that year as troops disbanded after the Italian campaign took it in all directions to their homes. By January 1496 it was described in Geneva and widely reported in France, before the end of the year it was in Holland and all over Germany; the first certain English mention was in 1497, by 1499 it had passed east of Prague. This transmission of the virus was rendered all the more disturbing by the publicity which press and woodcut were now able to provide. 'So repulsive is the appearance of the whole body', wrote a French doctor in 1495, 'so great is the agony, above all at night, that this malady surpasses in horror both leprosy and elephantiasis and threatens a man's life.' Preachers were not slow to welcome an ally to their rearguard action against illicit sex. Bishop Fisher of Rochester, in a sermon printed in 1509, described an England of men 'vexed with the French pox, poor and needy, lying by the highways stinking and almost rotten above the ground, having intolerable ache in their bones.' Nor did it spare the cultivated and wealthy. Konrad Celtis contracted it as early as 1496, his fellow humanist, Ulrich von Hutten, wrote a highly successful book about its cure but nevertheless died of it, Erasmus himself was a sufferer and so was Albert Dürer's friend and patron Willibald Pirckheimer. The number of bishops named raises the suspicion of gossip, but there is some cause to believe that Pope Julius II was syphilitic, even if this did little to daunt his heroic constitution. The disease, in fact, maimed far more victims than it killed, but its repulsiveness and the pain it caused sustained the horror that was felt.

Doctors were not slow to produce reasons, mainly astrological, for the outbreak of the scourge, together with remedies, though the first marginally effective one, the taking of mercury internally, was not proposed until 1512. Meanwhile public authorities took panic measures. In 1497 James IV of Scotland ordered all syphilitics into isolation on an island in the Firth of Forth. In Paris, early in the same year, notice was given by handbell throughout the streets that all infected residents were to repair to improvised quarantine quarters at S. Germain-des-Prés; all infected non-residents were to leave within 24 hours through two named gates where they were to sign for transport money and proceed at once to their homes. All this on pain of death. Such measures were too drastic to be taken seriously and the disease raged on through Europe as it was to rage through Polynesia some three centuries later. The German emperor Maximilian used syphilis as a sign that God, as the mystic year 1500 approached, was scourging mankind, and he urged his people to shun their evil ways and join the crusade he was attempting to raise against the Turks.

Violence and Death

To the uncertainty brought by disease to a man's estimate of his probable life span, violence, organised or casual, added another troubling dimension. The wars of this period were fought with far larger armies than had been raised hitherto and their laborious passage from one battlefield to another left a broad slime of distress where provision clerks had bullied, camp-followers stolen and soldiers looted. To casualties in combat, the slaughter of prisoners and the sacking of cities must be added the consequences of emptied village granaries, food scarcities and price rises that pushed thousands of non-combatants over the edge of subsistence into desperate want. Nor did the scourge of organised violence end here. Just as an army was laboriously built up of companies of men who traversed the country like legitimised bandits on their way to the point of assembly, at the disbanding of an army there were many who preferred the roving life of the would-be mercenary, who clotted into gangs and kept in touch with the possibility of employment through the rising class of military entrepreneurs, maintaining themselves in the interval by marauding. This was, of course, no new phenomenon. In 1477 a horde of young Swiss soldiers, discharged from the Burgundian wars, had vandalised their way from Lucerne to Geneva in a wave of looting. Christened 'the mad life', this mass delinquency reflected a problem with which no society was then fitted to cope: the reabsorbtion of its armed forces. Yet another cause of violence was the increasing effectiveness of attempts by governments to impose law and order. The bandits who swept down on travellers and held villages to ransom were not only the detritus of war but the waste products of de-feudalisation and centralisation, social unassimilables squeezed out by a closening contact between government and society as a whole. In addition to this displacement, violence could result wherever there was an attempt to alter old ways, from the murder in 1489 of the earl of Northumberland while trying to collect a royal tax in a Yorkshire village to the armed defiance with which the University of Paris tried to protect its exemptions from the law of the land.

The chief cause of urban violence was, however, sheer misery. Suspicion that merchants were hoarding grain against an increase in price or the rumour of a new impost could provoke popular outbursts of shopbreaking and arson. In France, the richest of European countries, there were riots of this sort in Bayonne in 1488, and in Montauban and Moissac in 1493. In 1500 the streets of Paris were overrun by men threatening to throw grain merchants into the Seine. There were food riots at Nevers in 1507. At Agen in 1514 the mob took complete charge of the town and, before the military could close in, clamoured for the equal distribution of goods and the exclusion of the rich from municipal government. With Lyons on the verge of a similar explosion in 1515, the magistrates forbad public meetings and censored all popular entertainments in case they contained egalitarian propaganda; two years later the city was given over to armed bands of artisans. It was small wonder that the carrying of weapons was prohibited and a curfew imposed on the streets at night in most European towns; any man abroad after dark had to carry a torch and explain his purpose to the watch, and frequently streets were fitted with chains that could be unwound from their drums and used to seal them off on any suspicion of trouble.

Considerable space was given in manuals of advice for confessors to the need to persuade parishioners to keep the peace; not to provoke others to quarrels, not to incite neighbours by noise or challenging gestures or by malicious gossip. Gambling was deplored as the age's commonest cause of affrays. Governments forbad it in taverns, captains on ships, gild statutes among apprentices – and vainly. This was class legislation. Henry VIII could lay his bets on chess, dice, cards, archery or tennis in the full light of court, the wager book of the Hansa merchants in Danzig shows them betting on the duration of a war, the results of an election or a tournament, on the price of herring, on the chances of a cook pointing to her landlord as the most probable father of her children; they could afford to lose. It was above all the poor man who was quick to feel himself cheated and reach for his knife, especially after drinking; court records are filled with tavern savagery and small brutal peasant vendettas. But there was an undercurrent of violence in all levels of society. It was present even in their pastimes. Jousts were expected to produce casualties. It was common for the mock-battles staged as pageants to become real ones. Such casualties were the sharp edge of an age brutalised by a habitual exposure to and indifference towards cruelty. Animal combats were common princely entertainments. Criminals were mutilated and butchered in public to large and excited audiences and their bodies, or fragments of them, hung on gibbets outside town-walls or at crossroads. At times torture was carried out in public, as when in 1488 the citizens of Bruges bayed for the spectacle to be prolonged as long as possible, and in another case cited by Johan Huizinga those of Mons 'bought a brigand, at far too high a price, for the pleasure of seeing him quartered, at which the people rejoiced more than if a new holy body had risen from the dead.'

Against this background the cruelties inflicted under the influence of greed or fear by the Portuguese and Spaniards against non-Christians are hardly surprising: da Gama's firing of a shipful of women and children, the actions of Tristaõ da Cunha's men in Somalia, where they cut off women's arms and legs the quicker to get at their bracelets, Balboa's loosing of savage dogs against the Indians of central America. Philosophers like Marsilio Ficino could bewail the 'beast-like' cruelty of men. More surprising, perhaps, were the prolonged efforts of the Spanish monarchs, Ferdinand and Isabella, to mitigate the cruelty of their settlers in the West Indies.

Mystery plays, mixing the holy with the horrible, brought the most bestial scenes of the torture chamber on to the public stage and showed considerable ingenuity in the neat substitution of a lay-figure at the moment when the pincers began to squeeze and the hot irons to burn. The woodcuts in printed chronicles with their detailed and often illustrated descriptions of monstrous births and carnage-strewn battlefields, reflect the same morbid appetite for horrors, and it occurs too in art, notably in northern versions of the temptation of St. Anthony and the scourging of Christ. This appetite is, clearly, a commonplace of all times. It does, however, appear with a sense of unusual feverishness at this period which can only partly be explained factually. The fascination with torture – to take but one example – is to be seen very clearly in France, yet in fact the penalties prescribed by French law were at this time becoming notably milder. Throughout western Europe the criminal law, when public order was not concerned, was unfairly summary in its processes but not savage. Practice varied from country to country – tongues were ripped out in Italy for a blasphemous swearing bout which in France would cost seventeen sous, and the law could easily be stampeded into panic violence, but the average man was not ill-protected; it was the powerful subject who might expect the complete arbitrariness which is the scapegoat's fate, from Henry VIII's propaganda killing of his father's unpopular financial agents Empson and Dudley to Machiavelli's object lesson, the politic assassination of Ramiro D'Orca as a sop to Cesare Borgia's Romagnol subjects. The enormous volume of litigation in spite of delays and high fees displays the law not only as a means of damping down violence but as an arena where combative instincts could seek a public, formalised and usually bloodless release.

The veneer placed over violence by the law, the Commandments and by reasonably prosperous times was, however, thin and easily broken, especially when God's apparent determination to scourge his people led to waves of panic. To the scourge of plague was added that of the infidel. The horror spread by tales of Turkish atrocities during the occupation of Otranto in 1480 was expressed not only in print, but in painting through a rash of Martyrdoms of the Holy Innocents. In 1496 a physician writing about syphilis was moved to ask not only whether the disease, as a punishment for sin, was beyond human cure but whether this was not true of all disease, a failure of nerve that underlay the growing – and novel – tendency to identify all mental illnesses with the operation of the devil and therefore with witchcraft. The millenarian death wish of the Middle Ages, exacerbated for some by the approach of the year 1500, took on a deepened morbidity in the many versions of the *Life of Antichrist*: a Jew begets the Beast on his own daughter, amidst adoring sycophants it circumcises itself and triumphs over those who deny him as they are sawn, burned, crucified or buried alive. As the end of the century approached, rumours and portents multiplied: monstrous births, rains of milk and blood, stains in the sky. The reports flowed in from France – a triple moon, Germany – a veritable plague of deformed infants, Greece – a corona of flaming swords, Italy – a thunderbolt crashing into the Vatican and toppling the pope from his throne. Even when the danger had passed the feeling of an impending doom persisted. Bloody rains continued to fall (Dürer drew a stain in the shape of a crucifixion left on a servant girl's smock by such a down-pour), wild preachers still announced the end of the world, and old-fashioned chroniclers, exhausted by their centuries-long tales of violence, assured their readers that the world was running down to its last days. In illustrations of the Dance of Death the skeleton hand touched the sleeve at an increasing number of untoward movements, pointed at a more detailed cross-section of society. Death was more seldom represented in the almost-consoling guise of the great leveller, or the gate-keeper to the true goal of life, salvation. A new theme, the Art of Dying, which concentrated not on death itself but the precise moment at which it comes to the bedside, was multiplied rapidly in woodcut books and the imagery of sermons.

How widely these fears were shared it is impossible to know. Suicide was rare, could indeed be satirised, as when the hero of Diego de San Pedro's romance *Carcel de Amor* (1492), rejected by his mistress, committed suicide by eating up her letters to him. Tomb inscriptions continued to take the interest of generations as yet unborn for granted, business men and politicians went on making plans, there was no extra rush of pious benefactions to catch St. Peter's eye. Humanists could still see an age of enlightenment ahead when they had polished and published the whole treasury of ancient wisdom. 'I believe I see a golden age dawning in the near future,' wrote Erasmus in a letter of 1518. 'I see from the depths a change coming,' wrote the Spanish scholar and educational reformer Vives in the following year. 'Among all nations men are springing up of clear, excellent free intellect, impatient of servitude.' And a year after that a school book taught the Latin for 'the golden vein or golden world (by revolution celestial) is now returned or come again'.

Time past was being mastered. Historians could now look back in perspective. Episodes which frequently had hovered timelessly in the medieval chronicle were now commonly located with reference to a chronological vanishing point. Historical characters seen in terms of a fairly realistic psychology became easier to imagine and identify with. A search for causation which explained events in terms of human weaknesses and ambition strengthened the narrative thread of history, and some discrimination in the use of sources enhanced its intellectual appeal. For information, patriotic reassurance, in search of wisdom or an enhanced sense of personal identity, or purely for escape, men entered this organised past in increasing numbers. Edition followed edition of Livy, Caesar, Josephus, Eusebius and Valerius Maximus (to take a sample from one printing centre, Lyons), medieval chronicles were revised and new ones issued in response to a demand from the whole reading public. For time to come, on the other hand, there were no guide lines save those, potentially ominous, projected forward by the church. There was no concept of secular progress save in the sense of a more effective recovery of the past: the consolation of ancient wisdom, the spur to emulate ancient achievements. There was no notion that man could improve his physical lot, that food could be increased, disease routed, life made more convenient or comfortable. Both the humanitarian and the technological motives for planning hopefully for the future were lacking. For the vast majority the future was not a zone where a man could project with some confidence his own achievements and those of his posterity nor speculate optimistically about society as a whole: it was filled by the image of death.

Mobility

The sense of time is partly objective, influenced by calendars, tasks and clocks, partly subjective, affected by seasons, hunger and the individual's attitude to the stages of life and to his life expectation, and it is intellectually conditioned by the ability to reach imaginatively into the past and the future. In a similar way the sense of space has a physical, an emotional and an imaginative or intellectual aspect. It is shaped by what is known – the immediate environment and the routes taken on journeys, by what is felt about what is seen, and by the ability to imagine what the eye cannot see. The first element is determined by mobility, the second by the feeling for nature, the third chiefly, at least, by maps.

Overwhelmingly Europe was an agricultural or, in vast tracts of forest, marsh and scrub, an almost uninhabited land. The great majority of men, possibly 85 per cent in western Europe, nearer 95 per cent in the east, lived on scattered homesteads or in small villages; they were born, they married and they died within sight of the same wood or parish church. In England and Wales there were some 810

market towns (with populations between 300 and 1–2,000) catering
for supplies that could not be made or grown at home; on average,
the distance a man had to travel to reach the nearest one was seven
miles. Taking less evenly urbanised areas into account, and the dawn
trek from fortified village to pastureland which characterised peasant
life in the Mediterranean islands and the plains east of the Elbe, we
should probably not be far wrong if we took the average longest
journey made by most people in their lifetimes as fifteen miles.

Towns, particularly those which lay on the most frequented routes,
were far more the centres of new ideas and social adjustments than
they had been even a century before. The isolated abbey, the monastic
village, though they might still house individual scholars of merit,
were no longer centres of learning. The day of small-town schools of
art, St. Albans, Aix, Siena, was over or waning. As the population of
Europe slowly, and notably after the middle of the fifteenth century,
recovered from the Black Death, the towns, and especially those
on the most travelled routes, had grown partly because more children
were born and survived in them and partly because of emigration
from the countryside. It was the large towns above all, with their
economic opportunities, their social variety, their printing presses and
cosmopolitan minority groups, their clustered monuments and the
patronage they extended to literature and the arts that drew the
restless and the work-hungry along the roads and rivers of Europe
to settle amidst new impressions or to collect them and pass on. For
most of the men who enlarged their spatial horizon by travel it was a
town that drew them to make the first move.

Hardship for the traveller was inevitable, and hazards great. The
Venetian government, which had the most elaborate diplomatic network in Europe, had to impose heavy penalties to keep its agents on
the move. In 1506, Francesco Morosini wrote from Turin to say that
in crossing the Alps on his return from France several of his suite had
died in snowstorms. Next year the papal legate returning from the
meeting between Louis XII and Ferdinand of Aragon at Savona wrote
that he had been sea sick 'usque ad sanguinem' and, indeed, he got
back to Rome so weak that he contracted a fever and died. Diplomatic correspondence is full of horror stories and complaints about bad
inns, rotten food, surly muleteers and (there was no waterproof
clothing and the roads were too rutted for heavy closed carriages)
constant exposure to wind and rain. The ambassadorial life was an
alternation between ceremony and discomfort. There was, too, especially in the unpeopled spaces of eastern Europe, the constant fear of
bandits. Even in the west travellers who were not rich enough to
travel with a small cavalcade waited for a merchant convoy before
passing through the more desolate regions.

Such regions were plentiful, as a glance at population figures, in rounded millions, will make clear: Germany, 12; France, 16; Russia (very uncertain), 9; Poland, 9; Castile, 6–7; the Balkans, south of the rivers Save and Danube, $5\frac{1}{2}$; Burgundy (including Artois, Flanders and Brabant), 6; England, 3; the kingdom of Naples, 2; the Papal States, 2; Portugal, 1; Aragon, 1; Sweden and Switzerland, both $\frac{3}{4}$. People, then, were thin on the ground. There was a tendency for large towns to become larger rather than for small ones to grow, or for villages to become towns. The traveller could have days of open country separating him from one oasis of comfort and another. Naples was an extreme case; with a population of well over 200,000 it was possibly the largest city in Europe, but there was no other town of even moderate size in the whole of southern Italy. London had 60,000 inhabitants; then came Norwich with 12,000, Bristol with 10,000, Coventry and perhaps a dozen others with about 7,000, a few, like Northampton and Leicester with 3,000 and the great majority with 200 or less. Paris had over 150,000 and was beginning to expand through its walls into the future Faubourg St. Germain, Lyons was half its size, and well below that came towns of the next rank, like Rheims or Bourges, with 10,000. The politically fissiparous condition of Germany produced a different pattern: no really large city, but more on the 15,000 (Frankfurt-am-Main, Ulm, Regensburg) or the 10,000 mark (Mainz, Speyer, Worms) and some above those figures: Cologne, 40,000; Nuremberg and Magdeburg, 30,000. In Castile, Burgos, Toledo, Seville had populations of over 50,000 and Salamanca possibly 100,000 (Madrid, not yet a capital city, had 12,000); below them the numbers tumbled precipitously: not for nothing was Spain reckoned by travellers to be the most deserted and uncouth of the west European countries. No other Portuguese town approached the size of Lisbon (40,000). Even greater was the contrast between Stockholm, at 6,500, Bergen, at 6,000 and other Swedish and Norwegian towns – or Moscow at a possible 150,000 and the other Russian towns, of which Novgorod alone was of significant size. In Holland, only Leiden, Amsterdam, Delft and Haarlem passed 10,000, in Switzerland, only Geneva with 12–15,000. After Naples, the largest cities in Italy were Venice, with some 100,000 inhabitants and Milan with about the same; the population of Florence was about 70,000. There was certainly no reason for the European pilgrim or trader to feel superior when he visited Constantinople (well over 100,000), Aleppo (65,000) or Damascus (57,000), or, above all Cairo, for which there are no figures but which seemed to Italian visitors to be capable of housing the combined populations of Rome, Venice, Milan and Florence.

These figures must be treated with caution. Governments had little interest in population statistics for their own sake, the tax returns from which they can be compiled are often incomplete – or incompletely understood. But, from the point of view of the traveller, the picture is clear. Plotted on a map, the large, the safe, the hospitable towns amount to a few widely scattered dots. Only on the chief trade routes were inns to be found at intervals of ten to fifteen miles. Only the rich could afford to take enough food, bedding and armed men to diverge from the main routes. But though travel had its difficulties, anyone who wanted to move, could, and at speeds which hardly varied until the coming of the railways. From Paris to Calais, for instance, took $4\frac{1}{2}$ days, to Brussels $5\frac{1}{2}$, to Metz 6, to Bordeaux 7, to Toulouse 8–10, to Marseilles 10–14 and to Turin 10–15. From Venice it took Philippe de Commines 6 days to reach Asti, 'for the road was the best in the world'. Other average times from Venice were to Rome 4 days (though there is a record of a courier doing it non-stop in a day and a half), to London 26, to Madrid 42, to Constantinople 41. These are times taken by merchants or diplomats in a hurry. Along routes where there was an organised postal service the times could be still further clipped. In 1516 letters sent from Brussels via the postal system operated by the Taxis family reached Paris in summer in 36 hours, Lyons in $3\frac{1}{2}$ days and Rome in $10\frac{1}{2}$ days. Once off the main routes, however, and above all if a sea passage were involved, the times were impossible to forecast with any degree of accuracy.

The heaviest traffic consisted of traders, their goods and their agents, the traffic being at its height at the four seasonal fairs held at Lyons where, for a fortnight of intense activity, merchants brought samples from all over western Europe. Good roads, navigable rivers, a central position and royal protection made Lyons at these times the busiest of European cities. The city was also thronged by the stewards of wealthy families who travelled far to load a mule train with exotic supplies. The account books of one such purchaser, the agent of Princess Philiberta of Luxembourg, show how widely the net of commerce was cast. His purchases included spices from Venice, wine from Crete, currants from Corinth, salt fish from Flanders and dried Spanish anchovies, fabrics from England, Italy and Holland, leather goods from Spain and Germany: dog collars, jesses and purses. The Lyons fair is only one, if the greatest example: in France alone there were also annual trade fairs at Paris, Rouen, Tours, Troyes, Dijon and Montpellier. And the fairs only brought into focus an activity that was continuous; European mobility was, above all, mercantile.

Next in volume was a multiplicity of men looking for work. The population of Europe was growing but slowly, but faster than agriculture or the labour demand of towns could readily absorb. This was especially true of Castile, the mountains of central Europe and the less fertile islands and coasts of the Mediterranean. There was a steady flow of men from these areas seeking jobs, above all, as soldiers. Albanian mercenaries were found as far afield as Spain, though most sought service in Italy and were relied on particularly by Venice. Called stradiots because they were always on the road (Italian *strada*), they were joined there by men from other sterile regions wandering in search of wars which others were too prosperous to risk fighting in themselves. Luck, and a captain short of men, could make a tramp into a soldier overnight; it was almost the only way an entirely unskilled man could better himself. English evidence shows how hard it was for the unskilled vagrant, the farm labourer, to establish himself by travelling. He was not wanted, except, perhaps, seasonally, in other agricultural districts, he was not wanted at any time in the towns. On the other hand the possession of an acquired skill and the ability to serve an apprenticeship, did make travelling worth while. An analysis of two London companies showed that nearly half their apprentices had come from northern England.

Some men could travel, indeed had to travel, in the fairly confident expectation of being employed. Village clocks were made by itinerant clockmakers and churches often by itinerant masons: the great mosques of Contantinpole were built by renegade Christians, just as the guns that had shattered the city wall in 1453 had been forged by renegade Christian gunsmiths. Printing was, for some, an itinerant profession, as was proof-reading. We hear much of itinerant bands of actors, jugglers and musicians, something of itinerant professional football and tennis players but almost nothing, alas, about the most symbolic wanderers of all, the gypsies. Treated most tolerantly in Scotland and Scandinavia, they were expelled from Spain (by law if not in fact) in 1499, from Burgundy in 1515; they were harassed elsewhere. That in spite of this they flourished, the widespread influence of their music shows, and from time to time the picture lightens; a gypsy band played at the wedding of Matthias Corvinus and Beatrice of Aragon in Buda in 1476 and they were mentioned as playing at court in 1483. On Corfu, under Venetian protection, a hundred gypsies formed a community exempt from galley service and the usual peasant labour services.

Wanderers almost as compulsive were students and scholars. Degrees could be built up piecemeal by residence at one university after another; for each student there was an ideal curriculum available, based on books by and hearsay about famous teachers, to be followed by moving not from one lecture hall but from one country to another. The study of Latin, Greek and Hebrew had produced a new and revolutionary mood in scholarship, both secular and Christian, and to take advantage of it scholars had to hurry from one spring to another as it bubbled through the rocks of traditional scholastic learning: to confer with colleagues, to exploit an eager publisher, to settle for a while under the wing of a sympathetic patron. To this end, More wrote in defence of his friend's restless itinerancy, 'Erasmus defies stormy seas and savage skies and the scourges of land travel' and goes 'through dense forest and wild woodland, over rugged hilltops and steep mountains, along roads beset with bandits...tattered by the winds, spattered with mud, travel-weary.' But he does this both to learn and to give, for 'as the sun spreads its rays, so wherever Erasmus is he spreads his wonderful riches'.

This defence of one man's migrancy can serve for European culture as a whole, which was marked in this period by an unprecedented speed in the internationalisation of styles – or, rather, by an unprecedented exposure of national or local styles to the challenges of outside influences. In the late fifteenth and early sixteenth centuries not only did Italian scholars introduce Roman Law and the study of Greek and classical Latin to Cracow university, but Italians worked on the city's cathedral and the royal palace on Wawel hill, leaving a lasting imprint on the Poles who worked under them. A similar permanent dye was given to Spanish culture by Italians patronised by Ferdinand and Isabella, a stain widened by the organisation of the court, which included tutors for the royal princesses and a school for the young aristocrats the monarchs took under their protection, and by the perpetual migrations of the whole court, so various in its composition, with troops, musicians, cooks, saddlers, dressmakers, surgeons and a host of officials, so glamorous and so large as to be an itinerant capital, affecting the way of life and the ideas of at least the noble class all over Spain. At the other end of Europe Ivan III introduced Italians to work on the final stages of the Kremlin. The Uspensky Sobor was completed by Aristotile Fioraventi in 1479 and the diamond faceted Granovitaia Palace, designed by Solari with the decoration of Ferrarese palaces in mind, was finished by 1491. Henry VII of England employed Flemish stained-glass workers. Some of his coinage had been designed by a Fleming, and the bronze screen round his monument by the Italian Torrigiano, was the work of a Dutchman. In France, in addition to Leonardo da Vinci, who died there in 1519, and the architects Francesco Laurana, Fra Giocondo, Giuliano da San Gallo and Domenico da Cortona, whole *équippes* of Italian craftsmen were imported. For work on his château at Amboise,

Charles VIII had architects, painters, sculptors, wood-carvers, marquetry workers, upholsterers, armourers and an organ maker. To this assembly Louis XII, in 1500, added faience workers from Forlí, complete with their kilns.

Musicians were characterised by a similar mobility. Orchestras were like armies: the best were composed of specialists from various nations. Just as Francis I employed Swiss pikeman so he enlisted, at the beginning of his reign, cornettists and trombone players from Italy. The Venetian organist, Dionisio Memmo, was called from S. Marco to London in 1516. While the flow of executants tended to be from south to north, and led to a marginal import of musical fashions – Henry VIII danced in the first Italianate masque in 1513 – the flow of composers and teachers was from north to south. The Englishman John Hothby (d. 1487) taught for twenty years in Lucca, but the majority originated in northern France and the Low Countries and spread the brilliant achievements of this area all over Europe. Johannes Tinctoris spent over twenty years (1474–95) at the Neapolitan court, where he demonstrated in practice, and through a number of treatises, the qualities of one of the period's most illustrious composers, Johannes Ockeghem. Ockeghem himself spent some time in Spain under Ferdinand, and his northern influence was confirmed when in 1516 Ferdinand's successor Charles brought with him a whole choir from the Netherlands.

Josquin des Prez, *doyen* of the composers of the period, was also a migrant from his home in Hainault; he worked in Milan, in the papal chapel in Rome and, at the turn of the century, at the court of Ercole d'Este in Ferrara. Thereafter he spent most of his time in France, dying there in 1521. These travels, plus the amiable practice whereby princes took their musicians about with them or lent performers to one another, meant that Europe learned, with remarkable speed, and by a process that happily reversed Gresham's Law, to speak a common musical language.

Administrative routines also drew many men away from their homes. Jury service, membership of a representative assembly, the need to plead at a superior court of law; these dislodged men, if infrequently and reluctantly, from an otherwise static existence and in a manner that was socially selective, for the richer or better born a man was, the more likely that in both church and state he would be expected to travel to the central tribunals of the nation. This trickle of representatives, litigants or petitioners to the centre was paralleled by a movement of officials – judges, financial agents, royal messengers, commissions of inquiry – from the centre to the periphery.

Though some of the old pilgrim routes, like that to S. James of Compostela had become less popular, and the habit had increased among those too busy or too lazy to go themselves of paying others, usually by bequest, to carry out a proxy pilgrimage, it is likely that more pilgrims were on the move in this period than ever before or since. There is the negative evidence of the thunders from pulpit and press against going on pilgrimage in too thoughtless or too carefree a mood. There is the positive evidence of the souvenir trade, the painted cockle shells and tin images of S. Michael at Mont S. Michel, the attendance figures noted by the gatekeepers at Aix-la-Chapelle where 142,000 pilgrims came to adore the reliquary of the sacred blood in a single day in 1493, the estimate that of the scores of thousands of pilgrims who came to Rome in 1500, a year of plague as well as of Jubilee, over 30,000 died there.

Their motivation was naturally various. The French humanist Lefèvre d'Etaples described the heartfelt single-mindedness of an old man, an ex-slave of the Turks, he met in northern Italy in 1491. 'I saw a man dressed in a sack who walked along barefoot and bare-headed. His belt was made of rushes and he carried a wooden cross. Careless of the rain and snow, very thick at that time, he went from chapel to chapel; if the door was closed he waited in prayer, kneeling in the snow. He lived on nothing but bread and herbs, fasted for long days at a time; his drink was water and his bed the earth.' At the other extreme was Friar Felix Faber who prepared himself for a pilgrimage to Jerusalem in 1483 with delighted zeal. He filled his cell in the Dominican cloister at Ulm with all the travel literature he could lay his hands on. Indeed, as he wrote in his open-eyed and carefree narrative, 'I give you my word I worked harder in running round from book to book, in copying, correcting, collating what I had written, than I did in journeying from place to place upon my pilgrimage.' This was the sort of curiosity that made Dr. Diego Chanca and Michele de Cuneo accompany Columbus on his second voyage purely out of interest, or urged Pigafetta to leave his native Vicenza to join Magellan's expedition 'to experiment and go and see with my own eyes'; that made Lodovico Varthema show 'the same desire to behold the various kingdoms of the world which has urged on others' so that in 1502, 'longing for novelty' he set off for Mecca disguised as a Moslem pilgrim and went on to trade with some success in Burma and Ceylon.

Feeling for Nature

Travel does not, by itself, condition the sense of space. It depends upon the individual's reactions to the scenes through which he passes, and here there is a formidable problem of evidence. Were it not for the independent record of Dürer's watercolour sketches of landscape, for example, his travel diaries would suggest that he was interested in little more than the number of miles travelled, the people he met and the prices at inns.

Much of nature was, in any case, marked off from a tranquil appreciation of it for its own sake. Apart from infrequent and widely-scattered communities of fishermen and isolated bands of salt evaporators, the sea coast of Europe was deserted, its rocks and marshes a *cordon sanitaire* the traveller or trader only penetrated to embark or disembark. Even maritime countries like Portugal and Venice suffered from a shortage of sailors; a poor living scratched from the soil was more attractive than life on shipboard. No holiday-maker sought the sea. It was dangerous, a wreckers' world, unwritten about save in tones of dismay, unpainted save as the background to a miracle or a foreground to the welcoming quays of town. Mountains too were zones of fear and could be admired – save by a stratigrapher like Leonardo – only if their pastures and hanging woods enabled them to be seen as useful to man. The forests which covered so much of Europe were rarely penetrated save by huntsmen and fugitives from justice.

Appreciation of nature was also limited by dusk. Fear of the night was universal. There was no movement in or out of villages, cottagers barred their doors. If a neighbour screamed in the street, his cries went unheeded. Wolves roamed in the suburbs, wild boars rooted up the young fruit trees, and robber bands had the highways to them-selves. This insecurity in an only, vestigially-policed world nourished nightmare stories of werewolves and kindred horrors. Night was the devil's day when his witches flew. With hearths smothered for fear of fire, outside the towns the night was spent in a state of physical and emotional siege.

It was an age, too, when health, and sometimes life, depended on the weather. Diaries were often hardly more than anguished records of exceptional rains and frosts. The countryside – what was left, when the coastal areas, forests, mountains and wastes have been subtracted – was above all the place where the food came from. A bad harvest and all but the rich suffered, the very poor starved; 'fertile' or 'infertile' rather than 'beautiful' or 'depressing' was the first reaction to landscape; humanist, merchant, monk, all had a farmer's eye. And agricultural Europe looked neither particularly lush – the result of later drainage and grass selection – nor pleasingly trim, for there was little enclosure by hedges. Nor, in spite of the thin population, was there sufficient productivity to ensure that a good harvest would tide over a bad one. About one third of the land was permanently out of action, lying fallow, for the shortage of livestock and the absence of artificial manures meant that the land could seldom support more than two crops in succession. The expensiveness and short supply of stout draught animals and the inefficiency of the ploughs most peasants could afford, meant that cultivation tended to be shallow, the land lacking in humus (English farmers spread the lanes with bracken, waiting for it to be mulched by passing traffic) and the yield light. Everything, then, depended on the weather; a subjective feeling for nature was checked by objective appraisal.

It was not only in the fields that delight was screened by a calculation of use; flowers, shrubs and herbs were seen primarily in terms of flavourings or medicines. It is doubtful whether the poor saw them in any other terms. Even for men who were well-to-do and educated there remained a screen: the conventional woodcut illustrations of the herbals, overlaying the flower itself with what was often a strongly divergent image which had struggled through the middle ages unrefreshed by direct observations since the days of Dioscorides. Herbals and bestiaries showed common flowers and familiar animals in a convention that contradicted everyday experience, but these images had two sources of power: they symbolised knowledge and authority, and they were the accepted hieroglyphs which demonstrated the diverseness of God's creation and His direct concern for man. At the back of the eye which looked at nature was a pseudo-botany, a pseudo-zoology, and a pseudo-topography, for there were conventional symbols for tree and river and mountain; even when artists had demonstrated their ability to portray a city exactly, printers continued to illustrate verbal descriptions of different towns with the same conventionalised woodcut view. How far this inner vision affected ordinary vision it is, of course, impossible to say. There is a gap between the eye seeing and the pen or brush recording that we cannot measure, but we may guess that for most men it was filled by associations that obscured a straightforward 'love of nature'; utility, images from the pseudo-sciences, the sense of divine purpose in which love of nature became diffused into worship of God. From his villa at Poggio a Caiano, Lorenzo de' Medici could see that 'the olive on its gentle, open slope appears green or white according to the wind'. That is a flick of direct observation. In other poems by Lorenzo – in whom the feeling for nature was fresher than in almost any other writer of his age – the freshness is hardly more (and here he is more representative) than a scent clinging to motifs from medieval tapestries and classical literature: '*Cerchi chi vuol le pompe* ... Let him who wants them seek pomp and honour, public squares, temples and grand buildings, pleasures and treasures which bring with them a thousand worries, a thousand pains. A green meadow full of lovely flowers, a stream which moistens the grass on its banks, a little bird that makes its plaint of love, these soothe our passions much better.'*

By the early sixteenth century withdrawal from the city to seek the tonic tranquility of the countryside had become a commonplace. In Italy the villa had already some fifty years of evolution behind it and elsewhere in Europe the country castle began to soften, as law and order gained more ground, into the country house. Moralists praised the innocent pursuits of rural life, poets took up the strains of Theocritus and the Virgil of the *Eclogues*, shepherds and shepherdesses entered the masque. In *c.* 1490 Signorelli gave this back-to-nature movement a tutelary deity with his *Pan* and in 1502 Sannazzaro's *Arcadia* caught the age's nostalgia for peace and innocence with a delicacy of mood and a firmness of structure that was to give the pastoral an enduring life. Though wild men of the woods were to dance at the court of the young Henry VIII, this was above all an Italian and, at least in part, an artificial mode. There were other reasons than love of the countryside for villa life. A landed property was a sound investment at a time when Italian commercial life was subject to alarming recessions. Again, as in the days of Boccaccio, those who could afford to do so withdrew from the cities in the hot months that so often brought the plague. The villa was not so much used to identify a man with country life as to enable him to disassociate himself from certain aspects of urban existence. There was a wave of fascination for northern chivalry, for the castle, the hunt and the social separateness that the Italian ruling class had compromised when, centuries before, they had chosen the jostling competitiveness of the towns. The villa permitted a de-militarised feudal life, still further removed from class suspicion by its classical associations. With their humanist-troubadours to entertain them, the republican leaders of Florence and Venice could ride out with hounds and falcon and safely play the composite rôle of Amadis, Cicero and merchant banker. For the aristocrat love of the country was probably subsidiary to the social convenience of the setting, and for those humanists who could afford to build a villa or modify a farmhouse for themselves, country life was hardly more than a bookshelf in the open air. A safer guide than verse is the evidence of woodcuts and engravings produced for a mass audience and which show the country as above all a place for love. From homes where there was no privacy, from mattresses sour with damp and hopping with fleas, the first warm days of spring drew lovers to the fields and woods. Not without reason are the age's two most tranquilly beautiful love scenes, the *Mars and Venus* of Piero di Cosimo and Botticelli, placed in the open air.

* Tr. Eve Borsook, *The Companion Guide to Florence* (1966) 244.

Art as a whole is a better guide than literature; while the achievements of the ancients in landscape painting were known from Pliny the Elder's descriptions of classical works there were no surviving examples to copy or be influenced by. Technically, landscape had been rendered with considerable exactness early in the fifteenth century; the river winding towards hills in the background of Jan van Eyck's *Madonna of the Chancellor Rolin* (1425) is a magnificent example. But in intention this is still nature as symbol. From about 1500 there was a change away from using landscape as a symbol of the creation or an allegory of a state of mind towards a feeling for nature for its own sake, as the self-sufficient encloser of a mood, not a finger post to some destination in the mind or soul. Technical progress helped prepare the way for this change. Mastery of compositional and aerial perspective meant that the painter – a Dürer or a Giorgione – could come back from the countryside with a whole landscape in his mind or in a sketch. It enabled painters to use landscapes which had a personal meaning for them so that they could record, easily and naturally, the setting of their own lives; thus the Arno valley was used in Baldovinetti's *Nativity* and Pollaiuolo's *Martyrdom of S. Sebastian*. These familiar backgrounds ceased to be symbols because they were seen and recorded as a whole, as a scene, not a working together of a river, a rocky hill, a forest, from the iconographical dictionary every painter carried in his head.

The quality of feeling is not easy to assess, however. Did Altdorfer dwarf the armoured saint in his *Forest with S. George and the Dragon* with the overwhelming foliage of the woods because he loved trees, or because they symbolised the part of the country that was the special preserve of the knightly class and their huntsmen? Indeed, did Pollaiuolo use the Arno valley because the receding river allowed him to think in terms of conventional linear perspective? All that can be assumed is that an undoubted delight in landscape for its own sake was recorded by few artists, and primarily for their own satisfaction. The majority of such scenes are drawings. A few are worked to a degree of finish which implies sale or gift, and hence connoisseurs who shared this delight. But no finished painting is devoted entirely to landscape. Though the literary pastoral, particularly a work like Pietro Bembo's *Gli Asolani*, with its intensely visual imagery, probably encouraged painters to concentrate on the landscape element in their work, the painter's vision was far more searching than the poet's. Lorenzo's description of the olive is unusually exact for a writer. This, however, is only one of many passages in which Leonardo describes the appearance of foliage: 'when your eye is somewhat below the level of the tree you will be able to see its leaves some on the top side and some on the reverse, and the top sides will be a deeper blue as they are more foreshortened, and the same leaf will sometimes show part of the right side and part of the reverse, and consequently you must make it of two colours'. Between notes like this and the *plein air* sketch on the one hand and, on the other, a finished studio work, the problems of translation were formidable. Apart from lack of demand it is possible that realistic landscape painting remained literally in the background because it was easier to render it in that way.

We can guess at the significance of the fact that among the itinerant groups there was a high proportion of those who produced and those – merchants, nobles, churchmen – who patronised works of literature and art, and that this may have had some bearing on the portrayal of nature. The impressions that affected their sense of space, however, were derived for the most part from well-beaten tracks or from the rural environs of a town, and for the most part travellers set out with a practical purpose – to get a job, take up a post, to study, trade or fight – and were blinkered by a specific aim. Erasmus expressed the typical attitude of the educated traveller; he tears himself away from his friends with reluctance and grits his teeth until he rejoins human society. Nature is something to grumble at – too much pain, too cloudy, too cold, the sea too rough – almost never to delight in: a vast unwelcome corridor connecting the warm halls of men. Even geographers and topographers whose eyes were professionally open to new scenes hardly ever express any feeling for them. Their concern was with place names, with productivity and with people; the town where all accused persons were hung and dug up and given Christian burial if they were subsequently proved innocent – anthropological bizarreries of this kind were more interesting than the landscape in which they were enacted. Columbus alone of the explorers expressed a delight in nature, but for all the nights he spent under tropical skies there is no mention of the stars except as tricky things to navigate by, and even his praise of landscape dwindled rapidly into utilitarianism: 'In that island Hispaniola there are mountains of very great size and beauty, vast plains, groves and very fruitful fields, admirably adapted for tillage, pasture and habitation.'

Exploration

It was above all a thoroughly practical search for useful products, especially gold and spices, that determined the sensationally rapid opening of the aperture through which Europeans could look at the world; the Cape of Good Hope rounded in 1488, the West Indies discovered in 1492, India reached by sea in 1498, Brazil described in

1500, the Americas recognized as a separate continent in 1513 when Balboa confirmed previous conjectures by sighting a 'new' ocean, the Pacific, South America circumnavigated by Magellan in 1520.

These voyages, epoch-making as they were, were largely the culmination of long familiar aims and skills. For centuries gold from beyond the Sahara and the pepper substitute known as grains of paradise had been available in the ports of North Africa, drugs and spices from the East Indies in those of the eastern Mediterranean. The desire to get to the source of these supplies had led merchants to cross the Sahara and to travel overland to China. But already, by the end of the fourteenth century, it was clear that the sources could only be tapped profitably by sea; overland transport costs, political insecurity, the time lost in passively accompanying one's bales as they were changed from caravan to caravan: these factors ruled out any exploitation of the experience of such travellers as the Polos.

By the fifteenth century, long sea voyages were commonplace. Venetian galleys plied regularly to England, Baltic traders to Spain, English fishermen were beginning to venture to Iceland. Frequent voyages into the Atlantic triangle Lisbon–Azores–Cape Bojador (mapped on the Catalan Atlas 1375) had provided a training school for ships and seamen that made them competent for exploration at any range. A series of Portuguese expeditions, working further and further down the west African coast, led to the crossing of the equator in 1473. In 1482, John II founded the port of Elmina on the Gold Coast and successfully by-passed the Saharan caravan routes.

From the 1420s, indeed, when these expeditions began, nearly all the preconditions for transoceanic, as well as coastal exploration, were in existence. The managerial basis was adequate; loans for outfitting, maritime insurance to cover unforeseeable risks, co-operation between backer and expert geographers. Christian trading posts and commercial enclaves in the Ottoman and Mamluk dominated Levant, the apportionment and administration of lands conquered from the Moors of Granada, the handling of slave or virtually rightless labour: these provided models that could be adapted for the exploitation of lands discovered overseas – had, indeed, been adapted to the Azores and the Canaries. From the technological point of view, ship design was improved during the fifteenth century, but in 1420 vessels were hardy enough, and sailed sufficiently close to the wind, to have made the crossing to the Americas and back. From the scientific point of view the pattern is the same. Navigational instruments, astrolabes and nocturnals, were improved, the astronomical tables on which their accurate use depended were refined. But in practice seamen did not rely on advanced position-finding techniques. Using the familiar compass and estimating distance travelled by experience, the feel of their ship and, while tacking, with the assistance of a simple traverse board, pilots well into the sixteenth century navigated by dead-reckoning. Accurate time-keeping is absolutely essential for determining longitude, only slightly less crucial for fixing latitude, and the only time-piece sufficiently practical for use at sea was the hourglass, never – on a pitching, swaying ship – a precise instrument even if an emergency did not lead to its remaining unturned. There was an unbridgeable gap between an evolving shore-based theory and what actually worked at sea. Mathematics, astronomy and precision instrument-making were not irrelevant to the process of deliberate and sustained exploration but they determined neither its timing nor its range.

These were determined by two things: a development in geographical theory and a shift in the way in which men imagined terrestrial space.

By 1480 geographers had devoted considerable attention to the *Geographia* of Ptolemy and to the maps derived from his text. The Ptolemaic world map showed the world as it had been known to intelligent Romans of the second century; a world that, thanks to Greek contact with India and guesses derived from rumour and trade about what lay still further east, gave a more or less accurate lay-out of Europe, the north African coastline and Arabia, and allotted generous space to the Indian Ocean – showing it, however, as an inland sea, its southern shore washing the vast (and entirely speculative) mass of Terra Incognita, which was shown north of and parallel to the Tropic of Capricorn, at which point it merged into Africa. It showed that ships could sail clear from Africa to the Indies (a term that telescoped the Malay peninsula, the East Indies and China), but it also seemed to show that there was no way of breaking into that route by sea; it gave a teasingly clear view of the treasure and, at the same time, locked the door on it. But Ptolemy was increasingly studied in conjunction with his predecessor, Strabo, who encouraged the idea that Africa could in fact be circumnavigated, as did a third author whose works received closer attention in humanist circles, Caius Julius Solinus.

The extent to which Ptolemaic theory had been modified by 1459 was shown by the world map designed by the Venetian monk Fra Mauro. Adopting a Ptolemaic shape for Asia, it shows an Africa which, while not taking even reasonably full account of Portuguese discoveries by that date (possibly as far south as Sierra Leone), is clearly circumnavigable. It was this changed view of the world that encouraged John II of Portugal not merely to be content with the gold of Elmina but to try to reach the source of eastern spices as well.

In an attempt to check the accuracy of his cartographers before investing in a trading fleet, however, he dispatched two expeditions in 1487. Bartolomeu Dias was sent south by sea along the west coast of Africa, while Pero de Covilhã was sent in the opposite direction, to enter the Indian Ocean via the Mediterranean and the Red Sea and pick up what information he could find (he could speak Arabic) among the Arabs who traded between east Africa and India. While Dias, blown off the coast and driven far south and west by storms, actually doubled the Cape unawares, Covilhã reached Sofala, just south of Beira. There he made inquiries about sea routes around southern Africa and, probably from stories of Arab ships blown round from the east as Dias was blown from the west, gathered that circumnavigation was possible. The result of the Dias–Covilhã pincer movement was to gain a reasonably clear impression of the whole African coastline, with the exception of the stretch where the two did not quite touch hands between East London and Sofala. The ground for Vasco da Gama's voyage round the Cape, up the east coast to Malindi and across to Calicut had been prepared, and almost certainly it was only John's subsequent illness that delayed Portuguese contact with India until 1498.

By this time Columbus was on his way to the West Indies for the third time. The discovery of America was in sharp contrast to the exploration of Africa and contact with India. Until Dias was forced out deep into the South Atlantic when he was some five hundred miles north of the Cape, the exploration of the African coast had proceeded handhold by handhold; seamen approached the unknown, cape by cape and beach by beach, from the security of the known. Once the Cape had been rounded and contact made with Mozambique, they entered a highly sophisticated trading area with maps, pilots using quadrant and compass and a busy traffic of large ships. The Indian Ocean resembled an Arabic-speaking Mediterranean, and with interpreters from the Iberian peninsula or North Africa, Europeans could master its intricacies without too much difficulty though not, of course, without facing much danger and inevitable hardship. Once geographical theory and, consequently, maps had accepted the circumnavigability of Africa, contact with the far east was a matter of will and courage rather than of an imaginative conviction that justified an enormous leap across mere ocean.

That Cathay lay westwards across a great ocean had long been taken for granted. The implementation of this knowledge however, required not only suitable ships, adequate navigating techniques and men prepared to hazard their lives, but a way of imagining space expressed in cartographic terms as actually and invitingly open to exploration. And the shift from thinking of maps as records of what was known or surmised to seeing them as diagrams of the possible, as invitations to journeys that could be seen as an extension of ordinary voyages, was influenced more directly by art than by science or by travel itself. By the late fifteenth century an artist like Leonardo could not only record a landscape accurately as he stood before it, but imaginatively project his spatial thinking to the wider prospect of a bird's-eye view and, wider and higher still, to a detailed map of a whole province. Art helped the mind to think spatially by first training the eye. By helping men to 'see' the countryside as a whole, rather than as a mass of separate impressions, and training their imaginations by presenting them with imaginary but perfectly believable landscapes, the painter was enabling them to project the imagination beyond the frame of a painting, beyond what was visible to what could be conjectured, and similarly to urge it from the known part of the map to envisage its unexplored regions as knowable. Certainly, from the 1490s maps determined the direction of voyages of exploration with a sense of positive invitation that was new – to such an extent, indeed, that scores of ships and hundreds of men were to perish in search of passages, straits and, in the case of Terra Incognita Australis, a whole continent, that existed chiefly in the guesswork of cartographers.

At the same time there was an increasing demand for maps and written descriptions for administrative and military reasons. 'I have been asked,' wrote a humanist physician of Zurich in the early 1490s, 'to describe the regions of our Confederation and their environs so that you may realise... how useful such a description is to all those princes who are about to take the field with their armies.' Historians began to use geography, 'the eye of history', to locate their subject-matter in space as well as in time, and patriotic zeal was yet another motive for city and regional descriptions. Politicians, too, without atlasses or maps that showed national frontiers, showed an increasing interest in visualising the scene of their diplomatic operations, relying on ambassadorial reports to eke out the still rudimentary maps of Europe.

By 1520, however, only a minute fraction of Europe's population had ever seen a map. No geography was taught in schools or universities, except for a very few, mostly in Germany, where Ptolemy was introduced. Without the habit of conceptualising space, a traveller going to war or work could not link his separate impressions to the nature of his route as a whole or extend them imaginatively to the unseen parts of the area through which he was passing; a man could not visualise the country to which he belonged; a landowner, unable to 'see' his properties as a whole was not concerned to concentrate his scattered holdings by sale or exchanges; a ruler, unable to 'see' his kingdom was not perturbed by bargaining away provinces that map-conscious generations were to see as essential to strategic frontiers; governments, informed by verbal descriptions, were unable to judge the resources in men and materials of their rivals; generals miscalculated their lines of communications and found it difficult to work to a systematic plan of operations. Certainly, in an age virtually without effective maps the bump of locality is likely to be well developed, and the hunt sharpened an eye for terrain and the judging of distance. If, however, there is an air of confusion and improvisation about the diplomatic and military events of the period it is, at least in part, because men were literally unable to see their goals.

The difficulty of collating written or verbal information with a visualised spatial concept also accounts (though again, only in part) for the general indifference of most Europeans to the astounding enlargement of their geographical horizons. The imagination simply could not follow the voyages, and accounts of what had been found were only attractive if they were laced with the marvels and monsters of medieval travel lore; the essential difference of the new lands and their peoples could not be grasped because the imagination tugged them back to Europe.

Narratives of voyages were printed from 1493, when an account of Columbus' first voyage appeared in Rome, but they did not acquire a significant readership until the middle of the sixteenth century. Portentous as first the economic and then the political consequences of trade and settlement overseas were to become, as yet, save to those directly involved with overseas trade or the planning of voyages of discovery, information about Africa, Asia and the Americas was irrelevant, and most humanist scholars were more concerned with the rediscovery of the ancient world, which could be carried on through words, the study of texts, than with paying attention to the discovery of the new, which involved a fresh visualisation of space. Thoroughly typical was the reaction of Marineo Siculo, who was teaching at Salamanca when Columbus was discussing geographical theory with his colleagues there and who was one of Ferdinand of Aragon's official historians. In all his voluminous writings there is only one reference to the New World. He records the discovery of a (presumed) Roman coin in Central America and smugly comments that 'this took the glory from our soldiers who were boasting of their navigation, since the coin is proof that the Romans had sailed to the Indies long before.' Marineo kept his mind's eye firmly on the past; to the great majority of learned men the more absorbing challenge lay not in space but in time.

2

Political Europe

The Political Unit

With hereditary, elective and joint monarchies, with broad-based and narrowly oligarchic republics, with independent and semi-independent confederations, with individual cities that operated as free agents and an emperor whose orders were virtually ignored by the vast majority of his subjects, the variety of ways in which government functioned is bewildering enough, even if we omit such anomalies as the papacy and the areas over which there was, to all intents and purposes, no government at all.* Yet in describing political events, whether they concern foreign policy and war, taxation and justice, struggles for power within a particular country, or the sense of relationship between a subject and his ultimate superior, the word government in this period has at least the merit of being less misleading than nation or state.

'Nation' then meant, as it had in the organisation of the General Councils of the church in the fifteenth century and still did in the social organisation of universities, a group of individuals with a common place of origin. It also conveyed a sense of the shared aims, experiences and sentiments which could be mobilised by government. It is, indeed, possible to speak of national feeling at this time and impossible to explain international affairs without stressing the strength of patriotism.† But the word nation in its modern usage calls up a more widely-felt sense of community than then existed and is inseparable from the notion of well-defined frontiers. Something like 'frontier thinking' was, indeed, involved when governments passed mercantilist economic legislation, or built fortresses to protect their territories, but being neither clearly marked except at the sea coast nor taken for granted as necessarily lasting, frontiers were for the most part little more than no-man's lands of varying depth, where local communities accepted now the law of one

---

* See Appendix. Europe c. 1500: a political gazetteer.
† See below, p. 73 seq.

side now of another as suited their convenience at the moment, and where the arm of government, weak from stretching far from an administrative centre, was frequently ignored by men who fortified their farms and churches chiefly with their own defence in mind.

Geographers could talk, as Johann Cuspinian did in his *Austriae Regionis Descriptio*, of natural frontiers, rivers and mountains. The French King Louis XI could say in 1482 that he wanted 'the kingdom to extend...up to the Alps...and to the Rhine', but twelve years later his successor, Charles VIII, renounced his claims to Franche-Comté and Artois in order to prevent Maximilian's interfering with his move to conquer Naples. There was in fact no general feeling that natural features were natural frontiers. No two countries were content to be separated by a river – so natural a bond between its banks at a time of bad roads and comparatively cheap water transport. Ivan III fortified the river Oka against raiders from the south, but he also established fortifications well to the south of it and settled a thick buffer of Cossack tribesmen there. During the wars fought in Italy from 1494 both Germans and Swiss got as far over the Alps and into the Lombard plain as they could; mountains split countries, but they did not suggest limits to expansion. Even the sea did not stop Henry VII from still considering Calais a part of England and trying to add Boulogne, or Aragon from seeking to control the kingdom of Naples. Theorists, again, tried to claim that language acted as a natural frontier; but in practice no ruler used this argument as more than an excuse for conquest; even within individual nations there was no feeling that all the subjects of one prince should speak the same language. Scholarship and the press were well ahead of the crown, for instance, in encouraging the spread of the French of the Île de France into the south. Charles V did not hesitate to rule the heterogeneous components brought to him by his election to the Empire in 1519, his inheritances in central Europe and the Netherlands and his marriage-trophy Spain as though they were one governmental unit.

In contrast to Asia, with its thinly spread populations and its gusts of supra-national religious enthusiasms, the European countries, especially in the west, were so squeezed together between the Atlantic, the North and Baltic Seas and the Mediterranean, their rivalries were so well defined, their conquests at one another's expense so small, their administrative systems so effective, that it is tempting to see them as modern states. But even discounting the most 'Asiatic' regions of Europe, the extreme north where Lapps and Finns fished and followed their reindeer without needing to know who for the moment was ruling them, and the region between the Dniester and the Danube, a vaguely politicised zone of nomads, slavers and refugees, Europe, seen from within, was still far from being a system of thoroughly self-conscious and methodically administered political entities.

From the point of view of international relations, Europe can be considered as a closed world of its own. The Turks withdrew from their foothold on Italian soil at Otranto in 1481 and thereafter, apart from a sea war with Venice from 1499 to 1503, they were too occupied with fighting on their eastern border against Persia or with conquering Syria (1516) and Egypt (1517) to be of major concern to the European powers. Overseas, though by 1520 gigantic strides had been taken in the establishment of Spanish and Portuguese empires since Columbus' first voyage of 1492 and da Gama's landing at Calicut in 1498, the Treaty of Tordesillas* had been effective in persuading the seamen of the two countries to keep out of one another's way, and the era of interloping and rival settlements on the part of other countries still lay in the future. As far as inter-national relations in Europe were concerned, the discoveries and the colonising movements which followed them had little more effect than to divert all of Portugal's and part of Castile's interest overseas. Aragon was hardly involved, and it was Aragon's ruler, Ferdinand, who was the chief architect of Spain's foreign policy.

The diplomatic hard core of the period 1480–1520 was formed by what happened in Italy between 1494 and 1515. They were both years of victory for France. In the first, Charles VIII invaded Italy and moved on to the conquest of Naples. In the second, the young Francis I recovered Milan after the battle of Marignano. The second victory was to prove as transitory as the first. The significance of these twenty-one years lies in the number of countries that were sucked into the struggle over the dismemberment of Italy, the size of the alliances which were formed for this purpose and the speed with which they broke up and were reconstituted. To give but two instances: Charles VIII protected himself before invading Italy by making pacts with Maximilian, Ferdinand and Isabella and Henry VII. In the next year, startled by his easy success, Ferdinand and Isabella and Maximilian changed sides, joining with Venice and the papacy to drive him out again. By 1509 matters had become more complicated, for the Italian states themselves had become less hesit-ant about using foreign aid for the settlement of scores against their domestic enemies. In that year Ferdinand, Maximilian, Louis XII, Pope Julius II, the duke of Ferrara and the marquis of Mantua formed the League of Cambrai, designed to defeat Venice and partition her

* See below, p. 48.

mainland territories. At the battle of Agnadello the League won a victory so resounding that the pope, caught in the dilemma of the sorcerer's apprentice, turned against France, which was eating up the lion's share of the spoils, and two years later, in 1511, had constructed an anti-French league which included (once more) Ferdinand and Maximilian together with the Swiss, Henry VIII of England and the recent victim, Venice. After the battle of Ravenna (1512) France was forced to withdraw – only to return, as we have seen, three years later.

While large-scale alliances were by no means novel (they had decided the course of the Hundred Years War, for instance) they had never before been constructed or reconstituted so rapidly. This was made possible by a transformation of diplomatic method. From the late fifteenth century the practice spread from Italy (where it was widely accepted) to the rest of western Europe of retaining diplomats *en poste* abroad for years at a time, so that the machinery for bringing about international agreements or changes of front was constantly in being. A second point is that the countries of Europe, especially those in the west, were to a hitherto unprecedented degree *able* to take a diplomatic initiative which could be followed up at once with cash and with armies.

Charles VIII was able to invade Italy with the largest army Europe had seen because his predecessor, Louis XI, had devoted a long reign (1461–83) to guiding France's economic recovery from the Hundred Years War. Ferdinand was enabled to intervene first on one side and then on the other because his joint reign with Isabella had restored order in the two kingdoms to such effect that the *reconquista* had been resumed, the Moorish kingdom of Granada conquered in 1492 and a well-trained army left idle. The end of the Wars of the Roses and the reign of Edward IV (1471–83) had restored peace and a re-tautening of government to England, a process that had been resumed under a Tudor monarch after the two-year rule of Richard III (1483–5). Thus Charles VIII had to bribe Henry VII not to invade France in 1494 and Henry VIII was able to invade France in his successor's reign with little regard for the cost. In 1477 the Swiss had defeated (and killed) their chief enemy, Duke Charles the Bold of Burgundy, at Nancy. This left them secure enough to supply large numbers of their highly specialised pikemen to the early French campaigns in Italy. By 1499, after an even bloodier battle than Nancy, they had defeated an army sent against them by Maximilian and, freed from any practical dependence on the Empire, took part in the Italian wars increasingly as a polity and less as the supplier of troops to others. Only Germany itself remained as disunited as it had been in the middle of the fifteenth century and as lacking in effective central administration. Maximilian, as a result, was the weakest of the contestants who fought in the peninsula.

This common and intense concern with Italy from 1494 to 1515 produced a new alertness on the part of each of the countries of western Europe to what the others were doing and encouraged a recognisably 'modern' method of handling diplomatic exchanges. It becomes even more tempting to think of international affairs being conducted in terms of a state system when Maximilian's grandson Charles, ruler of Spain since 1516, inherited the Habsburg lands on his father's death in 1519 and was elected emperor. Italy remained the battlefield but henceforward the struggle was waged between two blocs, Habsburg and (in the person of Francis I) Valois, together with allies who now appeared as little more than their satellites. By the end of our period, however, this polarisation had not produced the conscious search for a balance of power which was later to characterise international affairs in Europe. Information about the real strength of other countries was too uncertain, the pace of events too fast; above all, perhaps, there was little encouragement for long-range planning or the perception of an eventual balance because from the point of view of the non-Italian powers, the wars in the peninsula were wars for conquest not for survival.

Even with this reservation, however, the pace of international affairs makes Europe look as if it was made up of states in the modern sense, at least in the west, and the fact that it was internal unity and increased administrative efficiency that enabled them to enter the contest for Italy in the first place strengthens this impression. Before turning to the internal development of individual countries, therefore, it is worth making some general cautions against reading the word state in too modern a sense when it is used in this book.

In eastern Europe it is especially misleading. Ivan III (1462–1505) and his successor Vasili IV were engaged in transforming 'Muscovy' into 'Russia' through a series of conquests which remained only haltingly integrated into one governmental unit by 1520. The tie between Lithuania and Poland, the elective nature of kingship in Poland, Hungary and Bohemia which destroyed the possibility of administrative continuity, the virtual absence of a class of professional administrators who might have bridged this continuity to some extent: these difficulties in the way of achieving some recognisable statehood were compounded by the fact that the destinies of these countries were determined by the self-interest of a particular class, the nobles, and by the family ties of rulers who formed a 'ring' which looked on the lands between Germany and Russia as common property to be shared out according to dynastic convenience rather than national interest. A similar uncertainty as to where effective authority lay slowed the move towards uniform administration and a higher degree of harmony between people and government in the Scandinavian countries. In Germany the particularist sentiment of certain towns and princes was so strong that they preferred to ally among themselves rather than invoke the protection of the imperial government. Thus the Swabian League was formed in the south in 1488 to contain the Swiss and prevent the expansion of Bavaria under its aggressive Wittelsbach duke. Within this mosaic of particularisms there were territories where government was at least as effective as it was, say, in England. One such territory was the Palatinate, but even here there were anomalies. Its ruler the elector had to accept that some of his powerful vassals should promise to support him not in his rôle as count palatine but in his personal guise as, say, the lord of Weinsberg. The Burgundian inheritance resembled Germany. From Franche-Comté to Brabant and Flanders all its components were subject to one ruler and his council, but they were too disparate in size, economic function and historical conditioning to function with real coherence. The industrialised regions were not only averse to being joined with the agricultural regions in the southern parts of the duchy but were intent on pursuing their own traditional rivalries, province against province, town against town. They had, moreover, strong personal loyalties of their own. The Guelderlanders, for instance, looked on the Egmont family as their natural leaders, not the Habsburgs. The Netherlands was not actually unworkable as a unit, but the process of achieving a measure of consent was immensely wasteful of time and money. Finally, within the Swiss Confederation there was no central power. Each canton remained independent. When questions of general interest had to be discussed, one or two of the cantons, usually the richest, Bern or Zurich, took the lead and invited the others to send representatives to an *ad hoc* diet. The cantons did not consider themselves bound by majority decisions. It was also open to a group of cantons whose topography and common occupations gave them a specially close bond – such as the 'forest' cantons Uri, Schwyz and Unterwalden – to call a local diet without reference to the others.

Even when reviewing developments within the remaining countries of western Europe it is important to bear in mind not only the lack of a clear concept of frontiers but the omnipresence of enclaves, regions which were ill-adapted or unwilling to co-operate fully with the aims of government and which thus inhibited the development – part psychological, part a matter of administrative organisation – of a more or less uniform and willing response to universally binding governmental decisions.

In monarchies, the greatest enclaves were, paradoxically, the personal possessions of the ruler, vast estates which he could treat more favourably or exploit more effectively than the rest of his realm, areas which were 'his' in a purely personal sense although their revenues went far towards supporting a government which legislated for the country as a whole. Every country had an enclave in the form of the church, its territorial possessions and its courts. Each had enclaves in the form of areas as yet ill-digested by the solvents of central administration. In 1515 Francis I inherited a France whose boundaries were to remain little changed until the reign of Louis XIV. But he could still operate with real freedom only within the ancient nucleus of the country, in Picardy, Champagne, Touraine, Berry, Anjou and Maine – the 'real France' as an Italian traveller put it. Elsewhere his hands were tied by bargains made when lands were acquired: tax exemptions, legal exclusions, the need to consult local assemblies. Though heir to the richest and largest country in the west which professed allegiance to one ruler, in certain respects he was forced to administer it as though it were a federation of independent powers. In Aragon, Ferdinand's will was particularly hampered by the need to defer to local customs in Catalonia, as was that of Isabella in the remotest part of her nation, Galicia, where she had to grope and sue for support among its rival chieftains. The Tudor writ, too, began to run haltingly as it neared the Scottish border, and even nearer the centre of government there were patches of territory, like the palatinate of Lancaster, the 'liberty' of Richmond and the soke of Peterborough, which retained traditional rights of self-determination in matters of law and, to a lesser extent, of taxation. Even Milan, a duchy brought forward in evidence by Jacob Burckhardt for his thesis that in Italy the state became a 'work of art', was so little a work of art that Lodovico Sforza, strongest of its rulers in this period, had to allow some of the leading families in the Milanese to issue their own statutes and to allow them to accept oaths of fealty from men in their neighbourhoods.

Some Examples: Florence, France, Spain, England and Germany

If we take a republic, Florence, a monarchy with an undisputed succession of rulers, France, a joint monarchy, Spain, a monarchy with a new line of rulers, England, and the combination of independent federal and monarchical powers that was the Empire, narrative limits can be assigned to each of them which while by no means self-contained are something more than mere conveniences; they represent fairly well-defined periods of political development and they roughly coincide. For Florence, such a period runs from 1478, the year of the Pazzi conspiracy to murder Lorenzo de' Medici and his brother, to the election in 1523 of the second Medici pope, Clement VII; for France from the resumption of royal control over Anjou and the duchy of Burgundy in 1481-2 to the Field of Cloth of Gold in 1520; for Spain from the Union of Castile and Aragon in 1479 to Charles of Habsburg's election as emperor in 1519; for England from Henry Tudor's accession in 1485 to the consolidation of Wolsey's control over foreign policy in 1518; for Germany from the death of Frederick III in 1493 to Charles's election.

In Florence, because it was small, political events affected its people most closely. In 1478 the attempted murder of Lorenzo and Giuliano took place at high mass in the cathedral. With Giuliano dead and Lorenzo wounded, the assassins were pursued through the streets, vainly trying to rally support as they fled, and by nightfall four members of the Pazzi family, one of them an archbishop, were dangling from the windows of the palace of the Signoria in the full view of the populace.

By that time Lorenzo, who had inherited in 1469 the dominant role in civic affairs which had been granted since 1434 to his father and grandfather, had both tightened his political control and made enemies within the city and outside it. Together with his supporters he had increased the grip of the 'Medicean' council of one hundred over the organs of government that purported to represent more or less popular opinion. His marriage to an aristocrat and a non-Florentine, Clarice Orsini, had raised suspicions that the family were no longer content to be burghers among fellow burghers, and he had refused to cooperate with Pope Sixtus IV's attempts to increase papal control in the Romagna; the conspiracy of 1478 was devised by a jealous Florentine family with the support of the pope. And its aftermath was a war against Sixtus and his ally the king of Naples whose conclusion was a personal diplomatic triumph for Lorenzo, and the occasion for tightening still further the controls he and his supporters used to keep their potential opponents out of office. Though formally never more than a private citizen, when he died in 1492 leadership in the city passed without fuss to his son, Piero, as the focus that kept together, and thus in power, the group of families who had long associated themselves with the Medici.

By 1494 the decisions in Florence were made by a group comprising some three hundred individuals who staffed the chief governmental committees in rotation. In that year Charles VIII invaded Italy. On his march through Tuscany Piero hastened the king's exit towards Rome with bribes (assent to the occupation of key fortresses) so large that the agreement was denounced even by his own party and he was forced to flee the city. The resentments that came to the surface represented many shades of opinion, but they expressed themselves in two major arguments: that Florence should be governed by a fairly small number of experienced men, subservient to no one family, and that political control should be far more widely spread than it had been at any time in the century. By now the Dominican prior of S. Marco, Girolamo Savonarola, had attained a remarkable ascendency over a large number of all classes in the city, based on a powerful pulpit manner in the evangelist tradition, a series of accurate prophecies, including Lorenzo's death and the coming of the French, and a down to earth concern with public issues. Almost certainly his support of the 'popular' argument enabled it to be put into effect. The constitution was redesigned with safeguards against the formation of parties and with a new feature that was as radical an inversion of the Medicean council of one hundred conceivable in the Europe of that time, a Great Council whose membership was open to one out of every four or five lay adult males living in the city.

The new form of government was at once put to the test of war, not through the direct participation of the citizens, but through heavy taxation for the hire of mercenaries, the psychological pressure of diplomatic isolation (for Florence stuck to the French alliance inaugurated by Piero), and actual threats to their territories from invading armies and from local crises such as Cesare Borgia's attempts to consolidate the fragmented political units of the neighbouring Romagna. Closest to Florentine hearts was the war that dragged on from 1495 to 1509 to regain Pisa; occupied by French troops as a guarantee that Florence would not cut Charles VIII's communications during his Neapolitan campaign of 1494–5, the city refused to return to Florentine domination when the French withdrew. And when that prolonged crisis was over another began, caused by Florence's resistance to the urging of Julius II to join the league he formed in 1511 to rally all Italy against the French. Continued opposition to that project led to the re-imposition of the Medici on the city by force of papal and Spanish troops in 1512, the abolition of the Great Council and a return to the constitutional forms of Lorenzo's last years.

Factional jealousies and impatience with the fumbling procedures of the 'democratic' government had led to the re-emergence of a pro-Medicean party which welcomed the events of 1512. There were malcontents. Two of them planned a repetition of the Pazzi conspiracy in 1513 which foundered through its betrayal – a betrayal in which Machiavelli was involved and to which we owe the great works of his years of banishment from public affairs, *The Prince* and *The Discourses on Livy*. But radical republicanism, the republicanism that saw the Great Council as its symbol, was pushed underground.

In 1512 the head of the Medici family was Lorenzo's son, cardinal Giovanni. In the following year he became pope as Leo X and Florence began to be governed increasingly from Rome, though formally it remained a republic which merely paid a special deference to the members of the family resident in the city. The link between the Medici palace and the Vatican formed one difference between the Florence of 1494 and of 1513. Another was largely a matter of tone; related to a pope and married into princely families, the new generation of Medici brought with them a whiff of a world that did not take republics for granted. Hope among republican shades of opinion revived with Leo's unexpectedly early death in 1521. But the new head of the family, cardinal Giulio, was shrewd enough to disarm opposition by inviting it into the open in the form of written suggestions for changes in the constitution and two years later he, too, became pope as Clement VII. Under Leo X, papal policies had not cost Florence too dear in terms of cash, and branches of the city's banks in Rome flourished. Clement was more formidably burdened by French and Spanish political pressure and could no longer ignore the spread of anti-Catholic feeling in Germany. He needed increasingly huge sums of money and he turned regularly to Florence for it. Opposition mounted within the city, fostered by the unpopularity of the family's current representatives there. In 1527 Rome was sacked by Clement's enemies and the Florentines once more expelled the Medici and re-constituted the government in the form in which Savonarola had known it.

For Florence the story that dates can tell is above all a constitutional one. For France it is predominantly one of wars. From the death of Louis XI in 1483 one king followed another without question or tumult, Charles VIII being succeeded by Louis XII in 1498, Louis by Francis I in 1515. Louis XI's policy of enforcing internal peace, keeping clear of major foreign entanglements, encouraging trade and agriculture and taking advice from men who shared his own taste for unglamorous hard work had succeeded well enough to allow a country naturally rich in natural resources to recover from the Hundred Years War. At the end of his reign two strokes of luck nearly doubled the area of France directly belonging to the crown. In 1481 the death of the last male representative of the great feudal house of Anjou brought in the extensive provinces of Anjou and Provence. In 1482 the Treaty of Arras settled the problem of what was to become of Charles the Bold's territories after his death in 1477 by giving Picardy and the duchy of Burgundy to Louis. In marked contrast to earlier periods, from 1482 to the conquests of Louis XIV the history of France is that of very much the same geographical area – apart from Brittany. This duchy had traditionally conducted itself as an independent power. Again, a fortunate death came to the aid of the crown. In 1488 Duke Francis II died, leaving the duchy to his daughter. Among her numerous suitors Charles VIII proved most persuasive because in 1491 he invaded Brittany with a large army and granted terms only on condition that she marry him.

This recognisably modern 'France' continued to be governed on lines firmly sketched by Louis XI: the concentration of authority within the king's council, definition of the competence of the other central organs of state, notably those dealing with finance, and their relationship to that council, steady erosion of local privileges in the interest of a uniform administration operating from Paris. This last policy proceeded slowly enough to avoid any major confrontation between either powerful individuals or corporations and the crown. The fact that the estates general were not convened after 1484 until 1560 has caused that year to be seen as a landmark of sorts, but in fact there was little popular support for the idea of a meeting of representatives of France as a whole and kings continued to consult with their subjects through local assemblies; from the point of view of the crown getting what it wanted, and the regions having a chance to present their grievances, there was no significant change involved.

Charles VIII and his successors inherited the most productive tax system and the best organised military establishment in Europe. Stable at home, they took their country unhesitatingly to war. In 1494 Charles entered Italy with the intention of taking up the Angevin claim to Naples. Entering at the invitation of Lodovico Sforza, unopposed either by Florence or the papacy, his army proceeded to Naples as fast as the quarter-masters could chalk up the marks on the lodgings appointed for it. Naples surrendered after the briefest of campaigns and though Charles had to fight hard to gain the Alps again in the following year, the inconclusive battle of Fornovo allowed him to extract most of the troops he had not left in garrison in Naples.

Though the Neapolitans quickly rebelled against their new governor, Louis XII could look on his predecessor's venture as a success. His target was broader. To the crown's claim to Naples he added the claim of his own family – through the marriage of one of his forbears to a Visconti – to Milan. In the second year of his reign, 1499, he invaded northern Italy and by the following year was master of the Milanese. His next move was to reconquer the kingdom of Naples; not all of it, for Ferdinand had expressed Aragon's traditional interest in southern Italy by sending troops to help the Neapolitans expel Charles VIII's garrisons, but half the kingdom, grudgingly accepting that he would have to share the spoils with Ferdinand. In 1502 Naples was invaded and divided, but inevitably there were quarrels over the division of the spoils, and led by a general of genius, Gonsalvo da Cordoba, and supported by reinforcements from Sicily and Spain – France's inadequate sea power was never made good during her interventions in Italy – Spanish troops expelled the French once more, and this time finally, in 1504.

By now military adventures in Italy had become something of a fashion. France's next attempt at conquest, through the League of Cambrai of 1508, was as part of an assault whereby France, Spain, Maximilian, Pope Julius II and the duke of Mantua were to partition the territories of Venice between them. The diplomatic preparations for Louis's part in this venture were necessarily elaborate. Louis was far more of a working monarch than Charles VIII, who could sign his own name only with difficulty, but though reasonably intelligent he was neither subtle nor patient and was fortunate in having a Wolsey in the shape of Georges, cardinal of Amboise, to take most of the burden of administration and negotiation from him. The allies' victory at Agnadello was complete but as in the case of Naples, occupation was followed by mutual jealousy. The allies, as we have seen, re-shuffled; Ferdinand and Julius and later Maximilian, joining forces against the French who by 1513 were forced not only out of the Veneto but out of the Milanese as well.

Flamboyant and cultivated, Francis I differed from his predecessors in every respect but militancy. Within a few months of his accession he was across the Alps and by the battle of Marignano convincingly won back Milan. The concordat of Bologna, in terms of both what was conceded to Francis and what was withheld, reflected Leo X's grudging acceptance of the probability that France had come to Italy to stay.* So did the much-trumpeted Treaty of Cambrai of 1517 and its sister blue-print for lasting peace in Europe, the Treaty of London of the following year. On Maximilian's death in 1519 Francis even put himself forward as a candidate for the Empire. That glamorous if half-hearted bid, followed as it was next year by the portentous entertainment of the Field of Cloth of Gold, is chiefly notable because it represents an expenditure that, added to the costs of war in three reigns, could only come from a country so prosperous and – by the standards of the age – so orderly that any summary of its political history must deal primarily with events that took place outside its borders.

For Spain, in contrast, such a summary must be concerned equally with internal and external acts of state. Both Isabella's and

* See below, p. 167.

Ferdinand's predecessors as monarchs of Castile and Aragon had been men of mediocre competence whose reigns had been plagued by the revolts of dissident nobles and a wide-spread lawlessness. Isabella's succession in 1474 was, moreover, followed by a civil war which was not settled conclusively in her favour until 1479, the year in which Ferdinand became king of Aragon. The union of the two crowns which was then published was based on a tried working partnership. Ferdinand had married Isabella in 1469, and had supported her with diplomatic advice and military aid throughout the war; the mutual respect they showed for one another was an essential contribution to what was to seem in retrospect the most extraordinary two generations in Spanish history.

Though Spain was unified in their persons, no attempt was made to improve constitutional or administrative unity. Castile as the larger and greatly the more populous country absorbed much of Ferdinand's time as well as most of Isabella's. Governing through an itinerant royal council linked to Aragon itself and its sister regions, Catalonia and Valencia, through viceroys and local councils, Ferdinand deferred enough to traditional local institutions to keep his own tri-partite realm content, and staffed them carefully enough to minimise the consequences of his absenteeism. The reconsolidation of fractured royal power in Castile began during a lull in the civil war when in 1476 a meeting of the *cortes* (the national assembly) agreed to unite the multitude of local self-help agencies, the *santas hermandades*, into an organisation directly responsible to the crown for police work and the suppression of brigandage throughout the realm. But if Isabella needed a base of law and order from which to work, she also needed cash and the ability to bribe or reward the nobles whose independence she was determined to reduce. By establishing in that same year the principle that the crown had the right of appointment to the grand masterships of the immensely wealthy military orders she made a remarkably bold stroke towards achieving this aim, too. She offered the first that fell vacant, that of Santiago, to Ferdinand, and he prudently refused. But this refusal meant that there was no serious opposition to his acceptance of the remaining two. Altogether, the affair of the grand masterships exemplified the successful union of talents as well as of crowns, with Ferdinand's astuteness balancing his wife's approach, a blend of impulsive pragmatism and – especially in religious matters – idealism.

The union itself was quickly followed by another measure designed to produce cash and cut down the power of the nobles *vis-à-vis* the crown: the Act of Resumption of 1480, whereby they were required to hand back all crown lands they had occupied during the disturbances since 1464. In the same year the royal council of Castile was reformed on lines that seriously maimed the initiative of the great feudatories. And in 1482 Isabella diverted their energies and gave her new administration time to stabilise by re-opening the centuries-long crusade against the Moors, now concentrated in the Muslim kingdom of Granada.

For ten years the history of Spain was largely one of war in the south and consolidation at the centre, and if there is any recognisable break in the period we are treating it comes in 1492. In that year Granada finally fell and was incorporated in Castile. Six months later Christopher Columbus at last got the backing he had been demanding for years and set off to make the first recorded European contact with the West Indies. In one sense this voyage, and those that followed it represented a transference of the mood of *reconquista* overseas. But just as the war against Granada had combined the service both of God and of internal order, the transatlantic voyages were designed to produce both Christians and gold. More purely idealistic, or at least more singlemindedly doctrinaire, was the third chief event of that year, the forcible expulsion of all professing Jews.*

The bull *Inter caetera* whereby Spain obtained exclusive rights over her New World discoveries from the Spanish pope Alexander VI in 1493, and its secular counterpart the Treaty of Tordesillas of the following year, which divided the as yet undiscovered parts of the globe between Spain and Portugal, were almost exclusively in the interest of Castile; though individual Aragonese were permitted to settle in the Americas, trade and the profits of settlement were vested in the Castilian crown. But whereas up to 1494 the political theme had been one of settling Castile's internal affairs and launching the country on its amazing career overseas to the west, from that date Ferdinand's initiative became predominant and was directed towards Aragon's traditional area of influence, the eastern Mediterranean, and the theme becomes one chiefly of foreign policy and war.

In 1495 Ferdinand was largely responsible for the alliance of Italian powers designed to hound the French out of Italy, and he remained firmly committed to that policy, in spite of his agreement reached by the Treaty of Granada in 1500 to share the kingdom of Naples with Louis XII. By 1504 the possessor of Naples, he joined the anti-Venetian League in 1508 – another occasion on which he joined with France only so long as it suited his convenience. In 1512 it was largely thanks to his troops that Julius II was able to force France's last ally, Florence, to surrender and to accept back the exiled Medici. And taking advantage of Louis' embarrassment in Italy he

---

* See below, p. 143–4 seq.

annexed the kingdom of Navarre and thus rounded out Spain to its present borders.

Isabella had died in 1504, and true to the essentially personal nature of the union, she was succeeded not by Ferdinand but by their daughter Joanna, wife of Maximilian's son Philip. Accordingly, in 1504 Joanna became queen of Castile. For two years Ferdinand was legally restricted to the government of his own kingdom, but in 1506 Philip of Habsburg died. Joanna was by now insane and Ferdinand became regent for their heir Charles, who was then six years old. Though supported by Isabella's chief counsellor, Archbishop Cisneros, Ferdinand's position in Castile was complicated by the interference of Charles' Netherlandish advisers. Nevertheless he was able to continue her policies in two respects: he moved the crusade against the Moors across to the north African coast, where Oran was captured in 1509, and he obtained from Julius II the right to appoint to all ecclesiastical benefices in the New World, a right he and Isabella had already obtained for Granada.

This was the first of the policies of the Catholic Kings (the title Ferdinand and Isabella had been granted in 1494 for their services to the church) which Charles followed after Ferdinand's death in 1516. His advisers persuaded the pope to grant the crown the right to appoint to bishoprics throughout Spain, thus obtaining the most tractable of all the national branches of the Catholic church in Europe. It was some years before he picked up the other threads of his predecessor's policies. Arriving in Spain in 1517, unable to speak Spanish and surrounded by Flemings, his personal unpopularity brought a resentful halt to political changes of moment until he learned to govern Spain as a Spaniard in the years after his election to the Empire in 1519.

As with Spain, the first responsibility of government in England was the imposition of law and order and the reestablishment of effective royal power. In England the task was eased because the means of exerting the crown's authority were already established by long precedent and incorporated in financial, judicial and consultative institutions, which, given favourable circumstances and sound leadership, could produce strong and orderly rule. In Castile and to a lesser extent in Aragon, the sovereigns had to invent; in England their chief task was to restore.

Some progress was made in this direction during the 1470s by Edward IV, not so much in checking the slide towards the sort of unplanned decentralisation that resulted from the retaining of private armies and from the feuds that persisted between the supporters of York and Lancaster, but in putting the central organs of government back to work in the interest of the country rather than of a clique.

Edward died in 1483. The succession of his twelve-year-old son Edward V provoked the closet-skirmish that was the prelude to the last of the Wars of the Roses: a struggle for control of the government between the boy-king's mother and his uncle, Richard, duke of Gloucester that ended when Richard persuaded parliament to proclaim him king on the score of the boy's possible illegitimacy. This manner of taking the crown was a source of offence to some, the disappearance of Edward and his brother which speedily followed was another, yet a third was his checking opposition not so much through the law as with the axe. In this atmosphere his attempt to govern peacefully in the tradition of Edward IV was seen in terms of personal ambition, and when the representative of the rival house of Lancaster, Henry Tudor, arrived from France in 1485 he found enough support to win him both the battle of Bosworth and the crown itself.

With his rival dead, Henry lost no time in encouraging men to take it for granted that he and his heirs now represented the true line of English kingship, a claim that could not have been proved either by law or genealogy. Parliament agreed to this, as it had in Richard's case. Henry's marriage to Elizabeth of York did something to placate the potential opposition that remained and he deprived it of its natural leader by putting the Yorkist heir, the young earl of Warwick, in the Tower.

That Henry VII was able to found a dynasty that ruled England for over a century was – apart from his highly developed sense of the possible – a matter of timing. By 1485 not only were a majority of the magnates who considered themselves Yorkist prepared to put security above the chanciness of yet another conflict, but this feeling was even stronger among those non-noble landowners and merchants who, while well-to-do and proud of their local influence, were more concerned with livelihood than loyalty. It was to these men that the measures which Henry took to break the private armies of retainers, to stop juries from being brow-beaten and to protect tenure, contract and public order through special courts directly answerable to the crown appealed. It was they who served him willingly as justices of the peace in the counties and who gave him their voice when he sparingly ordered them up to London to sit in a parliament. Latent opposition remained. Around Lambert Simnel, posing as the imprisoned earl of Warwick, rallied enough disaffection for Henry to have to lance it with a battle, the rout at Stoke in 1487 which left Simnel a prisoner in his hands. A graver threat, and a much more long-lasting one, was Perkin Warbeck, posing as Edward V's brother the duke of York. That Henry's problems were not ones merely of domestic order was shown by the support Warbeck obtained first in France, then in the Netherlands and successively in the Empire, Ireland and Scotland before he found himself let down by the men of Cornwall, whose traditional resistance to central authority he had relied on to give him an army. His career as an imposter had lasted for six years before he surrendered in 1497. Two years later Henry was still concerned enough about plots against the regime to have both Warbeck and the still imprisoned earl of Warwick executed.

Yet by this time Henry had already taken steps to protect himself through a ring of foreign alliances. By the treaty of Medina del Campo in 1489 his two-year-old son Arthur was contracted to marry Ferdinand's daughter Catherine. The treaty of Étaples with France in 1492 put an end to the support Henry had been giving to Brittany's struggle for independence; support given partly in his role as claimant to the throne of France and partly because friendship with Brittany was the surest way of keeping down piracy in the Channel. By 1496 a peace settlement with the Netherlands reduced the danger of support for a rival coming from that source, in spite of continuing economic rivalry. Nearer home, Ireland was punished for having supported Warbeck by laws ('Poynings laws') passed at Drogheda in 1494 which theoretically made Ireland completely subservient to the English crown, and in 1502 a marriage was arranged between princess Margaret and James IV of Scotland. Internally the reign was less a matter of events than of processes. Financially the crown was given a greatly enhanced freedom of action by an act of resumption in 1481 which paralleled Isabella's of 1480, but apart from that Henry played the role of the good steward rather than of the constitutional innovator or the dashing proprietor. Even the most strenuously worded statutes of his parliaments, like the act on retaining of 1504, did little more than add teeth to legislation already in existence.

In 1509 the seventeen-year-old Henry VIII stepped unchallenged into an inheritance that included a tried core of councillors and bureaucrats, a balanced budget, a society which while rough and criminous was not potentially rebellious, and a clearly recognised if modest stature on the international scene. Apart from executing two of his father's more unpopular ministers, Empson and Dudley, the new king let domestic affairs continue on the lines laid down by his father, but he scooped deep into the late king's treasury in order to cut a more impressive figure abroad. Married to Arthur's widow Catherine, he welcomed the Aragonese connection which gave him a card of introduction to the protagonists in the widening drama of the Italian wars and justified aggression against France. In 1513 he tasted blood in person on an expedition that took Thérouanne and Tournai and routed a smallish French army at the battle of the Spurs, and through the victory of his deputies over France's ally Scotland at the more decisive battle of Flodden. Thereafter England's role in international diplomacy became more marked, especially when after 1515 Wolsey's personal ambition led him to relate English affairs very closely to those of the papacy. In 1518 English initiative, expressed through the treaty of London, spread a glossy if thin veneer over the hostility of the western European powers, and the period ends with tremors of apprehension being transmitted through the entire European diplomatic network as a result of the personal meetings between Henry and Charles in England and the Netherlands and between Henry and Francis on the Field of Cloth of Gold in 1520.

Germany figures large in the diplomatic history of this period but for the most part its interventions had little more than ritual significance. Threats of war were more common than actual mobilisations and military attacks usually petered out with nothing left to show for them. Yet Germany was both large and populous.

This disparity between aims and means sprang from the disparity between geography and constitution. The emperor spoke as the political leader of Germany but the Germans did not back him up. This was only to a small degree because of the elective, rather than hereditary nature of the imperial title. To all intents and purposes the Empire was hereditary in the Habsburg family; Maximilian succeeded his father Frederick III in 1493 and was succeeded in turn by his grandson Charles in 1519. The chief reason was the lack of an imperial machinery to connect the policies of the emperors with the pockets of the multitudes of princes, knights, and cities who treated their constitutional place within the Empire as peripheral to their own interests. This constitutional place was not ignored. Indeed, it was acknowledged that certain problems, brigandage, private war and, in the south west, population pressure, could not be dealt with on the local level. Both the components of the Empire and the emperor himself wanted parts of the machinery to work, but their efforts were hamstrung by a failure to agree on how it should work. And this failure, and hence the failure of the emperor to receive backing outside his own hereditary lands, was thrown into relief by the consequences of the Burgundian Duke Charles the Bold's death at the battle of Nancy in 1477.

Thanks to his marriage to Charles' daughter Mary, Maximilian received the lion's share of the duke of Burgundy's lands. He had to fight France for them but by the Peace of Senlis in 1493 he retained Franche-Comté, Luxembourg and the wealthily industrialised Netherlands, governed on his behalf by his son Philip from 1494 and then, on Philip's death in 1506, by the young Charles, chiefly under the influence of his aunt Margaret. It was this acquisition of land in the west that brought the issue of reform of the imperial constitution into urgent relief. Emperors habitually put the interest of their own territories before those of Germany as a whole. Now, to the political interests of the old Habsburg lands – hostility to Venice, defence against the Turks, fishing in the dynastic waters of Bohemia and Hungary – was added the challenge of having an unfriendly France as a neighbour. And this came at a time when France, plunging repeatedly into Italy, was showing itself to be the most aggressive of the European powers. And this challenge came during the reign of an emperor* whose character was particularly susceptible to the chivalric, religious and militant overtones which the phrase Holy Roman Empire still preserved. Maximilian, therefore, was determined to play a heroic role in Italy as prelude to leading a European crusade against the Turks. His subjects were determined that he should do nothing of the sort.

Hoping for French support against Venice, Maximilian did not oppose Charles VIII's invasion of 1494, indeed, he married the daughter of Charles' ally Lodovico Sforza of Milan partly for the sake of her dowry, partly to give publicity to the fact that Milan was a fief of the Empire. But the ease of Charles' victory over Naples gave him pause. To raise money to join the forces of the league raised to confront Charles on his way north, he approached the *Reichstag*, the imperial diet which comprised the electors together with representatives of the princes and the cities, at Worms in 1495. Such money as he got from it came too late to turn a hazardous retreat for the French into a defeat. The diet insisted on discussing constitutional reform, and from it emerged two decisions that were to endure: the banning of feud and private war within the Empire and a *Reichskammergericht*, or imperial tribunal, which was to enforce this ban. It was composed of twenty-five judges, only five of whom were appointed by Maximilian, though he appointed two more as proprietor of the Habsburg lands. Five years later, in 1500, the diet met again at Augsburg. By this time Maximilian had had to swallow the winning by the Swiss of their independence from the Empire in the Swabian war of 1499 and to watch the conquest of Milan by Louis XII in the same year. Again, his demands for money for troops were met by demands for reform. The measures of 1495 had only been against the emperor's interest insofar as they compelled him to share his supreme judicial authority. In 1500 he had to accept the *Reichsregiment*, a supreme governing body of which he was president but

---

* Maximilian was not formally emperor because that title depended on coronation by the pope, which he did not receive. But from 1508 he adopted the title emperor-elect. Hitherto, his correct title was King of the Romans.

which could legislate for the Empire without him. His military plans
again petered out, but at least he had the satisfaction of seeing the
new council wither away as an effective organ of state within a
couple of years. It was the last serious attempt at reform before
Maximilian's death.

But if subsequent diets were slightly less critical, the emperor
continued to cut a poor figure abroad. In 1496 he had vainly attacked
the Tuscan port of Livorno as Lodovico Sforza's ally against Florence.
In 1509 his only contribution to the war against Venice was the
unsuccessful siege of Padua. In 1516 he invaded the Milanese but
ran out of money after he had been in Milan for a single day; his
troops deserted and he returned to Austria in humiliation.

From 1493 to 1519 the history of the Empire is only marginally the
history of Germany. That is above all the history of the individual
principates, the self-governing ecclesiastical territories and the great
cities which made up the German-speaking world. Maximilian tried
to give them a common destiny through fervent propaganda on
behalf of a revived imperial leadership. And he failed. His success
lay in the government of his own lands and in a dynastic policy that
made his successor the ruler of more than half of western Europe.

Internal Development

Except for a few instances, the chief domestic aim of government, in
these five states as elsewhere, was not to innovate but to restore.
However, as Guicciardini pointed out in his comments on Machiavelli's *Discourses*, any attempt to reproduce something that has happened in the past necessarily produces something novel because of
intervening circumstances. What gives the governments of this period
some air of novelty was the number of precedents they exhumed or
refurbished and the speed with which they did it, the fairly general
acquiescence of their subjects (except in Germany), and the existence
of larger permanent bureaucracies which ensured that what had been
taken back under central control would be kept there.

Though no Christian government could challenge the Ottoman
Turks in this respect, the growth of central control was a phenomenon that can be observed almost all over Europe from Russia, in
the conquests of Ivan III, to the Papal States, where popes from Sixtus
IV to Julius II and Leo X fought to regain territories that had fallen
away under their predecessors and thus increase the reserves of men
and money on which their thrusting role in international as well as
peninsular politics depended. Effective centralisation was, however,
hampered by poor communications, especially where the capital was

eccentrically placed with regard to the periphery, as in England and France, and by the lack of standing armies, save in the form of royal guards and garrisons, which meant that governments had to temper change to what subjects were prepared to accept.

The areas open to central control were cleared by the crown's resumption of rights that had lapsed in periods of anarchy, by reviewing charters that enshrined (or purported to enshrine, for there had been much forgery to this effect) exemptions and privileges, by enlarging the category of offences that could be interpreted as breaches of the 'King's peace', and simply by offering quicker or fairer justice than the individual could find in the manor house or town hall. All justice had to be paid for in fees and fines, and royal justice leaned as hard as it could against enclave justice not only because by so doing it broke down purely local loyalties but because this produced what was, in effect, a lucrative but invisible tax.

In the field of justice, government was seen as giving more than it took; in that of taxation the exchange was less congenial, and it had to move warily. No French king, for instance, dared invade the tax exemptions of the nobility. Nearly all governments had to come to terms with assemblies which claimed to represent the tax-paying classes. In Poland there was the *seym*, in Sweden the *ting*, in the Empire the *Reichstag*, in Castile and Aragon the *cortes*, in France and the Netherlands meetings of estates, in England parliament. All these bodies had been shaped primarily by the crown's need for special taxes for military purposes and for the public support that was necessary if they were to be collected. They were susceptible to manipulation by the crown, particularly if the nobility were on its side, but the principle of redress of grievances in return for grants of cash was common to all of them, and rulers were naturally loath to summon them except in case of great need. Before the costs of her and Ferdinand's wars in Italy mounted seriously, Isabella let fourteen years elapse without calling the Castilian *cortes* together; Henry VII only called one parliament between 1497 and his death in 1509. The period was in general a testing time rather than a turning point in the development of national assemblies. At its close the decline of the French estates general was not yet confirmed; at the other extreme, the regular partnership of crown and parliament, later to be characteristic of English government, was hardly anticipated.

A more important development was the increasing number of professionals employed in government, for they provided continuity, a concept of service detached from blood or possession, a sense of impersonal, pervasive and accreting activity on behalf of government rather than of a particular ruler. From royal councils to local administration the number of men employed for their skill alone increased.

From Russia to the Palatinate and Spain and England the secretary
became a key member of the administration. It is no accident that the
Empire, where the civil service was weakest, failed to produce either
an effective imperial or federal administration – yet even there the
spirit of the more impersonal state-to-be was expressed by one of
Maximilian's learned councillors who complained that nothing ever
got done because the emperor himself was constantly meddling.

This move towards an impersonal element in government in no
way diminished the personal rôle of the ruler or the image he presented to his people. Every subject, said Charles VIII's chancellor
when introducing him to the estates general in 1484, must long to
see his king. 'Look with joy, then, upon his face. How radiantly it
displays such beauty, such serenity! How clearly it reflects a noble
and illustrious nature! What promise it offers to all of his sagacity in
the future! Is it not worthy to be obeyed: to deliver you from fear, to
bring perpetual calm to the terrors of the whole world? There is no
doubt that, with the aid of the confidence we feel in him, he will
accomplish his work in such a way that within his lifetime the age of
gold will return among us and everywhere cries of happiness and
rejoicing will resound!' The notion that government was the embodiment of a personal relationship between ruler and ruled, which this
harangue conveyed, did not imply mere obedience. It was accepted
that the prince should protect as well as make demands on his people.
Feudal conventions had indoctrinated Europe with the idea of contract, coronation oaths stressed the ruler's duties as well as his
powers, and when given an opportunity subjects were not slow to
speak up for their own side of the relationship.

When Henry VII rode into Worcester in 1486 he was greeted by a
pageant actor with the words

> 'O Henry! much art thou behold to us
> That thee have raised by our election.'

In 1514, the estates of Bavaria lectured Duke Wilhelm in still plainer
terms: 'What is a prince but an administrator of a territory, a servant
of servants, as even the pope has called himself? A prince remains the
first in his land only as long as he leads all his subjects in virtue. If
not, he need not be praised, nor honoured, nor obeyed.' Henry VII
was a new king with a title to the throne that was not altogether
watertight. Wilhelm was being actively opposed by his younger
brother Ludwig. But though these examples are special cases they
do reflect a general, if by then old-fashioned, idea that there was a
special and direct bond between the ruler and his people. Kings
continued to acknowledge this convention by explaining the reasons

for their actions in certain cases: Charles VIII explained his reform of the Rouen exchequer to the local estates, invited the towns to endorse his pre-invasion treaties of 1493 and justified the invasion itself to them. Monarchs still extracted personal oaths of allegiance from individuals and towns, thus indicating that the crucial loyalties were expected to be felt for the sovereign rather than for the state. Henry's visit to Worcester was part of a programme followed by all rulers to show themselves to the people. Erasmus warned the future Charles V that 'nothing so alienates the affections of his people as for [the ruler] to take pleasure in living abroad, for then they seem to be neglected by him to whom they wish to be most important.' In illness and old age, Louis XI, terrified of assassination, shut himself up at Plessis-les-Tours, strengthening it with spikes and iron pillboxes from which archers could shoot at anyone trying to gain an entrance. He dismissed most of his attendants for fear that they should poison him. Yet in order to make it clear that though in seclusion he had not ceased to rule, he increased his diplomatic activity and invented excuses to correspond with countries with which diplomatic negotiations could not credibly be carried on. According to Commines he sent to Spain for mastiffs, Valencia for 'little shaggy dogs', to Sicily for a mule, to Naples for horses, even to Sweden and Denmark for elk and reindeer.

So far were they from trusting to administrative forms and centralising policies to preserve loyalty to the man as well as obedience to the machine that rulers up-graded their titles. The grand duke Ivan III of Russia had himself styled 'sovereign of all Russia', his successor, Vasili, referred to himself as tsar, or emperor. From the neutral and objective 'king' Henry VII had become by 1504 'our most dread sovereign lord'. The titles given in proclamations emphasised the wars were between rulers, not between states. In 1485, when England and France were on friendly terms, the French king was referred to as Henry's 'most dearest cousin, Charles of France'. Five years later, France was an enemy, its ruler simply 'Charles the French king'. In 1492 alliance brought Henry to refer to 'the right high and mighty prince his cousin of France'. War in 1513 led to a return to the formula 'Louis the French king', the truce of 1514 to the style 'the right excellent, high and mighty prince, King Louis of France.' It was during this period that a ceremony was elaborated to conceal the fact that a French king was actually dead until the moment he was placed in his tomb. An elaborately lifelike effigy was made of the newly dead monarch, to which all honour was paid as if it were the man himself. In the funeral procession to S. Denis the king's body lay naked in a coffin, but the effigy wore his crown and carried his sceptre and staff of justice. Not till the body was actually lowered into the ground was the cry made 'King Charles is dead; long live King Louis.' As yet this ritual, so powerful because it tapped the appeal of both pageant and mystery play, was not an acting out of the doctrine that the king never dies; in that formula something like the state, as opposed to the personality of the ruler is implied. It expressed, rather, a conviction of the importance of prolonging the homage and glory due to a king to the very edge of the grave.

Logically, a ruler's court, as an extension of his personality, became more gorgeous. Henry VII, though frugal with the country's money in other respects, was prodigal in the banquets and entertainments he gave at court. The purpose of court life was, of course, not only to arouse interest and awe at home but to impress foreign visitors. The expense of Henry VIII's Westminster tournament of 1511 would have covered the construction of sixteen or seventeen ships of war, and this inflation of princely spectacle was a widespread phenomenon; it could be seen in the courts of Milan or Vienna or Moscow and in the progresses during which the French kings and Ferdinand and Isabella showed themselves off as the visible embodiment of their nations. It was, moreover, a bait to attract nobles and thus fulfilled a straightforward political purpose: the expense of a glamorous court and the pensions handed out to courtiers was less than that caused by disaffection, let alone revolt.

A feeling of identity with a ruler did not necessarily lead to an identification with his policies. So a hitherto unprecedented use was made of propaganda. The means used were various. Proclamations and manifestos were distributed for reading from the pulpit. Yea-saying men of letters were employed to trumpet their employers' fame and the rightness of their causes. The fine arts were pressed into service even when the audiences they impressed were necessarily small. Threatened by proposals to call a general council of the church, Sixtus IV commissioned Botticelli to warn the conciliarists of the fate that befell rebels to God's appointed by means of his fresco The Punishment of Corah. Julius II, conscious that heretics who attacked the doctrine of transubstantiation were also attacking the priests who alone could produce the miracle, had Raphael paint the Miracle of Bolsena, with its wafer stained with blood.* Medals were struck with political slogans. Even everyday coins could carry a political message. After Isabella's death Ferdinand, though legally no more than regent in Castile, had coins minted with the inscription

---

* To memorialise Sweden's release from the coils of Denmark Sten Sture commissioned Bernt Notke to make the equestrian statue of St. George and the dragon – an action paralleled by the erection of Donatello's Judith and Holofernes in front of Florence's civic palace to symbolise the expulsion of the Medici.

'Ferdinand and Joanna, King and Queen of Castile, Leon and Aragon'. Nor was the drama neglected. Sannazaro's *The triumph of fame* celebrated Ferdinand's conquest of Granada for the benefit of his cousin Ferrante of Naples. Konrad Celtis wrote a play which commemorated Maximilian's defeat of the Bohemian army in 1504 and coupled with it an exhortation to the emperor to take a crusading army to Constantinople – a project for which Maximilian had long sought money and troops. Whether the poet and dramatist Pierre Gringore was actually sponsored by Louis XII is not clear, but his writings certainly followed the king's policies very closely: anti-Venetian in 1509, when France was about to attack Venice, anti-papal in 1512, when Louis was trying to bully Julius II with the help of a general council of the church.

The use of popular phrases in Gringore's propaganda plays suggests that they were written for audiences with a mixed social background. Still wider audiences were reached by the woodcut, which played something like the part of the modern political cartoon. No ruler used the woodcut to such various ends as did Maximilian, from crude and cheap broadsheets justifying particular political moves, to the elaborate 'Triumphal Arch' (of which self-glorifying work seven hundred copies were printed) and the massive illustrated books, *Freydahl* and *Teuerdank* which gave, under the gauziest of disguises, a vision of Maximilian as a multi-talented superman under the special protection of the gods. Printing made the propaganda leaflet possible – Louis XII issued them during his campaigns in Italy. Heavily slanted political songs were printed as well as sung.

Propaganda could, of course, work both ways; a leader could use it to tell his followers, or subjects, what they ought to think, subjects could use it to put their own case to a leader. In 1515, when Maximilian's grandson Charles came to the Netherlands, the citizens of Bruges, losing business fast (partly because the river was silting up) to Antwerp, felt the need of support. They staged a pageant entry for the young prince in the course of which he 'was led before two scenes which went to the heart of the situation. The first showed a despairing lady named Bruges being deserted by Business and Merchandise. The next one did more than present the problem: it suggested the solution. In it Law and Religion were forcibly preventing Business and Merchandise from deserting the lady.'*

In the case of such animated petitions and the answering proclamation that could follow them, something like a dialogue between ruler and ruled was possible – though it should be born in mind that

---

* G. R. Kernodle, *From art to theatre: form and convention in the Renaissance* (Chicago 1944) 69.

pageant programmes were planned by guilds and municipal councils and not by representatives of all income and occupation groups. Even when a pageant tableau was purely congratulatory, however, as when in 1515 Lyons greeted Francis I with a scene which showed him as Hercules taking the golden apples from the garden of the Hesperides (Milan), issue and ruler were identified before a mass audience which was then extended still further by published descriptions.

The effect of realism in the fine and graphic arts and in portraits on medals and coins, of the press and of the newly elaborate pageant and the masque-play was to make the image of the ruler so vivid that for the majority of men exposed to these media it helped to obscure the growth of bureaucratic institutions and the increasing grip of government on the nation as a whole. Printed collections of statutes, proclamations and legal decisions helped to give a circle of educated men, for the most part lawyers, a clearer view of government as a substantive, evolving whole, though as the volume of original law-making was still small and the citation of centuries-old statutes frequent, the potential power of government to interfere progressively and minutely with men's lives was difficult to grasp. And this was particularly true at a time when diplomacy, wars and highly publicised dynastic marriages were continually drawing attention to the personal rôle of the prince or his *alter ego*, a Wolsey in England, an Amboise in France – in decisions affecting the destinies of peoples.*

International Relations and War

Before describing Utopia, Thomas More's imaginary traveller, Raphael Hythlodaeus, was asked why he did not put the wisdom he had accumulated overseas at the disposal of some ruler in Europe. His answer was that 'many have done it in published books' but vainly, because princes do not want to be told to rule uprightly. 'Come now,' he continued, 'suppose I were at the court of the French King and sitting in his privy council. In a most secret meeting, a circle of his most astute councillors over which he personally presides is setting its wits to work to consider by what crafty mechanisms he may keep his hold on Milan and bring back into his power the Naples which has been eluding his grasp; then overwhelm Venice and subjugate the whole of Italy; next bring under his sway Flanders, Brabant and, finally, the whole of Burgundy – and other nations, too, whose territory he has already conceived the idea of usurping.

* See further on this topic, below, p. 73 seq.

'At this meeting, one advises that a treaty should be made with the Venetians to last just as long as the king will find it convenient, that he should communicate his intentions to them, and that he should even deposit in their keeping part of the booty, which, when all has gone according to his mind, he may reclaim. Another recommends the hiring of German *Landsknechte*, and another the mollification of the Swiss with money, and another the propitiation of the offended majesty of the emperor with gold as an acceptable offering. Another thinks that a settlement should be made with the king of Aragon and that, as a guarantee of peace, someone else's kingdom of Navarre should be ceded him! Another proposes that the prince of Castile be caught by the prospect of a marriage alliance and that some nobles of his court be drawn to the French side by a fixed pension.

'Meanwhile the most perplexing question of all comes up: what is to be done with England? They agree that negotiations for peace should be undertaken, that an alliance always weak at best should be strengthened with the strongest bonds, and that the English should be called friends but suspected as enemies. The Scots therefore must be posted in readiness, prepared for any opportunity to be let loose on the English if they make the slightest movement. Moreover, some exiled noble must be fostered secretly – for treaties prevent it being done openly – to maintain a claim to the throne, that by this handle he may keep in check a king in whom he has no confidence...

'Suppose I proved that all this warmongering, by which so many nations were kept in a turmoil on the French king's account, would, after draining his resources and destroying his people, at length by some mischance end in naught and that therefore he had better look after his ancestral kingdom and make it as prosperous and flourishing as possible, love his subjects and be loved by them, live with them and rule them gently, and have no designs on other countries since what he already possessed was more than enough for him. What reception from my listeners, my dear More, do you think this speech of mine would find?'*

More's reply, of course, was 'not a very favourable one'. His own revulsion from war-mongering was such that he made the Utopians prefer assassination, supporting rival factions, bringing an enemy's rivals on his back: anything in fact, that intelligence could invent rather than having recourse to the humiliatingly animal-like phenomenon of combat.

---

* Tr. G. C. Richards in *The Complete Works of St. Thomas More*, vol. 4, ed. Edward Surtz and J. H. Hexter (Yale U.P. 1965) 87–91. Myron P. Gilmore drew attention to the illustrative value of this passage in *The World of Humanism* (N. Y., 1952) 155.

His portrait of the council meeting was only mildly a caricature and was based on the actual policies of France at the beginning of Francis I's reign. Looking back from 1516, indeed, a man of peaceable mood born, as More was, in 1478, could hardly fail to reflect on the number of wars that had taken place in his life-time and the scant changes in prosperity, frontier or regime to which they had led in Europe. It was only in the east that war had led to dramatic and lasting changes. Turkish expansion into Europe had already overwhelmed Serbia and Bosnia and reached the Adriatic. The occupation of Otranto and the even more daring raid that took Turkish cavalry round Venice into the neighbourhood of Vicenza in 1499, were mere demonstrations, though shocking ones; the reluctance of Turkish troops to winter away from their homes put a geographical limit to their actual conquests. But in 1516 and 1517, in two superbly energetic campaigns, Selim I conquered Syria and Egypt with long-term consequences to Mediterranean trade greater than any produced by a purely European conflict. In Russia, too, armies built Ivan III's control outwards from Moscow and supported his successor Vasili's completion of the control of Ryazan and the coup which abolished the independence of Pskov. Armies cut the threads held in Hungary during the reign of Matthias Corvinus, and from his death in 1490 Silesia, Moravia, Moldavia and Wallachia swung away into other orbits; Polish, Lithuanian or Turkish.

Further west, however, where populations were denser and more evenly spread, the links between local and central government closer and borders more tradition-bound, while wars were frequent their results were less impressive. Leaving aside the civil war that gave England the Tudor dynasty, the quasi-civil wars within Maximilian's dominions – the Flemish revolt of 1488, the unsuccessful attempt to control the Swiss in 1499 – and such small-scale wars as the failure of Venice's attack on Ferrara in 1483, the Bavarian–Palatine conflict of 1503 and the action taken by the Swabian League against Duke Ulrich of Württemberg in 1519, and limiting the view for the moment to conflicts which did not have extensive international backing, only the Spanish conquest of Granada in 1492 had consequences of real importance.

The wars which More/Hythlodaeus had principally in mind, however, were those in which successive French kings had sought to conquer territory in Italy, and though the French invasions did not positively 'end in naught' until 1525 – when Francis I was taken prisoner at the battle of Pavia, the losses in territories doled out to allies and in cash spent on invading armies far outweighed any positive advantages to the French crown, let alone to the French people.

French military activities worked, as we have seen, like an infection on other nations. Even the powers who could not hope for pickings of Italian territory for themselves found their attitude to foreign affairs affected by the changing pattern of domination in Italy, the varying fortunes of France, Spain and Germany, the appeals for aid from the threatened Italian peoples, the exhortations now to support one side, now the other, of the papacy. From London to Constantinople national policies were conditioned, at least intermittently, by what was happening in Italy. The first invasion of 1494 had caused little stir outside France and Italy. In 1518 the treaty designed to quiet ambitions in Italy was subscribed to by France, Spain, Germany, England and the papacy, and opened to Scotland, Denmark, Portugal, the Swiss, Hungary – and the much punished states of Italy.

This Utopian project foundered with the imperial election of the following year and wars in Italy – for Francis could not expect to conquer Charles' heartlands themselves – started up on a larger scale than ever. Even within Italy itself, while there were many changes of régime as the states paid off old scores among themselves, changed their own governments, sought foreign protection or found themselves temporarily occupied, there were only minor adjustments of borders. Nor were the campaigns outside Italy which were fought as by-products of the chief struggle notably successful. Ferdinand did not conquer the whole of Navarre. Henry sold Tournai back to France five years after taking it. Writing when the fate of Milan and Naples was still in doubt, it was natural for More to suggest that the gains of war did not justify the sacrifices made for them. Indeed, apart from the Spanish conquests in northern and southern Italy the lasting changes in political control in this period were not the result of war. Venice obtained Cyprus from its ruler Catarina Cornaro in 1488 as the result of a cash bargain, albeit backed by the threat of force. The kings of France were indebted for the extension of their power not so much to arms as to confiscation for treason (the Armagnac and Alençon territories), failure of heirs (Anjou, Maine, Provence) and marriage (Brittany). The greatest accumulation of power of all was brought into the hands of Charles V by election and inheritance. Why, then, was there so much war-mongering?

Almost everybody in Europe took wars for granted. In Bohemia a few descendants of the Hussites believed that Christ had come to deliver the world from war, that Christians should verily turn the other cheek and meet violence with non-resistance. More and Erasmus were among the very few who put forward pacifist ideas on humanitarian grounds. The church's doctrine of the Just War – that it was legitimate to fight on the authority of a legally constituted superior, for a just cause and with righteous intent – was not in itself

ignoble, but, as Erasmus pointed out, 'among such great and changing vicissitudes of human events, among so many treaties and agreements which are now entered into, now rescinded, who can lack a
pretext...for going to war?' And in fact no campaign was undertaken that failed to obtain the blessing of a nation's clergy. Indeed,
with bishops liable in law to produce troops at the crown's bidding,
and popes themselves raising armies for the extension of their own
secular power and constructing alliances for joint military action it
was a rare preacher – John Colet was such a rarity – who would
think it appropriate to raise his voice against an impending campaign. Bishop Seyssel included a section on new conquests as a matter
of course in a political treatise written for the young Francis I. It was
not the churchman but, occasionally, the sensitive scholar or chival-
rically conscious gentleman who deplored the spread of firearms.

War, after all, had been endemic in Europe as long as anyone could
remember or any chronicle record. It was war above all that had
nurtured patriotic pride and national consciousness and that formed
the most attractive reading matter in histories. So far were men of
affairs from thinking that Christ had brought peace into the world
that Commines, hard-headed servant of the French crown, could
write that God had so planned it that each European power had an
enemy placed at its side: 'thus to the kingdom of France He has
allotted England as an opponent, to the English the Scots, to the
Spanish kingdom, Portugal.'

The battlefield, too, was seen as a natural court of appeal for suits
between rulers, especially over matters of inheritance. If France had a
claim on Naples, as Charles VIII believed, or on Milan, as was clear
to Louis XII, and the local authorities rebutted these claims, how else
was justice to be obtained? Theoretically the papacy was an international arbiter, but no one believed this in practice, and only a
power which had reason to believe that the pope would arbitrate in
its favour was prepared to submit to its decision. Ferdinand did this
in order to secure Spanish rights to further exploration and settlements in the Americas. In 1493 he got what he wanted, the bull *Inter
Caetera* – but from a Spanish pope, Alexander VI. Hand to hand
combat between individuals as a way of letting God judge a case
which confounded the wisdom of men still lingered in judicial
thought, and war was but an extension of this notion. In a primarily
agrarian world the bulk of litigation was about land. Land was avidly
grasped however far away from the chief estate, however unproduct-
ive or difficult to administer. As the greatest landlords in their countries, rulers applied the same standards to territories as distant as was
Naples from Paris, and warfare in these circumstances was but
litigation pursued by other means.

The lack of a clear idea of natural or linguistic frontiers is crucial to an understanding of this state of mind. So is the equation: power equals land. Land for the subject still carried with it an aura of private justice and personal homage even though governments were doing their best to dissipate it. Outside the burgher republics, social standing was above all a matter of acres, forests, tenants, petitioners in the forecourt, retainers at the common table, muniments spelling out privileges – even if they no longer obtained. For the ruler as inheritor or conqueror, land had a value for its own sake. To chide the kings of France for striking south to Naples, which produced little more than grain (a commodity which France seldom had to import) and could only be reached by immensely vulnerable lines of communication, is reasonable but unrealistic. Henry VIII has been scolded* for seizing territories in France which were bound to be impermanent. Why did he not spend the money on making Calais, already English and commercially valuable, really strong instead? To conquer France itself, to assert his fragile claim to its throne: these things were impossible. Yet Henry's coinage continued to style him king of France. So strong was the urge to acquire land that it lingered symbolically long after the actuality was dead. Catarina Cornaro, dwindled to proprietress of the tiny town of Asolo, styled herself queen of Cyprus still, and queen, too, of Jerusalem and Armenia.

Maximilian's plan to obtain Brittany in 1490 by a secret marriage to its duchess at a time when he was in scant control of his own south German inheritance, was, given the temper of the times, bizarre neither for its geographical reach nor for its method. Much of the time spent by diplomats was concerned with dowry politics, an international traffic in heiresses, or potential heiresses, almost regardless of their age. It is true that this plan of Maximilian's did not succeed; Charles VIII persuaded Anne's representatives to break the contract and married her himself – breaking his own contract with Margaret of Austria to whom he had been affianced since she was two years old. But the Habsburg empire which Charles V inherited was largely constructed from Maximilian's own marriage to Mary of Burgundy, and the marriages he arranged between his son Philip and Ferdinand's daughter Joanna and between his granddaughter Mary and Louis, son of Ladislas of Hungary and Bohemia.

From one point of view empire-building by marriage was a peaceful pursuit. It was, however, deplored by More and condemned by Erasmus, partly because it deflected a ruler's interests away from a care for his own people and partly because at any moment the resurrection of an old claim could provide an excuse for war.

---

* Very severely indeed in *Army Royal* by C. G. Cruikshank (Oxford 1969).

Moreover early deaths meant that uncertainty and therefore tension was always in the air. The fortunes of the marriages arranged for their children by Ferdinand and Isabella can be taken as an example.

They married their eldest daughter to Alfonso of Portugal who died a few months later; re-married to his successor she died in childbirth of a son who lived only two years. Their daughter Catherine married Henry VII's short-lived son Arthur and her failure to provide his brother, Henry VIII, with an heir was to provoke the most hazardous divorce in English history. They married their son, Juan, to the Emperor Maximilian's daughter Margaret; in six months he was dead, leaving Margaret pregnant of a child who was still-born. By these accidents the Spanish succession devolved on another daughter, Joanna, who was subject to bouts of madness, and to the son, Charles, she had by Philip. Thus a welter of unseasonable royal deaths contributed to the air of hectic impermanence that characterised so much of the diplomatic activity of the time, and tension was further increased because the chain reactions that followed from war were not checked by any clear concept of neutrality. A country could try to stay out of trouble, but old allegiances would be invoked, rights of passage called for; more persuasive than the plea 'I want to be left alone' was the counter-argument 'My cause is just, therefore as a Christian government you should support it.'

Economic motivation played but a small part in a decision to go to war. Piracy, endemic in the Baltic, the English Channel and the Mediterranean, was dealt with by reprisal, licensed counter-piracy and confiscations on the part of individuals, rather than by war. Over the centuries, market agreements between neighbour nations, the establishment of staple towns, international fairs and trading companies – an accumulation of devices had been worked out which enabled imports and exports, raw materials or finished goods to flow in reasonable accord with the economic needs of individual countries. Rulers were more easily moved by the past than by a vision of future balance sheets, Ivan by the desire to recover 'all the Russian land of old', Maximilian to reassert the centuries-old claims of the Empire in north Italy, Charles VIII and Louis XII to reactivate their own families' claims in the peninsula. Though the opportunities occurred in the present, the justifications for war were to be found in history, a litter of claims that could be resurrected with a fine show of legality and could commonly be associated with the grievances of exiles or malcontents: Louis XII's claim to Milan went back to a marriage of 1389 and his first invading army was led by a Milanese, Gian Giacomo Trivulzio, who had been banished by Lodovico Sforza.

The medieval doctrine of the Just War assumed that the decision to open hostilities was a personal, not a collective decision. The position had not changed during the intervening centuries. 'The common folk do not go to war of their own accord,' wrote More, 'but are driven to it by the madness of kings.' And Erasmus similarly laid the blame for 'that madness of war that has persisted so long and disgracefully among Christians' at the door of the European princes. The personal initiative of the ruler, his role as the fount of chivalrous honours, as the natural leader of an army were taken for granted. Feudal society had been organised for war and kings were still seen as the armed tip of the social pyramid. Charles VIII, Louis XII, Francis I, Henry VIII, Maximilian all led armies in person. Monarchs like Louis XI, Henry VII and Ferdinand, who preferred to plan rather than execute, were the objects of surprised (though among intellectuals like Machiavelli and Commines, respectful) comment.

A king's councillors, especially the professional bureaucrats among them, might urge caution but in the immediate circle of advisers to the crown nobles were in the majority, men who as leaders of the second estate had been educated for war. Whether kings actually sought opportunities to wage war in order to satisfy aristocratic yearnings for something more satisfying than the hunt and the mock-war of the tournaments is doubtful, above all in the west. In Hungary, when Matthias Corvinus' successor adopted a policy of peace and retrenchment, the aristocracy revenged themselves for this thwarting of their natural way of life by harassing their peasants, and maimed the power of the crown itself by refusing to co-operate with its policy of centralisation. In the west, as we shall see,* court service, diplomacy and estate management were becoming increasingly attractive. However, there was never a shortage of nobles and gentlemen to officer a war, including the 'unchivalrous' artillery arm, not only younger sons with financial prospects squeezed by the custom of primogeniture, but the greatest nobles of the land; all the same, it would be difficult to show that rulers were stampeded into war by a restless aristocracy. Even in France there were complaints that the second estate was not fulfilling its predestined armed role.

Nations were still in theory organised for war. In England, where the practice whereby nobles surrounded themselves with armed retainers was closely limited by law, they were expected to produce fighting men at the king's command, and parishes and municipalities were likewise required to produce men already trained in the use of their weapons. But such an army was no longer an effective fighting force. The noble cavalryman was a dwindling asset in the face of pike and

* See below p. 157 seq.

gun. The local levies were seldom properly trained, their arms and equipment were frequently inadequate or missing and were in any case old-fashioned: sword, bill and bow at a time when pike (which required regular group training) and hand gun or arquebus (expensive and distrusted in lower-class hands in peacetime) were becoming the key infantry weapons. When to this is added the reluctance of townsmen to leave their occupations and peasants their harvests for the uncertainties of a campaign, it is apparent that the old system had to some extent broken down; those who planned wars had to take into account the engagement and pay of mercenaries. The extent of discussion about the rival merits of native *versus* mercenary troops, *ad hoc versus* permanent armies, points to the same conclusion.

This debate was least urgent in Castile, whose mainly pastoral economy led to underemployment and made recruiting easy, and in Switzerland, another pastoral country and one, moreover, accustomed to defending its independence by arms. It was liveliest in Italy, particularly in the republics, where unbellicose burghers had long relied on hired professionals to do their fighting and were perturbed by the difficulty of controlling them, but the issues were also of concern to France and England. Mercenaries were trained men who brought their own equipment. But they were expensive and had to be paid promptly, their commanders did not always see eye to eye with the native leadership, discipline was more difficult to keep in multi-national armies, orders more difficult to pass. National resentment could cause trouble when mercenaries were used for garrison duty. A permanent national army avoided delay in starting a campaign, meant that trained men were always at the ready, cut down the need to enter into alliances simply in order to obtain extra troops, enabled the lessons of one war to be incorporated in the methods used in the next. On the other hand it was expensive to maintain a military establishment in peacetime, and a standing army might become a revolutionary one.

These were not new issues. But, although unresolved in this period, they were discussed with new urgency. Armies were getting larger (between 25,000 and 40,000) thanks to the emphasis on balanced arms and the considerable supply corps of carpenters, smiths, carters and pioneers needed to service the artillery. Yet governments were trying to cut down the semi-independent military powers of the greater nobles and bring law and order into the countryside at large. The need for larger armies coincided with the need to demilitarise and pacify; social and military policy conflicted.

This did not mean that governments could not go to war when they chose. The aristocracy in the main was still prepared to fight and exemplify its role as the natural military leaders of society. Townsmen could be critical of expenditure on foreign wars – or at least claim to be in order to receive some sort of favour in return; but Gringore himself defended the Italian wars because French honour was at stake, and under a veneer of grousing, towns paid the taxes demanded of them. Little can be known about what the illiterate and unrepresented man thought about war, but to a populace whose margin of survival was at the whim of weather and murrain the prospect of regular pay, coupled with ignorance about the actual conditions of service abroad, was likely to be attractive. The habit of obedience, natural restlessness or desperation (it is doubtful whether 'a sense of adventure' can be applied to men with such circumscribed lives), loyalty to or at least comforting knowledge of a local captain: for one reason or another men joined the ranks. Apart from Germany, where Maximilian found it extremely difficult to get troops together (though cities and princes could for their own quarrels) the national element in an army could always be found. The chief problems faced by governments involved equipment, transport, supply, the payment of mercenaries and relations with allies.

These problems were seldom faced realistically. Spare equipment to replace arms that were damaged or lost was commonly underestimated, as were the number of weapons required and the difficulty of hiring carts and draft animals when passing through country where the farming season was in full swing. Frequently there was not enough coin to pay the troops, though experience had shown that this was bad for morale in the case of native troops and disastrous in the case of mercenaries, who could desert *en masse* or even turn on their employers. But this very unrealism made it easier for war to be declared when a king and his entourage decided on it. And it was reflected in the reliance placed on allies.

The freedom of England from civil wars, the consolidation of French territory coupled with a striking economic recovery from the Hundred Years War, the union of the Spanish crowns and the end of the crusade against the Moors, the succession of the would-be warlike Maximilian on the death of the more cautious Frederick III: these developments produced an atmosphere in international relations in the late fifteenth century all the more tense because of the common interest in Italy and in the bargains that could be struck among the powers competing there. Both the tempo and the temper of diplomacy were affected. Though the resident diplomat was usually of a social rank too low to sign a treaty, he could urge negotiations to a point at which a more formal embassy could endorse it. On the other hand, though it was easier to induce in these agents a sense that their business was to serve the interests of their home governments and not to make up their own minds nor apply their own moral scruples to political matters, they found it more difficult to get information or be treated with real confidence than did the traditional noble or episcopal ambassador. Nor did their home governments always treat the information sent back in despatches with the confidence due to them. And information continued to be sought by other means, through spies and tapping the mercantile news networks. There is little doubt that the presence of rival diplomats at courts, the bribes and other underhand methods they were at times forced to use, added an air of distrust to the diplomacy they helped to speed up.

Though there were a few lasting themes – English use of Flanders to counter French intrigues with Scotland; Spain's reliance on England when plotting against France; English dependence on the Empire when threatened by France – it was largely a period of flux. And as Henry VIII discovered in 1514 and 1517, when his allies were secretly preparing to change sides, an alliance did not mean lasting security or that negotiations with other powers could safely be dropped. Yet though the possibility of being let down or positively betrayed was acknowledged, there was a stubborn belief among rulers (not necessarily shared by their agents) that each new engagement, so solemnly sworn to, often so pompously celebrated, would actually work.

War is not only relevant to an understanding of international relations. The search for money to enable rulers to take military action was, together with attempts to obtain dynastic (or, in the case of republics, class) security, the chief factor that underlay constitutional and institutional developments before the Reformation. Rulers of course spent money on other things: on their backs, their courts, their palaces, their officials and diplomats, but the financial needs of war enormously outstripped any other need.

3

Individual and Community

Christendom

This was not an age in which the individual had grown away from the need to be linked with others. Indeed, it is probably true that from the points of view of emotion, self-interest and intellect these links were stronger than ever: the family a more self-conscious unit, the gild a more stalwart protector, the town a source of greater pride, membership of a nation somewhat more meaningful, the international fellowship of scholarship certainly more warming. Only the always vague notion of belonging to the super-community of Christendom was on the wane.

Christendom as a notion was a commonplace, but in the main it was kept alive by two elements well removed from practical politics: nostalgia for the days of the crusader, nourished by chivalrous literature, and the individual's hope that he could cancel out his sins by contributing to the recapture of the holy places – a motive considerably weakened by the efficient tourist service run by the Mamluk rulers of the Bible lands.

Most popes, indeed, took their crusading duties seriously. In 1481 Sixtus IV, with immense effort, raised a fleet and an army to dislodge the Turks from Otranto. He had hoped to persuade this force to cross the Adriatic and recapture the Dalmatian fortress town of Valona, but their immediate task accomplished, the ships and troops slipped away to their homes. In 1484 Innocent VIII called on all the rulers of Europe to send ambassadors to Rome to plan a crusade. His legates were still trying to rouse the powers to interest in 1488. In 1500 Alexander VI issued a similar summons, which was similarly ignored. In 1517 Leo X worked out a scheme which even went so far as planning how the conquered territories of the Turk should be divided among the crusading nations. No one volunteered for a part in this grand drama of Christendom in action. It is true that Charles VIII had let it be thought that he had some intention of using Naples as a stepping-stone for a crusade when he entered Italy in 1494. Maximilian, conscious of the responsibilities of the Holy Roman Emperor, and an ardent believer in the values (and, in his hotch-potch realm, the political usefulness) of the chivalrous ideal of personal loyalty and Christian service, revived the old crusading Order of St. George with himself as its head. Gusts of enthusiasm could still shake a congregation or set the pages of crusading chronicles turning in a scholar's study, but for practical politicians the sword of idealism was firmly rusted to its scabbard.

In the years following the fall of Constantinople, it had become apparent that a *modus vivendi* could be worked out by trading interests in the Levant; in consequence the Venetians, when they had to fight, fought to contain and not to provoke. Trading and diplomatic links had brought understanding, pilgrims had found that the Muslim was not as Satanic as they had been conditioned to believe. There was a growing interest, and a respectful one, in Turkish administrative institutions, and Machiavelli praised the discipline and morale of Turkish at the expense of those of Christian troops. When the Turks were in occupation of Otranto Lorenzo de' Medici's sculptor Bertoldo struck his superbly idealizing medal of Mohammed, while Alfonso of Calabria hired a company of Turkish cavalry to help in his war against the pope! A German friar, visiting the city in 1482, was scandalised to see the Venetians welcoming a Muslim military mission and even giving these 'dogs, and right enemies of the sacrament' a place in the solemn Corpus Christi procession.

With so little cutting edge to the crusading mood in Italy, it is not surprising that monarchs further afield turned a deaf ear to crusade appeals. But the erosion of their zeal certainly owed much to the extent to which princes were busy with the organisation of their own states and anticipating the treachery which prevailed among one another. At the turn of the century the sultan Bayezid assured his viziers that nothing would come of European projects for a crusade. 'The Christians,' he pointed out, 'fight constantly among themselves... One says to another, "Brother, help thou me to-day against this prince, and tomorrow I will help thee against that one." Fear not, there is no concord amongst them. Everyone takes care of himself only; no one thinks of the common interest.' In 1516 Erasmus confirmed this observation in *The Education of a Christian Prince*, written for the future Charles V: 'Every Angle hates the Gaul, and every Gaul the Angle, for no other reason than that he is an Angle. The Irishman, just because he is an Irishman, hates the Briton; the Italian hates the German; the Swabian, the Swiss; and so on throughout the list. District hates district and city hates city.' And indeed, when the Venetian ambassador asked Henry VIII in 1516 for aid against the common foe of Christendom he got the following answer:

'you are wise, and in your prudence will understand that no general expedition against the Turks will ever be effected so long as such treachery prevails among the Christian powers that their sole thought is to destroy one another.' Ivan III, theoretically well-placed to organise a flank attack, preferred negotiation to crusade. Florence took advantage of the fact that Bayezid, who succeeded Mohammed the Conqueror in 1481, was more eager to consolidate than to extend his power, to increase its trading colony in Constantinople.

As for the Iberian peninsula, since the beginning of Portuguese exploration down the west coast of Africa there had been a more profitable and, for the western powers, politically more purposeful outlet for the crusading impulse. When the Portuguese passed on from the gold of Guinea to the spices of Calicut, King Manuel explained in a letter of 1499 to Ferdinand and Isabella that 'the principal motive of this enterprise has been, as with our predecessors, the service of God our lord and our own advantage.' And Columbus, well aware that the Catholic monarchs wanted a cash return from his voyage, knew too that they would be glad to hear that conditions in the West Indies were 'propitious for the realisation of what I conceive to be the principal wish of our most serene king, namely, the conversion of these people to the holy faith of Christ.' The discovery of America coincided with the end of Spain's own crusade to rid the peninsula of the Moors and redirected this drive away from Europe and the Levant. The missionary efforts of Spain and Portugal produced Christians without strengthening the notion of Christendom. The Turks were already settled deep into Europe and Europeans were settling overseas. Both processes helped to diminish the geographical meaningfulness of the term, and a renewed interest in the legend of a Christian empire in Africa ruled by Prester John, together with debate about the spiritual conditions of the peoples encountered in India and the Americas (could the gospel have already been preached to them? Were they potentially or, in some sense actually, Christians?) helped to dilute its spiritual coherence. Until Suleiman the Magnificent became sultan in 1520 and in the following two years captured Belgrade and the island of Rhodes, the mood of European feeling towards the Turks – where it did not amount to actual indifference – was one of guarded interest or inactive idealism.

State, Region, *Patria*

The individual looked for three things from government, all of a highly conservative nature: the preservation of law and order so that men could pursue their traditional tasks without danger to life and limb; fair, cheap and quick justice; as light a tax burden as possible. In helping stem crime and disorder governments could reinforce local peace-preserving devices like the hue and cry by sending in troops or commissions armed with emergency powers to administer summary justice, or by reorganising and strengthening local self-help organs, as Isabella did the *Hermandades* of the towns of Castile. Though the means, as in this last case, might be new, and though government action was to increase, restricting the freedom of movement of the potentially violent unemployed, for instance, the suppression of brigandage was one of the traditional duties of the crown and did not carry with it any associations that might shift attention from the personal responsibility of the ruler.

Similarly with justice. There was a steady advance of royal at the expense of local or personal justice, but whether this was administered by a familiar face, like that of the English justice of the peace, or a royal judge on circuit or by one of the central appeal courts, the image was not of an impersonal law but of a king acting out the most traditional of his roles, composing the differences of his subjects. The higher the plaintiff fought his way through the courts, the nearer he came not to the majesty of the law but to the majesty of the king. And in recognition of this role rulers continued to accept individual petitions for the redress of a grievance either, as through the English parliament, at one remove, or, as was Ferdinand and Isabella's practice, in person on a day set aside for this purpose. And they continued to make liberal use of their prerogative of pardon.

The third expectation, that rulers should live off the income from their personal possessions as much as possible and impose the minimum tax that would make the running of a war possible, was increasingly disappointed. Burgeoning administrations, larger, more specialised and thus more highly paid armies: the costs of government were rising and had to be passed on. Not everyone was threatened by banditry, not everyone went to law, but customs dues and sales taxes – especially on essentials like salt – made taxation a matter of almost universal concern. But, again, the common reaction to unpopular taxes was not to sense an inexorable extension of central control but either to bargain for a straight *quid pro quo* in the form of redress of grievances or the grant of privileges, or to complain that the king was ill advised, the victim of corrupt ministers and greedy courtiers.

Though agents of central government were inserted into local administration this was most clearly seen to be happening by the very small minority of Europeans who lived in towns. A linked development, the decreasing use of national representative bodies, meant that government, in the sense of the ruler's chief officers and their staffs, were actually negotiated with less frequently. Together with the common assumption that it was the ruler's function to preserve, protect and restore, to honour some vague, antique provision – the Salic law, the Code of Magnus Lagabøter – rather than to change: these factors helped to veil the advance of governmental power from all but a small minority.

In the city republics, of course, matters were different. The rotation of public offices every few months, the principle of selection by ballot, the fact that the scale was so small (Florence could be walked across in twenty minutes) that everyone was known or at least gossiped about by everyone else, meant that an interest in politics was widespread. Yet even here the chief interest was in personalities, in who was in and who, for the time being, was out. Just as in large nations the occasional nature of the contacts between government and people prevented the emergence of a concept of 'the state', the reverse phenomenon, close familiarity with those concerned with government, had a similar effect. Even Machiavelli, writing as an ex-career civil servant, frequently used the word 'state' in the sense of 'those individuals in power for the time being'. Only perhaps in Venice, where a legally defined caste system damped down class rivalries and where economic life was unusually homogeneous – commerce playing a far greater role than banking or industry – was there room for a concept of an impersonal state as well as for patriotic sentiment.

Everywhere, indeed, except among some intellectuals and many professional administrators, the region, the zone surrounding a man's own birthplace, was more important to him than his country as a whole. Most Germans, even the Swiss, felt a vague sense of belonging to the Empire, but homage to the idea did not influence action.* 'France' was a glamorous word, because men knew from chronicles and ballads what great deeds had been performed by French monarchs and their armies. But there was a widespread shrinking from the idea of a general assembly of representatives from all parts of the country or, among southerners, from an assembly which would require them all, from Toulouse to Provence, to dilute their regional identities. An Italian coming home from a sojourn in the north might long to be back in 'Italy', but once home his horizon shrank to a desire to be in his own native land, Florence or Rimini or Naples. It is understandable that in Bohemia, where many of the merchants, prelates and landlords were German, it was difficult for the lower reaches of society to look towards government with any sense of identification with it. But in most parts of Europe 'state' law had a tough

---

* Folk songs from many areas glamorised Maximilian and reviled his rivals, the French, but any attempts to raise money to fight them raised storms of protest.

struggle to supplant local law, which however imperfect, was thought
to be more 'natural' than the justice administered by the highly
trained appeal judges of the capital. There was widespread anger in
Germany over the inclination of princes to employ judges and chancery officials trained in Roman law. This was a capital mistake, said a
Bavarian knight in 1499, 'for these men of the law do not know our
habits, and when they do, they are not prepared to accept our
customs.' Expressing the same anti-centralising vein was a protest
from the estates of Württemberg in 1514; the duke should only
employ men who will 'judge according to the ancient customs and
usages and not trouble his poor subjects.'

By the time Francis I came to the throne in 1515 France was the
supreme example in Europe of what a deliberately centralising policy
could achieve. What it could not achieve, there or elsewhere, was an
extension of the range of the individual's loyalties, a broadening of
the circle of causes for which he was prepared to make sacrifices. The
great magnate might become a provincial governor, acting for the
crown, but the loyalty and awe with which he was regarded was not
thereby channelled to the capital. In every town, even in some large
villages, one or two of the leading inhabitants were employed as
royal officials, usually in conjunction with their normal occupation
of merchant or lawyer. They were linked by couriers and itinerant
administrators to the judicial and financial courts in Paris. But these
officials were still regarded as local men, and they had a continual
struggle to impose royal decrees on local habits. An extract from the
journal-chronicle of Benoit Maillard, prior of the abbey of Savigny,
near Lyons, gives something of the atmosphere in which these
changes were taking place. 'On the last but one day of the month
of April in the year of our Lord 1487, a certain Jean, a shoemaker
and a thief, having fled to this town of Savigny and been imprisoned
there on the plea of a poor woman of St. Clement-de-Valsonne whom
he had robbed, realising that the local police were going to hand him
over to those of St. Clement to undergo the penalty for this theft,
namely, execution, commended himself to the Virgin Mary and,
bending the stout iron bars of the door of the Chamarier prison
and breaking away its lower part, escaped and took refuge in our
church, witnessed by several of the monks. Thus, by the aid of the
Virgin Mary he escaped the hands of justice and was saved.' And in
1493 he recorded how the king's candidate for the archbishopric of
Lyons had to be installed by force of arms, even though he was a
cardinal and his appointment had been confirmed by the pope.

Maillard, like most of his contemporaries, looked up to the crown
through a web of local concerns, ecclesiastical and secular; the king,
almost turned into a god by the sacred character of his coronation

ceremony and able, unlike other men, to perform miracles of healing, should not have interfered with the Lyons election; though Maillard is proud to see the person of the king on his visits to the Lyonnais he trembles to think of the desolation caused to the villages around him as the royal armies trudge to and fro on the king's wars. Indeed, when pay was late and the opportunities of loot were scant, the armies themselves tended to break up. 'If we do but consider,' Commines wrote of Charles VIII's Italian expedition, 'how often this army was inclined to disband since its first arrival at Vienne in Dauphiné...it must of necessity be acknowledged that God Almighty conducted the enterprise.' As the bureaucratic state emerged awkwardly from its feudal chrysalis the officials, mostly lawyers, who delivered it, were forced to compromise between blue-print efficiency (for which models existed in Roman law and in the working of individual large estates, both lay and monastic) and tradition, to defer to local sentiment and to woo co-operation by invoking the glamour of the royal name. No reverberation emanated from 'the government'; appointments, proclamations, edicts had to come from the king.

The king's name was familiar in every court where royal justice was administered. At Nottingham sessions, Henry Gorrall was presented because it was said that he 'on the 26th day of September in the 13th year of the reign of King Henry the Seventh (1497) with force and arms, to wit, with a club and knife, threw out a dead and putrid horse into the streets of our Lord the King at Nottingham aforesaid, to the grievous nuisance of the lieges of our said Lord the King, and against his peace.' There was keen public interest in royal births, marriages and deaths. Pamphlets recorded the ceremonial visits of monarchs to cities in their realms and woodcuts commemorated their coronations. This constant citing of the monarch's name, this feeling for royalty did little, however, to link men into a nation-wide community of subjects. In 1495, during an attempt to settle a demarcation dispute between Languedoc and Provence, a commissioner from Provence (which had been annexed to the crown in 1481) was sent to set up the provincial arms on the Îles du Rhône. In so doing he came across a post to which the royal arms had been fixed. His reaction was revealing. He removed his hat and knelt before this symbol of royal power, then stood up, removed it and left it in the sacristy of a local church 'where relics are conserved'.

Inheritance, dynastic marriages, the fortunes of war: it was taken for granted that the limits of a country's jurisdiction might fluctuate; the image of 'France' was still further weakened by the accompanying notion, 'the lands ruled for the time being by the French king'. Moreover, when French royal power made a step forward it did so to a modern end but by medieval means, by invoking inheritance or feudal law, or by answering an appeal for aid or protection; each new link with a district or town was thus seen in isolation from any centralising policy as a whole and in terms of the feudal contract, theoretically revocable and based on the mutual performance of obligations. The machinery of the nation state of the future was being built among peoples as yet unaware of it.

While princes, then, and their officials sought to drive procedural highways to the capital (or its itinerant substitute, the court) through the dense scrub of local custom, for most men the effective patriotic horizon remained a restricted one. Outside the towns, among the great majority of the population, where there was little mobility and less literacy, it is doubtful if one can speak of patriotism at all, 'politics' being visitors to the local lord, the gossip of returned soldiers, and glimpses, through the words of a judge or a tax collector, of the distant majesty of the king.

As for nationalism, where it existed in something like the modern sense, it was literary, the invention of intellectuals. It was the idealised version of the common man's dislike of foreigners in which history was ransacked to provide evidence of the cultural leadership of the writer's own country. The revived knowledge of ancient history was made to serve a national purpose. Spiridon's world history asserted that the Russian royal family was descended from the brother of the Emperor Augustus, and thus reinforced the powerful fiction that Russia was 'the third Rome'. Lithuanian writers bolstered their national pride by relating that their people were descended from a boat-load of Roman legionaries blown away from Julius Caesar's forces by a storm in the North Sea. But it was above all among the countries neighbouring Italy and most conscious of the peninsula's intellectual leadership that legend was combined with ancient and medieval fact to produce deliberately patriotic history. French authors pointed to the sterling character of the Gaul as revealed in Caesar's *Commentaries*. Germans emphasised the valour and nobility of mind of Arminius in the *Annals* of Tacitus, and were sure that if other classical works, concealed by jealous Italians, were to become available, they would elaborate the virtues of the ancient German race; 'let them give back to us the entire History of Tacitus which they have hidden away', demanded Albert Krantz, 'let them return Pliny's twenty books on Germany!' 'Rome conquered Gaul', wrote Valeran de Varennes in 1508, 'but after Rome's decline is was the Gauls who conquered Germany [Charlemagne] protected the papacy [Pepin and Charlemagne] and freed the Holy Land [the crusades].' Rome had brought cruelty and subjugation in her wake, Christophe de Langueil pointed out in 1510, but the Gauls had always acted with

justice and virtue. 'In arts and sciences', moreover, 'France is superior
to Italy: she has produced from her own soil more men eminent in all
ways than all other nations put together.' No wonder that the humanist lawyer Guillaume Budé was moved to dedicate one of his treatises,
the *De Asse* of 1515, which dealt with Roman coinage, simply 'to the
Genius of France'. No wonder, on the other hand, that the Alsatian
Jacob Wimpheling denied that the descendants of the Nervii had ever
conquered the descendants of Arminius. The French claimed that the
good German land between the Vosges and the Rhine belonged to
them. 'Where are there any traces of the French language?' he asked,
'there are no books in French, no monuments, no letters, no epitaphs,
no deeds or documents.' As for the Italians, what need was there to
defer to them? They had been sunk in ignorance while the tenth-
century German nun Hroswitha was writing the plays which Celtis
had re-discovered and dedicated to the Elector Frederick. Instead, the
Germans should assert the European leadership that was theirs by
character, culture and history. 'Truly', wrote von Hutten in his dialogue *Trias Romana*, 'it is a great and excellent deed to bring it about
by persuading, exhorting, driving and impelling that the fatherland
come to recognise its own debasement and arm itself to win back its
ancient liberty.'

This jingoism of the intelligentsia evoked little public response.
Pope Julius II could remind all Italians of their common inheritance
from ancient Rome when calling on them to back his determination
to expel the 'barbarians'. But the Italian states, when they did form
alliances, combined only so that when the common danger was past
they could continue to differ. Florence had rejoiced when Naples had
been conquered by foreigners in 1501, it gloated when Venice was
stripped of its main land possessions by the 'barbarian' coalition of
Cambrai in 1509. In a burst of literary enthusiasm in the last chapter
of *The Prince* Machiavelli could call for some form of united leadership, at least for Italy's strategic centre, but in answer to a friend's
inquiry in the same year, 1513, about an alliance of the Italian
powers, he said flatly 'don't make me laugh.'

The moulds of nation-wide patriotism were slowly in the making:
common language, unified administration, the elevation of a glamorised monarchy into full view above the great men of a locality,
the proliferation of full-time government servants, the elaboration of
a literature designed, at whatever cost to truth, to trumpet the fame
of one people. Much of the reality these forms were to clothe were
present: awareness of different national characteristics, political and
economic competitiveness, resentment of outside interference. But
most men lacked the vision, the knowledge and above all any need
to think, save fitfully, of the nation as a community. Its boundaries

were too vague, its people too diverse in speech and habits, its ruler too distant and his interests too separate. Meaning lay in the familiar and the near.

The 'Foreigner'

Men's close sense of identification with their own region and their much dimmer sense that it was linked to a larger polity were both conditioned by their attitude towards what was different and foreign. But in trying to assess the notion of 'foreignness', we have the impression not of looking here and there through a telescope but into a kaleidoscope. There were no geographies or general histories of Europe, no gazetteers or accurate maps to aid in the allocation of visual impressions, foreign tongues, proverbial national characteristics and tales of victory and atrocity to particular parts of Europe.

Of visual impressions the most intense were probably those of costume. Within certain limitations – no difference in cut or cloth between clothes worn in summer and winter, men's fashions changing more swiftly than women's – there was, where money sufficed, an infatuation with personal adornment. The visual and tactile responses to clothes were acute. A sizeable part of the European economy, indeed, depended on the pleasure taken in the feel of different stuffs, from furs to brocades, velvets and taffetas. Artists painted clothes with absorbed attention and some actually designed dress fabrics. The body, trained to the dance, adjusted itself with quick sympathy to weight and cut. Clothes were symbols of allegiance. Rulers dressed their servants in a uniform livery – red for the household of the Palatinate, scarlet and white for Aragon. Pope Leo X's musicians wore his white, red and green. The habit was repeated in noble households. Clothes were indicators of class, occupation and condition: virgin, wife or widow. All over Europe sumptuary legislation tried to curb sartorial extravagance in the interest of class harmony (the burgher's wife should not ape the noble's, nor the noble's flaunt her status), of decency (don't emphasise breasts or genitals), of morality (curb vanity and extravagance) and protectionism (don't buy imported materials). Constant repetition shows how impossible it was to check the appetite for variety and display.

Vain, too, were exhortations from the pulpit. 'Ladies', pleaded the Franciscan Michel Menot in a Lent sermon, 'in this time of penitence the church covers its saints with a veil; for the love of God do the same to your breasts.' On another occasion, 1508, he attacked the extravagance of their coiffures. 'O ladies, you who go in for finery, who often fail to listen to the word of God although you could do so by crossing the street, I am certain that it would take less time to clean out a stable of forty-four horses than it takes you to pin up your hair.' Vain were the laments of poets: in 1509 Alexander Barclay mourned that

> 'Man's form is disfigured with every degree,
> As knight, squire, yeoman, gentleman and knave...
> Alas thus all estates of Christian men decline,
> And of women also, disforming their figure.'

The pace at which fashions changed continued, indeed accelerated, with sleeves now wide as a monk's, now almost too tight to draw on, as another preacher complained in Strasbourg. And not only fashions in dress; 'An honour 'twas a beard to grow, Effeminate dandies now say no!' wrote Sebastian Brant in his *Ship of Fools.**

With so much concern for dress at home, it is not surprising that foreign costume was a matter of absorbing interest. 'Don't the Spaniard, Italian, Frenchman, German, Greek, Turk, Saracen dress differently?' asks a character in Erasmus' *Colloquies*. 'And in the same land how much variation of dress is there even among persons of the same sex, age and rank! How much do Venetian, Florentine, Roman differ in appearance, and within Italy alone!' Dürer procured illustrations of Irish and Livonian costume to copy and made drawings which minutely contrasted the dress of Italy and Germany.

Fashions spread through paintings and dance troupes, through commercial, military and diplomatic contacts. 'The fashions in clothing,' Celtis wrote in his description of Nuremberg, 'change continually, being influenced by the different nations with which trade is carried on.' The costume of the Burgundian court was being copied in northern Italy in the 1480s; by 1515 Henry VIII had one costume 'in stiff brocade in the Hungarian fashion' and another 'in white damask in the Turkish fashion'. A traveller noted that the women of Genoa, the prettiest in Italy, he thought, had begun in 1517 to dress as though they were Spaniards. Such importations could arouse patriotic resistance. 'See the trousers', wrote Johann Geiler, 'they are divided off like a chess-board, and the making of them costs more than the material. All these fashions come to us from Italy and France; they are a shame to Germans, who, though the best people in the world, allow themselves to fall into the follies of other nations and to be made monkeys of by foreign tailors.' In some of the Swiss cities embargoes were placed on the wearing of foreign styles and

---

* Here and elsewhere I use the translation of Edwin H. Zeydal (Columbia U.P., 1944).

strangers coming to reside were given one year to adjust their wardrobe to local convention.

The sartorial 'map' was a confused, though vivid one. This was also true of the linguistic 'map', of which every traveller and every inhabitant of the big commercial towns had at least a vague impression, as had those who possessed the many multi-lingual song books of the period.

Thanks to trade, diplomacy, the administration of multi-lingual realms and the employment of multi-lingual armies, a smattering of foreign languages was not an unusual accomplishment. Except among churchmen and at the universities, spoken Latin was becoming restricted to purely formal moments, like the presentation of an ambassador's letters of credence, or to bridge gaps in the understanding of a modern language. In his *Education of a Prince* (1518 or 1519), Budé stressed the importance of learning modern languages so that the ruler could endear himself to his various peoples and not be at the mercy of an interpreter. Maximilian jotted down his own achievements in a manuscript of his veiled autobiography, the *Weisskunig*: German as a child; Latin from the school-master; Wendish and Bohemian from the peasants; French from his wife, Mary of Burgundy; Flemish from the circle of Margaret of York, Charles the Bold's widow; Spanish from diplomatic correspondence; Italian from army officers; English from archers in his pay. For diplomatic purposes King Manuel of Portugal learned Spanish and Henry VIII, with the aid of a resident tutor, learned French. Though the French were reluctant to learn other languages and, partly for this reason, their tongue was taking over from Latin as the major diplomatic language, Commines could carry on negotiations in Italian. Itinerant scholars, however passionately they felt about Latin, could not rely on it: Cornelius Agrippa learned French and Italian in addition to his native German. Purely as a polite accomplishment Lucrezia Borgia added French to the Spanish of her father's homeland and the Italian of her upbringing. The discoverers showed some interest in native tongues: a glossary of Malayan words was brought back by da Gama, and Pigafetta compiled one in Patagonian during his voyage with Magellan.

This accomplishment was seldom deep. The production of vernacular grammars, let alone dictionaries, was only begining: the first thorough teaching aid was the Castilian grammar of Elio Antonio de Nebrija, printed in 1492. Most men continued to be content with little handbooks which, like Caxton's *Dialogues in French and English* (1480), followed the traditional *Livres des Mestiers* with their model commercial letters and their simple conversations about buying and selling, finding an inn and hiring horses.

The extent to which any degree of familiarity with a foreign language helped men to visualise the country where it was spoken is impossible, of course, to estimate. Any possibility of seeing Europe in terms of a number of linguistic units was hampered by the fact that commonly the ruling class spoke differently from the mass of the people and that in all counties there were striking regional differences. Though centralising administrations, and writers who rejected Latin because it was being polished into a dead language no longer hospitable to neologisms and pungent or merely useful vernacular phrases, were helping to standardise national language, the process was very far from being complete. An anecdote told by Caxton in the preface to his *Eneydos* (1490) is of wide applicability. 'In my days,' he wrote, 'it happened that certain merchants were in a ship in Thames for to have sailed over the sea into Zeeland and for lack of wind they tarried at [the South] Foreland and went to land for to refresh them. And one of them, named Sheffield, a mercer, come into a house and asked for meat, and specially he asked after eggs. And the good wife answered that she could speak no French. And the merchant was angry, for he also could speak no French, but would have had eggs and she understood him not. And then at least another said that he would have "eyren". Then the good wife said that she understood him well. Lo, what should a man in these days now write?' And Caxton concludes that 'between plain, rude and curious' English he stands perplexed. In France the *langue d'oïl* of the north was incomprehensible to those in the south who spoke the *langue d'oc*, and within the former there were a number of regional divisions; when Maître Pathelin, in the popular farce of that name, shammed mad to foil a creditor he raved in Norman, Picard, Limousin and Breton. The 'ik-isch' still divided the retreating northern zone of Low from High German, and even then, when the first Low German translation of the Bible was published in Cologne in 1479, it had to have low Frankish and Low Saxon in parallel columns. More confusing still was the situation in the Netherlands. In Antwerp, for instance, the language of local administration was Flemish, of correspondence with the court or with the duke's representatives French, of the ecclesiastical courts Latin, while a swarm of translators aided commercial transactions in German, Italian and Spanish. In Russia there were three linguistic divisions, Great Russian, Ukranian and Belorussian, but travellers were as likely to be greeted in Church Slavonic as in any of these. In Norway the ruling officials and most of the merchants spoke Danish. There were tiny pockets in southern Italy where Greek was still spoken, and the vernacular differences between the major states provided fuel for endless literary controversy. His own contribution to this controversy

(*A Dialogue on Language*), Machiavelli hoped, would establish the primacy of Florence and 'disabuse those who are so ungrateful for the benefits they have received from our city that they are content to confound her language with those of Milan, Venice and the Romagna, and with all the filthy usages of Lombardy.'

Any impression of a foreign country was in any case still further blurred by a stubborn folk-lore of phrases which purported to hit off national character in vivid shorthand. To the German authors of the *Letters of Obscure Men* (1515–17) it was axiomatic that Poland was the land of thieves, Bohemia of heretics, Saxony of drunkards, Florence of homosexuals. In this folk-lore the French were frivolous, Flemings were gluttons and preternaturally clean, the English foul-mouthed, avaricious and insular; it was with no sense of discovery, but a delight in spelling out a truism, that an Italian visitor to England explained that 'the English are great lovers of themselves, and of everything belonging to them; they think that there are no other men than themselves, and no other world but England; and whenever they see a handsome foreigner they say that "he looks like an Englishman", and that "it is a great pity that he should not be an Englishman"; and when they partake of any delicacy with a foreigner, they ask him "whether such a thing is made in their country?"' As masters of the oath the English had a rival; 'to swear like a Scotsman' was a popular phrase among the French, but the deepest insult, nurtured by centuries of animosity, that a Frenchman could use to describe an Englishman was 'coué', tailed. In his *De Cardinalatu* Paolo Cortese warned a prince of the church who was setting up house in Rome not to employ Italian servants; the Romans were too violent and unreliable, the Florentines too grasping, the Venetians too uppish, the Neapolitans too lazy.

The epithets and phrases which peopled Europe with grotesque puppets sprang from a variety of antipathies. Political rivalry was naturally a common source. The Scots had long salved their wounds by calling the English cowards. But more pervasive were opinions based on social or cultural differences. The English despised the Irish because they lacked firm royal government and a stabilising law of primogeniture. The southern nations despised those of the north *en bloc* as stolid guzzlers, the north scorned the untrustworthy and conceited people of the south. Feeding habits are a constant refrain. 'Remove that old infamy of the Germans,' Celtis implored in his inaugural lecture, 'in writers who ascribe to us drunkenness, inhumanity, cruelty and every other evil approximating bestiality and irrationality.' When Charles V's entourage brought northern eating habits to abstemious Spain, Peter Martyr expressed his dismay at men 'whose only god is Bacchus followed by Cytherea' and an

Italian ambassador in Switzerland was appalled by the way in which his hosts 'spend two or three hours at table eating their many dishes and barbarous spices with much noise.' Erasmus made Charon declare that he had nothing to fear from ferrying Spaniards across the Styx, but the English and the Germans were so crammed with food that they nearly sank the boat. Trivial as these insults seem, they had weight in an age when food was often scarce and gluttony was one of the most vividly realised of sins in sermon and popular art. Coprophagist carvings in northern churches suggest how the imagination could be perverted by the tension between greed and guilt.

In spite of the literary culture of Burgundy and the artistic achievements of the Netherlands, Italians clung to their conviction that north of the Alps Europe was in the hands of the barbarians. Writing to Leo X from sophisticated Brussels, Raphael's pupil Tommaso Vincidor complained 'I have much to bear, away among foreign barbarians.' Visiting the shrines of the Holy Land, Pietro Casola noted fastidiously that 'I always let the ultramontanes rush in front.' Christopher Scheurl angrily quoted in 1506 a Venetian saying that 'all the cities of Germany are blind – except Nuremberg, and that sees with only one eye!' On the other hand, 'we must make allowances', wrote Zwingli with lofty sarcasm, 'for Italian conceit... They cannot bear to see Germany out-stripping them in learning.' France, too, wished to import Italian culture uncontaminated by the Italian character. Singers from Milan had much to teach the Parisians, but Jean Marot could not forbear exclaiming that they sounded like the birth pangs of a nanny goat; they were also likened to piglets squealing in a sack. Learn from, but don't imitate: this was the message of Pierre Gringore's 'There is nothing worse, on my faith, than an Italianate Frenchman.'

Whether at the level of boys giving a tang to their games by playing French against Germans or of official propaganda, this moral chauvinism perhaps helped men to identify with international rivalries that were decided on solely by their rulers. But neither the phraseology of mutual recrimination, nor the awareness that other groups of men spoke different languages and wore different clothes, did much to bring about any clear sense of personal involvement with an individual's own country, let alone with Christendom as a whole.

Local Associations

This sense of involvement was all the weaker because of the vigour of local associations and their ability to cater satisfactorily to the desire for mutual aid, spiritual fraternity, recreation and simple gregariousness.

In the countryside the rural parish, though responding faintly to pressures from government and more regularly from the local lord or his steward, was a self-administering and fairly democratic unit where the church brought everyone together not only on Sundays and festival days and for births, marriages and deaths, but on all the perilous stepping-stones of the agricultural year, to pray for rain to start or stop, to give thanks for harvest-home. This combination of church as community centre and parish as small administrative unit roughly corresponding to the land worked, if not owned, by the village, was not to be found all over Europe. Its basis was the strip system whereby large fields were divided up among many cultivators. With holdings scattered among several fields, and decisions where and when to plough, sow and reap needing to be taken in common, a village was the natural centre of operations, whether the houses ran along a street or two, or were grouped pell-mell within a stockade, as in the Slavic 'ring-fence' village. Where share-cropping was common, as in southern France and Tuscany, or where land had been reclaimed from forest or was too mountainous or barren to support a nucleated population, or where migrant pasturage was the rule, peasants lived on scattered farmsteads or tiny hamlets made up of three or four families. These settlements contained a minority of the peasant population of Europe. Scattered from northern England through central Brittany, the Pyrenees, the Alps, the Apennines and the once marshy banks of the Weser and the Elbe to the northern regions of Scandinavia and Russia, they remained semi-Christianised, brutal in habit, breeding grounds for those solitary fantasies which stoked the witch-fires. Not that village life elsewhere was decorous or enlightened, but it allowed the struggle against nature and, as we shall see, the tensions of the home to relax within a purposefully organised gregariousness.

The urban parish played a similar role, related to the rest of the town as a whole but uniting an enclave of neighbours within it. Sizeable towns were divided into wards for administrative purposes. These, too, gave opportunities for co-operation, in peace-keeping, fire prevention, militia organisation and the overseeing of neighbourhood markets. The slow population recovery since the fourteenth century meant that most towns still retained large open spaces within the walls; in plan the town often resembled a group of villages, congregations of streets, of one- or two-storey houses for the most part, separated from the next nucleus by orchards or open spaces. This scattering of village-like districts was fostered by the police, customs and economic functions of the main gates which tended to become foci for inns, stables, markets and the shops and crafts dealing with the goods arriving along particular trade routes. The cathedral or largest church, and the town hall, exerted, of course a centralising pull, but even where the 'villages' blended into one another they preserved a warmly identifiable personality; with all classes working at home there was no morning or evening movement from one district to another. The tide might flow to the cathedral to hear a visiting preacher, to the town hall to listen to a proclamation, to a particular recreational area, but then it would flow back into the ward, to a self-contained and small-scale life, its homogeneity reflected in the inter-district rivalry of those horse races or football combats still commemorated in Italy.

Streets took their names from the trades practised in them, from local families and from local landmarks, church, brewery or inn, and shared occupational interest meant that kinsfolk usually lived in the same part of the town. Similarly, gild activity was frequently localised. There was no slackening of the social and economic purposes that had created the medieval gild. Constantly refurbishing their statutes to protect themselves from the 'foreigners' who were entering the towns in increasing numbers, they continued to care charitably for their members, to commission works of art for their chapels in the local church and to demonstrate that passion for their 'own' law which all occupation groups wished to preserve against the encroachments of municipal and royal legislation. The gilds represented an economic need, but the appetite for associations beyond such needs and beyond the circle of kin was stronger than ever. The *Meistersinger*, amateur musicians drawn from all trades, grew in numbers and enlarged their schools in the German towns. Religious confraternities flourished. The fraternal element could be very strong. The confraternity of San Ildefonso at Valladolid, for example, not only looked after sick or poor or imprisoned members and cared for widows and orphans, but enjoined that before each formal annual reunion all quarrels should be settled between members and that 'those who are not on speaking terms with one another' should be returned to amity; there was, moreover, to be no poaching of labour, no unfair competition. In some towns, particularly in England, the corporate body of the borough took the orphans of burgesses into its care until they came of age. New lay brotherhoods were founded, part devotional, part recreational. Associations like the Netherlands chambers of rhetoric commissioned and performed plays, held literary debates and poetry readings. The inherent conversability of the humanists displayed itself in a rash of academies and sodalities. Often informal, like the Florentine Platonic Academy, where Plato's works were discussed under the chairmanship of Marsilio Ficino, or those meetings in the Oricellari Gardens where Cosimo Rucellai's friends talked about Roman history and its relevance to Florence's constitutional agonies, the tone of these groups can be caught in numerous works that echo their discussions, though none retains the warm sense of human contact so well as does Castiglione's *Courtier*, which claims to record conversations which took place in the ducal palace at Urbino in 1507. The literary club flourished as widely in Germany as in Italy. There were *sodalitates* at Linz, Ingolstadt, Leipzig, Augsburg, Olmütz and Strasbourg. Celtis foresaw the creation of clubs for the four regions of Germany: called the Rhenana, the Danubiana, the Vistulana and the Baltica they were intended, through discussion and correspondence, to revitalise the cultural life of the country and recapture the lead from the Italians. As in Italy, the membership of these associations was not restricted to scholars, it included doctors, lawyers, educated burghers, churchmen and schoolmasters. Men with more perilous interests bound themselves together by oaths of secrecy and mutual support. Cornelius Agrippa belonged to a secret society of occultists, another group formed around the magician and mystic Mercurio da Correggio.

By means of such associations town life catered for business, religious, cultural and recreational interests. Conditions varied from town to town. Perhaps Venice was unique for the vivid role played by the gilds in the church festivals and state processions which made the Venetian calendar at once so formal and so gay. Nowhere else, perhaps, was there so much informed public interest as the Florentines showed in the great civic and gild commissions to painters, sculptors and architects. The extent of the control of the civic fathers over every detail of life, from the price of bread to the cut of clothes and the censorship of plays, was perhaps nowhere so complete as in the cities of Germany. But all towns offered a complex and satisfying system of relationships which left men with little inclination, save in the realm of business, to look outside to those larger and vaguer communities: the state, partnerships of states by alliance, Europe itself. In 1497 a traveller wrote of Calais: 'Every day in the afternoon, when the inhabitants take their rest, the gates are closed; and this also happens on holidays, only, instead of once, as on working days, it is done twice, the first time when services are being held in the churches, and a second time, as before, when the people are having lunch. At these times sentries and guards keep watch from the town's walls on all sides.' The town works, rejoices, takes its siesta like one huge, well-guarded family. In time of war the town's first thought was the defence of its walls. 'Politics' meant first and foremost civic politics, the elbowings and factions that can be suffered and seen.

Pride was above all civic pride. The Parisians boasted of their new Pont-Notre-Dame, swinging easily over the Seine with its twenty-foot roadway and lines of shops; its cost of a quarter of a million *livres* was met more easily than any tax imposed by the state for a national purpose. In times of festival or when the entry of some great man was celebrated, a city could minister still further to this pride by appearing in disguise, fountains turned into stands for *tableaux vivants*, chariots of Love or Venus, or Death or Fortune, dragged by strange-costumed figures through streets where the familiar façades were transformed by lath and painted canvas into Rome or the aisles of forests and ended in triumphal arches from which, securely strapped, the rapscallions of the neighbourhood piped of Augustan pomp or the loves of Pan. Jacob Wimpheling, writing in 1505 a history of Germany, wrote it in terms of Alsace, his own province, and reserved his finest eulogies for Strasbourg, the city he was writing in. He looks up at its cathedral: 'I would say that there is nothing more magnificent on the face of the earth than this edifice. Who can admire this tower sufficiently? Who can adequately praise it?...It is almost incredible that such a massive structure could have been raised so high! If Scopas, Pheidias, Ctesiphon and Archimedes lived today they would have to admit publicly that our people exceed them in the art of architecture and that they prefer this building to the Temple of Diana at Ephesus, to the Egyptian pyramids, and to all the other works counted among the seven wonders of the world.' *Campanilismo* could hardly be demonstrated more literally.

The Family and Personal Relationships

As far as the individual was concerned the most important form of association was, of course, the family. The ties of kinship were strong even among those whose names have some symbols of 'individualism'. Popes accepted the scandal of nepotism. Michelangelo, though elevated to the epithet 'divine' cared restlessly for his unpromising brood of relatives. Dürer, who in his great engraving *Melancolia I* stressed the essential loneliness of the creative artist, wrote with detailed, thoughtful sadness of his mother's death. Family records, reminiscences of dead ancestors, commissions for portraits and busts, multiplied; so did the ordering of masses for the dead, the purchase of indulgences, the building of chantries. Books described the perfect household. Princes were proud not only of illustrious lineage but to be known as the fathers of their people. Though conservative churchmen still deplored the necessity of the married state, an increasing number of men saw the godly life as something to be achieved as easily within the context of the home as of the cloister. Respect for the familial *pietas* of ancient Rome coupled with distrust of monastic morals produced an idealisation of life in the family.

The solidarity of the family owed much to its being the centre of, not a retreat from, production. In the country the entire family worked on the land and, in winter, shared their home with the animals for the sake of their warmth. The craftsman worked in his own house, as did the shopkeeper. Servants and apprentices lived as members of the family segregated from the ordinary life of the household only by their duties. Under the partnership agreements that were common among French peasants different families lived under the same roof, all their property, down to kitchen utensils, being held in common. A more conscious feeling for family unity led to the production of household scenes in illumination, painting and woodcut, sometimes as backgrounds for, say, the Birth of the Virgin, but frequently as straightforward genre scenes. Servants ministered to masters with little sense of social divisiveness. Wife and husband ministered to one another as a necessity that might be affectionate and respectful even if it was rarely self-sufficient from the points of view of passion and understanding. The father was expected to rule, though his authority might be under heavy siege, and the atmosphere was gregarious; desire for privacy was still tentative (even in wealthy families very few girls had, as had Carpaccio's St. Ursula, a bedroom of their own).

The functional solidarity of the home makes it difficult to judge the quality, the emotional tone of family life. A high death rate meant frequent remarriages; not only were marriages planned by kinsmen and thus lacking, at least in the initial stages, in romance, but the speed with which a new marriage partner was brought into the home suggests a certain emotional casualness. Three successive marriages were not uncommon. Again, in wealthy families it was customary to send children out to a wet-nurse for the first months and also (though infrequently in Italy) to send them to be educated by growing up in some great household, a 'finishing' that began at the age of seven or eight. That the family did not always care for its oldest members as a matter of course is suggested by contracts whereby an old person made over his property to his children in return for a guarantee of support, in sickness and health, as long as his life should last. And that the atmosphere of the family was not necessarily such as to keep children absorbed and law-abiding is shown by the tirades of preachers and satirists against juvenile delinquency, in which parents are blamed for not keeping an eye on their offspring and for allowing them to read trivial romances and to strike up undesirable acquaintances. Late marriage for men and a high death rate at 35–40 possibly meant that many children were fatherless by the time they reached adolescence and that few would have a grandfather's eye upon them.

More common than comments on relations between the generations were those on relations between the sexes. It is probable that the status of women had, as a whole, declined. When men were absent at war, or for purposes of trade, the law had accepted that their wives were competent to run their estates and manage their businesses. With wars waged increasingly by mercenaries and trade conducted increasingly by agents, women had a less prominent rôle to play in affairs. In some trades – especially those which depended on female labour, ribbon-making, dressmaking, embroidery – women were admitted to gild membership, but seldom to positions of authority. Shopkeepers' wives looked after customers as an extension of their domestic duties. There were women barbers in France, a few women money-changers in Germany, some women musicians have been recorded, and while women were generally excluded from religious drama they were admitted to ministrel groups and performed in *tableaux vivants* and moralities. When visiting Antwerp, Dürer bought a manuscript illuminated by an eighteen-year-old girl. 'It is very wonderful that a woman can do so much', he commented. What women were really capable of only appears in exceptional circumstances. Caterina Sforza defended Forlì in the Romagna against Cesare Borgia with a bravery any man would have envied. Zoe Paleologus, wife of Ivan III, played an important part in the Italianising of Muscovite culture. The refinement of the courts of Ferrara, Mantua and Urbino undoubtedly owed much to the influence of a few highly educated women like Isabella d'Este and Elisabetta Gonzaga. Born to rule, or with the possibility of ruling, an Anne of Brittany or a Margaret of Austria could show herself the equal of men. By chance the shopkeeper's daughter Sigbrit, mother of Christian II of Norway's mistress, had an opportunity to show that a shrewd bourgeoise could run a state better than a feeble king; by chance a peasant girl, Maroula of Lemnos, showed that a woman could rally a wavering garrison and lead it in a successful counter-attack against the Turks, an action for which she was offered a dowry and the pick of an officer husband by the Venetian state. Literature offered a few vivacious and independent-minded heroines but for most writers, women's place was firmly in the home, their interests restricted, as in Fernando de Rojas' portrait, to '"What did you have for dinner?" and "Are you pregnant?" and "How many chicks have you got?" and "Take me to lunch at your house" and "Point your lover out to me" and "How long is it since you saw him?" and "How are you getting on with him?" and "What are your neighbours like?"

and other things like that.' Vespasiano da Bisticci, the Florentine bookseller and biographer, would not even grant them this liberty. Women, he wrote, should follow these rules: 'the first is that they bring up their children in the fear of God, and the second that they keep quiet in church, and I would add that they stop talking in other places as well, for they cause much mischief thereby.' The same note was sounded in England; 'there is nothing that doth so commend, advance, set forth, adorn, deck, trim and garnish a maid as silence', warned an anonymous English tract. Among the patrons of William Caxton's printing press was that vigorous woman Margaret Beaufort, countess of Richmond and Derby and co-founder of Christ's and St. John's Colleges at Cambridge, but the printer described a more passive ideal when he wrote that 'the women of this country be right wise, pleasant, humble, discreet, sober, chaste, obedient to their husbands, secret, steadfast, ever busy and never idle, temperate in speaking and virtuous in all their works, or at least should be so.' A rare exception, Cornelius Agrippa, wrote in 1509 a little treatise in praise of women, designed to catch the eye of Margaret of Austria. His contention was bold: that only masculine tyranny and lack of education prevented women from playing a role in the world equal to man's. But floundering for arguments to support his thesis he was forced to use such unconvincing ones as that 'Eve' has more affinity than 'Adam' with the ineffable name of God, JHVH, and that physically women were finished off more neatly than men. It is a failure of nerve that is easy to understand in an age when a scholar could scribble 'becoming mad, he took a wife' against a colleague's name in the matriculation roll of the University of Vienna.

Save in court circles and some exceptional bourgeois households women were educated casually, if at all. The wealthier the family the earlier were marriages arranged in the interest of property and inheritance; thus the girls most likely to receive a good education were also those most likely to have it cut short. In law the Roman notion that 'in foemina minus est rationis' was gaining ground, leaving it open to judges to impose less severe penalties on women because they lacked the mental and moral force necessary to constitute wrongful intent in the full force of the term, and there is some indication that laws entitling widows to a proportion of their husbands' effects at his death were being set aside. Moreover, to judge from the (admittedly biased) evidence of sermons, parents showed less concern over a strict upbringing for girl children. Josse Clichthove, not by any means an alarmist preacher, took it for granted that his congregation would accept his picture of a society where the education of girls was neglected and where they were allowed a dangerous liberty to rove and mingle with bad company. There was thus a suspicion that once a girl had been 'bought' by a husband, she would have to be watched.

Though authority in the family, and in the determination of inheritance was legally vested in the male, his authority, according to satire, was seldom to be taken for granted. A favourite theme in popular art was the battle for the trousers, in which a man and wife wrestled for who was to wear them; victory (sometimes determined by a delighted demon) usually went to the termagant wife. Other woodcuts and engravings dwelt alarmingly on famous cases of men being dominated by women: Adam tempted by Eve, Samson shorn by Delilah, Holofernes decapitated by Judith, Aristotle bridled and driven by Campaspe. The hen-pecked husband was a stock character in the drama. In a farce by Cuvier, Jacquinot's mother-in-law reminds him that he 'must obey his wife as a good husband should'. She and her daughter pen a lengthy list of his obligations and force him to sign it. He is to get up first, light the fires, prepare the breakfast, wash the children's soiled clothes, in fact 'come, go, run, trot, toiling away like Lucifer'. The dénouement comes, much to the relief of husbands in the audience, when his wife falls into an enormous wash-tub and begs him to pull her out. 'It's not on my list' is his answer to each plea, and he only rescues her in return for a promise that henceforward he will be master in his own house. This is caricature in humorous vein, but behind it is the fear of a darker form of domination, for this was a time when women were introduced into crucifixion plays gleefully forging the nails for the cross, and when a misericord could portray a woman heaving a man off to perdition with a rope round his genitals.

Fear of woman's sexuality appears to have been widespread. 'Where, alas!' sighed the foremost student of the printed sermon literature of late fifteenth-century England, G. R. Owst, 'where is our merry medieval England?' The church, of course, drew on a long tradition in which woman was identified with *luxuria* and described in terms of pathological disgust. But it was not only clerics who believed, with Michel Menot, that 'luxuria etiam breves dies hominis facit'. Etienne Champier, a doctor as well as a poet, warned the readers of his *Livre de Vraye Amour* that too much lovemaking led to gout, anaemia, dyspepsia and blindness, and he was doing no more than repeat a medical commonplace. Both clerics and doctors reflected a fear that had its roots in the darkness of folk terrors. It was expressed in that most popular of travel books, the *Travels* of Sir John Mandeville. He describes the inhabitants of an (imaginary) island 'where the custom is such that the first night they be married, they make another man to lie by their wives for to have their maidenhead...For they of the country hold it so great a thing and so perilous for to have the maidenhead of a woman, that them seemeth that they that have first the maidenhead putteth him in adventure of his life...And I asked them the cause why that they held such custom: and they said me that of old time men had been dead for deflowering of maidens that had serpents in their bodies that stung men upon their yards, that they died anon.' A similar story is told by the traveller Lodovico Varthema, and there is little doubt that the plot of Machiavelli's *Mandragola*, which hinges on the fact that a gulled husband believes that a drug his wife has taken will kill the first man who sleeps with her, refers, for all its comic implications, to an unacknowledged fear of woman as castrator. To this fear, and to the teaching of church and medicine we must add another factor. The bourgeois literature of the time harps on the theme of women devouring, pestering, exhausting their husbands. Girls and wives were not insulated from sex. Bedrooms were not private places (though domestic architecture was beginning to reflect a desire that they should be), language and gesture were bawdy and woman's sexual appetite openly acknowledged.*

At the poorer levels of society a natural sexual relationship between man and wife was complicated by economic circumstances. 'Little property and many children', as a Flemish proverb put it, 'bring great distress to many a man.' The church and, to a lesser extent, military service did provide opportunities for employment outside the local community, but the family was commonly preserved as a self-sufficient unit (even if only a marginally viable one) by a series of voluntary restraints. One was postponement of marriage itself, for poor men frequently until between thirty and thirty-five. A second was making love in ways that could not lead to conception – ways in which the clergy were briefed to inquire about in the confessional and which they sought to combat. A third was abortion, again condemned, and, indeed, punishable with death, but common. The last recourse was exposure, and here, at least in the towns, foundling institutions accepted, wet-nursed and put out discarded infants to foster-parents, a system supported by a fairly general lack of social, if not legal, prejudice against the bastard. Thanks to these restraints and the high incidence of death due to disease, the average household probably did not number more than the parents and two or three children, though as kin usually lived in the same district, if not in the same street, this figure may conceal some redistribution of

---

* 'It is convenient that a man have one several place in his house to himself from cumbrance of women.' (William Hormon's Latin phrasebook of 1519). A similar work of the same date, John Stanbridge's *Vulgaria*, shows something of the tone of conversation. Boys learned the latin for male and female genitals and for words like 'fart', 'stynke', 'shyte', and 'pysse', and for phrases like 'tourde in thy teethe' and 'he lay with a harlot at night'.

children among childless or slightly better-off relatives. Even so, it is difficult not to suspect that the confessions in witch trials involved a hysterical shifting of responsibility for the fantasies and aberrations caused by a fear-haunted sex-life, as did, in all probability, the accusations of sexual interference laid by men, with the assistance of celibate inquisitors, against the night-hags.

The contrast between precept and appetite was not only deep but open. Almost all the practices forbidden by the clergy can be illustrated in popular art, in books or in public entertainments. It was a mortal sin to take pleasure in watching the couplings of animals. In 1514 a widely publicised animal entertainment was put on in the Piazza dei Signori in Florence. Particularly noted was the moment when a mare was sent in among some stallions. In the opinion of one observer, the pious diarist Luca Landucci, 'this much displeased decent and well behaved people'. But in the eyes of another diarist, Cambi, it 'was the most marvellous entertainment for girls to behold.' Erasmus, in his very widely read *Colloquies*, takes lesbianism for granted as a hazard for young nuns, and among the popular stories attributed to Priest Arlotto Mainardi was one of a peasant who confessed not only to stealing the priest's corn but to masturbation; the jovial absolution was 'take your beater out prominading as often as you like, but do not steal any more; leave other people's property alone, and above all give me my wheat back!' In art, themes like Potiphar's wife, Susanna and the Elders, Bathsheba, Lot and his daughters gave an opportunity for painters to display a directly sensual appreciation of the nude. In stone and wood carvings in churches, figures of *luxuria* strained the use of allegory into simple carnality and straightforward phallicism. In woodcuts and engravings the 'influence' of Venus was demonstrated by scenes of lovemaking, Folly and Death were shown presiding over brothel scenes in which the didactic convention was used as an excuse to celebrate the pleasures of sex in the same way that, in a playfully scholarly guise, patrons like Federigo Gonzaga and Alfonso d'Este could indulge a taste for mythological erotica with Ios and Danaes; coaxing, in the case of Alfonso, the genial *Feast of the Gods* from one of the greatest of all painters of religious subjects, Giovanni Bellini, and a broodingly sensual *Leda* from Michelangelo. When to this we add the jokes which Castiglione in his *Courtier* tells as suitable for mixed company, the sexual content of the French *chanson* and the Italian carnival song (lutes and song books were among the 'vanities' burned by Savonarola) we get a picture of the pleasure of sex, either completely open or employing, as in the case of Lorenzo de' Medici's 'Song of the fir cone sellers', an easily-translated sexual imagery, but in any case flouting conventional Christian morality.

There was a clear confrontation. On the one hand a printed (Italian) anecdote like this: 'Because of his excessive addiction to lust, Febo dal Sarasino was gradually losing his eyesight. When he turned completely blind, he said "The Lord be praised; now I will be able to indulge all I want without fear of going blind"!' and, on the other, a sermon preached in Paris by Olivier Maillard in 1494 in which he asked 'Are you here, printers of books?...O miserable booksellers, your own sins do not suffice you; you print vile sensual books, books on the art of love, and give occasion for sin in others; you will all go to the devil.' Dürer, fervent draftsman of the Apocalypse, teased Willibald Pirckheimer about his taste for young men, and Pomponius Laetus brushed off criticism of his homosexuality with a reference to Socrates; yet preachers warned the Italians that disaster after disaster, from the French invasion of 1494 to the Venetian earthquake of 1511, was a punishment for sodomy. For many the black of conduct or day-dream could apparently contrast with the white of Christian teaching without strain, men turning easily from sin to absolution, helped by a church which, realistically, was more lenient in court and confessional than in the pulpit. But it is clear that not all could accept this simple dualism, the tension perceptible in sexual obsession was too apparent. In the course of the French mystery play *The Vengeance and Destruction of Jerusalem*, Nero orders an operation to be performed on his mother so that he can see the precise place where he had been conceived. Chastity belts were made, and shown in art, even if they were not used. The tension inherent in the secular version of Christian morality worked out in the chivalrous romance – in which there was a revival of interest at this time – was shown by woodcuts spelling out the real object of the heroes' worship. The mingling of sexual and devotional imagery in the poetry of Skelton shows how that other etherealisation of feeling for women, the literature of Mariolatry, could be penetrated by imaginings of the grossest sort.

All this, of course, is evidence to be treated with great caution. The fashion (in some places) for low cut dresses and (mainly in Germany) for codpieces of aggressive cut and colour tells us little: it is impossible to recapture the emotional effect of a past fashion. Similarly, we can draw no conclusion from the proliferation of the lifelike nude in art. Suggestiveness has little to do with realism. Besides, the nude could still draw on a tradition which associated it with shame or humility: it was in this guise that Memling painted Tommaso Portinari kneeling naked, his wife beside him, in the scales of judgement. We may doubt, however, if anyone took sex as neutrally as the Utopians, among whom it was lumped with the comparable offhand pleasures of scratching and defaecating.

Nor can there be any doubting the existence of true, sympathetic understanding between men and women. Nevertheless, Christian morality and the problems of voluntary birth control within the family had produced a state of mind in which women could readily be seen in terms of categories. There was the woman of romance, the ideal day-dream partner of man's intellectual, fantasy-building self. There was woman as sexual recreation. And there was woman as wife, a stereotype of house-minding and child-rearing, too ignorant to be mentally intriguing, too familiar in background and too much the product of a largely business-like negotiation to arouse curiosity. Trapped amid fears and cares the married man looked, in imagination or reality, outside the home for romance or for unworried lust. There is a long list of popular dirges (all written from the male point of view) with such titles as: *The Newly-wed's Complaint* and *The Shades of Marriage*. The French poet Coquillart described at bitter length how love flies out of the window as a wife becomes physically repulsive through child-bearing and breast feeding. A German drawing symbolised marriage by depicting two trunks growing from one tree stump; they end in crossbars on which a nude man and a nude woman, both blindfold, are crucified. It is an attitude later summed up in Luther's rueful 'Yes, one can love a girl. But one's wife – ach!'

In his *Courtier*, Baldassare Castiglione defended marriage unless there were great inequality in age or temperament, but talking of joking and banter between men and women he made one of his characters say that women 'can taunt men for lack of chastity more freely than men can sting them; and this is because we ourselves have made a law, according to which a dissolute life is not a fault or degradation in us, whereas in women it is such utter disgrace and shame that a woman who has been slandered once, regardless of whether the charge is true or false, is disgraced for ever'. In his obituary character sketch of Louis XI, Commines noted with amazement that he had remained faithful in his last years 'considering that the queen (though an excellent princess in other respects) was not a person in whom a man could take any great delight.' Antonio de Beatis wrote of the young Francis I that 'although of such slight morals that he slips readily into the gardens of others and drinks the waters of many fountains, he treats his wife with much respect and honour.' Johann Cuspinians's eulogy of the Emperor Maximilian stressed that 'unlike other princes' he was always virtuous in his relations with women. This double standard of morality was not peculiar to princes, and that it was avenged is shown by prints in which the lover slips from the bedroom as the husband enters. The Utopians were anxious guardians of sexual morality. 'The reason why they punish this offence so severely,' More explained, 'is their fore-knowledge that, unless persons are carefully restrained from promiscuous intercourse, few will contract the tie of marriage, in which a whole life must be spent with one companion, and all the troubles incidental to it must be patiently borne.'

It is not surprising that prostitution flourished, government and, much more grudgingly, the church, seeing it as an essential safety valve. Recruitment was kept up by poverty, especially in times of dearth when families could only survive by prostituting their daughters. The demand was maintained by population figures that point to a considerable imbalance between the sexes, men being well in the majority. There were (unreliable) estimates of 6,800 for the prostitutes of Rome in 1490 and 11,000 for those of Venice in the early sixteenth century. Their regulation differed according to the views of the municipal authorities. Coquillart represents the streets of Paris haunted by a familiar figure: 'Woman who goes torchless by night. And murmurs to each "do you want me?"' while in Nuremberg prostitutes, though protected by statutes of their own, were required to stay in state-licensed brothels. The introduction of syphilis made little difference to this open mindedness; caution, not panic, was the main reaction. It was indeed during this period that the prostitute came into her own. The substitution of the word 'courtesan' for 'sinner' reflects a growing tolerance for the profession as a whole, and in Italy, and especially in Rome, the prostitute catered for romantic companionship as well as lust. From the home then, men looked out to gild or confraternity comradeship, to the consolations of less workaday love, and the satisfactions of friendship. In societies such as Florence, where it was common for girls to marry at about twenty and men in their late thirties, the imbalance encouraged homosexual relationships as well as prostitution. But in general, and apart from the routine companionship of business and administration and the strong feeling of solidarity among men as a whole *vis-à-vis* women, it was an age of strong and unaffectedly sentimental relationships between men. The chivalrous ideal of linked knights errant contributed something to this, so did the mutual watchfulness and shared confidences encouraged by the lay piety of the *Devotio Moderna* in the interest of spiritual self-improvement. Cicero's much reprinted *De Amicitia*, the stories of famous friends in ancient Greece and Rome, Pylades and Orestes, Theseus and Perithous, Scipio and Laelius, together with the widely penetrative ideal of Platonic love focused attention on the art, as well as the advantages, of friendship. Friendship was not limited to neighbours or fellow-townsmen. Formal posts, indeed, were few, and were usually restricted to the diplomatic correspondence of the states that had introduced them. The University of Paris had a system whereby students could keep in touch with their families in the country. The Hansa merchants had their own postal service, so did big international firms like the Welsers and Fuggers. With the appropriate contacts, men could use these organised systems, though they were expensive, but letters were also carried by merchants, bailiffs, clergy; at some cost of time and convenience correspondents could use the ceaseless traffic of men going on errands of their own. In the twelve months from August 1st 1514 Erasmus, sending letters himself from Louvain, Liège, Basel, St. Omer, London and Antwerp received correspondence from Strasbourg, Freiburg, Louvain, London, Paris, Arlon (a village in Belgium), Tübingen, Schlettstadt, Augsburg, Halling (near Rochester in Kent) and Rome. And a more enduring link was available. In 1517 he commissioned Quentin Matsys to paint his portrait and that of his friend Peter Giles and sent both to More 'in order that we may be always with you, even when death shall have annihilated us.'

Generally, however, a messenger's verbal report meant more than the letter he carried, the gift for expressing spontaneity in writing being uncommon. The ability to sustain a relationship by correspondence was rare; men liked to see and jostle one another, to drink and pray and argue and conduct business together. What they could not see and hear they found difficult to imagine, and any discussion of governmental changes, foreign relations and war must take this into account.

4

Economic Europe

Continuity and Change

Taking the economy of Europe as a whole this was not a time of dramatic change. In the west prices began to rise slowly towards its end, but in spite of wars, fresh outbreaks of plague and local dearths it was a time of muted overall prosperity. There were no demographic surges, no industrial booms or slumps, the next wave of state bankruptcies was not to come until the middle of the sixteenth century. The new injection of precious metals from the Spanish colonies in America was not yet strong enough to upset a monetary metabolism already used to infusions of African gold from Portugal.

Though statistics are not sufficiently full for assurance on this point, it seems likely that the prosperity of the Milanese–Veneto–Tuscany area of Italy slowly lost its pre-eminence to south west Germany, and there is no doubt that pre-eminence in banking passed in the same direction; though the Medici and Fugger banks were both exceptions, the decline of the former in the late fifteenth and the rise of the latter in the early sixteenth centuries were related to circumstances affecting the two areas as a whole, notably the increased importance of minerals north of the Alps and the increased difficulty of getting raw wool for the Italian clothing industry. To some extent this contrast also reflects a wider shift in the relative importance of the Mediterranean and Atlantic coasts in terms of potential economic growth. Nothing like a transference of leadership from one to the other was as yet taking place; that ports like Lisbon and Antwerp were growing faster than were Florence and Venice was no more than a harbinger of what the future was to hold. For from a commercial point of view Europe was still almost entirely a self-contained unit, full of areas servicing one another on more or less equal terms rather than many areas polarised towards the few which trafficked on a large scale with the lands then in process of discovery.

The exploitation of these lands had, indeed, proceeded at a remarkable pace, By 1515, the end of the Portuguese viceroy Affonso d'Albuquerque's period of office, fleets were returning regularly from the west Indian coasts, protected as they assembled by the fortified ports of Diu, Goa and Cochin and from Arab raiders on their way across the Indian Ocean by ships based on Ormuz and Mombasa. A fort at Malacca, moreover, acted as a forward base for the continuing exploration of Malaysia and the Moluccas. Before Cortes landed in Mexico in 1519 Spain had established settlements in the West Indies in Santo Domingo, Jamaica, Cuba and Puerto Rico and was building Darien, in Colombia, into the first Spanish town on the mainland. As yet, however, it is doubtful whether either of the great colonising powers made more out of their overseas empires than they put into them. Much of the capital for the voyages was raised from Italian and German bankers, who had to be repaid. Portuguese spices brought an initial profit to Lisbon, but as they were increasingly forwarded to Antwerp for distribution the retail profit fell to non-Portuguese hands. And though enough gold was coming to Spain from the West Indies to begin the rise in prices that was to infect Europe as a whole by the end of the century, Spain's real wealth was to come from the silver mines of South America which were as yet undiscovered. The European economy was only marginally affected by the consequences of the voyages of Columbus and da Gama by 1520.

The direction of the flow of basic foodstuffs and raw materials in Europe remained constant: flax and furs moving westwards from Poland and Lithuania, Sicilian grain and cotton moving northwards, wool from Spain and England moving eastwards, and salt fish moving south from the Baltic and the North Sea. The areas of dense population and of manufacture, the chief absorbers of these commodities, did not shift; the centre of gravity of Europe's financial and industrial life continued to be the southern Netherlands and north-eastern France, south Germany and northern Italy. The Rhine, with its floating race of men and women who were born and reared on the barges they seldom left, remained Europe's busiest river. Within this pattern were towns which continued to be so specialised that they were largely dependent on the chief streams of commerce: great entrepôts, like Venice, smaller centres like Pskov, with its crammed streets of iron and silversmiths, minute ones like Waldsee, which exported fine quality wind-instruments. But there were also many regions which had developed such a diversity of economic activity that they were, and remained, largely self-sufficing. Characteristic of such regions was Yorkshire, which fulled and wove fleeces from its own sheep, built in its own Pennine stone, fed itself from its river and sea fisheries, mined and smelted its own iron; lead for roofing and guttering and the steel wares of Sheffield were available for export, and Hull provided an outlet for them to the burly merchant cogs of the North Sea. Such regions could be connected to the overall pattern of European trade more or less at will, depending on supplies and prices.

Prices continued to be determined above all by transport costs. The purchaser of Indian spices in Toledo paid twice what he would have paid for them at Lisbon. Seventy-five per cent of the cost of grain at the port of Archangel was due to the cost of transport from Moscow, six hundred and fifty miles away. The price of the same commodity rose by one third on the short haul from Rouen to Amiens. The bulkier the commodity the higher the charge: only 5 per cent of the price of delivered timber represented the forest price, the rest was absorbed by transport. These charges included the costs of freight, loading and unloading, insurance and customs duties, and, depending on the route, tolls, compulsory escorts and other passage charges. Goods moving from Paris to Rouen up the Seine paid fifteen different tolls before facing the dues charged by Rouen itself. Between Nuremberg and Frankfurt, some hundred and fifty miles, four different escorts had to be engaged as the wagons passed from one territorial jurisdiction to another. And at Frankfurt itself there were gate charges to pay.

A multitude of seigneurial rights and municipal privileges came between the producer and the consumer. Attempts were made to improve roads as an alternative to the use of rivers especially burdened with tolls; in France associations of merchants were formed to bargain with riparian landlords. But transport costs continued to determine prices, and therefore wages. It was, again, transport costs that maintained the essentially regional nature of economic activity, with small market towns serving and being served by hinterlands with a radius of fifteen to twenty miles; transport costs that ensured that apart from raw materials, like wool, and basic foodstuffs, grain, oil, salt and wine, long distance commerce catered almost exclusively for the rich. With the possible exception of a single outfit of holiday clothing, it is doubtful whether the great majority of men possessed any object whose maker they were not in a position to know personally. Because of distribution costs merchants strove, in the teeth of governmental regulations, to establish monopolies, the great trading companies to increase their profits in rare but essential commodities like copper and alum by establishing cartels. Nor did the basic characters of large firms alter in other respects. They played safe by diversifying their interests as had their medieval predecessors, combining banking with commerce and industry, and they continued to make loans to princes in exchange for trading privileges: the Hansa helped Edward IV to the throne of England, the Fuggers and Welsers paid for the electoral votes that gave Charles V an empire.

While the basic conditions of economic life remained stable there were, of course, regional changes. The rapid development of Icelandic fishing grounds at the expense of those of the Baltic damaged the prosperity of Bergen, which had been for centuries based on the salting and re-distribution of herring and cod. The shortage of precious metals for coin, especially for purchases in the Levant and the Indies and, on a lesser scale, for the payment of armies, led to a notable development of the silver mines in Saxony and Bohemia and made the fortunes of the firms which managed them. The old silver mining towns of Saxony increased at a rate that radically altered the balance of town–country interdependence and led to a rise in the price of foodstuffs and fuel that made the peasantry and the urban proletariat of this region the most revolution-prone in Europe. New towns, like Annaberg, near Chemnitz, were founded and quiet mountain valleys were filled with thrusting communities dedicated exclusively to this one purpose and strikingly homogeneous in character. By the 1520s the number of men employed in mining and metallurgy throughout the Empire was reckoned in the neighbourhood of one hundred thousand. The exploitation of the Bergslag district of Sweden led the Stockholm cornmarket to be renamed the ironmarket in the 1490s. Iron-bearing districts as a whole benefited from the growing demand for cannon, hand guns and pistols as well as for armour, and the traditional armaments centres, Malines, Moscow and Milan all grew in importance while others (London, Paris, Nuremberg, Brescia) emerged as rivals. The effects of war itself are difficult to assess: they were deeply entwined with others. The constant interruption of communications by sea and land with Italy from 1494 certainly worked to the advantage of Catalan and French shipping and of the big trading companies of southern Germany. But being the military cock-pit of Europe did not have a really drastic effect on Italy's economy as a whole. Florence remained a banking centre, though the names of the most prosperous banks changed. The canal and irrigation systems of Lombardy continued to maintain the Milanese as one of Europe's most prosperous agricultural areas. The development of silk weaving, using domestic raw material, continued to compensate somewhat for shrinking supplies of foreign wool for cloth. Indeed, at the very time when France and Germany and Spain were trying to carve up the peninsula they were responding to a shift in taste, a desire for comfort and a social pretension that led them to purchase increasing quantities of the luxury goods the Italian artisanate was so well trained to provide. The market for Italian silks, brocades, damask, silver thread, glass, faience, jewellery and devotional objects had never been so strong.

Even the most famous blow of all, the arrival at Lisbon in 1501 of the first Portuguese cargoes of spices bought in India, left but a painful bruise and not a permanent gash on this arm of Venetian trade. In 1504 Portuguese spices were on sale in London, and in the same year Venetian galleys found none at either of the two chief spice outlets in the Mediterranean, Alexandria and Beirut – ports at which they were accustomed to finding three million pounds weight or more. The shock of these first years, and the panic that accompanied it, did not last long. The empty quays were the result not of Portuguese monopoly but of the temporary dislocation of the Arab distribution service across the Indian ocean to the Red Sea and the Persian Gulf: not the holds but the guns of Portuguese ships were to blame. By the beginning of the 1520s the links with Arab distributors had been re-established. Henceforward Venetian spices had to compete with those of Lisbon, but the purchase price at both ports was roughly the same and the demand was higher than ever. Spices (chiefly pepper) were only one of the commodities handled by Venetian shipping, though they were the most valuable. Apart from importing other eastern luxury goods the city and its *terra ferma* had begun slowly but profitably to weave cloth. The production of glassware and printed books was increased. This diversity, plus the resumption of spice imports, led to Venice's being more prosperous in the 1520s than it had been during the 1480s. War with the Turks from 1499 to 1502, the news from Lisbon, bank failures and heavy subsidies to allies, shattering defeat at Agnadello in 1509: Venice weathered all these crises. It was in these years that the process of converting the wooden bridges over the canals into stone ones was begun. The Fondaco dei Tedeschi, burned down in 1505, was at once rebuilt on a grander scale than ever, as was the district on the other side of the Rialto when in 1514 it, too, was destroyed by fire.

Changes did occur in the respective importance of cities and arms as well as of whole regions. Freer trading practices and protection pushed Antwerp well ahead of its old rival Bruges. The international fairs at Lyons continued to draw business away from those of Geneva. Amsterdam became one of the busiest fishing ports in northern Europe, largely at the expense of the Baltic ports. Even more dramatic was the expansion of south German banking and trading firms at the expense of the Hanseatic group of companies in the north and those of Italy. The Augsburg firms of Hochstetter, Welser and, above all, Fugger, insinuated their agents – at times veiling their connection with the parent company – into the chief cities of central Europe, took over the management of papal revenues and, thanks to the indebtedness of the Habsburgs themselves and of other princes in

Germany and Hungary, received concessions for the working and sale of the very commodities for which almost every government had experienced an increase in appetite: silver and copper. All the same, the resilience shown by Venice demonstrates the essential conservatism of European trade and industry and the endurance of the overall patterns of supply and demand.

The Tone of Economic Life

It is impossible to generalise about the degree of economic competitiveness to which these conditions gave rise. A great French historian has likened the merchant of this period to a soldier, 'a man of swift decision, of unusual physical and moral energy, of an unrivalled boldness and determination'.* There is much to be said for this definition. It was a time of ingenious cornerings of commodities in desperate demand, of ferociously defended monopolies. It was said that when Jacob Fugger was urged to sit back and enjoy his wealth he answered that 'he had no intention of doing so, but wished to make a profit as long as he could.' Columbus was stressing the contrast with Europe when he wrote of the San Salvadorians that 'they are so ingenuous and free with all they have that no one would believe it who has not seen it; of anything that they possess... they invite you to share it and show as much love as if their hearts went with it.' Russian monasteries charged up to one hundred and fifty-six per cent on loans to impoverished landowners. A missionary priest in Malacca startled his vicar by proclaiming that 'he would not be satisfied unless he had secured 5,000 *cruzados* and many pearls and rubies within the space of three years.'

On the other hand, Dürer was drawing on widespread condemnations of idleness when he engraved a bourgeois sleeping by a stove, his coffer closed, and dreaming, under the influence of the devil, not of profit but of Venus. The Venetian diarist Girolamo Priuli ascribed a similarly non-militant posture not to the devil but to a resting on economic laurels. 'Our ancestors were brave, fierce, impatient of injuries, quick to strike, prone to fight. Now we are of milder mind, meek, long-suffering, shy of a blow, shrinking from war. And this, I take it, because in olden times we all lived by trading and not on fixed incomes; we spent many years of our lives in distant lands, where we dealt with different races and grew courageous... Now few of us live by trade. Most subsist on their incomes or on their official pay.'

---

* Lucien Febvre, in *Revue des Cours et Conferences* (1921) 63.

For Priuli, then, the soldiering age was over. He spoke of Venice, but there was a widespread increase in the number of *rentiers* and those who aspired to the security of administrative office. Indeed, with the possible exception of Antwerp, where a local boom led to an intense competitiveness among the swelling foreign communities and native traders, it is easier to see the bourgeoisie as above all cautious in business, with a strong sense of duty and obligation to civic affairs, distrustful of new ideas and genuinely religious. 'And since our Lord God is the giver of every good', runs a passage in a Florentine parnership agreement of 1506, 'they are agreed that of the said profits of this firm, they shall give every Sunday as alms to orphan children 2 florins for every 100 florins they have received during the week, either as a firm, or else each member himself shall distribute according to this rule.' Far more representative than Jacob Fugger's remark is the tone caught by Luca Pacioli in his statement that 'the purpose of every merchant is to make a lawful and reasonable profit so as to keep up his business.'

There were, in any case, few areas of economic activity which held out the temptation to get very rich very fast. The metal market was one, and this was cornered by the south German houses. Loans to princes and tax farming were others, but few men had the capital available to try the first and the second offered opportunities only to a few. Commercial profits were damped down by transport costs, industrial ones by gild restrictions. How much energy was imparted to the economy by the desire of the work force to save money in order to better itself it is impossible to say. One out of every thirty of the inhabitants of Venice had a bank account, commonly a very small one. On the other hand Clichtove repeatedly deplored the habit of breaking off work when the Angelus rang at noon on Saturdays; did his congregation not realise, he asked, that the devil was prompting them to observe the Jewish Sabbath as well as the Christian Sunday?

Economic progress for the individual commonly depends on obtaining a loan, credit for expansion. And in a society in which both lender and borrower is seeking to improve his position a loan involves repayment with interest. Against the taking of interest were the voices of both Aristotle and Christ. In the *Politics* acquisition by agriculture and animal breeding was termed natural, while acquisition by means of usury 'is justly censured because the gain in which it results is not naturally made but is made at the expense of other men.' And in the Sermon on the Mount Christ said 'lend, hoping for nothing again: and your reward shall be great, and ye shall be the children of the Highest.' Medieval fulmination against this essential activity of the merchant, money-lender and banker had been constant and became more sweeping than ever in the early sixteenth century.

In the *Adages*, the most widely distributed of all his works, Erasmus complained that 'indeed it is against nature, as Aristotle said in his *Politics*, for money to breed money. But now this thing is so widely accepted among Christians that while the tillers of the soil are despised...usurers, on the other hand, are considered to be among the pillars of the Church. Nowadays the rage for possession has got to such a pitch that there is nothing in the realm of nature, whether sacred or profane, out of which profit cannot be squeezed.' When John Eck, a cleric and professor at the university of Ingolstadt, argued at a debate in Bologna in 1515 that a trading loan could properly carry five per cent interest (the Fugger banking firm had paid his travelling expenses), his friend Pirckheimer, himself scion of a wealthy merchant family, wrote 'it pains me to see you meddling with a subject that cannot but stain your conscience', and he warned Eck that he was merely being used for propaganda purposes.

Neither the direct prohibitions of canon law, nor a steady stream of pulpit reprimand, had succeeded in stopping economic self-interest from using the loan, or trading for the maximum profit that could be obtained. Sometimes the convention was blandly ignored. In Russia it was the monasteries which were the pacemakers in business techniques; in certain towns, like Geneva, the authorities, albeit with certain qualifications, legitimised loans involving interest; in Lyons merchants were allowed to charge 15 per cent in deals among themselves. Most frequently it was sidestepped by fictions: a loan was disguised as an investment or a partnership, or, rather more baldly, repayment sums which concealed the interest involved were named in contracts, or loans were repaid in foreign currency, thus representing an exchange or reciprocal purchase. Or a bank would pay what amounted to interest in the form of an annual gift; as long as expressions of gratitude to the depositor were not a condition of the deposit no infringement of canon law was involved, indeed, as the bank might go up in flames, or the money, invested by the banker in, say, a trading fleet, might go to the bottom, the depositor was facing a conjectural risk and was entitled to some compensatory payment. All these devices were already familiar by the fourteenth century. It is doubtful whether the usury laws had any effect whatsoever on economic productivity in Europe as a whole, but they possibly affected the channels into which economic activity was directed, and they did provide a climate of opinion to which the individual had to adjust with varying degrees of comfort. As the most straightforwardly wicked interest-bearing loan was one made to a consumer who found himself in financial straits, and the church was more tolerant to loans (as long as there was no named, fixed interest rate) made for commercial purposes where the risk to the lender was greater, there was a tendency for the scrupulous businessman to prefer commercial investment to straightforward money-lending; certainly all banks involved themselves in commercial loans and the banker avoided most of the opprobrium levelled at the pawnbroker and the street-corner money-lender. This creative diversion of investment into production rather than into the support of consumption was balanced, however, by the uncreative diversion of investment into speculation with foreign exchange, another comparatively legitimate way of making a profit. The atmosphere which helped to condition these choices was charged not so much by the threat of actual prosecution as by the ease with which a debtor could dodge his obligations through invoking the protection of the usury laws.

This atmosphere was compounded of contradictions. In Florence small money-lenders, though tolerated, were denied access to the sacraments and Christian burial, though almost all citizens of any substance had holdings in the *Monte*, the consolidated public debt which paid interest on the sums invested in it. When the Lippomani bank failed in Venice in 1499, Priuli, himself a merchant and banker, wrote 'the Lippomani were of such quality and had in the past been so esteemed and honoured in Venice that none could be more so. But now they are arrested, imprisoned and cursed by all. And this is the moral of these events: whoever placed his hopes in earthly things is in the end deceived, for the wheel of fortune cannot stand for ever at one point.' Another Venetian, Marino Sanuto, noted that when on one occasion the state was hard pressed for coin to pay its troops, permission was asked for the mint to work on religious holidays. This preoccupation with money scandalised the Patriarch who refused; but, he said, if the men nevertheless did work – he would absolve them afterwards. The boom town of Antwerp was a setting where in practice few financial holds were barred, yet the communities of foreign merchants carefully chose confessors whose opinions they canvassed until, torn between canon law and the practical advantages of having wealthy penitents, the unlucky clergy either became permissive or shifted their responsibility by applying for rulings to the university of Paris. Uneasiness about the moral status of the business life was probably at its most perturbed in the first generation of the sixteenth century. The edgy religiosity which was a characteristic of this period had something to do with it. In addition, the first tremors of what was to be a widespread rise of prices faced the consumer with a phenomenon which, in the absence of realistic economic theory, he put down to the wicked machinations of business men, to *Fuggerei*. And with the rise in prices came a ripple of extra profits available for re-investment, thus drawing still sharper attention to the breeding of money by money.

It was, of course, possible to make a fortune in business, to move from rags to riches, but such careers were made against a prevailing wind of unadventurous protectionism. State intervention was hamstrung between a bullionist impulse to cut imports and stimulate home production on the one hand, and on the other a desire to damp down luxury consumption and keep the prices of basic consumables and foodstuffs low. Nor, among municipal bodies, was there any change in the medieval assumption that the duty of the city fathers was to keep prices down and quality high. Towns proliferated with inspectors of meat and poultry, measures of cloth, testers of wine and beer and bread, assayers of jewellery. This did not conflict with the mood of most producers. The general trend in Europe was for gild organisations, whether self-governing or responsible to king or town council, to deny any impulse to freedom of trade or manufacture, to become monopolistic and to make the master-apprentice-journeyman system more rigid. In Amiens, where the number of crafts which hardened into gilds increased from twelve in 1400 to forty-two in 1500, the Sisters of Mercy were forbidden to make goods to sell for the benefit of their charitable funds. The age of the all-round man was also the age in which the hilts, the blades and the sheaths of swords were made by different gilds, when a saddle was the work of three separate crafts: the wooden frame made by one, the padding added by another, the decoration by a third, and when *rotisseurs* and poulterers clamorously argued their exclusive right to sell roast goose. The multiplication of industrial and trade gilds in France under royal licence was directly advantageous to the crown; they disciplined their workers, their officers, among the most substantial citizens in each town, became gratefully dependent on central authority, and through payments for the approval of their statutes and on many of their activities, like the enrollment of a master or the indenturing of an apprentice, they provided revenue. They also became well-defined targets for royal and municipal taxa- tion. Not all economic activities were covered in this way. In Lyons, for instance, the number of such corporations was kept down to four by the city government in order to attract foreigners to establish themselves in business. But this overall move towards state control could not have been made had the economic community not favoured it. From the tiny craft gilds of remote English country towns with their restrictions on 'foreigners' coming to look for work to the wealthy Hansa merchant communities in Cologne, Dortmund, Brunswick, Lübeck, Danzig, Visby and elsewhere, the tone was one not of free enterprise but of control, of equality of opportunity among members, of security rather than risk.

Concern for the training of craftsmen, regulation of quality: these old motives were still present. But they were overtaken by the desire to create monopolies and permit a rigidly policed method of entry from a labour force which was growing at a disturbing rate. And the creation of monopolies was not so much in order to stimulate the accumulation of new fortunes as to reduce competitiveness, less to create new conditions than to stabilise and regulate the old. Restraint was, then, the prevailing mood in the large section of the bourgeoisie concerned with manufacture. It was among those who did not devote themselves to the making and marketing of a particular product that commercial militancy was to be found, merchants who bought in one place to sell in another, men whose temperaments led them to speculation rather than production and who often speculated in currency as well as in goods and acted as part-time bankers through the manipulation of loans. It was here that the greatest opportunities lay, together with the greatest risks, and it is because circumstances were encouraging the differences between these two chief types of bourgeois activity that no easy definition of the urban middle and upper classes can do justice to the variety of their lives and aims.

Even among the supreme opportunities, however, it took more than one generation to bring about a significant change in a family's purchasing power and the esteem in which it was held, and it was above all a combination of mercantile wealth and administrative position which produced the most dramatic examples of mobility from one social environment clear into another. The career of Jacques de Beaune is conspicuous almost to the point of caricature. Son of a moderately well-to-do merchant, he married into the circle of royal officials, and helped by these connections and the skill with which he multiplied his fortunes as merchant and banker, he became purveyor of plate to the crown, treasurer to Queen Anne and, in 1495, receiver general for Languedoc. Having inherited 3,112 *livres* on his father's death, by the end of the century he was worth more than 100,000 and by 1518 was able to lend the crown 240,000 for building operations at the châteaux of Amboise and Plessis-les-Tours. Ennobled by Louis XII in 1510, he received the barony of Semblan-çay in 1515 from the Queen Mother, Louise of Savoy, whose financial affairs he administered in addition to his receivership. Meanwhile his personal business concerns continued to prosper and a succession of gifts flowed from the individuals and towns he dealt with in his official capacity. In 1523 he reached the peak of his career. Already one of the richest men in France he became, as *trésorier de l'épargne*, the chief financial officer of the kingdom. Four years later, after proven charges of peculation, he was hanged.

Finally, little if any challenge to re-thinking the ways in which money could be made came from the business community itself, or from mathematic or applied science. There was no important change in business techniques. Already by the end of the fifteenth century partnerships and companies with distant branches were a matter of course. There were no bank-notes, bills of exchange and promissory notes were seldom transferred by endorsement or cashed before the date of maturity marked on them. But paper and credit were familiar aspects of international trade and were trusted by the private investor. In hazardous times or to evade taxation or the obligations of charity rich men used the Augsburg banks somewhat after the manner in which the banks of Switzerland are used today. Luther was scandalised when on the death in Rome of the bishop of Brixen in 1509, no gold or silver was found, simply a slip of paper 'as long as a finger' tucked in his sleeve, which a Fugger representative accepted as being worth three hundred thousand florins. In Italy double-entry book-keeping had become a commonplace, but just as the thinking behind the bill of exchange stopped short at the point when it might have achieved the extra advantages of the endorsable cheque, book-keeping practice very seldom produced a balance sheet, and when it did, this was usually due to death, bankruptcy or the dissolution of a partnership. The actual state of a business's affairs could be established at a given moment only by combing laboriously through a number of ledgers and journals. Everything was written down, but balances, so important an aid to forward planning, were, outside Italy, seldom struck. Nor was the way in which things were written down standardised. As Pacioli complained, 'each clerk likes to keep the books in his own way'.

Society as a whole was only patchily numerate. Even men who could be reckoned literate in that they could read, write and learn from books, were seldom able to do more than add and subtract, double and halve. Fractions other than halves lay among the *arcana* of mathematics, penetrable only to the few. Few learned the multiplication table, none used plus, minus, equals or multiply signs. Addition and subtraction were hampered by being carried out from left to right. There were (this is part of the reason for Pacioli's complaint) at least eight methods of multiplication, even more of subtraction. Still more baffling, both to accountants and to our understanding of the psychology of the business man, was the widespread retention of Roman numerals for calculation in preference to Arabic ones; time, space and accuracy were all sacrificed to this prejudice. Outside Italy, confusion about numbers was responsible for much mercantile and agrarian litigation, and even the highest reaches of accounting practice were not exempt. Roger Doucet, editor of the financial records of the French crown for 1523, has pointed out that 'errors in calculation are to be taken for granted. An accurate addition sum is the exception. The errors are often considerable, sometimes beyond the order of one hundred thousand *livres*.'

The trader's life was complicated by the multitude of different coins. Pacioli mentioned only a few of those in common use in Italy: Venetian ducats, papal, Sienese and Florentine florins, *troni*, *marcelli*, papal and Neapolitan *carlini*, Florentine *grossi* and the *testoni* of Milan. The situation was worsened by the fact that as none of these coins was milled they could be clipped or filed by unscrupulous dealers. They were, moreover, beaten out and impressed not by machine but by hammer strokes: the thickness was therefore variable. A further difficulty was the variety of units of measurement, from 'the iron yard of our lord the King' in England to the numerous *passi* of Italy. It is true that these complications were taken in the merchant's stride; he valued coins by weight, there were printed tables for the conversion of measures, and he had measuring sticks for the units most commonly used for the goods he handled, but constantly weighing, measuring, handling for quality, performing calculations with counters on a squared board or cloth: a plethora of sense impressions appears to have inhibited more than a most elementary use of mental arithmetic by the merchant and possibly explains the retention of Roman numerals with its consequent toll of errors. Just as in medicine there was little contact between the theoretical teaching of the universities and practical doctoring, so the mathematics (mainly geometry) of higher education offered no lessons to men engaged in trade.

There was a similar gap between university-based science and everyday technology. To the Turks, Europe was a huge laboratory from which they filched assistants to build galleys, cast cannon and make gunpowder, design fortifications, draw maps and work in metals; the Ottoman advance into Europe was spearheaded by Christian renegades. It was, however, a laboratory without new ideas. The key metallurgical discovery, the *saiger* process for extracting silver from silver-bearing copper ore, dated from the mid-fifteenth century; the most complex machine in industrial use, the multiple silk thrower, had been introduced before the end of the fourteenth. Water power was used increasingly for fulling cloth and grinding steel. In Holland there were wind-driven saw mills. Tread-wheels worked by dogs drew water from wells in Rouen, horse treadwheels were used to pump out mine shafts in Germany. Many of the technological drawings of Leonardo were devoted to showing how the forces of nature or the use of cogs, gears, pulleys and levers can replace manual labour or make it more productive. But there was no new principle involved and machines of any complication played but a small role in industry. In part this was due to the expense of constructing and servicing them, in part because labour costs were not so great as to make the widespread use of machinery imperative.

It is difficult to resist the feeling that there were other, less tangible reasons. The love of ingenuity for its own sake, for instance, acted as a check on the implementation of mechanical ideas on a large and economically useful scale. Many of Leonardo's contraptions could not have worked in practice: they were obsessed doodles, elaborating a single mechanical principal *ad absurdum*. Or they could be made to work, but not without an expense of human energy justified only by a five minute spurt past the chief review stand of a carnival procession; his 'tanks' were like the machines recorded by Landucci in his account of a wild beast hunt of lions and buffaloes in Florence, when 'they had made a tortoise and a porcupine inside of which were men who made them move along on wheels all over the piazza [della Signoria] and kept thrusting at the animals with their lances'. Similar, again, were complex clocks which symbolised the cosmos, with sun, moon and planets revolving round the earth, but which told the time indifferently, or multi-barrelled pistols, or crossbow- and pike-gun combinations, technically fascinating but well-nigh useless weapons.

Then, as Roland Mousnier has pointed out*, there was a widespread inability to learn from experience. He instances the agricultural practice of Poitou, where crops sown on land where chalk outcrops were ploughed into the soil yielded particularly well. Yet there was no attempt to mix chalk with the soil elsewhere, even though this was well within the technical competence of the farmers in the area. Finally, there was almost no flow of ideas, in any directions, between science, technological ingenuity, and craft or industrial experience.

Industrial plants were too small to present a challenge to the organising power of the capitalists and managers who ran them or to tempt them to look outside traditional ways of working. The industry which employed the largest number of workers, the making of cloth, involved something like twenty stages between the raw wool and the final product. Only two of these stages involved the use of anything that resembled a factory where large numbers of men worked together: fulling, done in large yards, and tentering (stretching), which was carried out on simple frames in long sheds,

* In *Études sur la France de 1494 à 1559* (Cours de Sorbonne, Paris, n.d.) 38–9.

as was the plaiting and tensioning of rope. The other stages were carried out on a family or group basis. The organisation required was a fairly simple matter of timetable and transport; the investment in plant, and therefore the attention paid to equipment, was tiny compared with the money sunk in raw material and wages.

The largest industrial plant in Europe was the Venetian Arsenal or shipbuilding yard, which employed some 4,000 workers in busy years. In some years the alum works at Tolfa, in the Papal States, employed even more, but with the failure of the Volterra supplies at the end of the fifteenth century and the collapse of French attempts to process their own deposits at a reasonable price, Tolfa remained the sole example of this quite sophisticated extractive industry. Coal mining was more competitive, especially with the development of the Liège area. Most coal, however, was dug from surface veins without specific mining crafts, crafts which were required above all for the excavation of metals, iron, silver and copper. Together with the manufacture of glass, in which Venice retained a clear lead, it was metallurgy that involved the greatest number of men and the largest investments of capital in a process that involved engineering skill, machine and natural power (for crushing and washing) and chemical knowledge. To judge from the publications on metallurgy that began to appear from 1500, and allowing for a reluctance to pass on 'secrets', this knowledge was based on rote and did not deepen. A more important reservation is that while there were plants scattered over a wide area from the Corinthian Alps to the Pyrenees, very few of them employed more than a thousand men. Even with the demand for pots, bells, bullion, guns and the huge pans used for evaporating salt, the metallurgical industry, like other industries, played but a small role in shaping the way in which more than a very few men indeed thought about technology, the organisation of labour or business methods. Neither the nature of industry nor its scale acted as a leaven tending to make the economic life of Europe stricter in its standards of calculation or more consciously progressive. Perhaps there was one exception: printing. Though firms which employed as many as a hundred men, as did that of Anton Koberger of Nuremberg, were rare, the techniques of book production had become rationalised. The design of presses, the lay-out of founts, the arrangement of the shops were all designed to speed output without sacrificing accuracy. The change from the sedentary to the standing posture of the compositor, slight enough in itself, is significant as the result of a time-and-motion study elsewhere to be observed only in labour-saving changes in the rigging of ships.

Economic Policy and Taxation

The extent to which governments intervened in the business affairs of individuals and corporations varied, but all did intervene and all had the same objectives, to encourage native products and protect them from foreign competition, and to prevent the flow of bullion abroad by making their countries as self-supporting as possible. The economic element in nationalism was the first to be widely appreciated and acted upon.

Because the French linen industry was languishing and Frenchmen were importing the fabric from England, Italy and Spain, Louis XI encouraged the linen producers of Arras, Rheims and elsewhere by granting tax concessions to the towns concerned and by increasing the import duties on the foreign cloth. His successor forced the other trades in Poitiers to give subsidies to the linen industry until it was back on its feet. To encourage the iron industry, Louis exempted miners and smelters from taxation and compelled local land-owners to supply iron-masters with timber for fuel. Maritime governments commonly offered subsidies to firms building merchant ships large enough to be converted into fighting vessels in time of war; though this was a way of getting a navy on the cheap it was also in line with laws, like the Castilian edict of 1500, which required a nation's goods to be exported in native shipping. In addition to customs dues, a further means of cutting down imports was the use of sumptuary laws forbidding the wearing of foreign products. To give an example for the observation of these laws, no Venetian public official was permitted to wear cloth that had not been made in Venice or its *terra ferma*. In a (vain) attempt to protect the Catalan coral industry, which produced ornaments much prized abroad, it was forbidden to export the special tools which would have made coral working easier for others. Government action could determine the economic prosperity of individual towns. The choice of Calais as sole export outlet for English wool is one example, the sacrifice of other towns to Moscow, whither merchants and artisans were compelled to move by royal edict, is another. A third, the deliberate building up of Lyons as an international trade and banking centre, was successful enough to provoke widespread criticism of the crown from less favoured French towns.

It was, however, in France that the principle behind much of this governmental direction was stated most clearly. 'Money', as a speaker at the estates general of 1484 put it, 'is in the body politic what blood is in the human body: it is then necessary to examine what bleedings and purgings France has undergone.' The two major bleedings were papal taxation and the purchase of luxury goods from abroad. The effects of the first could be countered by political action, the second by 'drawing gold and silver into the country'. The need to create a favourable balance of trade was all the more urgent because the value of coinage, and therefore the cost of living, was determined by the price of gold, and gold was in short supply. The widespread belief in bullionist theory among traders encouraged them to look for guidance to the crown, especially as the monarchs of Europe had long claimed the sole right to mint coin and to settle the respective values of gold and silver money. In this period, moreover, governments, whether of kings or independent princes, were effectively pressing their rights to all seams of precious metals, no matter who owned the land above them.

This monetary centralisation was undoubtedly beneficial to the economy as a whole. It was also profitable to the governments concerned. In addition it suggested the creation of other national monopolies – the extraction of saltpetre and the making of gunpowder, for instance – and the supporting, for a consideration, of monopolies already established or desired by private companies. Nowhere was the development of monopolies under crown protection more notable than in Spain. In 1497 Ferdinand and Isabella granted a charter of privileges to the chief inland transport organisation, henceforward to be known as the Royal Association of Teamsters, which exempted it from local tolls and gave it pasturage rights on all common and waste lands. In 1497 they licensed the *consulado* of Burgos which made that city the funnel into which all Castilian wool ran before being exported to northern Europe. In 1503, following this model, the *Casa de contratacion* was established in Seville as the sole receiving and distribution point for goods from the Americas. But the most dramatic of these sleeping partnerships, whereby the crown channelled commerce through its own pocket, was contracted with the *Mesta*, the association of Castilian sheep farmers. The flocks were of enormous size, some three million in all. Because of the nature of the country they were moved from mountain pasture in the summer to winter grazing in the plains over distances of as much as four hundred and fifty miles. Along the routes they followed there was a natural conflict of interests. Agriculturalists wanted to increase the amount of land put down to corn, vines and olives, all commodities in high demand, the sheep owners wanted huge corridors of pasturage. From 1489 Ferdinand and Isabella published a series of edicts in the interest of the *Mesta*, of which the most important, issued in 1501, guaranteed to members the undisputed tenancy of lands on which flocks had been pastured in the past, regardless of any subsequent change of intention on the part of the owner of the land.

Others secured shepherds against imprisonment as securities for the debts of their employers and exempted them from military service. Another, sacrificing the oldest of crown monopolies to its most recent monopolistic *protégé*, exempted the *Mesta* from the tax on the loads of salt which accompanied the flocks.

How far this descent of the crown into the market place was prompted by governmental initiative and how far by requests from merchants and manufacturers is difficult to say, but it sprang from the very naturalness of an interplay between government and production. When Louis XI, after consultation with manufacturers, published an ordinance in 1479 (repeated and elaborated in 1512) which regulated the quality, the number of threads and the length per piece of cloth for the area within the jurisdiction of the *parlements* of Paris, Rouen, Bordeaux and Toulouse, he was simply carrying out a function at a national level which had habitually been carried out at a local level by gilds and municipalities. The fixing of prices by government was another transference of a familiar municipal duty. Such transferences fitted easily into the view of a king as father and protector of his people. They were also in tune with the growing reliance on central rather than local justice. The publication of national economic ordinances went hand in hand with the codification of laws as rationalisations which were in the interest of both government and the individual. Again, parallel with the increasing tendency of nobles and lawyers to look for posts in government or at court, the bigger merchants were becoming less absorbed by the economic and administrative concerns of their towns and more interested in their personal fortunes. For both psychological and financial reasons, therefore, they looked beyond the city wall to the central government, and in consultative assemblies gave their support to royal patronage of local trade and craft associations and to national economic policies. And, finally, there was a somewhat clearer notion that such phenomena as rising prices and vagabondage were not simply punishments inflicted by God but the result of economic factors (the supply of specie, enclosure for grazing and the like) which could best be countered by governmental action.

This realism was still sporadic. Economic cause and effect was difficult to grasp. Theory was expressed in pseudo-explanations like the apothegm of the Portuguese Tomé Pires, 'a kingdom without ports is like a house without doors' and mercantilism was seen uncritically as the universal panacea. Even so, theory ran ahead of practice. In 1482 Louis XI attempted to set up a merchant marine subject to overall control by the crown. But the scheme called for a degree of co-operation among shipowners and merchants for which they were not ready, and it got no further than the paper on which it was written. In Portugal, merchants were prepared to accept the system whereby eastern imports had to be assembled at four collecting points, Ormuz, Goa, Malacca and Macao, shipped home in government organised convoys, and distributed through a central agency in Lisbon. The snag here was that thanks to the complexity of regulations and the lack of straightforward methods of clearance, Lisbon became the tightest bottleneck in Europe; the pioneer exploring country also pioneered the constricting use of red tape. Spain provides a third example of the hazards faced by the move towards overall planning. After the union of the crowns of Aragon and Castile, the advanced gild structure of Aragonese crafts was, in the interest of uniformity and of convenience, introduced into Castile, thus constricting rather than encouraging production there. Favour shown to the *Mesta* at the expense of arable farming led to a socially perilous rise in the price of foodstuffs. Cumulatively, these factors were even more disadvantageous to the country's economy than the expulsion of the Jews, whose economic role was gradually taken over by foreigners.

All plans to use government as an instrument of economic change were hampered by a lack of trained bureaucratic specialists. Above all they were hampered by unmethodically kept records and inadequate statistics. Governments could only guess at what would happen in the future because they had no clear figures which showed what had happened in the past. At a time when there was considerable vagueness as to a country's population, let alone its trade balances, when generals could misjudge the number of men under their command by as much as one third, when even Venice, a business state run by business men, could build more galleys than it could possibly man – when these errors in calculation are taken into account, a hit-or-miss element in commercial plans must be taken for granted.

The same is true of fiscal plans. The idea of an annual budget, a balance between national income and expenditure, was by now commonplace, as were attempts to forecast expenditure in the coming year. In small countries, especially where the tax burden fell predominantly on one large city, as in the case of Florence, a balance could be struck with some regularity, though it was never possible to estimate it at any time between the major audits. In large countries like France, it was seldom that the returns from outlying administrative districts turned up in time to make the annual balance complete, and even then it was tentative until teams of auditors could travel to check accounts on the spot. Accounting procedures, moreover, were still designed to deal primarily with individual sources of income rather than with conflated figures, nor did they distinguish between recurrent and non-recurrent income. The national budget served as little more than a rough guide to tax requirements and to expenditure. There was a similar distinction between large and small countries with regard to population statistics and therefore to the estimated yield of a tax. From income returns, hearth tax returns, registers of births and deaths, the Italian cities had a reasonably clear idea how many taxpayers they were dealing with even in the rural areas under their direct control. Elsewhere, uncertainty about population figures was a major cause of the yield of taxes often being strikingly below the anticipated sum. A war grant from parliament to Henry VIII, for instance, which promised about £100,000, turned out to yield less than £60,000. Other features beside ignorance accounted for gaps of this sort. Assessments of property, goods and income could be years, sometimes generations out of date. Local assessors and collectors were frequently bribed. Smuggling, everywhere endemic in Europe, reduced the estimated yields on customs or exercise taxes. And though the payment of taxes was represented as a public duty and some form of consent was obtained from representative assemblies for most forms of unusual taxation, the reluctance to pay was universal. The practice at Nuremberg whereby citizens assessed themselves and placed their municipal tax, unsupervised, in a communal money-box, was looked on by outsiders with some scepticism.

There was a stubborn conviction, especially among the poor and the fairly poor, that taxation was not really necessary at all, that while plagues and wars might require taxation to be imposed for a while, there was something unnatural about paying duty on such God-given products as bread, salt and wine, for which men had already paid with their sweat. This idea of a fiscal Golden Age did not simply express the innocence of the ignorant. The Three Estates division of society led nobles to refuse to pay taxes because their swords and their blood were permanently on offer to government, and clerics grudged serving a country with taxes because they were already serving it with their prayers (they were in fact taxed separately from laymen, and more lightly). At the end of the fifteenth century, when the Milanese came temporarily under French rule, the city council of Piacenza refused to pay excise duties because of an extraordinary rumour that in France – probably the most heavily taxed nation in Europe – no one paid taxes unless he chose to. In France itself another tradition – by now so outmoded as to be hardly more than a superstition – that the king could live on the income from his own domains alone was taken perfectly seriously by the estates general of 1484. In all monarchies a distinction was made between ordinary revenue, the personal income of the king, and extraordinary revenue in the form of taxes, duties and loans. Henry VII, whose personal income was reorganised and exploited with some thoroughness, still needed the export duty on wool and leather and the import and export duties on wine even in years of peace. Indeed, government everywhere was becoming a more expensive business but, except in the case of war, it was difficult for the taxpayer to see why this was so, and this was another element in the reluctance to pay.

Addressing the young Charles of Habsburg, who, as the Emperor Charles V, was to be Europe's greatest taxmaster, Erasmus took it for granted that a king would try to live without taxing his subjects unless 'some taxation is absolutely necessary and the affairs of the people render it essential.' In that case he should penalise the rich and tax 'the extravagant luxuries and delicacies which only the wealthy enjoy', among which he named jewels, silk, spices and dyes. For 'a good prince will tax as lightly as possible those commodities which are used by the poorest members of society, e.g. grain, bread, beer, wine, clothing and all the other staples without which human life could not exist... But it so happens that these very things bear the heaviest tax in several ways; in the first place, by the oppressive extortion of the tax farmers..., then by import duties which call for their own set of extortionists, and finally by the monopolies by which the poor are sadly drained of their funds in order that the prince may gain a mere trifling interest.' More painted an even darker view of the people's oppression. 'Picture the councillors of some king or other debating with him and devising by what schemes they may heap up treasure for him. One advises crying up the value of money when he has to pay any and crying down its value below the just rate when he has to receive any – with the double result that he may discharge a large debt with a small sum and, when only a small sum is due to him, may receive a large one. Another suggests a make-believe war under pretext of which he would raise money and then, when he saw fit, make peace with solemn ceremonies to throw dust in his simple people's eyes because their loving monarch in compassion would fain avoid human bloodshed. Another councillor reminds him of certain old and moth-eaten laws annulled by long non-enforcement, which no one remembers being made and therefore everyone has transgressed. The king should exact fines for their transgressions, there being no richer source of profit nor any more honourable, than such as has an outward mask of justice.'

For all these forms of extortion, from the cut taken by the tax farmer to the re-implementation of moth-eaten laws, Erasmus and More could have cited chapter and verse in contemporary practice. And they could have mentioned others. The German princes extorted protection money from towns and individuals. In the Palatinate men were forced by law to plant vines so that they would have to pay the tax on wine production. Louis XII of France extended the deplorable convention whereby administrative posts went not to the best qualified man but could be bought for cash. The moth-eaten laws were above all those relating to feudal tenure. At the bottom of the social scale medieval dues like pannage and the heriot were re-imposed, at the top, rulers set their lawyers to ferret out titles to land so that the old rights of wardship, livery and relief could be demanded of tenants-in-chief. This process was nowhere carried out with more determination and ingenuity than in England. Casualties during the Wars of the Roses meant that many estates could be shown to have escheated to the crown for lack of heirs. Heirs who were minors were declared wards of the crown, which administered their lands and took its profits until they came of age – at which point they paid a livery fee to take up their inheritance. Henry VIII, in a notable stroke of legal archaeology, persuaded parliament to accept his levy of feudal aids for the knighting of his eldest son and on the marriage of his eldest daughter.

The example of England shows how effective a bait was held out to fiscal efficiency and centralisation by the possibility of increasing revenue. In the reign of Henry VII alone, income from crown lands, customs duties, feudal rights, and legal fees and penalties almost tripled from about £52,000 to some £142,000 a year. In France, too, the income from crown lands was increased as well as the national revenue as a whole. But increased efficiency did not include taking stock of the social effects of a system which included, indeed was based on, the faults to which Erasmus drew attention. Unlike England, the French government relied heavily on a permanent extraordinary tax, the *taille*, an income tax which produced something like 83 per cent (in 1483) of the total revenue. As nobles, the clergy, judges and many other officials, together with certain towns, were exempt from this, the burden fell on the classes least able to bear it, especially on the peasantry. In addition, sales taxes (*aides*) were not only imposed on luxuries like silk, spices, dyes and jewellery, but on almost the whole range of staples: wine, grain, meat, poultry and fish, on woollen goods and shoes, on building materials and on coal and charcoal. Again, the poor were hardest hit. This inequity, least noticeable in England but characteristic of all European governments, was not only socially hazardous and involved formidable collection costs, it also encouraged evasion and smuggling.

In general, then, old methods were improved and in some cases extended, but there was no radical re-thinking of fiscal policy. Nor were governments able to keep the whole process of revenue collecting in their own hands. Lacking sufficient public servants, they put taxes out to farm, sacrificing the full potential of a tax to the certainty of receiving regularly a sum mulcted by the farmer. Lacking more than a hint of the notion of contingency planning, they had recourse to loans, often at very high interest rates or secured on specific items of revenue. Even when representative assemblies agreed to special war taxation, loans usually had to be resorted to as a means of bridging the gap between the vote and its implementation, and private financiers added their charges to the bill that finally had to be met. Reasonable fiscal steadiness in peacetime was in strong contrast to the way in which governments paid for wars. The pawning of valuables was commonplace. Isabella pawned her jewels to raise money for the campaign of 1489 against the Moors. Maximilian's superb collection of gold- and silver-smith's work was all in pawn at his death. Henry VII's personal treasure was, with the same eventuality in mind, kept chiefly in jewels and plate. The speed with which his successor disposed of anything that might have been left on wars for which there was little, if any, economic justification, illustrates the double standard that affected national accounting: on the domestic front, method and ingenuity and, with respect to trade, some imagination, in foreign affairs a mood of incautious improvisation.

5

Class

Definitions and Attitudes

Between 1515 and 1519 Nicolas Manuel painted for the Dominicans of Bern a Dance of Death which reflects the number of categories into which an intelligent townsman divided his social world. The church was represented by pope, cardinal, patriarch, bishop, abbot, canon, monk and hermit; noble blood by emperor, king, duke, count, knight and a member of the Teutonic Order; commoner blood by an academic and a practising doctor, a jurist and an advocate, an astrologer, a councillor, a rich merchant and one of lesser standing, a magistrate, a bailiff, a soldier, a peasant, an artisan, a cook and a painter. Death came to interrupt the occupations of each of them, as he did to take away an empress, a queen, an abbess, a nun and a prostitute and five allegorical figures: girl, wife, widow, bachelor and madman.

Conservatives still saw society as divided into three mutually-supporting estates. Caxton's *Mirror of the World* (1481) put the traditional formula of the commons who work, the knights who fight and the clergy who pray, in its simplest form. 'The labourers ought to provide for the clerks and knights such things as were needful for them to live by in the world honestly; and the knights ought to defend the clerks and the labourers that there were no wrong done to them; and the clerks ought to instruct and teach these two manner of people, and to address them in their works in such wise that none do [any] thing by which he should displease God nor lose His grace.' This ideal of harmony and balance was popularised through the commonplace analogies of the day: society existed in terms of three estates as God existed within the Trinity; the game of chess depended on the King being supported by knights, bishops and common pawns all working together; man's life depended on the co-operation of his members: the prayerful head, the protecting arms, the energy-producing body. Seen in terms of an actual body politic, Spain, for instance, the proportions are grotesque: head, 3 per cent, arms 2 per cent, body 95 per cent. And that the conservatives were aware of the problem of the size of the third estate and the variety within it is shown by Edmund Dudley's insistence in *The Tree of Commonwealth* (1509) that it should function as one member of the social trinity, although 'therein be all the merchants, craftsmen and artificers, labourers, freeholders, graziers, farmers, tillers and others generally the people of this realm.'

Broadly speaking, men of letters – and this includes politicians in oratorical mood – flinched from close observation of the third estate, with its extremes of banking wealth and proletarian misery. The prestige attached to land, with its ancient aura of local law-giving and political power, led to formulations on 'churchmen, landed, landless' lines. Alternatively, authors turned to Aristotle, ignoring his most practical division of classes, which included not only wage-labourers, peasant proprietors and artisans but a 'marketing class' which 'includes all those who are occupied in buying or selling', and settling for his crudest division between the very rich, the reasonably well-to-do, and the poor, who 'know only how to obey'.

At least this upper-middle-lower division of secular society enabled an analysis of society to be made in terms not of duty or service but of purchasing power. It was adopted by the most 'sociological' observer of his time, Claude de Seyssel. The purpose of his *La Monarchie de France* (1515) was to show how the new French king, Francis I, should preserve social harmony. Seyssel's categories do not include the clergy: he leaves them on one side as representing rich, well-to-do and poor in parallel to secular society. His first estate is the nobility, conventionally seen as specially privileged defenders of the realm; his second, merchants together with royal officials, the bureaucrats concerned with the administration of justice and finance; the third is composed mainly of producers, peasants and artisans, but includes petty officials, merchants in a small way of business and the lower ranks in the army. It is an inferior, a dependent estate 'according to reason and political necessity, just as in the human body there must be inferior organs, the servants of those of higher worth and dignity.' Tropes aside, and granting the influence of the medieval preoccupation with triads, the Seyssel formula was in accord with reality. And an added note of observation is given in a chapter 'How one moves from the third to the second, and from the second to the first estate' in which Seyssel explains that ambition can lead a commoner to prosper his way into the second estate, and outstanding public service can lead the king to ennoble members of the second estate into the first, whose ranks are, in any case, constantly shrinking thanks to death in war and, a significant point, poverty. This mobility, he notes, acts as an essential safety valve: without it 'those whose ambition is irrepressible would conspire with other members of their estate against those above them.' As it is, mobility is such that 'every day one sees members of the popular estate mount by degrees into that of the nobility and numberless into the middle estate.' And being a man of his times, for whom observation was not enough, he added that this reproduced Roman practice, whereby plebeians could rise to become knights and proceed to the patrician class.

The distinction between aristocratic blood on the one hand and, on the other, varying degrees of wealth was regularly made by governments in their tax and social legislation. The English sumptuary regulations of 1517, for instance, were designed to cut down extravagance and ostentation in the giving of meals, and clerics were included. The noble categories were: cardinal (nine dishes per meal); archbishop and duke (seven); marquis, earl, bishop (also seven); lords temporal under the degree of earl, abbots being in the House of Lords, mayors of the city of London, Knights of the Garter (six). The others were allowed, according to goods possessed or to income, five, four or three dishes. And 'it is ordered that in case any of the estates or other before rehearsed shall fortune to dine or sup with any other of a lower degree, it shall be lawful to the person or persons with whom the said estates or other shall so dine or sup to serve them and every of them according to their degrees, after the rates before specified', i.e. a merchant with goods worth £500 could put on a seven-course meal for a bishop but only three when he dined alone or with his financial equals. This blood and wealth division was modified for non-aristocratic officials to enable them to enhance their prestige. Thus the mayor of London, whatever his unofficial estate or degree, was allowed six dishes, and there was a special provision for judges, the chief baron of the exchequer, members of the king's council and sheriffs of the city of London: all were allowed five whatever their status in private life.

The notion of the three estates was to die hard, however. All over Europe the clergy, and in most countries the nobility, were subject to different forms of law from those affecting the third estate. In almost every country where there was some form of consultative assembly it was divided into clergy, nobility and commons – naturally, for monarchs wished to tap the wealth of the clergy, the nobles' income from land, and the merchants' profits from trade. The most coherent estate, in its own eyes and those of the others, was that of the nobility. It contained a wide range of ranks and incomes, but it was small in number and entry to it was policed by heralds and determined by the personal intervention of the monarch. It was surrounded, too, by the aura of a special code of behaviour, and in certain countries, France and Sweden, for instance, and in some parts of Germany, it was exempt from taxation. The clerical estate was larger in size and far more varied in its social and economic composition. With bishops' palaces, monastic farms, begging friars and chantry priests on starvation wages, the life of the clergy ran into that of the laity, rank by rank. From the point of view of the style in which he lived, the archbishop had more in common with a duke than with a parish priest; similarly, the corn or wine merchant in a country town may well have been happier bargaining with the steward of the neighbouring monastery than in the presence of an itinerant judge. In spite of this, the clergy, as responsible to Rome, as celibates, as administrators of the sacraments and as butts of an inclusive anticlericalism, presented the appearance of a separate order scattered through, but essentially different from the rest of society.

Where the formula really broke down was over the third estate. With municipal corporations, law merchant, gilds, confraternities, different procedures for free and unfree tenures, the third estate was broken up into occupations, interest and status groups even in the eye of the law. In representative bodies, from the English parliament to the Catalan *cortes* or the Bohemian diet, the third estate covered a broad social spectrum, from middling merchants to widely-acred gentlemen. In practice no one felt 'part of' the third estate but part of a specific occupational group, and, within that, of a specific income group. When polemicists, preachers or satirists looked round for social targets they attacked the nobility as a whole, the clergy usually under two heads, bishops and parish priests, and monks and friars, and the third estate in terms of a number of groups which were felt to practice a way of life that distinguished them from others. Cornelius Agrippa, in his *De vanitate*, attacked merchants (cheats and usurers), lawyers (shysters) and doctors (quacks) before passing to a blanket condemnation of the poor (stupid, superstitious, crude). Olivier Maillard, preaching in 1500 in Bruges, singled out princes and courtiers, then officials, merchants and lawyers. In his *Ship of Fools* (1494) Sebastian Brant attacked artisans,

> *Every apprentice would be a master,*
> *For all the trades a great disaster,*

lawyers, doctors

> *And while he thumbs the folios*
> *The patient to the bone-yard goes,*

merchants and their wives

> *A burgher's wife now often wears*
> *Clothes better than a countess bears,*

peasants

> *The peasant folk had simple ways*
> *In not extremely distant days*

and servants

> *Pay any wage, it will not please,*
> *Still they will spare their energies.*

In each group he sees laziness, deceit, ostentation and, above all, social climbing.

> *All lands into disgrace have got*
> *And none's contented with his lot,*
> *And none remembers now his sires,*
> *The world is full of fool's desires.*

There were, of course, local characteristics within the structure of the third estate: in England the yeomen, country proprietors who were expected to apply for knighthood if they prospered sufficiently, were regarded as a separate group, though a man's own estimate of his status might well differ from that of his neighbours. In Florence there was a sharp political, and a reasonably clear social division between members of the greater and the lesser gilds; in some parts of Germany master artisans had to swear that their gild candidates were 'free and no one's serf, nor the son of a bath attendant, barber, linen-leaver or minstrel.' But we can say that contemporaries saw the third estate as divided broadly into these classes: proprietor farmers, agricultural labourers, government officials, merchants, indentured craftsmen (apprentices, journeymen), domestic servants, urban labourers. Lawyers were considered a separate professional class, doctors were almost so, but not quite. Hovering beside these categories, not easily seen in terms of estate, degree or condition and not associated with a definite income level but pursuing a specific way of life, were certain identifiable groups: professional humanists,* artists, printers, miners and mercenary soldiers. Either because of itinerancy, or novelty, or changing attitudes to their social position, these groups did not fit easily into any stratified view of the third estate; nor did such a view take note of Jews, gypsies or slaves.

Complicating this already imprecise impression was one overriding prejudice, stronger probably than the barrier to sympathy between

---

* See below, Chapter 8 seq.

layman and priest; the townsman's prejudice against the countryman. Yet it is not as though rural and urban life were out of touch with one another. From Lisbon to Moscow vegetables were grown within the walls and the citizen relied on milk and meat from his own cows. The city fathers of Frankfurt-am-Main had to pass an ordinance forbidding citizens to keep pigsties on the street side of their houses and in other German towns wine growers and market gardeners formed special gilds. In Dijon artisans – furriers, carpenters, coopers and others – had vineyards and sold what wine they did not consume themselves. And if country occupations were a commonplace in the towns, the need for many countrymen to have two sources of income brought town occupations to the country, spinning, weaving, nail-making; most of the craftsmen who brought their baskets, saddlery, pots and pans to local markets were seasonal agriculturalists. Apart from the small merchant and the town-based bailiff or steward, few tradesmen moved about far in the country, but towns received a steady drift of farm labourers in search of work. There was interchange higher up the social scale: the yeoman's son who settled in a town, and whose family moved back to the country after two or three prosperous generations, was not an uncommon phenomenon. The majority of nobles, though they might have a town house and spend some time following the court, passed most of their lives on their country estates, were familiar with every detail of the agricultural year and were led by hawk and hound through every rural scene.

Yet for all these contacts there was an emotional gulf between town and country dweller, narrowest among the rich, widest when all other classes contemplated that universal butt, the peasant, most pungently expressed in the most highly urbanised countries, Italy, Germany and the Netherlands, but audible everywhere in literature and almost always visible in art, where the hulking, bent figure of the countryman is rendered commonly in caricature or with amused condescension. Country folk are sub-human, growled Felix Hemmerlin, a humanist canon of Zurich; it would do them good if their houses were burned and their farms laid waste every fifty years.

The convention of the rustic squire, the country cousin, the yokel come to gape at the wonders of the capital has a long history. Tales like Machiavelli's *Belfagor* (between 1515 and 1520) in which a peasant outwits the devil, are rare exceptions to the rule that rural workers are to be despised ('wild, treacherous, and untamed' was Sebastian Franck's opinion) or laughed at. In plays the countryman is a clown, in anecdotes he is a gullible ignoramus. It is in *The Courtier* that an early version occurs of the practical joke in which a man asks a bystander to hold the end of a piece of string while he goes round a building to measure it; once out of sight he ties the string to a nail and goes away. In *The Courtier* it is the device whereby a student of Padua robs a peasant of two chickens. Yet it was in Italy that Arcadia played its most charming imaginative role, where nymph and shepherd elaborated their pastoral loves and the pipes of Pan whistled provokingly from dense thickets of verse. And it was in the urbanised Netherlands that the country administered a sharp rebuke to the town. Among the *tableaux vivants* arranged for the entry of Charles, count of Flanders (the future Charles V) into Bruges in 1515, was one in which the inhabitants of the surrounding countryside featured themselves as the true inheritors of the Golden Age. As the printed description put it 'in the first Age and archaic crudeness of the human race, under the rule of the gods and goddesses represented in this enclosure, men lived in huts and cottages, entirely and peaceably on agriculture and stock-raising, for they sought no gain nor fruit save from the earth and from brute beasts', and the moral was that a simple, unaggressive life had been ruined by the growth of cities, which had broken the 'bienheureux circle aurian du glorieux Saturne'.*

This antagonism drew on centuries during which towns had bargained and fought their way to some measure of self-government against church, noble and monarch and had thrown off the taint of servility that still clung to the countryside. And as the standard of living and the level of education in the towns grew, the contrast of manners came to constitute another barrier; More had his Utopian citizens educated in the country and forced to return to agricultural tasks from time to time in order to break it down.

The burden of satire – 'All lands into disgrace have got, And none's contented with his lot' – is that this was a period of vigorous social change, of scrambling competitiveness. When searching for the psychological causes of war, civil faction and popular disturbances, historians almost unanimously pitched on ambition as the prime mover. Wherever we turn we find complaints that men are not content with the conditions in which they have been bred. 'The people have taken on airs', wrote the Lyons chronicler Symphorien Champier, 'and entertained evil ideas...and the servants, who once were humble in the presence of their masters and were sober and poured much water into their wine...now wish to drink better wine, like their masters, without any water or admixture whatsoever, which is a thing against all reason.' Handbooks for confessors admonished the clergy to warn their parishioners against envying the possessions or social position of others and not to eat or dress above their station.

---

* Elizabeth Armstrong, *Ronsard and the age of gold* (Cambridge U.P., 1968) 3.

Clichthove complained in sermon after sermon about congregations who treated the church as an extension of the market place, passing contracts about and discussing business deals. A German preacher described in 1515 a world that seemed to him to have gone money mad. 'Everyone thinks he will grow rich and put his money out to the best advantage. The artisan and the peasants invest their money in a company, or with tradesmen. They think to gain a great deal, and, often they lose everything. This evil did not exist in former times; it has grown up in the last ten years.' In England, Alexander Barclay inveighed in his *Shyp of Folys* (1509) against the pretensions which lead farmers to aspire to the gentry and butcher's boys to transform themselves into bailiffs (in that same year Wolsey, son of an Ipswich butcher, entered the service of the young Henry VIII as almoner and councillor). Why should men strive so? Death levels all at the end. 'Therefore methink of all thing it is best/Man to be pleased and content with his degree.' Folk lore told the same story. In an Italian popular play, the *Farce against taking a Wife* (c. 1500) a peasant girl is walking to market with a basket of eggs balanced on her head. As she goes she day-dreams about the future. She will sell the eggs, buy more, raise chickens and sell them, buy land and become rich. Then she will say to her father that she wants a husband, and not a farmer, not a gentleman, not even a noble. Her father will say 'It is the emperor that you want?' and she will say, bowing her head at the splendour of her dream come true. 'Yes, sir.' And Fortune concludes: 'On bowing her head the basket fell, and the eggs within, and so were spoiled, and with them the plans which this poor girl had made.'*

The individual's chief concern was to increase his standard of living within his class, whether noble, bourgeois, churchman or peasant-proprietor. The most desperate drive was to maintain a standard of living among those groups nearest the subsistence level, the peasant and the urban wage labourer. The most conscious drive was among those 'unplaced' groups, including artists and professional humanists, who, frequently of the humblest birth, were determined to find a social, as well as an intellectual welcome among the traditionally defined classes who patronised them. Corporate class feeling was expressed in terms of hatred of those with the power to oppress or starve at a particular moment in a particular town or, more rarely, in a particular region. Most commonly it was the price of bread that determined these outbursts of resentment. Sometimes it was a specific tax. 'Kill all the gentlemen!' was the response of the poor in Oberhasli when the men of substance in their canton voted to raise money

---

* I follow the synopsis given in M. T. Herrick, *Italian Comedy in the Renaissance* (University of Illinois, 1960) 36.

to provide the French with troops. But in general there was no class antagonism in the sense of one class wishing permanently to dispossess another.

When Adam dug and Eve span
Who was then the gentleman?

lingered on as a slogan, not a policy. Among the lowest ranks there was insufficient strength, among the moderately well-to-do sufficient upwards mobility, to ensure that social pressures were for the most part contained within the various compartments of the hierarchy of wealth and honour. The poor, especially the poor immigrants to towns, were feared less as potential revolutionaries than as the carriers and breeders of disease. Moreover, discrepancies of income were of an order that inhibited rather than encouraged class rivalry. In the neighbourhood of Valladolid the count of Benavente's annual income was seventeen hundred times that of a labourer; in the town itself, the income of a patrician of modest means was eighteen times that of a skilled craftsman and twenty-nine times that of an unskilled man. Social stratification, moreover, was broken up by clan affiliations, gilds, fraternities and clientage systems which restricted the ability to think in horizontal class terms and protectively associated men of low income with their betters.

Social tension in Europe was in any case far from uniform. At its most complex in countries with fairly dense populations, many towns, much commerce and well-established conventions defining the relations between government, corporation and individual – England, France, northern Italy, the Low Countries, central and southern Germany – it was also least disruptive there. In countries like Norway, Sweden and Spain, in which an urban middle class formed the thinnest of buffers between possessors and non-possessors, there was little occasion for tension within classes, and thinly dispersed populations, a vigilant church and a securely established customary law reduced the danger of tension between them. Moving eastward, however, beyond the limits of the Austrian Danube, where governmental and ecclesiastical institutions were firmly entrenched amid a racially homogeneous population of peasants, townsmen and nobles, the further we go towards the Black Sea or up into the Ukraine and Poland the simpler the social structure becomes and the more violent, with a weakly organised church, governments powerless to police vast areas of plain and forest, no well-defined citizen class and an aristocracy who still saw themselves as conquerors, and looked on the peasants, into whose lands their Magyar ancestors had ridden, as their scarcely-tolerated prey. The vicious suppression of the

Hungarian peasant revolt in 1514 was but the bloodiest example of a tendency at work throughout eastern Europe; with Danzig–Vienna as an axis, the balance of peasant freedom was rising in the west and dipping into serfdom in the east. The social composition of the eastern states seems, it is true, more starkly simple than it was because of the nature of the sources: monastic chronicles written, as it were, behind carefully bolted doors, saga-like royal chronologies, a minimum of personal correspondence or family records even from old established commercial centres like Novgorod. But certainly nowhere in the east was there a stratification so close as to justify a satirist venting his spleen on such minute ostentations as the cut of a doublet.

Even in the west the opportunities for social mobility, from occupation to occupation or class to class, were restricted to a very small minority, and changes of occupation that led to a change of living standard were very rare indeed. Some 90 per cent of the population of Europe lived outside the towns where alone there was some reasonable chance of climbing socially within a generation or two, and even there such mobility was hampered by the difficulty of accumulating capital; perhaps five per cent of townsmen, given opportunity, temperament and luck, might be able to better their position in their lifetimes. Poor countrymen might seek a new urban occupation, but as like as not they simply became poor townsmen. Movement from class to class provided too small a target to be worth attacking; pretension within classes fired the satirist because it was a deviation from the norm. It was attacked because it represented a breakdown in the ideal of service, of filling a useful place in society by devotedly serving a superior in return for his protection, an ideal that was not merely part of the nostalgia of chivalrous literature but still ensured harmony within the tradesman's house between master, apprentice and servant as well as within the complex social apparatus needed to run the vast households of the nobility. The ideal meant nothing – and never had – to men desperately on the make, it could wear thin in the relations of humanists to their patrons, and though it had risen within the military structure of feudalism it was openly denied now by professional soldiers who struck on the eve of battle for higher pay. However, it was from an understanding of the emotional satisfaction that service gave, as well as from its proved value as a social emollient, that the attacks on men's desire to change their station came.

In handbooks for merchants the emphasis was not on how to get ahead, how to make a fortune, but how to live up to the skills and virtues expected by society of a merchant. The same preoccupation with things as they were is shown in the many painted and engraved representations of the dress and occupations of different ranks, from emperor and money-changer to craftsman and beggar. They were shown for their own sake, or linked in a series like Manuel's in which death dances off with every man, whatever his position or trade, or, as in the engraved 'Tarocchi Cards', they were included with figures of the planets and virtues as part of a pre-ordained and unchangeable pattern of existence. Tableaux of occupations figured in public entertainments like the Schembart festival of Nuremberg, each distinguished by the costume which marked a man out in the street as a lawyer, a doctor, a shopkeeper or a smith. This visual cataloguing of class and occupation, like the increasing rigidity of craft organisation, the codification of laws and the working out of lists of precedence to determine who should enter when and sit where at diplomatic functions, reflects a tendency to see society as anything but open. The solemn state and religious processions in Venice were like animated diagrams of the three estates theory: doge and senators in one mass, the clergy in another, the separate crafts and occupations represented by their gild officers in a third: all sharply distinguished by their dress. Life was public, colourful and conformist: hence the alarmed savagery with which anomalies like Jews and gypsies could be treated.

Sumptuary legislation, through which all governments expressed the conviction that men and women should not dress or entertain above their station, was motivated, as we have seen, by a variety of aims. The church wished to curb vanity, the state to discourage the flow of currency abroad and to prevent large sums from being withdrawn from productive use. But the chief aim was to preserve the traditional layering of society, to make behaviour correspond with rank or occupation and, above all, to prevent the nobility – or, in cities, the patricians – from spending themselves out of effective public life or being reduced by extravagance to a manner of living inappropriate to their 'true' place in the social hierarchy.

By pointing to the fame that could come to writers and artists of humble birth it is possible to represent this period as one of the careers open to talent, but this is because fashion occasionally tore some of the meshes of the social net to give free passage to it. It is possible to group passages from the pages of speculative writers that would stress the role of man the maker, *homo faber*, and his freedom to affect his own destiny, but this has nothing to do with social advancement. The career open to talent – insofar as it was possible – was the product of specific demands by art patrons with walls to populate and of thriving administrations with jobs to fill; it was not the consequence of a new attitude towards social mobility. Dependent on an aristocracy, or on a patriciate that was aping aristocratic manners, the humanists spoke of freedom in tones adjusted to a conservative view of society. Reared on classical authors whose heroes were rulers, philosophers, artists and intellectuals and, in the main, disdainful of the results of contemporary ambitions which imperilled peace and coarsened thought, humanists were concerned to change hearts and minds but not to urge a foot to cross a class barrier.

Again, it is possible to find passages in discussions of the nature of true nobility that do seem potentially disruptive of social divisions. To cite Erasmus again, whose works had a far wider distribution than those of any other intellectual: 'let others paint on their escutcheons lions, eagles, bulls, leopards. Those are the possessors of true nobility who can use on their coats of arms ideas which they have thoroughly learned from the liberal arts'; or, à propos unworthy nobleman, 'why, I ask you, should this class of person be placed on a higher level than the shoemaker or the farmer?' But this suggestion that nobility is essentially a property of the cultivated mind exerting itself in the interest of the common good was in earnest only at the level (a high one) of comment on the moral nature of man: transposed into actual social terms it was no more than a cosily risqué debating point. Castiglione raised it, only to head it smartly off. The unwelcome suggestion that the baseborn can achieve rank was countered by the argument that good comes from good; the gentleman therefore would be careful not to besmirch his caste. The advice that followed was straightforward: the courtier should not wrestle with a peasant (it would damage his status if he lost); he should only dance with abandon among equals; he should mix sparingly with the people lest familiarity should breed contempt. Such advice shows how shakily realistic was the thesis that the good shoemaker was more worthy of respect than the bad noble. Were not aristocrats (thus Edmund Dudley, in grotesque parody of Pico) inserted by God in His scheme of degrees between ordinary men and the angels?

Nor did those shavings from the block of humanist thought, Fortune and Opportunity, express an approach to social mobility. From paint to the cheapest woodcut, images were multiplied of Opportunity, the sprite-goddess with bald pate and waving forelock which the resourceful man could clutch before she dashed past him. In bronze and prose Fortune teetered on her globe or puffed the sails of her own ship, personified Whim, less deterministic than Fate, less mechanically efficient than the Wheel of Circumstance. Machiavelli, in a key chapter in his essay in the politically possible, *The Prince*, likened Fortune to a woman who could be shaken into submission. But if the message of these images was that man was free to shape his career and need not grovel to fortune, it was applied only to the challenges within the context of one class, not to the effort required to move from one to another. Humanism enriched the subjective vocabulary of the individual's despairs and hopes while accepting the traditional social limits of his actions. Bearing in mind these indications of exclusiveness and restriction we can understand why Leonardo, when designing an ideal city, foresaw it as being on two levels: 'the high-level roads are...solely for the convenience of the gentlefolk. All carts and loads for the service and convenience of the common people should be confined to the low-level.'

Special Cases

Jacques de Beaune's career was highly exceptional but it contained features echoed in many less sensational ones; bourgeois birth, evidence of financial acumen that brought a socially advantageous marriage, and official posts which were themselves an occasion for making more money. There was nothing new about kings using men of bourgeois origin as advisers and administrators and many of the highest offices in the state were still reserved for nobles; it was the fairly rapid expansion of royal and princely administrations that made the bureaucratic career the one, above all, open to talent. In France in 1512 there were some 86,000 men whose lives were devoted wholly or part-time to administrative work. They varied in importance from a Semblançay to a small-town surveyor of weights and measures, from chancellor to the rummager of wool bales for the customs service. The motives which led men into this service were several. The deliberate glamourising of the role of the prince rubbed off on those who served him, even from afar. It could be 'placed' within the biblical picture of approved occupations. The royal notaries and secretaries of France formed a religious confraternity under the protection of St. John because, as they put it in 1482, 'he was the chief and highest of the secretary-evangelists of our saviour Jesus Christ.' The bureaucracy by now offered reasonable security of tenure. Some offices were even, in effect, hereditary. It was a career that could not only lead to ennoblement but meant mingling with nobles both at court and in provincial centres on terms of mutual interest: satisfying in itself at a time when the aristocrat was the most widely revered social type, and for the opportunities this relationship gave for marrying into the noble class. Finally, thanks to the convention, commonest in France, whereby offices were actually sold for cash, it was possible for a merchant to buy his way in. It was a career in which few men climbed far, but because of their mixed social origin – noble, bourgeois, clerical – the nature of their occupation and the specific loyalty it encouraged, and because of the blend of respect and distrust with which they were regarded, the officials demand a place in the list of special classes to be considered before turning to the broader categories of country and town dwellers, and to the nobility.

The notion of the three estates was based on a view of society in which each estate aided the other two. The officials in the popular view, constituted a group which lived off, not for, the others. And with them were associated two other occupations, also seen as dedicated to self-interest at the expense of the rest of society: doctors and lawyers. Medicine was an academic subject in high repute – it was the best paid chair in most universities – but it was almost entirely a bookish subject, and shaded readily into astrology. Simon of Pavia, for instance, who doubled as physician and astrologer to Louis XI and Charles VIII, married into the aristocracy and died rich. Without a tradition of empirical research and increasingly dedicated to explaining the principles of classical medicine, doctors sought explanations in the stars rather than in the bloodstream, and preferred magical to clinical experiment. To retain the monetary advantage of being thought to be practical as well as learned, they were tempted to claim wondrous but secret cures and thus expose themselves to the charge of quackery. Wisely, the public relied mainly on herbs and traditional lore, invoking the physician only in moments of real desperation – moments when a case had usually gone far beyond the ability of medical science to cure it. The popular image of the doctor was, then, of a man who charged heavily for failing to do his duty, and the figure of the man with a urine bottle in one hand and a bag of gold in the other was already a literary and dramatic stereotype.

Pierre Gringore included lawyers with doctors and officials as men 'stuffed to the eye-balls with the people's substance'. Already a tradition, abuse of the lawyers grew in volume and bitterness. Jurisprudence, like medicine, was a subject of the highest prestige. Universities bid against one another for the services of outstanding professors. It is, moreover, by a study of law, rather than of politics or religion or literature that the *disjecta membra* of a past society are articulated; law therefore was at the heart of the humanist excavation of the ancient world and carried a cultural as well as a professional prestige. A legal training, again, was a passport to promotion in the administrative or diplomatic services of both church and state. Patrician families in the Italian republics, nobles in Germany, France and England, sent their sons to law faculties as a means of respectable advancement. The tendency was particularly clear in England, where legal education was the concern not of the universities but of the Inns of Court in London. Thomas More was transferred by his shrewd father from Oxford to the Inns and Erasmus noted, with considerable exaggeration, however, that in England 'there is no better way to eminence, for the nobility are mostly recruited from the law.' Alexander Barclay watched the same phenomenon with his usual sardonic gloom: 'Lawyers are lords, but justice is rent and tore.' For while all over western Europe lawyers were achieving high office and some were becoming ennobled, and while almost all state business passed at some stage through the hands of men with a legal training, little was being done to increase the promptness, and decrease the expense, of the ordinary citizen's dealings with the law. The conflict of laws and the increasing thoroughness of legal training made litigants all too familiar with delays (Robert Pilkington's property suit lasted from 1478 to 1511), hairsplitting and the transference of a suit from court to court. More himself banished lawyers from Utopia rather than have his citizens enmeshed in 'so infinite a number of blind and intricate laws'. And over and above their normal charges lawyers were universally accused of taking bribes. To have an appetite 'as indiscriminate as a lawyer's wallet' was already a proverbial expression in France. What is the most delicate thing in the world? A lawyer's shoulder: if you do but touch it his hand shoots out for money. In a multitude of expressions like this literature expressed society's distrust. Lawyers might be ministers of state, town clerks, bailiffs or manorial auditors, they were scattered up and down the ladder of incomes, but whatever their other functions, in whatever style they lived, they were seen, and saw themselves, primarily as men trained in the law, their numbers sustained by the litigiousness of the public and inflated by the need of bureaucracies for the nearest thing the age possessed to a higher technical education and an organised profession.

Proficiency in humanist studies could also lead to a career. To read and, still more, to write Latin with elegant fluency was a talent leading to such jobs as secretary to bishop or noble, historiographer to a ruler or a city, or to a chancery post which required adding the prestige of the fashionable Ciceronian style to official correspondence, proclamations, treaties and the formal allocutions with which diplomats presented their credentials. It was probably rare for a man to come to the law from a poor background, but many humanists had relatively humble origins – origins that could be concealed by the classless latinising of their names: Aesticampanus for Sommerfeld, for example or Laticephalus for Bredekopp. Celtis (born Bickel) was a peasant's son. Wimpheling's father was a saddler. Marineo Siculo was born to poor parents in the little Sicilian town of Vizzini. Illiterate until he was twenty-five, he learned to read from his nephew, his sister having married a little above her birth. He was then taken up by a kinsman priest and, by dint of fierce application, found a post as tutor in Palermo. From this shelter he achieved such a reputation that he went to a Chair in Salamanca in 1484 without having attended a university himself. The freelance secular intellectuals were still a rare enough and a new enough phenomenon to be seen as a separate class, though as their talent was not hereditary they did not attract the critical attention that the multi-generation lawyers and officials drew on themselves. It is, in fact, extremely difficult to sense the attitude of other classes to the career humanists. They tapped some of the prestige associated with humanistically educated aristocrats and merchants. They were valued because their wares were timely; Italy was still, and the rest of Europe was increasingly, interested in antiquity, not only for intellectual refreshment but as an amulet against the charge of ignorance. They were honoured by gifts, respected as experts in patrician or aristocratic discussion groups, could aspire to coronation with the poet's laurel crown. On the other hand they inherited something of the indulgent condescension accorded their minstrel and chronicler forebears, were open to the charge of toadyism and pretension, and their marriageable state, and the frequent dissoluteness of their lives, were anomalous in an age when professional learning was traditionally the province of the celibate and theoretically chaste and sober clergy.

This uneasiness was paralleled in the social position of the artist. In 1520 a Portuguese diplomatic visitor to Ethiopia came upon an Italian who had been long settled there. 'He was a very honourable person', remarked Francisco Alvares, 'and a great gentleman, though a painter.' This is a reasonable summing up of the artist's somewhat equivocal status. In the Middle Ages painting (unlike music) was not one of the Liberal Arts, it was not even (unlike farming and wool-carding) one of the Mechanical Arts suited to men of free birth. This was no more than a theoretical stigma, but the painter, forced to be a gild member, was, like other tradesmen, expected to work to order, and while his talent could lead to a proliferation of commissions and might bring him a degree of wealth and fame, this did not necessarily enhance his social standing. On the other hand, 1520 was the year of Raphael's death; he left a very considerable fortune (16,000 ducats) but more than this, though a painter, he had lived, entertained and been received in a style appropriate to a gentleman. Two years before, Leo X had written to the governor of Civitavecchia warning him to prepare a sumptuous reception because he was bringing some writers and painters with him 'and these are persons of great importance and most dear to me'. Four years before that, Lorenzo Costa, court painter to Francesco Gonzaga, duke of Mantua, had flatly refused to paint the ducal children; Francesco's comment was a mild 'he has his quirks like most men of genius'. In about 1512 Andrea del Sarto and *il Magnifico* Giuliano de' Medici became fellow members of the convivial Society of the Trowel in Florence. And (according to Vasari) in 1506, when Michelangelo, who had walked out on a commission for Julius II, was shepherded back into his presence by a bishop who begged the pope to excuse him because 'such men as he were always ignorant', it was the bishop on whom Julius's wrath fell for his outmoded view of an artist's personal qualities. This is all the more revealing for the fact that Michelangelo's father, in whose veins was a faint trickle of noble blood, had tried to beat the boy's determination to be a sculptor out of him.

Apart from Michelangelo's frail gentility, the nobly-born Gianfrancesco Rustici, and Leonardo's illegitimate begetting by a prominent local notary, artists were predominantly of commoner birth. Piero della Francesca's father was a cobbler, Botticelli's a tanner, Fra Bartolommeo's a muleteer, Andrea del Sarto's a tailor and Antonio and Piero Pollaiuolo's a poulterer. And Lucas van Leyden, who married into the titled van Boshuysen family, was one of the very few exceptions to the rule that artists did not better themselves socially by marriage. The gentleman-though-painter status was given willingly to individuals whose works were in especial demand, but it left no residuum after death or fall from favour. On the other hand, the accumulation of information Vasari was able to collect about this period for his *Lives* is itself an indication of the interest taken in painters, sculptors and architects. He would hardly have found the same harvest of facts if he had been accumulating material for a history of the apothecaries. Nor, it is fair to say, would he have found it outside Italy. In Robert Wittinton's Latin phrase book of 1520 'carvers, gravers, image-makers and painters' were placed firmly between plasterers and glaziers and thatchers and other 'labourers'.

As with the career humanists, the success that could lead an artist into a way of life dramatically at odds with what was customary for men of simple birth was rare, non-hereditary and possible only where humanism provided a shared range of interests between painter and patron.* The idea of a separate estate of intellectually and creatively gifted individuals was germinally present, but it affected the way humanists and artists thought about themselves rather than the way others regarded them; in spite of an Erasmus or a Raphael the age thought more in terms of experts and special skills than of intellectuals and genius. It was above all in the main printing shops of the

* See p. 203–4.

continent that something like an estate of arts and letters could be seen in action, where scholar-capitalist, humanist advisers, academic proof-readers, artists and literate typesetters worked in an atmosphere half way between factory and academy. The multiplication of presses had been greeted with almost universal delight. There was some objection raised by collectors of manuscripts, some moderate caution against too wholesale a switch from script to print – 'though we had thousands of volumes', warned Abbot Trithemius in 1492, 'we must not cease writing, for printed books are never so good' – but the enthusiasm of lay scholars was matched by that of clerics. Already in 1476 the sponsors of a press in Rostock had justified their project by calling printing 'the common mother of all sciences, the Church's helper' and in 1487 the bishop of Augsburg's physician wrote to the printer Radtot that 'it would be difficult to estimate how deeply all classes of society are indebted to the art of printing which, through the mercy of God, has arisen in our time, and more especially is this the case with the Catholic Church, the bride of Christ, which through it receives additional glory and meets her Bridegroom with new adornment of many books of heavenly wisdom.'

Though the staff of a printing office was small, the capital outlay on press and founts, and the delay between the printing of an edition and its sale at the outlets of a slow and costly distributive system, meant that only a prosperous man, like the Parisian Jean Petit, who came from a family of master butchers, could set one up on his own. Alternatively a scholar could enlist support, as did Aldus that of Pico della Mirandola's family. Under these respectable social and financial auspices the best brains of the local community were enlisted to help with editing and proof-reading. When to this is added the collaboration of artists of the calibre of Dürer, Holbein, Burgkmair and the anonymous illustrator of the Venetian *Hypnerotomachia Polifili*, the attractiveness of the milieu to professional and dilettante scholars is easy to understand. Printers like Badius in Paris, Amorbach and Froben in Basel, Schürer in Cracow and Aldus in Venice ran institutions which, because of their continuity, their independence from the familiar centres of intellectual activity – universities and monasteries – and the social variety of their collaborators were far more influential in propagating the notion of an intelligentsia than were the temporary liaisons between painter, patron and scholarly adviser that characterised some of the great decorative cycles of the period.

Recognition of such a milieu had to some extent been prepared by the nature of the mid-fifteenth-century scriptoria. The printing houses, however, generated a quite novel excitement. While conservatives could interpret the use of Greek fire to prove that the ancients had known about gunpowder, printing was incontrovertibly an invention of the moderns. And the possibility of mass-production occurred at a time when governments were keenly aware of the value of propaganda and when humanism had awakened a demand for critically edited texts which could not be met, either in volume or uniformity, by copyists. When to this we add the fact that an increasing number of local schools were turning out semi-literates with nothing to read, the spread of printing was assured. By the end of the fifteenth century the number of books printed has been estimated at six million, composed of about thirty thousand different titles produced by something like one thousand different printers. A professional copyist, working at pressure, took six months to cover four hundred folio leaves; it is not surprising that the printing offices were a phenomenon which to some extent numbed conventional social judgement. In the 1470s Vespasiano da Bisticci, the doyen of Florentine manuscript purveyors, had been lampooned for hob-nobbing with his social superiors, whereas some forty years later the Emperor Maximilian had himself portrayed in a printer's workshop. Lastly, printing depended on a new class of skilled artisans. Block-making, type-setting, these were occupations that demanded intelligence and literacy as well as manual dexterity, and were highly paid. The press was a ganglion to which flowed the latest news, the latest ideas. It was an industry liable to seasonal unemployment when credit was overextended or when the demand for such a staple as legal forms shut down during the vacations. Many presses were tiny, producing only a few books before going out of business altogether. These factors combined to stamp a characteristic image on the wage-earning printers. Their literacy led them to claim a higher status than that accorded to the mechanical trades – symbolised by the demand for permission to carry arms; unemployment and migrancy made them stubborn bargainers for better working conditions; contact with news and ideas gave this stubbornness an edge of intelligent radicalism.

To know that a man was a printer then, was to know more about him than the words 'saddler' or 'weaver' conveyed as to the nature of the practitioners of these crafts. Possibly the only other wage-earning occupations to convey so sharp an image of character as well as work routine were those of the miner and the professional soldier.

By tradition, miners were looked on as forming a separate caste. This impression, based on the toughness of their work and the isolation of the seams, was now strengthened by improvements in drainage and ventilation that enabled them to work further underground and in still wilder regions. To the folklore of smith's work and mountain region – *Bergleute*, mountain people, miners were called in

Germany – was added the prestige of some of the most important technological advances of the time: pumping and crushing machinery, the surveying and construction of adits, the utilitarian chemistry of refining and smelting.

The miner could thus be an expert. Louis XI recruited miners from Germany and Ivan III imported German specialists in 1491 to prospect for copper and silver along the river Pechora. Because of the value of his craft and the isolated but compact communities in which he worked, he was also a man accustomed to privileges. Miners were treated by governments with some caution, in Sweden they even sent delegates of their own to meetings of the estates. In time of war recruiting officers turned above all to the mining areas in their search for hardy, resourceful and quick-witted soldiers and pioneers.

In a similar way, the mercenary soldier represented an old trade given a new aspect by changing conditions. He thereby made a fresh impact on contemporary opinion and acquired a more formalised view of his own separateness from the rest of society. Wars were still fought by a majority of part-time soldiers, raised for a specific campaign and returning to their peacetime occupations at its conclusion, gentlemen and a few rich bourgeois on horseback, peasants and poorer townsmen on foot. The cost of maintaining an adequate standing army of professionals was too great to permit the breaking of this formula altogether, but its drawbacks were becoming increasingly clear. Peasants had always been reluctant to be long away from their crops, tradesmen from their shops. Though in most parts of Europe laymen between the ages of sixteen or thereabouts and sixty were required to keep weapons at home or in a local armoury, these were seldom, in spite of constant admonition, kept in good repair. And now, after the convincing and widely publicised defeats of the Burgundian armies by the Swiss in the 1470s, two lessons had been learned. One was that heavy cavalry, the traditional noble arm, could not on their own defeat pikemen, and that armies now needed a more careful balance than any one country could easily muster – heavy and light horse, pikemen and halberdiers, archers and arquebusiers; the second was that a higher standard of training was desirable than the part-time soldier was prepared to invest in against a crisis. For garrison duty, therefore, for permanent personal guards (like the Scots guard of the kings of France), for the keeping in being of sieges and the occupation of foreign conquests, the professional soldier, who would go anywhere and serve for any time, could provide continuity, just as his experience could stiffen the scarcely trained bodies of troops to which his companies were attached on the battle-field.

Mercenaries were of mixed social origin. The cavalry included not only knights and retainers of noble birth but poor men whose service was rewarded by the gift of horse and armour. The infantry covered the whole spectrum from the knight who no longer thought it unbecoming to a gentleman to fight on foot, to exiles, escaped criminals, bankrupt merchants and discontented tradesmen. In 1509 the conservative Frenchman, the Chevalier Bayard, refused to dismount and storm Padua along with the *Landsknechte*. 'Considers the Emperor it to be a just and reasonable matter' he complained, 'to peril so much nobleness together with his infantry, of whom one is a shoe-maker, another a farmer, another a baker, and such like mechanics?' But the place accorded the mercenary in the popular imagination was not so much concerned with his social origin or fighting ability, as with his temperament, behaviour and appearance, a composite image fostered by actual images, especially prints by artists, Nicholas Manuel and Urs Graf among them, who had been mercenaries themselves. Wandering adventurers with no loyalty save to their captain of the moment, killing for cash and squandering their money on drink, women and gambling, dressed in tattered finery, blasphemous, neglectful of their families – it was in these terms that the mercenary became a hackneyed bugbear to preachers and moralists. With streaming banner and jutting codpiece they were represented, not without a trace of grudging envy, as slashing and hiccoughing their way through every decent convention, outraging every law save that of supply and demand.

Social antipathy had a four-fold base. Fear of loss or damage was one. Lawyers and mercenaries, however necessary, could abuse the trust put in them for their own gain. So could millers and tanners, both universally reviled as men who were needed to process others' products but who could set aside or snip aside part of these products with little fear of detection. Moral disapprobation was a second. Bath attendants' sons were excluded from gilds because the public baths were commonly places of prostitution as well as the most convenient way of getting clean. A third was unabsorption into legally constituted society: hence the German scorn for the linen-weavers, who had no gild, no voice, therefore, in civic affairs, hence too the distrust of wandering entertainers, however beguiling their talents. The fourth was a latent hatred of those whose moral standing was unknowable, who were not only without an acknowledged place in the social hierarchy but were spiritually alien as well. Most prominent in this category were the Jews.

By the late fifteenth century an uneasy compromise between Jew and Christian had been worked out. It involved the yellow badge (or its equivalent) and sudden and arbitrary taxation, but it secured freedom of worship; the separateness was hardly more galling than that of the localities into which communities of foreign Christian merchants might be herded, and wealth could buy exemptions. Not only in trade and banking, but as physicians, musicians and scholars the Jews made significant and welcomed contributions to some of the mainstreams of European life. An interest in Hebrew was growing* but this interest in the language of Moses, of God's commandments to men and of Christ himself was the thinnest of ice over the centuries-long prejudices of westernised Christianity. Since the Vulgate Bible of St. Jerome, God had spoken to Europeans in Latin: Hebrew was the tongue of Judas, the betrayer. In painting after painting the Christ child blessed mankind among the ruins of the Old Law of the Hebrews, the fractured arches of the stable symbolising the shift from Palestine to Rome. Passion plays featured debates in which synagogue was dialectically routed by church. When a new pope moved in procession to St. Peter's he was met on the bridge of St. Angelo by the representatives of the Jewish community in Rome who offered him the scrolls of the Mosaic law. As successor of St. Peter he imperiously rejected them before moving on to his enthronement. This symbolic ceremony was enacted elsewhere; in Corfu, for instance, where a family was exhibited to tourists as lineal descendants of Judas Iscariot, a new archbishop was presented with a scroll of the Old Law for him to wave aside and the Jewish community also had to cover the streets with carpets which the archiepiscopal feet could tread into the dust.

Herding, the badges of infamy, spiritual bullying: in settled times these were hardly more than a humiliating charade, but they kept alive the Jew's vulnerability as a scapegoat. An unexplained disappearance of a Christian child could lead to charges of ritual murder, arrest, torture and the burning of synagogues. A preacher could enlist the breast-beating penitence of his congregation the more readily by diverting some of the blame for the wickedness of their environment to their tolerance of the crucifiers, as when in 1488 Fra Bernardino of Feltre unleashed Jew-baiting mobs in Florence – an action for which he was subsequently banished. In the fear and lapse of political direction that followed the defeat of the Venetian army in 1509 the inhabitants of towns like Verona, Treviso and Asolo turned on the Jews, looting their houses and (till soberer times returned) expelling them and their families. Always frail, this compromise coexistence had become even less secure with the realisation that the economic role for which the Jews had been tolerated had been taken over in practice and to some extent in theory by Christians. To

* See p. 229–30.

borrow money, to pawn belongings, it was no longer necessary to go to the Jews. In the 1480s and 1490s anti-Jewish rioting was in many cases the result of a municipal government's setting up a public savings bank for making loans to poor men. Dependent on interest but backed by the Church, these *Monti di Pietà*, as they were called in Italy, removed the irksome need for tolerance. When the Florentines established a long-discussed *Monte di Pietà* under Savonarola's urging in 1495, the Jews were given twelve months to prepare to leave the city.

Though the first formal ghetto, a district actually closed off from sunset to sunrise, dates from 1516 when the Venetian Jews were sealed off in this way, the Jews by a natural exclusiveness had lived in a privacy which was an affront to the gregariousness of their neighbours, and a cause of suspicion: how was it that the Jews, who lived apart, almost, as it were, in secret, always seemed to have more money than the frank, open and loan-seeking Christian? Officially the church could accommodate itself to co-existence with the Jews as the church could co-exist with slavery, judicial torture, firearms, anything society appeared to need to keep it going, but individual clerics and, above all, public opinion found it difficult to accept the Jewish infection of the third estate. 'Why do the Jews not want to work with their hands?' asked the preacher Geiler of Kayserberg. 'Are not they, as we are, subject to God's explicit commandment, "In the sweat of thy brow shalt thou eat bread"?' The Spanish chronicler Andres Bernaldez pointed out that the Jews 'never wanted to take jobs in ploughing or digging, nor would they go through the fields tending cattle, nor would they teach their children to do so; all their wish was a job in the town, and earning their living without much labour.'

In 1498 they were expelled from Nuremberg because (in this city based on the profit motive) of their 'evil, dangerous and cunning usurous dealings'. In the same year they were expelled from Würzburg, Salzburg and Württemberg, in 1499 from Ulm, in 1500 from Nördlingen, in each case with the permission (and to the financial advantage) of Maximilian. In France, expelled from certain towns (among them Tarascon, Saint-Maximin, Arles) they found refuge on papal territory at Avignon. In 1495, and again in 1506, they were banished from the whole of Provence; de Beatis commented that if the Jews went the few yards that separated papal from French jurisdiction 'anyone could put them fearlessly to death'. In 1502 Ivan III withdrew the measure of protection he had extended to Jews in Russia. But it was in Spain that social jealousy, religious euphoria, political calculation and, perhaps, population pressure produced the real catastrophe: in 1492 practising Jews were summarily expelled

and with such savage vigilance that it has been estimated that possibly as many as one hundred and fifty thousand actually fled the
country. In 1494 Torquemada ordered that the descendants of all
those found guilty by the Inquisition of having formally but uncon-
vincingly renounced Judaism should be excluded from a list of occupations which to all intents and purposes was a definition of the
middle class. They 'may not hold or possess public offices or posts or
honours, or be promoted to holy orders, or be judges, mayors, con-
stables, magistrates, jurors, stewards, officials of weights and measures, merchants, notaries, public scriveners, lawyers, attorneys,
secretaries, accountants, treasurers, physicians, surgeons, shopkeepers, brokers, changers, weight inspectors, collectors, tax-farmers,
or holders of any other similar public office.' In addition to the
expulsion of the practising Jews in 1492, the efforts of the Inquisition
led to the burning of two thousand condemned *conversos* and one
hundred and twenty thousand more fled the country. The vacuum left
in the middle ranks of society was not filled. The poor lacked talent
and capital, the aristocracy scorned the life of the trader and banker.
It was, above all, foreign Christians who took over the direction of
Spanish economic affairs, Genoese, Germans, Flemings; in the interest of one faith and one race Spain began her period of Empire
overseas and hegemony in Europe grievously maimed in the social
composition of her people.

To some extent Spain compensated for this reduction in the distributive class by an increase in the productive class through the
institution of slavery in the New World. The inhabitants of the
West Indies proved incapable of sustaining the heavy labour of
mining or, later on, of cultivating sugar. In 1501 the first cargo of
African slaves arrived. Though the introduction of slavery in the
Americas coincided with a fall in the number of slaves at home, its
path was smoothed by the fact that the use of non-Christian slaves as
domestic servants and agricultural labourers had long been taken for
granted in southern and eastern Europe, and with the connivance of
the church, which put the possibility of conversion from paganism
above the certainty of loss of personal liberty: better a Christianised
slave than an unregenerate freeman. The missionary orders did come
to show – and it took considerable courage – a deep humanitarian
concern for the lot of the indigenous populations of the Americas, but
the importation of slaves from elsewhere had become too commonplace to prompt more than a flicker of concern about the institution
of slavery itself.

The Portuguese had been importing African slaves for their own
use well before they supplied them to the Spaniards for the mines and
plantations of the New World. Some 150,000 had been shipped by

1500. Early in the sixteenth century an observer wrote, no doubt with some exaggeration, that 'one could almost believe that in Lisbon there are more slaves, male and female, than there are Portuguese of free condition.' In Italy, slaves had long been a familiar feature of wealthy households, and if their numbers were declining at the end of the century – though there may have been some 3,000 in Venice alone – this was not due to a change of attitude but to the blocking of a main source of supply by Turkish control of the Black Sea and Levantine ports. Henceforward the Turks absorbed the multi-racial products of the Kaffa market, and Italian, Spanish and Portuguese merchants were left with Ethiopians, Moors from the north African littoral and a few Greeks and Slavs picked up in Dalmatia. Black slaves were, besides, becoming more expensive, and in bourgeois households had proved a tiresome moral problem: their chattel-like availability enabling their owners to test an already well-developed lore about the potency of the African. They were now bought principally as pets, welcome as a note of dusky exoticism in the fashionable *ensemble* of a court. Ippolito de' Medici's negro wrestlers, the one hundred Moors, a present from Ferdinand to Innocent VIII in 1488, whom the pope distributed among his cardinals and the Roman nobles he wished to favour, had a productive value of zero. This is probably true of south-western Europe as a whole (slavery had long disappeared in the north-west) by 1500. The Mediterranean galley-slave is a phenomenon of the mid-sixteenth century. Though ship's captains used captured natives overseas, on voyages from Europe the men chosen for pump duty or to be left en route to 'Europeanise' patches of coast for the benefit of shipwrecked or supplyless explorers, were criminals whose sentences had been commuted. This erosion of use did not lead to a weakening of principle. Indeed, the revived study of ancient political theory led to a renewed interest in the slavery on which ancient society had been based. It was from this basis that the exquisite aristocratisation of Castiglione's view of society took wings, for 'some...are born and devised and ordained by Nature to obey, just as others are to command...There are also many men concerned solely with physical activities, and these differ from men versed in the things of the mind as much as the soul differs from the body...These, then, are essentially slaves, and it is better for them to obey than to command.' Principle did not, of course, lead to action. But it is difficult to doubt that the clearer view of the structure of Greek and Roman society which emerged from humanistic studies added something to the note of contempt which led every writer on politics in this period to pour scorn on the masses.

Slavery in the east declined more slowly. At the turn of the century slaves were used in Russia as domestic servants in princely and boyar

houses and on some of the larger estates as labourers, but both in
Russia and Lithuania slavery was being turned into serfdom, as it had
already been in Poland. Southern Lithuania was, however, a source of
supply for the slave raids of the Crimean Tartars. Protected by an
alliance with Ivan III, who needed their support against Kazan and
the Khanate of the Golden Horde, in 1482 they arrived in force as far
north as Kiev, sacking the city and carrying off large numbers of its
inhabitants to Kaffa. Self-transporting in an age of high transport
costs, slaves were a highly profitable investment, and there was no
slackening of demand among the Turks, both from wealthy individuals who wished to enhance the variety and pomp of their retinues
and from the sultan's own agents. In a country where the sultan
himself was the son of a slave the word had different connotations
from the always degrading and sometimes fearful associations it
aroused in the west. Adult slaves might find themselves rowing in
Turkish galleys, but most were employed as servants or bodyguards.
For boys from the age of twelve or so, either bought in slave markets
or recruited as part of the human tribute levied by the Turks among
the Albanians, Serbians, Croatians, Bulgarians and Greeks, the possibility of social mobility – apart from legal status – was enormously
greater than in the west, a factor which caused many Balkan parents
to welcome the four-yearly posse of child inspectors, and even
prompted Muslim families to pay Christians to pass off their children
as their own. The administrative and military services of the Ottoman
state, were recruited from re-educated young Christian slaves, and a
career started in an Albanian hovel could lead to a generalship, a
capacious harem and a household running into thousands. The lot of
the tribute children was in dramatic contrast to that of the negro
plantation worker in Hispaniola or of those still less fortunate Gui-
neans sold by the French to their cannibal associates in Brazil, the
Potiguara, as food.

The Agricultural Community, Town-dwellers, Aristocracy

From government officials and painters to miners and slaves we have
been dealing with anomalies within the third estate. Work was overwhelmingly a matter of tilling the soil, and the population of Europe
was overwhelmingly a population of peasants. In 1510 Lucas van
Leyden commemorated this fact in a moving engraving of Adam and
Eve. The two figures walk across a landscape of stones and coarse
grass, backed by a tree pollarded by gales. Eve, as the prefiguration of
Mary (Quos Evae culpa damnavit, Mariae gratia solvit) and the
symbol of all motherhood, fits into this toilsome background but is

not of it; with brooding face and flying hair, her body and dress a marvellous blend of gothic with the antique, she cradles a child who sits in her arms like a plump baby abbot. Timeless and classless, mother and child are escorted across the picture by a figure that seems to have grown out of the landscape and is doomed to stay in it; an old man, with wild beard and hair, his neck stooping from enormous shoulders, dressed in a torn skin and carrying a wooden spade.

Peasants no longer wore skins, but a spade, and for the most part a wooden one, was still the badge of their work, for the peasants' job was, above all, to break the ground for grain. In spite of peasant shepherds in Spain, peasant viticulturalists in Burgundy, peasant bee-keepers in the Russian forests, it was primarily on wheat, oats, barley, spelt and rye that Europe lived. Poor communications meant that no one area could be an effective breadbasket for its neighbours (even in France there were no districts exclusively devoted to vineyards) and shortage of manure and shallow ploughing with small-framed cattle meant that to produce a surplus for merely local consumption very large areas had to be kept apart for grain, even when the land was more suited to grazing or fruit or market gardening. Apples and apricots, flax and beans, chickens and donkeys: the variety was there, but what gave the peasant his characteristic status and social organisation, recognisably similar from the Atlantic to the Ural mountains, was tillage for grain.

The long medieval centuries had produced innumerable variations in peasant tenure and services, from the right-less slave, through the serf, able to catch the eye of the law of the land through the fence of his lord's control, to the prosperous freeholder. The nature of the land produced its own variety; the rancorous independence of the Breton peasant, walling off his thin-soiled patch from his neighbour, con-trasting with the broad open fields south of the Loire with their corporate triumph of harvest-home. But some generalisation is poss-ible. The essential social difference was between those with a plough and animals to tow it, and the majority who had only a spade or could contribute but one or two beasts to fill a richer man's team. Illiteracy was the rule. Physical tiredness; constant vigilance against incursions into strips or patches undefined by hedges or fences; isolation; these factors produced the 'peasant mentality' and appeared to justify the stream of urban jest and abuse. Certainly they produced a conservatism in agricultural practice and a tenacious bloody-mindedness of which governments and would-be improving landlords had to take account. With no privacy – the majority had one or two-roomed hovels which doubled as barn and stable – and few possessions, a table, a chest (for storage and to sit on), an iron

pot and a kneading trough, with children who were set to scare birds
as soon as they could toddle and a wife who worked as hard as he,
the peasant was unfitted to become involved with changes in the
superstructure of the civilisation of which he was the foundation.
The voice with which he speaks from the written sources is violent,
litigious, full of crude superstition. But this is because we hear him
most clearly when he is up against government or being denounced
from the pulpit. His endurance, his ability to work with others, his
urge to collect land and stock of his own: these can best be seen in the
land itself and the marks of his work in it, and for the rest we must
turn to the peasants of modern Europe, of, for example, Montenegro
or Sardinia or Ireland, to see how an ignorant conservatism can
include generosity and humour.

A quick survey of Europe from west to east will show the regional
variations against which these generalisations must be measured and
how wide was the contrast between the reasonably prosperous peasantry of England and France and the declining status and living
standards in Poland and Russia.

The variety in England was especially great. A gradually rising
population meant that men with little or no land of their own, who
relied on being employed by others, were meeting greater competition and being forced into reliance on charity. The same factor
brought insecurity into the lives of the large number of cottagers,
men who owned a house and a few acres of land but who looked to
seasonal work for others to keep their families safely over the subsistence level. On the other hand, during the labour shortage after the
Black Death significant numbers of peasants had bought or bargained
their way into small farms of their own (or, if not absolutely their
own in law, capable of being handed on without question to their
heirs). The result was to increase the gap between the landless man
and cottager and the smallholder who, while still working himself on
the land, employed shepherds and labourers. Such a man might look
forward to the time when his descendants could eschew labour with
their hands and glide by the path to which no legal or universally
recognised rules applied, but only local judgement and a reasonable
prosperity, into the broad spectrum of the squirearchy or gentry;
profits on farming were small and holdings could be built up only
slowly, generation by generation.

In England the yeoman owed much to the comparative stability of
his polity and the peace it brought to the countryside. Above all, he
was indebted to the fact that the Hundred Years War had been fought
on French soil. In France, though the proportion of independent
small-holders was probably less, and the yeoman class did not have
the 'weight' that local opinion accorded them in England, there were

large differences in the size of land holdings and, in spite of considerable vestiges of feudal and seigneurial law, possibly more freedom of
action and security of tenure; for in their effort to reactivate estates
devastated by war, landlords had made large concessions in order to
tempt a tenantry back from dispersal and hiding. By the late fifteenth
century there was still land waiting to be restored to productivity, and
the *métayage* system, whereby rent was paid in produce in return for
tools, seed and the use of the land, enabled men without capital to
reclaim land and settle there securely, even though the profit to be
made from a *métairie* was unlikely to lead to a rise in status. That our
period – almost precisely our period – was one favourable to the
French peasant who wished to buy land and increase his stock is
suggested by figures collected by Mlle. Bezard. To buy a hectolitre of
maslin (mixed wheat and rye) a labourer would have had to work for
six days under Louis XI, two and a half under Charles VIII, two and
three-quarters under Louis XII and eight under Francis I; to purchase
a cow, twelve days under Charles VIII, forty-three under Francis I; to
buy a hectare of land, forty-four under Louis XI, twenty-one under
Charles VIII, one hundred and forty-six under Louis XII and nearly
four hundred under Francis I.*

If the wealth of published material relating to English and French
rural life makes generalisation hazardous, any conclusions about the
position of the Spanish peasantry are temerarious for the opposite
reason. A decree of the *cortes* held at Toledo in 1480 abolished servile
tenure in Castile and feudal services were abolished for Catalonia in
1486 in return for a cash compensation. How far the peasantry
actually benefited from these measures, in contrast to Aragon,
where feudal relationships remained in force, it is impossible to say.
There were enough prosperous peasant proprietors in Castile to be
recognised as a social type in literature, but the possibility of a poor
man's improving his status was severely inhibited by the massive
support given by the government to the pasturage routes for the
giant sheep flocks organised by the *Mesta*. In the peninsula as a
whole it was further inhibited by the weight of seigneurial dues,
state taxes and church tithes; for most peasants a life of desperate
toil left their fortunes exactly as they had inherited them and provided no insurance against the indebtedness that followed a bad
harvest. In Portugal rent, feudal dues and tithe could account for
seventy per cent of a peasant's produce.

Yet this was not, in Spain or Portugal, a time when peasant revolt,
let alone peasant war was feared. King John of Denmark (1481–
1513) could safely refer to the peasants as men born to servitude (a

---

* *La vie rurale dans le sud de la région Parisienne de 1450 à 1560* (Paris, 1929) 236–9.

condition into which, in contrast to Sweden, they were declining in his reign). The French proverb 'Jaques Bonhomme has a strong back and will bear anything' took the peasant's passivity for granted, as did the German 'a peasant is just like an ox, only he has no horns' – though peasant wars were to break out in southern and central Germany in 1524–25 and were preceded by clandestine associations like the *Bundschuh* movement of 1502–1517. For its size and the heterogeneity of its institutions, Germany was, of all European countries, the one about which it is most dangerous to generalise, but the status and prosperity of the peasant (and therefore the range between poor and well-to-do) seems to have been highest in the south-west and to have dwindled towards the north-east. Speaking of Alsace, Wimpheling wrote 'I know peasants who spend as much at the marriage of their sons and daughters or the baptisms of their infants as would buy a small house and farm or vineyard.' Moralists' evidence is always suspect; on the other hand, an ordinance issued in 1497 at Lindau forbad 'the common peasant to wear cloth costing more than half a florin the yard, silk, velvet, pearls, gold, or slashed garments', evidence that the effects of the luxury trade routes through the Rhineland were not confined to the towns. Of greater concern to moralist and town council was the independence nurtured by the example of the neighbouring Swiss, who, by means of a largely peasant war, had not only thrown off the feudal dues which were still common (though no longer a badge of dependence) in south-west Germany but had created an independent community. It also reflects two crucial but at present immeasurable factors that bore on the position of the peasantry in western Europe as a whole; the mounting costs of bureaucratised administrations – state, civic and princely, which were passed on to the sector of society in which objection was least likely to be mobilised; and the professionalisation of war, which meant that landowners, denied profits from pay, loot and ransom, turned to the exploitation of their own properties. The *Junkers* of Prussia are a clear example of this second tendency; dormant feudal rights were reactivated in a movement to reduce peasant status to that of the numerous Slav bondmen whose labour was entirely at the disposal of their employers.

Clear, too, is the distinction between the ways in which magnates sought to secure enough labour on their estates east and west of the Elbe. Westwards, the tendency was to reduce, commute or abolish labour obligations, to rely on goodwill and voluntary contract rather than force. Eastwards, landlords intensified their demands for labour and their efforts to tie that labour to the land. This move to serfdom was backed by the governments of eastern Europe: urban life, always less vigorous than in the west, was in decline; rulers faced bankruptcy if they could not woo the financial, as well as the political support of the wide-acred class of noble or gentry landowners. In 1497 the Bohemian diet affirmed the servitude of peasants. In 1519 the service due for a peasant holding was declared by statute to be one day a week (in lieu of from one to six days a year) and was in practice considerably heavier; by a series of laws passed from 1496 to 1511 neither a peasant nor his sons could leave the land without his master's consent, and during the same period right of appeal from seigneurial justice was removed from all but church and crown lands. In 1514 all Hungarian peasants outside the royal free boroughs were condemned to 'real and perpetual servitude' to their masters. The same debasement in status and freedom of action proceeded in Lithuania and Russia, with increased demands both for money dues and labour services and with a firmer tying of the peasant to the soil; by the Russian Code of 1497 a peasant could only leave his lord during the two weeks following St. George's day and only then after paying heavy fees for the privilege of being a free man for one twenty-sixth of the year.

A prime cause of this descent into serfdom was the declining importance of towns and of influential urban classes in eastern Europe. Noble resentment of the rival marketing activities of the towns, the high prices charged there for manufactured goods, the refuge they gave to runaway peasants and the consideration given them by rulers in need of cash subsidies; these factors led to a successful pressure on governments to reduce the independence and the commercial activity of the towns. And this pressure came at a time when the Hanseatic League, itself in decline and harassed in the Baltic by English and Dutch shipping, could no longer act as an example of urban energy in north-eastern Europe, and when the westward overland trade routes virtually dried up when the Turks occupied the north coast of the Black Sea. In 1500 townsmen were excluded from representation in the Bohemian diet; they regained it in 1517, but the tendency was clear: nobles, with the support of government, confronted the peasants without the political and economic buffer of the towns.

This is not to say that bourgeois activity ceased in the east: men continued to sell and exchange goods they did not themselves produce, to devote themselves to loans and currency exchange, but they did this increasingly as agents or factors employed by the territorial magnates, or as glorified pedlars taking advantage of the customs concessions on imports which were (at least in Poland) lifted for the nobles but not for the towns. But the word 'bourgeois' means little if it cannot be linked to a bourgeois culture, and for this four conditions are necessary: significant accumulations in towns of men devoted to the exchange of goods, services or cash; representation of their common views in national or regional, as well as local government; recognition of the nature and values of their own way of life as specifically different from those of the nobles or the primary producers, and an acknowledgement of that difference by others; the possession of sufficient wealth to make a physical and intellectual mark on the culture of their times by building and patronage. By these criteria it is difficult to locate a bourgeois culture east of the Oder, even in Cracow, Novgorod and Moscow.

The contrast between urban life (common to Europe as a whole) and bourgeois culture must, of course, be kept in mind when trying to assess the nature of the town-based classes in western Europe as well. A significant bourgeois culture was possible only in areas where thriving towns were near enough for their interaction to produce something more pervasive, more recognisable than the activity of an individual town: Flanders and northern Italy were fourteenth-century, southwest Germany and the Rhineland fifteenth-century instances. In Spain communications between the widely spaced big cities were too difficult to give interaction much meaning. The bourgeois life of London found little echo in the other, far smaller, urban centres of England.

Though the key French cities, Rouen, Bordeaux, Toulouse, Marseilles, Lyons, were widely separate, however, urban life in general had been stimulated by the economic policies of Louis XI; the towns looked to Paris for an element of encouragement and control; at the trade fairs, even more than at the meetings of the provincial estates, the bourgeoisie were impressively seen to constitute an estate of their own and the connection of some of the great merchant families with the royal administration gave an extra publicity to their status. Above all, perhaps, the increasing range of incomes and styles of living among the bourgeoisie as a whole caught the attention of contemporaries more vividly than before.

How wide the range of incomes among the bourgeoisie could be by 1500, may be seen from a reasonably thriving, middling large town, Hamburg, in which four categories have been distinguished:* the rich, with incomes varying from 5,000 to 40,000 Lübeck marks – the great merchants and property owners; those with incomes between 2,000 and 5,000 marks, mostly men engaged in brewing or shipping; the smaller brewers, prosperous shopkeepers, notably butchers and goldsmiths, with between 600 and 2,000 marks; lesser tradesmen and the numerous brewers who rented, rather than owned their premises – 150 to 600 marks. Below these categories came the

* By Heinrich Reincke, quo. P. Dollinger, *The German Hansa* (London, 1970) 133.

mass of poor artisans, municipal employees, such as street cleaners, porters and domestic servants.

Taken in conjunction with comparable studies at different times, such figures tend to show that there was a fairly general tendency in European towns for the contrasts both between rich and poor bourgeois and between the bourgeoisie as a whole and manual workers to become more marked. A case in point is Nuremberg, which shared the rise in production characteristic of many German cities between 1480 and 1520. The discrepancy here between the poor and the very rich has been described as 'enormous'* but no easy correlation can be made between wealth, status and political power. Political control was firmly in the hands of forty-three patrician families, themselves divided into three categories according to the antiquity of their association with civic administration. Formally closing admission into the ranks of the patriciate in 1521, the Council defined this class as 'those families who used to dance in the *Rathaus* in the olden days, and who still dance there' by formal invitation. Lower in public esteem than the patricians, and likewise distinguished by clothing and forms of address, was a specifically recognised class of those who had acquired affluence or professional reputation more recently: men whose income and style of living might be similar to, or more impressive than that of certain patricians, but who could not share their peculiar aura of authority.

Consciousness of class gradings within the third estate was equally minute in the Italian cities. Here again, while wealth was important, it was only one of a number of criteria which determined the respect in which a man was held and the value he set upon his own position in society. Antiquity of connection with the direction of civic affairs created a grading of its own, even if, like the Sienese *gentiluomini*, certain families represented a group whose political function had practically withered away: respect for lineage could survive the loss of power. Individuals were 'placed' socially not only with reference to their political influence and their personal qualities and possessions, but to the historical record of their family and the standing of the families to whom they were related by marriage. Social antennae were acute and tradition-conscious.

It is impossible to speak in general terms about the tone of bourgeois life. It was a far cry from the opulent decorum of Venice and the fastidiousness of Florentine deportment to the crude revelries of the Bergen merchants at the annual initiation of journeymen into the ranks of the fully-fledged *Bergenfahrer*. The lawyer satirist,

---

* By Gerald Strauss in his *Nuremberg in the Sixteenth Century* (N.Y. 1966) from which I take the following details.

Guillaume Coquillart, portrayed the bourgeois of Paris and his
native city, Rheims, as boors aspiring to be aristocrats. From what
is perhaps his most vigorous theme, relations between the sexes,
emerges a vivid picture of bosom fumbling, skirt throwing up and
bottom pinching on the one hand, and rare fabrics, elaborate
coiffures and finicking tastes on the other. One of his most sparkling
poems describes the quarrel between a prosperous couple about
whom their daughter should marry. The husband is content that
she should stay a 'belle *bourgoise*', the wife insists that 'on la
demoisellera'. Conquillart suggests that, meanwhile, she should
be dressed half in linen and half in velvet, 'moytie bourgeoise et
demoyselle'.

It was in fact probably more common for rich bourgeois to pass
upwards into the ranks of the aristocracy, by acceptance if not by
patent of nobility, than for a poor man to prosper his way into those
levels of the bourgeoisie where the real social weight lay. Urban
society was ancient. The distribution of power in municipal affairs
had long been stabilised among the representatives of various trades
or crafts and little allowance had been made for the economic
changes of the past century or so. Because recruitment into the
mastership ranks of the gilds was becoming increasingly restricted,
the industrious apprentice who makes good was too rare to be, as
yet, a symbol of social success. While a master could take his own
sons as apprentices without restriction, one or two outsiders was
usually the limit, and then, after an apprenticeship of from four to
eight years, the qualified journeyman had to find work for himself
until he could accumulate the fee which could purchase him a mastership of his own.

The tendency for the mastership class to become self-perpetuating,
and for status to be determined by tradition and family rather than
talent or response to market fluctuations, hardened at a time when
immigration into the towns was increasing and when rising prices
forced the salaried journeyman and the urban labourer either to a
restless itinerancy or to a nearness to the bread-line that caused a
further hardening of the ranks above them; the existence of a hard-
pressed proletariat was not a novel, but became a more noticeable
phenomenon. 'In all', it has been said of England, 'up to two-thirds
of the urban population lived near or below the poverty line; the
top third constituted a social pyramid rising to a needle-like point –
through prosperous artificers, tradesmen and professional men to the
single merchant who might alone pay up to a third of the subsidy due
from the community.'*

---

* Joan Simon, *Education and Society in Tudor England* (Cambridge, 1966) 18.

Desperate men, however, had neither the energy, nor the mutual trust, nor the ideology to combine effectively. There were companionships, proto-trades unions which gave a semblance of conscious class unity to working men and offered a form of social relief to itinerant labourers or journeymen on the look-out for work. There were strikes for better pay and better hours, especially among the mining communities of Germany. But the notion of collective bargaining was supported by no theory and the challenge it presented to the old notion of mutual service was so great that cities were prepared to lose a trade rather than improve working conditions by accepting demands made from below. It was only mercenaries who could strike with complete success: they alone could present demands that involved lives as well as livelihoods.

Among the upper levels of the bourgeoisie, increasing scorn and fear of the proletariat went hand in hand with the relish for aristocratic manners which Coquillart noted. And this was at a time when the European aristocracy – with many personal and regional differences, were experiencing a noticeable change in function and values. Certain ceremonies and forms of address (the Spanish 'it is our will') that aped royal procedures were abolished. Personal justice was sharply curtailed. Nobles could no longer strike money, ennoble others or release them from taxes. They still went to war, but at the king's invitation and on his wages. And their weakening position *vis-à-vis* the crown and the bourgeoisie was emphasised by a fairly general shrinking of income from their estates caused by a decline in the purchasing power of money – a decline that may have amounted to something like two-fifths between 1500 and 1520. Bowing to circumstances – the forbidding of private war and the building of fortresses, the wooing rather than the commanding of agricultural labour, the dwindling importance of the knightly cavalryman – the aristocracy became more rational as landlords, more appreciative of opportunities to serve government for a salary, more careful to resurrect or invent a part to play in regional and municipal politics.

The loss in political power of the west European aristocracy was to some extent balanced by its standing in the church. Bishoprics, abbacies, priorships: these key positions were commonly the prerogative of the younger sons of noble families. Especially in Germany, nobles dominated the cathedral chapters. Erasmus, informed that entry to the Strasburg chapter was open only to those who could muster twelve aristocratic forbears on both the father's and mother's side, commented that 'Christ himself could not have entered this college without a dispensation.' But for every magnate who lorded it over great demesnes fattened by shrewd marriage alliances and defended by the prestige of ecclesiastic relatives, there were many aristocrats who only just managed, snarling and miserable, to hang on to their increasingly anachronistic rôle. Writing to Willibald Pirckheimer, von Hutten described his life as a free knight of the Empire. 'Do not envy me my life as compared with yours... We live in fields, forests and fortresses. Those by whose labours we exist are poverty-stricken peasants, to whom we lease our fields, vineyards, pastures and woods. The return is exceedingly sparse in proportion to the labour expended... I must attach myself to some prince in the hope of protection. Otherwise everyone will look upon me as fair plunder... We cannot visit a neighbouring village or go hunting and fishing save in iron... The castle, whether on plain or mountain, must be not fair but firm, surrounded by moat and wall, narrow within, crowded with stalls for the cattle and arsenals for guns, pitch and powder. Then there are dogs and their dung, a sweet savour, I assure you. The horsemen come and go, among them robbers, thieves and bandits... The day is full of thought for the morrow, constant disturbance, continual storms... If the harvest fails in any year, then follow dire poverty, unrest and turbulence.'*

Within the aristocratic caste there were, indeed, clear gradations of dignity – in England from duke and marquis through baron and knight to esquire and gentleman – and one reasonably clear distinction of class: between the prepotent aristocrats and the men of heraldically recognised descent but moderate standing, a class identified with the gentry in England, the *petite noblesse* in France, the Polish *szlachta*, the Hungarian *Köznemesség*, the Bohemian *Ritterstand* and the Spanish *caballeros*; a class whose legal privileges differed from country to country but which was recognisably separate in kind from prosperous farmers or burghers. The sources hardly allow our sensing these gradations with the requisite delicacy. Just how nuanced the perception of status could be is shown by the *mestnichestvo* (place order) system observed by the Muscovite boyars in their search for office. 'The lineage of each candidate for a post and his place in the line of his descent (his *otechestvo*, as it was called) was compared... a remarkably complicated system, for it was based upon the relative ranks occupied by the ancestors of the man doing the comparing, as well as upon the place of these men in the line of descent from their ancestors. The fundamental principle of the system was that no one need serve under another person if he could show that one of his ancestors had held a higher position than had the ancestors of his proposed superior. Moreover, each servitor was responsible for the honour of all his living kinsmen and of all his

* Hajo Holborn, *Ulrich von Hutten and the German Reformation* (N.Y. 1966) 18–19.

descendants, for if he accepted a rank inferior to that warranted by his pedigree he set a precedent that would damage the careers of all his present and future relatives.'*

There were also national differences between the extent to which it was thought proper for aristocrats to adopt careers other than those of property administrator, ecclesiastic or royal office holder. In Russia to engage in trade was not considered demeaning. Trade was scorned in Spain in principle, not always in practice. The same was true of France, where an aristocrat thought it permissible to exploit his land – and this included mineral deposits and (because it depended on his timber) glass manufacture – but where the feeling that commerce cancelled nobility was strong enough for a form of financial suicide in the cause of honour, non-derogation, the avoidance of a rich bourgeois marriage, to be widespread. The English compromised, allowing their sons to range beyond the caste frontier into legal studies and, more rarely, into commerce.

The shrinking of political independence and a weakening economic position did not have a profound social effect. Among the nobility the transition from quasi-prince to grandee is easier to detect now than it was then. In some countries – France, Spain and Hungary among them – aristocrats were exempt from taxation; in all they were taxed separately, and their distinction from the bourgeoisie was thus still seen in high relief. New creations from bourgeois blood were numerous, but not so frequent as to maim the prestige of aristocratic birth. And an aura of social distance was enhanced by a revival of chivalric manners. Malory's *Morte D'Arthur*, printed in 1485 by Caxton and in 1498 by Wynkyn de Worde, suggested that 'all gentlemen that bear old arms ought of right to honour Sir Tristram for the goodly terms that gentlemen have and use...that thereby...all men of worship may dissever [distinguish] a gentleman from a yeoman.' The late fifteenth century Gothic revival of manners followed the spirit of this advice. The tournament was revived with full medieval ceremony and a new heraldic sophistication. It was sharply restricted to gentlemen; in England no one lower than the rank of esquire could compete, in Germany, to keep out the recently ennobled, the number of noble forbears necessary to qualify was increased to eight, even at times to sixteen. And alongside the freshened cult of the tournament there was a wave of legislation to restore to the knightly class their neglected hunting rights both over the 'greater hunting' of deer, wild boar, bears and wolves and the 'lesser hunting' of wildfowl and hares.

* J. Blum, *Lord and Peasant in Russia from the Ninth to the Nineteenth Century* (Princeton, 1961) 137–8.

It was a revival that both reassured the aristocrat that he was different in kind from other men and heightened the attractiveness of the aristocratic milieu to the bourgeois. For the neo-chivalry of this period was a fashion and fashion was something the bourgeois understood. Indeed, in some places he set it. 'Extravagance in dress has impoverished the German nobility', a German moralist wrote sadly. 'They desire to make the same show as the rich city merchants. Heretofore they were the leaders in fashion, and now they are unwilling that the wives and daughters of the merchants should excel theirs in costliness of apparel. But they cannot afford this, for they do not derive from their estates the twentieth part of what the merchants can earn by their business and usury.'

Even in the Italian republics a nostalgia for nobility had always been present. Knighthood, a patent of nobility: these gave status of a still coveted sort even if they had nothing to do with political power and little influence on the style in which their holders lived. They reached out to touch the fringe of the world of kings and emperors, to the honour due to blood rather than continual striving, to a form of status that was heritable and not dependent on the chance skills of an heir. This sentiment, in addition to the contact with French and Spanish manners during the Italian wars, led to a fairly widespread aristocratisation of the upper reaches of Italian life. Pulci's *Morgante* had domesticated chivalrous ideas, salted with mockery, in the circle of Lorenzo de' Medici. Boiardo, living in the semi-royal court of the Este in Ferrara, had carried their naturalization further in his *Orlando Innamorato*. The sixteenth century brought Ariosto's *Orlando Furioso*, and, with it, an Italian chivalrous literature that breathed a spirit entirely its own. It brought individuals like Luigi da Porto who fought in the campaign that followed the Venetian defeat at Agnadello in 1509; he fought as a mercenary, but in a mood of self-conscious chivalry, preferring single combat where his bravery could be seen to shine, elaborately courteous to friend and foe, doggedly in love and prone to write sonnets during lulls in the fighting. It brought, too, a belief in the political value of aristocratic manners. In 1516, when the Medici were cautiously trying to neutralise the republican institutions of Florence after their return in 1512, Lodovico Alamanni suggested that they should persuade the leading citizens to wear the cape of northern, princely fashion rather than the bourgeois cloak. At a time when in other western countries the aristocracy was adapting itself with varying degrees of gingerliness to non-feudal conditions, the Italian patrician, so used to legal and administrative life and to the notion of service to the community, showed signs of envying the individualism, or, rather, the comparative irresponsibility of the seigneur. Nor did he have to look across the Alps to see the seigneur raising troops, exercising personal justice or setting his bravos on officers of the state: in Milan and Naples the late fifteenth century saw a growing use of military tenures and feudal relationships.

Italian respect for the way of life of the invading aristocracies was not based on respect for their intellectual attainments. Castiglione expressed the hope that were the cultivated duke of Angoulême to succeed Louis XII (as he did) the French might at last acquire a culture that would begin to match their valour. Sebastian Franck wrote of German aristocrats that 'they have no occupation but hunting with dog and falcon, guzzling and carousing.' But no blanket condemnation of this sort is really revealing. German aristocrats' sons, for instance, went in impressive numbers to universities.

In the same way, the English aristocracy were probably literate in the main in spite of the humanist Richard Pace's famous anecdote about the outburst of an English squire: 'I swear by God's body I'd rather that my son should hang than study letters. For it becomes the sons of gentlemen to blow the horn knowledgeably, to hunt skilfully, and elegantly carry and train a hawk. But the study of letters should be left to the sons of rustics.' Changing conditions were showing that prestige and economic advancement called for hornbook as well as horn. Educated princes were seeking educated advisers and public servants, and were increasingly finding them among the bourgeoisie. That contemporaries recognised this is witnessed by a nervous spurt of anti-bourgeois satire sponsored by noble patrons. And that satire was not enough is shown in Edmund Dudley's warning 'verily I fear me the noblemen and gentlemen of England be the worst brought up for the most part of any realm of Christendom. And therefore the children of poor men and mean folk are promoted to the authority that the children of noble blood should have if they were meet therefore.'

6

Religion

Church and State

In 1498 the first party to sail direct from Europe to India arrived in Calicut. They were taken to a Hindu temple and shown its phallus-columns, the shrine of Parvati, the threatening demon-kings and the guardians of the cult of Shiva wearing the *sutra*, the triple thread that identified their caste. The occasion was described by the narrator of da Gama's voyage. 'When we arrived they took us to a large church, and this is what we saw. The body of the church is as large as a monastery, all built of hewn stone and covered with tiles. At the main entrance rises a pillar of bronze as high as a mast, on the top of which was a bird, apparently a cock. In addition to this there was another pillar, as high as a man, and very stout. In the centre of the body of the church rose a chapel, all built of hewn stone...within this sanctuary stood a small image which they said represented Our Lady... In this church the captain-major [da Gama] said his prayers, and we with him. We did not go within the chapel, for it is the custom that only certain servants of the church, called quafees, should enter. The quafees wore some threads passing over the left shoulder and under the right arm, in the same manner as our deacons wear the stole. They threw holy water over us, and gave us some white earth, which the Christians of this country are in the habit of putting on their foreheads, breasts, around the neck and on the forearms. They threw holy water upon the captain-major... Many other saints were painted on the walls of the church, wearing crowns. They were painted variously, with teeth protruding an inch from the mouth and four or five arms.'

Even making some allowance for the legend of the Apostle St. Thomas's missionary work in south India, this confusion bears striking witness to the extent to which Europeans were conditioned to see, as well as to think, in terms of Christianity. Centuries of crusading, trade and pilgrimages had done little to open Christian eyes to the nature of Mohammedanism, Christianity's neighbour and rival faith. There was as little attempt to understand the true nature of a faith practised in Europe itself: that of the Jews. When the Cabala was studied, by Pico della Mirandola and Reuchlin, it was as part of the literary archaeology of Christianity. The study of Hebrew was, indeed, undertaken seriously. Reuchlin's grammar was published in 1506 and the language was taught at several universities, among them Alcala, Louvain, Wittenberg and Oxford. But this was in the interest of studying the Old Testament, not Judaism. It was not a time of challenging heresies within Christendom itself. Relations between Catholics and Orthodox were on the whole calm; in Corfu Romans and Greeks shared in religious processions and once a year the church of St. Arsenios was discordant with their two styles of chanting. But the great debates, the efforts to reach formal reconciliation through mutual understanding, had ceased since the mid-century. To see a Hindu temple in terms of a Christian church was an extreme case, but it is not surprising that other explorers should show little interest in the beliefs of the peoples they came upon. 'They have no faith,' wrote Alvise Cadamosto of the inhabitants of the Canary Islands. 'They do not have or understand any belief' was Caminha's comment on the natives of Brazil. Spiritually, the non-European peoples were seen as *tabulae rasae* on which the elements of Christianity had merely to be scratched. Or when (as with the Aztecs) a flourishing priesthood drew attention to a systematised faith, it was above all the similarities to Christian practice that were commented on. It was not until widespread backsliding from superficial conversions became an outstanding missionary problem that Christians realised that it was necessary to study and to understand rival faiths in order to attack them at the roots, a development that coincided with the Reformation's redirection of interest to faith rather than morals.

Da Gama's men came from a civilisation where not only devotion but the whole cast of secular life was permeated by Christian observance. It is a point that need not be laboured. The physical appearance of city, town and village was dominated by churches. No crowd, no much travelled route was without its quota of characteristically robed clergy, its crucifixes and shrines along the way. In England the proportion of clergy to laymen was roughly one in seventy-five; in Italy it was considerably higher. Religious ceremonies marked the stations of the agricultural year, the meetings of consultative assemblies and gilds. University *viva voce* examinations took place in choir or chancel. Pots, beds and chimney pieces carried Christian texts, figures and symbols. Labourers carrying their tools waited for employment in cathedrals. Effortlessly, the church extended its arms to the new and strange: miners exposed to the hazards of blasting, and gunners to those of an exploding breech were offered the patronage of Saint Barbara. The protecting cloak of the Virgin, long-extended over the devout to protect them from the arrows of plague was offered as a defence from the new scourge of syphilis. Through its views on usury the church declared an interest in a man's business life. All countries had church courts, whose main purpose, apart from regulating the lives of the clergy themselves, was to watch over those matters which linked clergy to laymen administratively: marriage settlements, wills, contracts, the payment of tithes and other dues. And exhortations from the pulpit on moral issues were also backed up by canon law enforceable in the church courts, particularly with respect to sexual offences, blasphemy, slander and neglect of the sacraments. The church was responsible, too, for the ferreting out and trial of heretics.

At the institutional level lawyers might bicker about points where canon law appeared to conflict with civil law, but more significant to the sense of religion being diffused throughout secular life was the general assumption that the law of each land was also in accordance with the law of God, and that this was especially true when the nature of an offence threatened the stability of the regime. The preamble to an English statute of 1513 put this identity of interest very clearly. 'Forasmuch as it is often seen that man's reason, whereby he should discern the good from the evil and the right from wrong is many times, by seduction of the Devil...repressed and vanquished, whereupon commonly ensues discords, murders, robberies, divisions, disobeisance to sovereigns, subversion of realms and destruction of peoples,...therefore emperors, princes and governors of time past, for refraining of such inordinate appetites and punishment of those folks which rather eschew to offend for fear of bodily pain or losses of goods than for the love of God or justice, full wisely and politicly ordained divers laws serving to the same purpose as well in time of war as peace.' Cabral, following up da Gama's voyage, carried with him a letter to the ruler of Calicut warning him that now God had pointed out a way by which Europeans could dominate the trade of his country he should not wish to resist His manifest and known will. Machiavelli's 'crime' was not that by detaching political planning from the background of Christian morality he invited rulers to be wicked: by that criterion they were wicked anyway, but that he deprived actions of state from carrying with them the savour of divine approval.

Between the church's insinuation of its control into the privacies of domestic life and the suggestion that to break the law was to disobey God, a third aspect of secular–clerical relations affected the way in which men thought about religion: the connection between the church in a particular country and the papacy. Notionally,

Christendom was one. When popes called for a crusade, individual states had at least to expend some effort of ingenuity in explaining why they could not contribute to it. Notionally, popes were supreme diplomatic arbiters. 'It is the proper function of the Roman pontiff, of the cardinals, of bishops and abbots', Erasmus wrote in 1514, 'to compose the quarrels of Christian princes, to exert their authority in this field and show how far the reverence of their office prevails.' Papal assistance was indeed invoked to bring about an agreement between the Swiss and Milan in 1483, and to confirm the Anglo-French treaty of 1498. Leo X's bull of 1517 ordering a five year truce in Europe was followed by the treaty of London in 1518. But Wolsey, not Leo, was the actual architect of this pacification and, as in the instances of 1483 and 1498, the papal lead was followed only because the contestants were already exhausted enough to welcome a settlement.

And just as rulers used or ignored the papacy as universal arbiter in terms of their own convenience, they sought to create enclaves within the international machinery of church government, to check the flow of law-suits, taxes and fees to Rome and to moderate the extent to which the popes staffed 'national' churches with candidates of their own choosing.

Relations between England and the papacy continued to work harmoniously in terms of fourteenth century statutes which limited the scope of papal appointments and of appeals from English church courts to Rome. In strong contrast, the control of the crown over the church in Spain increased dramatically. The Inquisition, fully formed under the generalship of Torquemada in 1483, was a valuable political weapon, and the confiscations it imposed were an important source of revenue to the crown. In 1486 Ferdinand extracted from Innocent VIII a bull granting him the patronage over all churches to be set up in the recently conquered kingdom of Granada. In 1508 the Spanish Crown was granted the right of appointment to all benefices in its American possessions. In Castile and Aragon the tax exemptions of the clergy were reduced and an informal agreement reached whereby the papacy ratified the appointment of royal nominees to bishoprics. Taken together with the bull *Inter Caetera* and the title 'Catholic Kings' granted them by Alexander VI, the concessions won by Ferdinand and Isabella from popes in need of their diplomatic support were remarkable. Freedom from Roman control, however, meant no weakening of Catholic orthodoxy; future events, indeed, were to suggest that the popes served their faith most usefully not through their victories, but through their concessions.

In Germany Maximilian vaguely thought of a national church of which he would be (in a manner never clearly expressed) the spiritual as well as the secular head. Anti-papal feeling, however, though stronger in Germany than elsewhere, was impossible to mobilise among the competing interests of the Empire and remained in a state of baffled suspense, eased here and there by local 'concordats' granted to individual princes, and ventilated in meetings of the imperial diet as 'the grievances of the German nation' – complaints about the fiscal and jurisdictional greed of the papacy and the need for the moral reform of the clergy. Maximilian's cloudy Caesaro-papism was echoed more purposefully in Russia when Ivan III took advantage of the notion that now Rome (in Orthodox eyes) was heretical and Constantinople conquered, Moscow was the Third Rome, the true centre of Christianity. Ivan drew liberally on the image and on the ceremony of Byzantium. He promoted the idea of his protectorship of the church and pushed steadily for a real control over it, a tendency supported by churchmen themselves partly as a lesser evil than control by local nobles, and partly because an influ-ential minority believed that ecclesiastics should not possess material wealth. The secularisation of the possessions of churches and mon-asteries after the capture of Novgorod provided a model for a cau-tious policy of secularisation in the grand duchy of Moscow, and the Third Rome theory a respectable cover for this aim. For as abbot Filotheus (Filofei) wrote to Ivan's son in 1510, 'he [Ivan] is on earth the sole emperor of the Christians, the leader of the Apostolic Church which stands no longer in Rome or in Constantinople, but in the blessed city of Moscow. She alone shines in the whole world brighter than the sun.' In no other European country did the church see its mission as so intimately linked to the authority of the ruler.

The church in France had a clear image of itself as inheriting rights and liberties, summed up in the word Gallicanism, that gave it considerable independence from Rome and assumed a corresponding subservience to the crown. The monarch was termed 'Most Chris-tian'. The holy *ampoule* containing the chrism with which he was annointed at his coronation, entitled him to work miracles, curing sufferers from scrofula by touching them. In return, kings were care-ful to flatter their clergy; they honoured the formula in which the church in France was 'the eldest daughter of the church', superior in age and devotion to other national branches of Catholicism. Charles VIII and Louis XII invoked this tradition when seeking financial aid for their wars in Italy, so did Francis I when he put himself forward as a candidate for the Empire on the death of Maximilian.

The compromise within which king, pope and clergy tried to work was based on the concordat of 1472. It was more favourable to the king, giving him great freedom in appointing his own candidates to bishoprics, than to the clergy, for it left them open to stiff papal taxes.

It was resented by the theologians of the Sorbonne because it modified the earlier (1438) Pragmatic Sanction of Bourges, by the Parlement because it weakened the legal position of that body as a court of appeal in ecclesiastical cases; it was deplored by a hard core of ultramontanes because it did not grant enough power to the papacy. To look beneath the surface of the compromise represented by the concordat is to glimpse a seething resentment, a continual contesting of appointments. Provisions to benefices was the sorest issue. Who was to get an appointment: the king's man, the pope's, the candidate a cathedral chapter wanted from their own monks, or the son of a local magnate? Uncertainty about provision, plus the rivalry between Gallicans and ultramontanes, led to religion becoming ever more thickly smeared with politics. Even the saintly hermit Francesco di Paola, whom Louis XI had summoned to advise his dying days, became heavily involved in anti-Gallican intrigues, the centre of a web of information and the sender of smuggled messages to the pope. The situation was improved, but by no means cured, by the concordat of Bologna in 1516. By this agreement nomination to benefices was by the king, canonical institution by the pope: that is, the king could appoint whom he chose, depending on his needs and the nature of the advice he chose to take, while the pope rubber-stamped his choice (the ceremony of institution was, of course, of deep meaning to those capable of so seeing it) and elections were discontinued. The king did agree to certain principles governing nominations: candidates for bishoprics should be at least twenty-seven years old, for priorships and abbacies at least twenty-three, prospective bishops should have graduated in theology – there were other safeguards, but there were also enough exceptions (members of the royal household, 'personnes sublimes') to preserve something of the old, energy-consuming uncertainty. In sum, the churchmen in France looked less to the papacy and more – and in an increasingly place-seeking mood – to the crown. The sufferers from this narrowing church–state relationship were the population at large and the lower ranks of the clergy. The eldest daughter of the church was becoming the fine lady she remained until the Revolution of 1789.

In no case, however, is it easy to judge the effect of church–state relations, either internally or between a nation and the papacy, on the quality of religious life among the people at large. The nature of the clergy, the respect in which they were held, the effectiveness of their ministry, these were directly related to the way in which they were appointed. But while a pope might impose an unpopular foreigner, a king might appoint a favourite with no religious qualifications. Anticlericalism, omnipresent, and ranging all the way from pastime to passion, almost certainly affected the quality of men's spiritual involvement in their religious practice, and one element in it was the question of church property. Yet it was as rabid in Scotland and northern Italy, where land had been steadily passing out of the control of the church into the hands of laymen, as it was in Germany, where ecclesiastical estates were still of formidable proportions.

Clerics

The closer the links between church and state, the more natural it seemed to look on the life of religion as a career, in which, by stepping sideways from the aristocracy or the bourgeoisie to the adjacent niche in the ecclesiastical hierarchy, a man could expect accelerated increments of cash and, above all, of land. Georges d'Amboise, archbishop of Rouen and later cardinal, came from a rich bourgeois family but within a generation he and his brothers – who became bishops of Poitiers and Albi and abbot of Cluny – far outdistanced the prosperity of their secular relations. Nor need the transfer from one estate to another imply too drastic a change in manner of living. The aristocrat-cleric had to embrace celibacy, but he could still hunt, and he could still fight, as did the archbishop of Sens, who rode with Louis XII into Italy in full armour and lance in hand. The bourgeois-cleric found himself as fully engaged as ever in administering accounts, exchanging and accumulating lands, straining towards the luxury for which his secular colleagues were being so soundly abused. 'We see coming towards us', wrote the German chronicler Butzbach, 'our prelates, swollen with pride. They are dressed in the finest English cloth... Their hands, loaded with costly rings, are placed proudly on their thighs. They preen themselves on the finest horses and are followed by a numerous train of domestics in splendid liveries. They build themselves fine palaces where, amid sumptuous entertainments, they give themselves up to a life of orgy.' With a few pinches of salt, this description could hold good for a fair proportion of European prelates, above all in France, Spain and Italy, as well as in parts of Germany. Behind Butzbach's imaginary portrait lay actual prelates like the archbishop of Speyer, who retained his position and income as dean of Mainz, canon of Cologne and Trier, provost of St. Donatian in Bruges and parish priest of Hochheim and Lorch am Rhein, or, more dramatic, Albert of Brandenburg who, after becoming archbishop of Mainz in 1514, was allowed by the pope to retain the bishoprics of Magdeburg and Halberstadt. He was then twenty-five. The pope charged heavy fees for these privileges, which Albert had to raise by applying to the Fuggers for a loan, but to help him pay this Leo X granted him half the profits of the St. Peter's Indulgence sold in his dioceses: that famous Indulgence, designed to raise money for the building of the new St. Peter's in Rome, which helped Luther define his feelings about the religion of his day.

Scandal, of course, leaps to the eye, both for its own sake, and because it fascinated contemporaries. To supplement chronicles with diocesan records is to reveal bishops, possibly a majority, who ran their sees with an eye to their pastoral responsibilities. In England, lack of contact between bishops and the life of the parish was probably due as much to the great size of the dioceses as to their secular preoccupations or to pluralism, and possibly this is true of Castile, where Isabella sought to fill vacant bishoprics with men of proved devotion. An Albert of Brandenburg, however, was responsible for a thousand times the number of souls in the care of a 'good' bishop like Fisher of Rochester or François d'Estaing of Rodez. And absences on secular business, frequent migration from benefice to benefice meant that many sees were without effective leadership, governed by deputies who either sought to imitate their superiors or were forced to devote themselves to routine administration rather than actively supervising the priests who were primarily responsible for sustaining the faith of the people. The church was coming to resemble a business which, secure from competition, ploughs its profits into directors' salaries and leaves its sales force slack or despairing. All the same, consistency of behaviour as a badge of deep religious feeling was not then taken for granted. A peasant's faith did not die because he saw his bishop's face in a sweat from hunting any more than a journeyman thought a cathedral was less the house of God because he came to sell his labour there.

The same caution must be borne in mind when considering Rome itself and the influence on the tone of religion in Europe of the reputation of the remarkable popes of this period, notably Alexander VI, Julius II and Leo X, together with their hardly less remarkable entourage of cardinals. Alexander's election was unfairly believed to be the result of bribery during the conclave, and his unpopularity as a Spaniard and his unconcealed regard for his children led to a proliferation of scandalous stories. 'There is no sort of outrage or vice', declared an anonymous pamphlet in 1501, 'that is not openly practised in the palace of the pope...Rodrigo Borgia is an abyss of vice, a subverter of all justice, human or divine.' The case against Julius II was put, with a vigour that suggests a grudging admiration, by Erasmus in his superb propaganda (pro-French) dialogue *Julius Exclusus*. The spirit of the pope is challenged at the heavenly gates by St. Peter. 'The invincible Julius ought not to answer a beggarly fisherman. However, you shall know who and what I am. First, I am a Ligurian, and not a Jew like you. My mother was the sister of the great pope Sixtus IV. The pope made me a rich man out of church property. I became a cardinal. I had my misfortunes: I had the French pox, I was banished, hunted out of my country, but I knew all along that I should come to be pope myself in the end...I rose to the top, and I have done more for the church and Christ than any pope before me...I annexed Bologna to the Holy See. I beat the Venetians. I jockeyed the duke of Ferrara. I defeated a schismatical council by a sham council of my own. I drove the French out of Italy, and I would have driven out the Spaniards, too, if the Fates had not brought me here. I have set all the princes of Europe by the ears. I have torn up treaties, kept great armies in the field, I have covered Rome with palaces...And I have done it all myself, too. I owe nothing to my birth, for I don't know who my father was; nothing to learning, for I have none; nothing to youth, for I was old when I began; nothing to popularity, for I was hated all round. Spite of fortune, spite of gods and men I achieved all that I have told you in a few years, and I left work enough cut out for my successors to last ten years longer. This is the modest truth, and my friends at Rome call me more a god than a man.'* Leo X, promised a cardinal's hat at thirteen and elected pope when he was only thirty-eight, was soon under fire for his addiction to hunting, the lavishness of his expenditure on the pleasures of patronage and for deposing the duke of Urbino in order to install his nephew Lorenzo de' Medici in his place.

In general, and leaving aside accusations of personal immorality, none of which – once they had assumed office – can be proved, popes were criticised for excessive pomp, political militancy, manipulation of the college of cardinals, the sale of offices, and nepotism. The triple nature of the papacy (its spiritual leadership, its sovereign role in a political entity, the States of the Church, and its governorship of a financial empire) was thrown into high relief in this period by the almost constant threat of diplomatic pressure or actual war. As territorial princes the popes were weak: areas formerly belonging to their States had been annexed by others (Bologna and Urbino were two cases); they had not solved the problem of assimilating the local feudal baronage. They needed money (which the succession of concordats had reduced) to raise armies and play the diplomatic game from a position of strength. They needed loyal lieutenants, and popes, who apart from Leo, were old men when they were elected and who could leave no dynasty behind them, found it harder to secure them than did other princes. They strained the conventions,

* J. A. Froude's paraphrase, in his *Life and Letters of Erasmus* (London, 1894) 142–3.

then, selling offices to garner cash, and they used members of their families, whom they could trust. Like their fellow princes who were insisting on a greater measure of positive political control, the popes, by inflating the college of cardinals with their nominees and by-passing traditional chains of command, were putting themselves in a position to take quick decisions and have them acted upon. The need to behave like other territorial rulers, and their growing ability to do so, threw the secular aspects of the papal role into high relief. Even so, the multiple role was familiar to influential visitors, diplomats and churchmen, from the similar roles played by leading clerics in their own countries. Popes were criticised for particular policies, seldom for acting as politicians. Hearing of the death of Alexander VI in 1503, a Florentine merchant passed on the news to an associate abroad with no reference to Alexander's moral or spiritual qualities, or those to be hoped for in his successor. He simply prayed that 'with the help of God' a pope would be elected capable of keeping order in the Romagna, for 'business in all regions in this section is in such a state that it must be stimulated.'

It was, besides, less the popes than the bearing of the cardinals, of whom between twenty and forty might be in Rome at any one time, that gave the centre of Christendom its air of secular magnificence. Many were, of course, thoroughly worthy men, but among the massive creations of Sixtus (thirty-four), Alexander and Leo (forty-three each) many were hardly more than impressive placemen. Frequently appointed young, and coming from palace rather than parish, it is possible that a majority had never heard a confession or addressed a congregation. Some flavour of their manner of life was given by an abortive reform bull of Alexander in 1497. Cardinals were not to take part in tournaments or carnivals or go to secular plays, their households were not to number more than eighty, of whom at least twelve should be in holy orders, they were not to keep more than thirty horses and they were not to employ boys or young men as body servants.

Again, to the worldly-wise visitor there was nothing anomalous about such behaviour, nor was magnificence and ceremonial likely to do anything but impress the ordinary pilgrim, used to such ecclesiastical display as his local community could muster. Some visitors were shocked by what they found, though it is not always easy to distinguish spiritual protest from straightforward anti-clericalism and the anti-Italian feeling that was especially strong among German intellectuals. There were accusations that everything, including God, was for sale, that religion had become selfish and earthbound (Luther's reaction), that faith itself was imperilled in the shadow of the Vatican. These were not new complaints. Outside Rome itself, moreover, news of popes and cardinals was scant, and was robbed of immediacy by distance.

The condition of the monasteries offered a more widely visible target for contemporaries to attack. Towards the end of the century Andrea della Robbia's noble polychrome relief showing the fraternal meeting of Saints Dominic and Francis was set up in Florence. With the Franciscans at the throats of Savonarola's Dominicans it hardly expressed more than the pious hope of Sixtus IV's 'Golden Bull' in which the pope had urged the need for harmony between one religious order and another and between all orders and the secular clergy. All over Europe, in fact, order combatted order (on occasion scuffling for first place in processions) and parish clergy bewailed the 'poaching' activities of the friars, who, it was claimed, undermined pastoral discipline by granting easier penances and who even admitted the excommunicated to their services. When to this variety of complaints within the ranks of the church itself is added the complaints of the laity, a sorry picture emerges, even allowing for the fact that jokes and moans at the expense of monk and friar had such a venerable ancestry that they had lost much of their cutting edge.

The condition revealed by visitations and reform commissions was indeed deplorable; lax discipline, the neglect of vows, concubinage, ignorance, domestic squabbles. The accounts are most telling, perhaps, when they are least sensational, when they describe not the potations of wealthy abbots, or those Andalusian friars who chose – four hundred of them – to emigrate to Africa and embrace Islam rather than give up the embraces of their concubines, but isolated communities that had gone back, as it were, to the bush, coping with hardships and enjoying the rough pleasures of the ordinary rural hamlet, distinguishable from a settlement of peasants by little more than their dress, and not always by that; or those wealthier foundations, filled with the offspring of poor noble families, few in priest's orders, who with their hunting and hawking and brawling made their abbeys seem like baronial castles *en masquerade*. The causes of this decay were obvious enough. Men and women were admitted too easily and not instructed properly once they had entered; peasants sent their children for reasons of prestige, aristocrats treated monasteries and abbeys as privileged systems of relief from a too numerous brood. Yet in many monasteries the numbers had so dropped that almost every monk was needed to fill some office and it was impossible to discipline them by demotion. In others an abbot had been put in by force over the heads of the community and was treated with sullen resentment. The absenteeism of superiors, inadequate or intermittent inspection: there are explanations to be found in the structure of monasticism as a whole as well as in the quality of individuals. Challenged on moral grounds by the activist strain in humanist thought, there is also possibly an explanation of the decline of monastic morale in the changing attitude to work: in the attitude, revitalised since the labour shortage that followed the Black Death and by the fear of violence resulting from unemployment in the towns, that insisted on the biblical 'six days shalt thou labour...'. Against this growing work ethic, identified particularly with the bourgeoisie but preached with gusto by the secular clergy, the monks were seen, and possibly were made to see themselves, as drones, no longer exemplars of the ideal life but refugees from it.

In 1516 the Benedictine Charles Fernand set himself to rebut the conviction, held by many of his order, that the world was grown old and man become so weak that he could not be expected to undergo the rigours and penances that the great elders, Saint Benedict himself and Saint Antony, had taken in their stride. Nor was this ingenious pessimism shared by the other architects of monastic reform. Slack members were ejected, sometimes by force of arms, as in the case of the Paris Jacobins, and friars from stricter houses put in their place. New orders, like the French Minims, helped through their example. Reform did not overtake decline, but neither was reform everywhere necessary. Luther joined the Erfurt Augustinians because of their reputation for the strict observance of their rule. They accepted him only after the normal year's probation and it was under their instruction that he became an outstanding theologian. And any generalisation about the state of monastic life must take into account successful men, like Jean Raulin, who chose to withdraw to it from one of the pinnacles of the academic world in Paris.

Like many members of the religious orders, the mass of secular clerics, especially in village or small town parishes, were distinguishable from the lay environment from which they were recruited, peasant or petit bourgeois, by little more than a cassock and a theoretical celibacy. In church, during the mass, their separateness was immense, and recognised: only they could turn bread and wine into the body and blood of Christ. As for the other sacraments, it is doubtful how far parishioners recognised that their efficacy depended on the nature of the priesthood and doubtful how many priests would have been capable of explaining it to them. Baptism, confession, marriage, extreme unction: the practice of religion was deeply engrained as a social habit; the comfort brought by the sacraments was, for a largely illiterate population, independent of theological understanding. The lower clergy were theologically naive because it was becoming harder for really poor children to get into universities, whose bursaries, primarily intended for the poor, were taken up by the children of the bourgeoisie. For reasons of poverty, large numbers completed only a part of their university course while many more got no further than the four-year arts course which included no theology. Admission to the priesthood itself was perfunctory and unsearching and produced a mass of unpromotable clerics whose influence on their congregations depended on the accident of personal integrity unsupported by reasoned belief. Criticism and exhortation from above could do little. A reforming provincial of a monastic order at least had groups of men to deal with; a reforming bishop was hampered by the scattered nature of his charge. And his poverty made it almost impossible for a parish priest to better himself. His tithes had commonly been subjected to so many legal and landholding charges in the past centuries that he was left with but a fraction of them. A tax could reduce him to real misery. He depended, then, on fees. 'One year', ran an Italian anecdote of the time, 'the harvest of grain and fruit was excellent all over Italy and Tuscany, especially in the countryside around Florence. Everybody was rejoicing and talking about the large harvest of his land. One day priest Arlotto was with a group of men who were talking about their good luck; and after he had listened to them for a while, he said: "I had a completely different experience from yours; I can assure you that my best plot of land gave me a very poor crop." All the men who were in Arlotto's company were amazed and asked him how that could be possible, and what plot he was talking about that had produced such a poor crop. "It is the cemetery behind my church," he replied, "every year it gives me an income of from about fifty to about sixty *lire*, because every year I usually bury there from six to eight people; and for each body, which takes up three yards of land, I get ten lire. This year my cemetery hasn't produced anything at all because as yet no one has died, and that grieves me a good deal."'

As dependent on a harvest of fees as were his parishioners on their crops, the priest's attitude to worldly goods blended into theirs. And so, frequently, did the nature of his household. Concubinage was everywhere a cause of worry to reformers. The council of Seville in 1512 was forced to plead that priests should at least keep away from the marriages of their sons and daughters. Legitimisation of a cleric's bastard was a commonplace. And this parallelism of manners between priest and people was all the more widespread because of the alacrity with which the better educated holders of remunerative benefices left their parish duties to be carried out by vicars, deputies humble enough to perform their function for a small wage.

The Appeal of the Church

Denunciations of the church's slackness abounded, most notably from within the church itself. Colet, in a sermon of 1513, summed up the gist of much current criticism when he said that the church had become a machine for advancing men's interests by taking money from the poor instead of handing Christ's teaching down to them in love. The ignorance of the people was taken advantage of by a large itinerant population of false friars, false monks, sellers of fake relics and fake pardons; indulgence vendors stressed the effectiveness of the fee rather than the contrition and the good works on which the doctrine of indulgences insisted. If Christ were to come back to earth today, said the Franciscan Thomas Murner, preaching in Frankfurt-am-Main in 1512, he would be betrayed, and Judas thought to have earned his thirty pieces well. By multiplying such denunciations the church can be made to look ripe not only for reform but for the Reformation. The prestige of its learning, however, though dimmer than heretofore and less exclusive, was still active, a source of inspiration to those who in growing numbers clustered in the great centres of theology, among which the university of Paris remained pre-eminent, and penetrating downwards through printed books and the spoken word of the pulpit. There was no dominating figure; men looked back, and fruitfully, to the great seminal thinkers, Augustine, William of Occam and Aquinas. Scholasticism, the mode of study and expression characteristic of the faculties of theology, was under attack, but the attack was violent because of the vitality, not the flabbiness of what it was assaulting. The pastoral influence of theological controversies had always been scant: that had been the work of movements which, like the Franciscan, had started at the pastoral level and then influenced theological scholarship. Intricate and argumentative rather than morally passionate, insulated from the church at large, theology remained vigorous and controversial. The danger was not that the church had lost its reservoir of learning, its ability to train and stimulate, but that too many of its leaders were appointed to their positions without coming into prolonged or, indeed, any contact with it.

The church's attitude to secular latin literature was mixed. While Leo X was watching Terentian comedies in Rome, Guillaume Michel was continuing the medieval tradition of a christianised Ovid with his edition of Virgil's *Georgics*, 'translated [into French] and moralised'. Virgil had referred to a swarm of legless bees hatched in the body of a calf, a straightforward, if unusual, piece of rural observation; Michel was quick to compare them with 'the new man regenerated in the blood of Jesus Christ, with no power of his own to walk and make progress along the path of virtue.' While in Italy the followers of Pico della Mirandola were attempting to break the divine code concealed in pre-Christian classical literature, the abbess of the convent of St. Clara wrote to Konrad Celtis thanking him for sending her his description of Nuremberg and a copy of Latin love poems, his *Amores*. 'I cannot in truth deny that the description and praise of the earthly fatherland in your book, which pleased me very much, would be even more congenial and delightful to me if it were a description and praise of the heavenly fatherland, Jerusalem above, from whence we come to this vale of misery, calamity and ignorance and to which we ought to aspire with all our might... For we have here no abiding city, but seek one to come... Therefore out of our singular friendship I admonish your worship to abandon the evil fables of Diana, Venus and Jupiter, and of other damned pagans who are now burning in hell fire, whose names and memory all true men who agree with the Christian profession must expunge, detest and deliver to complete oblivion.'*

The church took the lead in censoring books. Local censorship dates from 1475, when the university of Cologne was authorised by the pope to investigate not only books, but their readers. In 1486 Archbishop Berthold of Mainz was authorised to supervise books printed in his province and in 1501 came the first papal pronouncement of a general nature, when, in the bull *Inter Multiplices* (addressed to Germany) Alexander VI, though welcoming the invention of printing as a means of disseminating true religion, drew attention to the danger that heretical views might also get a hearing, and instructed printers to submit their works to the archbishops for licensing. Monastic presses were not uncommon; in Florence there was even one in the convent of Dominican nuns of San Giacopo di Ripoli. The church, indeed, had little need to be frightened of the press. Tentative figures for books printed before 1500 suggest that at least 45 per cent were of a religious nature, and that the percentage rose rather than fell in the next twenty years. And this figure includes very few of the religious ephemeræ: woodcuts with a few lines of text under them, the total religious furniture of innumerable poor homes, broadsheets and cheap pamphlets retailing miracles, saints' lives, or a few thematically grouped texts, handbooks to take on pilgrimages, brief meditations on the joys of Our Lady or the last words on the cross. Perishable, turned by clumsy hands, their numbers can only be guessed at from a few frail survivors.

---

* Lewis W. Spitz, *Konrad Celtis, the German Arch-Humanist* (Harvard U.P., 1957) 85–6.

The number of religious books is all the more revealing when it is born in mind that the introduction of printing enabled a country's whole manuscript literature, from cookery books and chivalrous romances to chronicles and poems – works accumulating over centuries – to get into circulation for the first time at a reasonable price. The queue, as it were, was jammed, and yet among new books popular demand gave pride of place to books on religious themes.

The effect on men's religious attitudes is impossible to gauge. Of heretical works there was hardly a sign before the spread of Lutheran books began. Sebastian Brant, it is true, complained that

> *Creeds, dogmas false in every way*
> *Now seem to grow from day to day.*
> *The printers make the case more dire:*
> *If some books went into the fire*
> *Much wrong and error would be gone.*

But it is doubtful if he had in mind more than the pullulation of accounts of false miracles and trite interpretations of scripture that degraded but did not challenge orthodox belief. On the other hand, works were published which, while not criticising the church, enabled men to define the nature of their dissatisfaction with it. Before 1501 the Bible had appeared in over ninety Latin and, in six languages, thirty vernacular editions. One of the works most frequently reprinted was the *Imitation of Christ*, again in vernacular translations as well as in Latin. Only a small proportion of the population was literate and the distribution of such books, even assuming an edition of one thousand copies each and a readership of five for each copy, affected only a fraction of that population. Against this, inventories in wills suggest that even reasonably well-to-do families possessed very few books, probably most had only one or two, and one book, read and re-read, prized and protected, tends to become The Book. The church had always been suspicious of the unsupervised reading of the Bible, especially of the Gospels: a contrast between the manners of Galilee and Rome could be made too naively; the simple teaching of the living Christ would be compared with the multiplication of ceremonies and dogmas produced through the centuries by the living church. Thomas à Kempis' book could be read in the sense that truly to imitate Christ it was necessary to withdraw from institutionalised religion. In this way the printing of religious books, while witnessing to the essentially religious temper of the age, encouraged criticism of the church.

A German work of morality printed in 1483 related how there was once a 'holy man who met a devil carrying a bag'. He asked him what he was carrying. The devil answered 'boxes of different kinds of ointment. In this' (showing him a black box) 'is an ointment with which I close men's eyes that they might sleep during the sermon ... one sermon will rob me of souls I have had in my power for thirty or forty years.' The popularity of sermons is indisputable. Volumes of them were printed and many were translated from the vernacular in which they were delivered (except for sermons to clerical audiences, or those preached on occasions of state) into Latin and thus acquired an international currency. Their stock themes, common to all countries, included: life, from cradle to grave, is a miserable, vulnerable affair; man's sins are too many to count, but the main ones are pride, luxury and gluttony; men in general obey the promptings of the flesh and ignore those of the spirit; the church itself is full of simony and pompous worldlings. Their tone ranged from the immensely learned earnestness of a Colet to the preacher imagined by Angelo Poliziano, who, preaching on the Annunciation, asked 'What do you think, dear ladies, that the Virgin Mary was doing at that time? Dyeing her hair blonde? No, of course not! On the contrary! She had a crucifix before her, and she was reading the Book of Hours of Our Lady.' It ranged from the itinerant Franciscan, shouting and kicking the side of the pulpit to keep his congregation of rustics awake to a preacher for whom Poliziano felt an enthralled admiration: Savonarola. As a preacher, Savonarola was not superior to, or more popular than men like Olivier Maillard or Michel Menot in France or Johann Geiler of Alsace; they too appealed to all levels of intellectual sophistication, were masters of both anecdote and argument, could terrify, inspire and charm.

As with books, it is extremely difficult to gauge the effect of sermons. Many, certainly, were violently emotional. The apothecary Luca Landucci, a devoted follower of Savonarola, noted in his diary that when the friar began to preach again in defiance of Alexander VI's prohibition, 'many people went there, and it was much talked of on account of his excommunication; and many did not go, for fear of being excommunicated, saying: 'guista vel inguista, timenda est'. And he added, 'I was one of those who did not go.' If any moral can be drawn from the confrontation between Savonarola, the preacher we know best, and Landucci, one of the very few assiduous attenders of sermons who has left any trace of his reactions, it is that even at a time of political and millenarian tension neither faith nor psychological equilibrium was easy to shake. Again, it has been suggested that the contemptus mundi emphasis created an atmosphere of despairing alarm, that the constant attacks on the avarice of merchants, the luxury of the nobles and their indifference to those in need encouraged class antagonism. It is doubtful. These themes were centuries

old. When attempts to control preaching were made, as by the
Lateran Council of 1516, it was heresy and inflammatory prophecies
that came under scrutiny, not attacks on the rich or on the great, not
even on the clergy themselves; indeed, it is more likely that support
for the church was undermined by the continual washing of its own
dirty linen in the pulpit.

Religion had a dark side of anguish and morbidity but this was at
least as much the result of fear, physical fear in the face of plague,
dearth and violence, as of the soul which feels itself doomed never to
be illuminated by the presence of God, to be fouled eternally by sin.
The church was careful to leave escape routes for the sinful: the
mediation of the priesthood, the warnings of the confessional, the
possibility of good works. Unless there was suspicion of downright
heresy, its yoke was laid fairly lightly on the conscience of the
individual. The penances imposed by the church courts for offences
like adultery were mild, and the rights under testament of bastards
guarded; the ferocious penalties prescribed for blasphemy were commonly commuted to a small fine, or the gift of a candle to the
offender's church. Bishop Seyssel recognised that princes had in practice to tolerate the troops of prostitutes who accompanied armies on
the march 'just as the church tolerates brothels in cities without
approving the sin involved.' Contemporary literature shows how
easy-going the relationship between even illicit passion and religion
could be, at least for the sophisticated. In order to seduce his mistress,
the hero of Caviceo's romance *Il Peregrino* hides under an altar in
order to urge his suit while she kneels in prayer, and has himself
smuggled into her house inside a statue of St. Catherine. When the
hero of de Rojas' *Celestina* calls for divine aid to help his pimp bring
Melibea to his bed, it is not on Jove or Amor that he calls but on 'you
who brought the Orient Kings to Bethlehem, following a star, and led
them back to their own country.'

Tolerance was shown too in the way in which the church took
account of changes in the direction of popular devotion. There was a
widespread appetite to believe that the Virgin had been immaculately
conceived, that this most approachable figure in the life of Christ and
supreme example of womanhood was as free as her son from original
sin, that besides looking to the perfect man, the worshipper could
pray to the perfect woman. Without warrant either in the scriptures
or the writings of the early Fathers, the cult was approved by Sixtus
IV, though not as a dogma, and endorsed in 1496 by the theologians
of the Sorbonne. Welcome (short of dogma) was also given to the still
newer cult of St. Anne, the desire to believe that the Virgin's mother
had also been chosen from the beginning of time as part of the divine
plan of redemption and without bondage to original sin. 'Men began

to speak of Saint Anne when I was a boy', Luther wrote in 1523. 'Until then no attention was paid to her.' The first two decades of the sixteenth century saw the multiplication of the saint's image in churches all over Europe. It was in this period that the devotion of the Rosary became widespread after its beginnings in the 1470s, and that the stations of the cross became a familiar worship though, as the stations had not yet been fixed along the Via Dolorosa itself in Jerusalem, the ritual varied between one church and another. Nor was this flexibility shown only towards popular aspirations. Growing emphasis on the dignity of man among humanist scholars led to an insistence – particularly among Platonists – on the immortality of his soul. Because of the philosophical difficulties of this concept, the church had left the matter open as probable, but unsusceptible to proof. In 1513 the Lateran Council made this belief a dogma of the church.

This responsiveness to demand is shown not only by what the church allowed but by what it condemned. The most notorious example of this is the persecution of witches. There was nothing new about a belief in witches. In a sermon of 1505 at Tübingen, which reads like an encyclopaedic synopsis of common knowledge, Martin Plantsch reminded his congregation that witches raised storms, had cats as familiars, caused impotence, manipulated sickness and health, broke into wine cellars through closed doors, used powders, infusions, images and desecrated the sacraments. This was familiar folklore. What was new was sustained official notice. In 1484 Innocent VIII issued his bull *Summis Desiderantes Affectibus* which authorised the Dominican inquisitors Heinrich Krämer and Jacob Sprenger to stamp out witchcraft in Germany. Two years later they published the founding document of witch persecution, the *Malleus Maleficarum*, a recognition chart for witches with directions how to prosecute them which rapidly gained a European circulation. Innocent's bull, listing the enormities committed by witches, included damage to crops and animals, sexual impotence in men and barrenness in women. By providing scapegoats for a wide range of economic and personal calamities the church was satisfying appetites as urgent as those which sought new ways of expressing a spiritual need.

All the traditional aids to Catholic devotion were enthusiastically taken advantage of; indeed, it was in response to the vigour of these devotions that satire at the expense of superstition and the externality of religious observance was at its height in the late fifteenth and early sixteenth centuries. Belief in the power of wonder-working images and the sense that towns and cities were under the protection of a patron saint were undimmed. The appetite to visualise the faith, and, in the case of relics and cult objects like certain statues and tombs, to touch, was as strong as ever. An Englishman, questioned on suspicion of heresy, had imagined the miracle of transubstantiation so clearly that he believed that the host must be surrounded by 'very white bread the thickness of a small twine thread, for, he saith, that when a man or woman shall be houseled the edge of the host may happen to hit upon a man's tooth. And then, if the circle of bread were not there to keep in the blood, the blood would peradventure fall down without his lips.'*

Down the naves of churches in Switzerland and Italy Christ was still drawn on Palm Sunday on the back of a wooden donkey. On Ascension day, in the Great Minster in Zurich, Christ rose through a hole in the floor and was hoisted up through a trapdoor in the roof. The church still gave full weight to the opinions of St. Gregory and St. Bernard: emotion is raised more readily through the eye than through the ear; the memory is stimulated more by a painted than by a heard argument; art is the literature of the illiterate. Late in the fifteenth century the Augustinian Gottschalk Holle emphasised that men could be led to piety more effectively 'through a picture than through a sermon' and Geiler acknowledged that 'such articles of faith as are essential to man may be learned by the common people through contemplation of the pictures and stories that are painted everywhere in the churches.' From hastily daubed saints scarcely distinguishable in religious use from pagan amulets, to theologically sophisticated fresco cycles like those of Raphael and Michelangelo, painting echoed and encouraged every spiritual impulse. Imaginative or lazy, wisely or foolishly permissive, the church allowed the variety of religious experience to cover its walls and crown its altars. And the walls and altars continued to be built.

In France, Spain and Germany there were many new churches and new chapels inserted in old ones. In England, the glass of Fairford and King's College, Cambridge, the tower at Fountains and Bath Abbey are only among the best known examples of an impressive activity in the building of churches and the furnishing of them with tombs, chantries, new pews, pulpits and screens, and with the carved alabaster for which the country was famous. Still more impressive evidence of the continuing vitality of religious observance is found in the activities of the lay confraternities which gave the non-labourer townsman a personal stake in the apparatus and the devotional satisfaction offered by the church. In addition to the social import- ance of the schools run by some of them and to the charity they

* In Margaret Bowker, *The secular clergy in the diocese of Lincoln 1495–1520* (Cambridge U.P., 1968) 153. Spelling modernised.

extended outside their own membership the confraternities could be notable patrons. In 1517 the Venetian confraternity of S. Rocco began the building of the meeting house (*scuola*) for which Tintoretto was to paint a series of masterpieces spanning his career. In Florence, the confraternity *dello Scalzo* bought land next to their little church for a cloister which Andrea del Sarto began to decorate in 1511 with the most beautiful *grisaille* works of all time. At the other extreme were the little alabaster plaques carrying eucharistic emblems which were sold for a shilling or two to members of the York confraternity of Corpus Christi to keep in their homes.

Dissatisfactions

There were many rungs in the ladder that lead man to God. A window placed in Saint-Laurence in Beauvais in 1516 shows a man who kneels, begging Laurence's intercession; the saint in turn looks beseechingly to the Virgin, who looks to Christ, who looks to God. The number of those who wished to sweep the rungs clean of saintly relics, mariolatrous devotions and emblems of the eucharist in order to look directly and without priestly intervention to God were scattered and few, and their numbers did not noticeably increase in this period. Only in Bohemia was heresy, a legacy from the days of Hus, commonplace. The Utraquists, who practised communion in both kinds and read the gospels and the epistles in the vernacular, were socially of some standing, with powerful backers among the gentry and certain towns, and they were, for the most part, allowed to practise their mildly eccentric and socially unalarming rites. Far more extreme were the Bohemian Brethren, practically beyond the reach of orthodoxy among their mountains and forests. In a letter to Erasmus, Jan Slechta, a cultivated Bohemian of some means, described their opinions. The pope and all his officials they describe as Antichrist. They choose their own bishops, rude unlettered laymen with wives and families. They salute one another as brothers and sisters and recognise no authority but the Bible. Their priests celebrate mass without vestments, use leavened bread and only the Lord's Prayer. Transubstantiation they deny, and the worship of the host they regard as idolatry. Vows to the saints, prayers for the dead, and confession to priests they ridicule, and they keep no holy days but Sundays, Christmas, Easter and Whitsun.

The importance of the Brethren was largely the influence they had on the men who came to the mountains from all over central Europe to work in the silver mines. Not very different were the beliefs of the Waldensians, a sect strongest among the Alpine valleys of Piedmont and south-eastern France but with scattered communities in Italy, again in mountain regions like Calabria and the Abruzzi. Anti-sacerdotal, distrustful of any practice which could not be demonstrated from the Gospels and Epistles, they believed that any man of pure life could administer the sacraments which they received as symbols only of Christ's body and blood. They lived (perforce, for the most part) in poverty and were prepared to attend churches in order to divert attention from beliefs that had been condemned time and again since the twelfth century. From 1488 they were savagely persecuted and their numbers much reduced. The third fairly easily definable group were those English Lollards who continued to keep alive the notions of Wyclif: rejection of transubstantiation, confession, prayers for the dead and clerical celibacy. They distrusted all non-biblical ceremony and stressed the importance of reading the scriptures in the vernacular. Lollard ideas were in the main restricted to poor men. Legally punishable with death if, after conviction and recantation, they relapsed, the English bishops did not pursue the Lollards with fierceness. The numbers involved were small and most of them recanted at the first prosecution. How many men, not Lollards to the extent of being identified as such, were influenced by their arguments against ritual, clerical wealth and exclusiveness and their bitterness against Rome, it is impossible to say.

Outside these sects, each of which possessed (or, in the case of the Lollards, had possessed) some form of 'church' organisation of their own, all over Europe from time to time individuals, moved by some psychic tension, dashed the host to the ground and jumped on it, shouted aloud that the pope was antichrist or announced their intention of begetting a new Saviour. The lack of any firm notion of secular progress, plus the enduring tradition of medieval chiliastic dreams, meant that in moments of political or social stress the wildest forecasts of the coming of Antichrist or the end of the world could be scribbled on the future without appearing inherently unlikely. Mystical excesses led Spanish friars to claim that personal union with God delivered them from the ability to sin and saved them from the responsibility of performing good works. In Germany and the Netherlands similar notions, with enough common psychological and doctrinal ground to relate them to the centuries-old heresy of the Free Spirit, prompted men to claim that the entire organisation of the church was a fraud, that man has the ability to be God and that once he has recognised this is free to make love to his sister or his brother before the altar or to murder his children. Still more common was a simple sticking to the word of the scriptures, and not only among poor and ignorant men; 'I would give two shillings to anyone who could show me any passage in holy writ which commands us to fast during Lent', said Jean Laillier, rashly presenting a thesis at the Sorbonne in 1484 in which he rejected confession, absolution, clerical celibacy and the authority of tradition.

There were others, however, who quietly opted out of the church's complex hospitality, preferring a way of uncombative self-perfection, and this is where the real danger to the church appeared to lie, in a feeling that the church's ministrations were not wrong, but irrelevant. Thus the Brethren of the Common Life, men and women who lived in monastery-like communities, observing self-imposed vows of poverty, chastity and prayer, by putting meditation and right conduct above ceremonies and sacraments implied, without stating, a criticism of the church; it was from their wholly orthodox schools that Erasmus and Luther emerged to stress the Bible as the yardstick by which to measure belief and worship. The influence of the 'Devotio Moderna' practised by the Brethren was extensive; they had houses and schools throughout the Rhineland and from the Netherlands as far east as Saxony. The essence of their faith was the conviction that strength of character and love of God were sufficient support to the Christ-seeking soul, that to live piously man needed the minimum of support from rites and from priests, let alone from the theology of the academics endlessly disputing the borderland between venial and mortal sin. 'What is the use of pompously debating obscure and hidden matters of which our knowledge or ignorance will be irrelevant on the day of judgement?' The question is typical of the Devotio's central book, the Imitation of Christ.

The distrust of reason which was so marked an emphasis in the Imitation of Christ was also in part responsible for a heightened interest in magic among scholars. To the mystic, reason put a false veil of human cleverness before the face of God. To the magician it screened out the flashes of light that, by leaping from the creator to the human soul, could give the individual something of the creator's power over nature. Magical powers were not only appropriate to the high status in the scale of creation which some strands in humanist thought granted to man but a way of strengthening by incantation, talismans and spell-like songs, man's spiritual nature. Humanism itself grew from the study of pagan books, but it would be difficult to show that outright paganism was any threat to the church. Little significance need be read into the case of the man who, in 1503 in Paris seized the host from the hands of the priest and declared that 'Jupiter and Hercules are the only true gods.' More significant, and immensely moving, is the account left by Fra Luca della Robbia of the last hours of Pierpaolo Boscoli, sentenced to death for his involvement in an assassination plot against the Medici in 1513. 'Rid me,' he pleaded, 'of the memory of Brutus, so that I may die a Christian.' The friar claimed that after wrestling all night to rescue Boscoli from the values of his humanist education he succeeded. And doubtless this is true. Given the religious temper of the age it was a very rare man whose last moments were filled by a vision of the Elysian Fields rather than of the Christian judgement day.

The study of antiquity could lead to more dispassionate views about the merit of other religious systems than the Christian. Thus Machiavelli could praise the valorous patriotism that Roman religion gave the soldiers of the Republic, thus Mutianus Rufus, who had been a classmate of Erasmus in the 1430s, could teach that the philosophy of the ancients and the religions of the Jews and of the Christians were but different reflections of the steady outpouring of God's divinity. And this comparative approach could shade into deism, as in Celtis:

> 'You marvel that I never move my lips in any church,
> Murmuring through my teeth in prayer.
> The reason is that the great divine will of Heaven
> Hears the small inner voice.
> You marvel that you so seldom see me
> Dragging my feet into the temples of the gods.
> God is within us. I do not need to meditate on Him
> In painted churches.'

But there was seldom any doubt as to where the priority lay in moments of stress, of war, of personal loss, or at the approach of death.

To these and other needs the church responded by allowing accretions to its teaching and to its practice and by attempting to reform its so easily identifiable faults hampered as always by its own immense vested interests, by the expectation of laymen that priests and monks should be conspicuously more virtuous than themselves, and, above all, by the thirst for certainties that no institution can actually demonstrate but can only be experienced by individuals.

7

The Arts and their Audience

Music

When da Gama's men went on shore after rounding the Cape of Good Hope they were greeted by natives playing a kind of flute, 'thus making a pretty harmony for negroes who are not expected to be musicians'. It was to be expected, however, that the seamen would be able to answer in kind, and they did. The early voyagers took trumpets and drums which were used to assist company keeping and to give signals in fog but also for recreation. Erasmus was not indulging in sentiment when he expressed the hope that New Testament stories would be sung at the spinning wheel and the plough. Music, from the simplest unaccompanied song to the choirs of cathedrals and the orchestras of princely courts, provided the most widely shared and, arguably at least, the most deeply felt of cultural pleasures.

No description of the feelings induced by looking at a work of art had the intensity of Andrea Calmo's reaction to a concert; 'as for the manner of singing, I have never heard anything better. God! what a beautiful voice, what style, what fullness, what diminuendoes, what suavity that would melt the hardest hearts.' Dürer noted that in Venice, in the course of another concert, the viol players themselves were moved to tears, and one of Leo X's chapel masters, Elzéar Genêt, resolved to renounce secular music altogether because of the danger of arousing the wrong passions too strongly. In similar vein a German prayerbook of 1509, accepting that its readers would 'sing during your work in house and field, at your seasons of prayer and devotion, in times of joy and in times of sorrow', added: 'good songs are agreeable to God, bad ones are sinful and must be avoided.' To elevate the mind, to ease the working day: the power, the utility, the universal popularity of music were taken for granted in a way notably different from the praise accorded any other form of artistic expression.

The inclusion of music in the *quadrivium* meant, of course, that every university graduate, and thus a fairly high proportion of those capable of expressing themselves freely in correspondence and books, was already equipped to discuss the nature and the effect of music, even though the music course was theoretical and did not necessarily involve any executant ability. But singing and learning to play an instrument was a normal part of the schooling of middling and upper class families. The instrument would most commonly have been the lute, the staple of the age's *Hausmusik*. Domestic keyboard instruments were less common, but most large churches and many great houses possessed an organ, and Rudolph Agricola can probably be taken as speaking for many travellers when he reported his pleasure at finding when visiting Ferrara that he was able to indulge his 'weakness for the organs'. Wind instruments, in the opinion of Castiglione, should be left to professionals, as carrying (the idea came from Aristotle's *Politics*) a taint of servility, and in the main they were.

From Portugal to Lithuania and Hungary, itinerant singers retailed old ballads and fresh news events in rough verses, accompanying themselves on a lute or a simple bowed fiddle, national epics jostling with the gossip of court and battlefield in a sort of musical journalism which reflected popular tastes and interests more faithfully than any other medium except, perhaps, the sermon. Students, journeymen, gild members, mercenary soldiers: each had repertoires of songs as specific as their clothing and occupations, songs which are still scarcely charted as an aspect of men's ability to identify themselves with the nature of their work, their relationship to other groups within the local community, through 'news' songs to authority, and through national epics cast in ballad form, to their country as a whole. So widespread was the dance – that other occasion for popular music making – that in parts of Spain and Italy dances were incorporated into religious ceremonies.

The occasions on which music was played were frequently public, interludes in mystery plays, for instance, or processions, or the celebration of a victory, an alliance or a peace treaty, and most towns of any size employed a town band of trumpeters, fife-players and drummers. In Antwerp they even gave regular evening concerts. But there is an abundance of evidence to show that music was taken for granted in the home as well. From 1501 printed music began to appear, much of it divided into separate books so that each performer could have his own part before him; dedications show that a great part of this printed music, both vocal and instrumental, was intended for private homes.

The pace for changes in style and expertise of execution was set by the orchestras and vocalists attached, as a matter of course, to noble households. There was much competition for the services of composers and instrumentalists; singers at the papal court under Leo X could command salaries at least as high as those paid to men of letters. Lorenzo de' Medici placed a memorial to the 'family' musician Squarcialupi in the Florentine cathedral. Maximilian actually knighted his court organist, Paul Hofheimer. It is not at all out of keeping with the prestige of music among the other arts that Leonardo, in a famous letter in which he attempted to recommend himself to Lodovico Sforza of Milan, while setting out his competence as painter, sculptor and military engineer, gave special prominence to his ability as a lute player. Leo X himself composed music, as did Henry VIII. A list of princes and monarchs who could play an instrument would indeed be wearisome, and the point is only worth making because there was none who could paint or sculpt or – with the possible exception of Lorenzo de' Medici, who submitted a design for the unfinished façade of the cathedral in Florence – had any competence as an architect. The plethora of music-making angels in art, the use of musical instruments as a theme in *intarsia* work, Raphael's S. Cecilia (formerly a rare subject), the existence of music academies, in the sense of performing and discussion groups, in Siena and Rome: these examples are a reminder of the part music played in a culture which has become famous in retrospect chiefly for the visual arts.

In Italy the emphasis in court music was above all secular, though some princes took a close interest in the quality of the music performed in their chapels. Elsewhere, however, most of all, perhaps, in Hungary and Bohemia and Spain, greater emphasis was placed on sacred music, though this remained, of course, the special province of the church itself. In England an interest in complex musical settings of the liturgy was so widespread, even in collegiate churches of a medium size, that Erasmus, the defender of the vocal ploughboy, was moved to remark of church music that 'they have so much of it in England that the monks attend to nothing else. A set of creatures who ought to be lamenting their sins fancy they can please God by gurgling in their throats.'

The move to a more harmonic treatment of music in this period lay behind the growth in the size of choirs, for more came to depend on the effect of massed voices. So in addition to inter-church musical rivalry, with its attendant chorister-poaching, there was an increased demand for boys and men as singers. Monastic and parish choirs and musicians not only made music inside churches and chapels, they walked in processions, went out to bless departing armies and celebrate returning ones. And regular church music was supplemented by choirs and instrumentalists supported by the lay confraternities, some of which, like the Antwerp confraternity of Our Lady, were wealthy enough to instal organs of their own in the chapels reserved for them.

In general, then, and taking both secular and sacred music into account, there were by the turn of the century both more individuals actively concerned with making music and more occasions for hearing it than ever before. It was, in addition, one of the great formative periods in the evolution of musical style, an evolution particularly identified with northern France and the Netherlands and with such composers as Ockeghem, Obrecht, Isaac, Mouton and Josquin des Prez, but affecting the composition of music in other countries through the migrancy of musicians and composers and, to a much lesser extent, through the circulation of printed scores. Interchange was particularly fruitful between the Netherlands and Italy. Italy lacked composers of real distinction, but its strong instrumental tradition was a stimulus to the hitherto more vocally oriented musicians of the north, and the existence of such centres as Milan, Florence, Mantua, Ferrara and Urbino offered a wider range of secular patronage than was available there. Obrecht, Isaac and Josquin all worked for a while in Florence.

Thanks to the printing press, the correspondence of musically minded humanists and the competition between courts and churches, the names and the personalities of players, singers and composers were widely known and discussed. The emphasis on instrumental improvisation, the emergence of a vocal connoisseurship in which the quality of an individual voice was matter for eager discussion: these factors, too, worked to a similar effect. Increasingly composers signed their works. Ockeghem's death in 1495 was mourned not only in works by fellow composers but in an epitaph by Erasmus. As in the other arts, there was a self-conscious attempt to break from earlier traditions, particularly from the deeply entrenched Gregorian chant, the principle of successive composition (as opposed to harmonic composition, in which the parts were imagined simultaneously) and the subordination of the sense of the words to the pattern of the music. And against the background of this desire for novelty, composers stood out in stronger personal relief, as in an Italian letter comparing Isaac with Josquin des Prez and praising the former more highly because 'he will compose new things more often'. And disputes between rival theorists helped to sustain the notion of music as an evolving art form. That between the Spaniard Bartolomé Ramos de Pareja and Franchino Gaffurio, who held the chair of music at Milan and was also director of music at the cathedral, led to a widespread taking of sides, especially when the dispute sank to the level of personal abuse, with Ramos accusing Gaffurio of not only being a bastard and a drunkard but of having a voice like a raven.

Interest, opportunity, itinerancy, printing: these help to explain the speed of diffusion of one of the chief advances of the period – thinking in terms of chords rather than of successively added layers. But the creation of a harmonic structure also depended on an invention, the musical score, which came into use in the 1480s, and on the added freedom given to composers by Ramos in that same controversial treatise, his *De Musica Tractatus* of 1482, by his urging that thirds and sixths should be treated as consonancies, a suggestion which the ear had hitherto rejected under the influence of the mind's acceptance of an argument based on purely mathematical reasoning. But it was also related to the other great advance, the use of music to express the whole range of human experience by allowing its texture to be determined by the meaning of words.

The Utopians were, as usual, in the van of progress. 'All their music,' wrote More, 'whether played on instruments or sung by the human voice, so renders and expresses the natural feelings, so suits the sound to the matter (whether troubled or mournful or angry), and so represents the meaning by the form of the melody that it wonderfully affects, penetrates and inflames the souls of the hearers.' As far as the song was concerned this was not, of course, a new principle. Student drinking songs had never sounded like dirges. And the Utopians had already been anticipated by Josquin and Ockeghem who had brought the echoing of natural feelings into the higher reaches of complex polyphony. The combination of a writing for voices that made it possible both to hear the words clearly and to be directed musically to their literal meaning, with a chordal approach that under-scored their emotional significance: this helped to make music the most satisfying of all the media that attempted to mirror human experience while obeying its own formal laws. From the secular fun of making voices bray like asses or instruments imitate birds, crickets or chattering women, to the new eloquence with which the themes of popular devotion, the suffering on the cross, the sorrows of the Virgin, the tribulations of Job, could be rendered, music's new versatility is essential to an understanding of the social role of late fifteenth and early sixteenth century culture.

It did not develop in isolation. The nature of the university syllabus, the existence of music-loving scholars and of musician-painters: music had obvious links with learning and the other arts. Its emotionalism may have reflected the desire for a more personal religion, the emphasis on music following meaning almost certainly reflected the humanists' emphasis on the properly established text and their knowledge that Greek music had been closely moulded to the poems it enhanced. In imagining the effect of a score as a whole rather than as an accumulation of detail, composers were running in parallel to the practice of painters and sculptors. The links can be sensed more readily than they can be identified, but there can be little doubt that the extent to which men were coming to think of 'culture', of their relationship to the product of a number of forms of creative expression, was primarily determined by music. Numerically, more men and women listened to music and made it than was true of any other art. Qualitatively, the actual effect of music on the individual appears to have been greater. The 'all round' man was encouraged by his education to be aware of all the arts, of culture as a whole, but it was more likely to be through the lute than through brush or chisel that he would gain any practical experience of the formal and technical problems all forms of advanced art have in common.

Drama

Second only to music in the number of people it affected, and the extent to which it moved them was the drama. The range of dramatic entertainment was wide. At one end of the scale was the dramatic monologue, a single actor telling a story or giving a mock sermon or impersonating a variety of characters and voices in what amounted to a one-man play. At the other was the street pageant which could involve changing the appearance of thoroughfares and squares and might employ a sizeable proportion of the population as extras. In the same way that great men maintained their own orchestras, they kept troupes of actors, usually small, from four to ten; like orchestras, these troupes could be lent to other notables or sent to provide entertainment at weddings, as when Henry VII's players were sent to Edinburgh for the marriage of James IV in 1503. Normally their task was to act short plays as 'interludes' between the successive acts of that characteristic court entertainment, the proto-masque, in which members of the court or patrician palace acted out an allegorical story, usually of love, but sometimes of a political nature.

There were numerically more amateur than professional performers in 'real' plays (that is, situations expressed largely in dialogue form), and when we add the numbers who took part in entertainments in which, while there was little dialogue but a strong emphasis on mime, impersonation, or in being part of an acted story, the parallel with music becomes clear: the drama was an art which at all levels of sophistication could reckon on a high level of self-identification with its procedures. 'Real' plays included the still vastly popular mysteries, essentially based on stories from the Bible or the lives of saints, but incorporating, usually for comic effect, a good deal of business and dialogue drawn from everyday secular life. Morality plays, usually variations on the theme of man's choice between virtue and vice but sometimes based on a stronger narrative element, like the story of patient Griselda, or of the virtuous Blanchefleur, who cut off her hands rather than marry her father, were increasingly popular; so were the farces which even more easily than the moralities could adapt themselves to satire and the inclusion of contemporary references.

Latin plays, usually comedies modelled on Terence and Plautus, were performed by amateurs at universities and at humanist courts. None has been thought to be of lasting literary value, but this cannot be said for the secular comedy based on the same models. Machiavelli's *Mandragola* (1518) is the first European play since classical times to combine satisfactory construction with flesh and blood characters, and, apart from a few impenetrable local references, its satire, directed chiefly against the bourgeoisie and the church, is couched in a dialogue to which no indulgence is required even today. *Mandragola* is surprisingly independent of any specific classical source, though the act divisions, a little of the machinery for getting the plot under way, and one or two of the characters owe a debt to Plautus. Even more interesting in showing how readily classical models could be updated into contemporary terms is the same author's slightly later comedy, *Clizia*, for while this is firmly based on Plautus' *Casina*, the tone is that of 1506, the year in which Machiavelli places it, and the play splendidly exemplifies his belief that 'the aim of a comedy is to hold up a mirror to domestic life'. No other source gives so realistic an account of a day in the life of an early sixteenth-century Florentine bourgeois than the speech in which Sofronia laments her husband's infatuation with a young girl.

'Anyone who knew Nicomaco a year ago and came across him today couldn't help being amazed by the great change that's come over him. He used to be thought dignified, responsible, sober. He passed his time worthily; got up early in the morning, heard Mass, ordered the day's food, and then saw to whatever business he had in town, at the market or the magistrates' office. If not, he either discussed some serious topic or other with a few friends or shut himself in his study at home to balance and tidy up his accounts. Then he dined happily with his family and after dinner talked to his son, gave him advice, helped him understand human nature, taught him how to live, in fact, with examples from past and present. Then he went out and spent the rest of the day either in business or in some sober and respectable recreation. Every evening he was home by dark, stayed with us a while by the fire if it was winter, then went into his study to look over his affairs, and three hours after sunset he had supper in the best of humours... But since he's had this girl on the brain, his affairs have been neglected, his farms are decaying, his trade going to ruin. He's always criticising, and doesn't know why; he comes in and out of the house a thousand times a day without knowing what he's meant to be doing, and at meal-times he's never there. If you speak to him he doesn't answer, or his answer is right off the point. The servants see this going on and laugh at him, and his son has lost all respect for him.'

In *Clizia*, as in the early plays of Ariosto and the *Calandria* of Bibbiena, a knowledge of classical comedy helps to give firmness to dramatic structure together with hints on how to get an anecdote (the core of the numerous *novelle* which since the days of Boccaccio had had a lively influence on the Italian farce) promoted to the length and variety of characters required by a play. But the urge to involve the audience in the familiar and contemporary was at least as strong as the desire to flatter them with classical reminiscence, and this pressure towards realism can be seen in all forms of drama. The appetite for allegory and moralising was still strong, but when Henry VIII got up impatiently and 'departed to his chamber' in the course of a morality acted by his own players he was making a gesture symbolic of a desire to experience drama as a mirror of society rather than as a translation of abstract debate from the pulpit or the dialectic class. And the demand was not only for psychological realism; audiences who had been content for generations to accept a tree as a forest, a fountain as a pleasure garden and a rudimentary castle as a whole realm, now wanted, and were given, stage settings which attempted to mirror the physical appurtenances of real life.

Where skilled craftsmen and artists – and money – was available, painted backgrounds and complex stage machinery were employed to create genuinely illusionistic settings, adding the delight of recognition to the exercise of imagination. As with music, the drama was both refining its own rules and taking a step towards its audience. These audiences were at their largest for the mystery plays. Attendance figures for a three-day marathon at Romans in 1509 were 4,780 for the first day, 4,220 for the second and nearly 5,000 for the third. Stage machinery for the mysteries could be really elaborate, with apparatus for raising large groups of martyrs into Paradise at the same time, rain-making machines and hell-mouths with real flames. Dummies stuffed with animal bones and entrails added a *frisson* to burnings at the stake and in a mystery at Bourges in which an unusual number of figures from classical mythology figured, Proserpina's costume was so devised that her breasts not only dripped blood but from time to time emitted sparks. To the same effect auditions were held for gild mysteries in order to achieve a convincing level of acting and clerics could obtain permission to grow beards while preparing their parts.

The rapid alternations between tragic and ribald moments in the mystery, which had been a traditional feature of their writing and took for granted an emotionally volatile audience in whom tears and guffaws could alternate quickly and naturally, gave little scope for psychological realism: the broad effect was the aim. However, there was a tendency to clarify the action by having more dialogue in fewer scenes, to develop characters in a life-like manner and to play down the element of the merely grotesque or the purely miraculous. In 1486, for instance, Jehan Michel undertook to up-date an earlier version of the Angers passion play. He lopped off the Old Testament scenes, eliminated one in which the purpose of salvation was debated (as being too rarified and scholastic), added spice to the character of Judas by making him kill his father and marry his mother and added pathos to that of the Magdalen. After questioning those who had already seen Jesus about his age, complexion and the colour of his eyes, she decides to seduce him and goes to hear him teach in her most alluring costume. After trying in vain to attract his attention she falls under the spell of his words and his message and, moved by guilt and repentance dissolves into tears. Describing the comparable Alsfeld passion (1501), Kuno Franke wrote that 'in characters and scenes like these, the Christian legend, we feel, has come to be entirely acclimatised to German city life . . . it has come to be a perfect expression of the personal experience of the average citizen of those days.'*

The organisation of the mystery play was largely in the hands of the average citizen, though it may have been written or modified by a learned cleric. All gild or craft members responsible for particular scenes or series of episodes were expected to help pay for them. The timing of their performance, commonly once a year, was also deter-mined by moments of urgent local feeling: the need to intercede for rain, to beg God to keep the plague away or to give thanks for a good harvest. But the pace of revision and the nature of newly composed cycles were probably affected by texts being printed and widely read; comparisons could be made and tradition overcome in the interest of a demand for up-to-date realism difficult to achieve as long as the text was a quasi-sacred manuscript locked up in the gild headquar-ters.

Half way, as an art form, between the procession or cavalcade and the mystery cycle, the pageant was a dramatic entertainment using

---

* *Personality in German Literature before Luther* (Harvard, 1916) 137.

whole areas of a city as a theatre. In a procession, men were no more than resplendently themselves and the onlookers were merely watchers. In the pageant, though there was little dialogue on the stages set up at street corners or on flat well-heads along a thoroughfare, and there was much dependence on allegory and the formal speech, the mood was genuinely theatrical in that those taking part were representing someone other than themselves, and the onlookers, as they moved from tableau to tableau, were moved to an exercise of the imagination quite different from that involved in watching the familiar city fathers and a bishop or two pass by. A closer analogy would be the carnival, for then the instinct to take on a disguise, particularly strong in cultures with a demanding moral code and a sharply differentiated class structure, was open not only to those formally ensconced on pageant-cars but to others: a privilege granted grudgingly by civic authorities but when granted, as at Nuremberg for the annual *Schembartlauf*, savagely defended. Partly because of police control (masks and uncharacteristic clothing were associated with crime) and partly because they were usually mounted for a visiting dignitary, pageants were decorous affairs and the vast majority of the population had to be content with seeing only the actors and the streets themselves in disguise, but that was enough to generate a sense of theatre.

Thus from the toga-ed Latin play performed before select audiences – plays in which princes themselves might take a part, as did the Emperor Maximilian and his successor Charles – to the mystery and the pageant, a very large proportion of the men who commissioned, or simply looked at paintings and sculpture, together with the artists themselves, were familiar with at least some forms of dramatic entertainment.

Art

The connection between artists and the drama is in one sense straightforward. Andrea del Sarto painted theatrical sets, Leonardo produced pageant designs, Pontormo decorated some of the triumphal cars with which Florence celebrated the news of Giovanni de' Medici's elevation to the papacy as Leo X in 1513. The mystery of the passion produced twice a year in Vienna was directed by the prominent sculptor Rollinger. Dürer's Triumphal Arch woodcut was the echo on a flamboyant scale of the specially constructed arches where visiting potentates received addresses of welcome.

Less straightforward is the connection between the drama and the overall effect of the visual arts. There was a comparability of effect, at least, between the *tableaux vivants* of actors posed against a painted background which were dispersed along a pageant route and the way in which painters placed their characters – in an Annunciation, a Birth of the Virgin or a Last Supper – in an enclosed space. The feeling for unity and enclosure is very similar. In all likelihood the feeling for unity of setting had originally passed from painting to the stage, but it is possible that an interest in psychological realism had passed the other way, that painters had been aided in their expression of grief or anguish or expectancy by watching actors. A more important link, perhaps, was the attitude not of those who produced but those who paid for works of art. All, again, whether wealthy individuals, gilds or city fathers, were used to seeing men acting in the familiar stories of the Bible or the lives of the saints, or in the moralities and secular farces. They were used, in fact, to looking carefully at actual bodies in repose or movement, as though in an activated work of art. Passing then from the acted to the painted scene they might demand that the painted figures should be lifelike; they would certainly be able to follow an artist's intentions if this were his aim because the drama would have helped to break down the notion that painted figures and real people had to be looked at from different points of view. And the breaking down of this notion allowed the patron's eye to follow the artist's intention when he went against straightforward imitation of life in the interest of idealisation or deliberate distortion. Whatever other motives, then, prompted an artist's treatment of the human figure – a desire to imitate a description of an antique painting, a pre-occupation with musculature, reaction against a predecessor or a rival, or the desire to produce by selection the perfect and therefore unrealistic image – he was freed to follow his bent by purchasers visually trained by the theatre.

It is worth bearing in mind the ability of music to move men to tears and the endurance of mystery-playgoers (three days was by no means exceptional for a cycle), for the records of direct responses to works of painting or sculpture are thin. De Beatis' reaction to seeing the van Eyck altarpiece in Ghent was, indeed, enthusiastic: 'this painting, done in oils, is executed with so much perfection and life-likeness, there is so great a harmony between its parts, the flesh-tints are so well rendered, that one can say without any doubt that this is the most beautiful work in Christendom.' But it was also exceptional. Celtis ignored painting and sculpture in his long description of Dürer's own city. Machiavelli says nothing of his fellow-citizen Leonardo – or of any other artist.

That painting could have an effect comparable to that of music we can infer from Savonarola's inveighing against portrayals of religious scenes in which physical beauty arouses unspiritual feelings. Possibly Pollaiuolo's nudes at Arcetri were covered with whitewash under his influence. In a similar vein Erasmus recommended in the *Education of a Christian Prince* 'that artists should represent a prince in the dress and manner that befits a wise and serious prince...The princely halls should be adorned with wholesome pictures...instead of those which inculcate wantonness, vainglory or tyranny.' And Cortese, writing his description of how the ideal cardinal should live, stressed that in his bedroom he should only hang pictures which should provide him with some virtuous subject for meditation as he opened his eyes.

One source of a general interest in the arts was civic pride. Cristoforo Landino in 1481 cited Florence's painters and architects as one cause for the city's great repute. Felix Faber, writing about a new church in his description of Ulm, his own city, proudly remarked that 'it is larger than any other parish church...and more majestic than most cathedrals' and, though he does not dare compare it with Santa Sophia in Constantinople, nevertheless 'our church is more beautiful than all others.' And he went on to cite a third reason for its uniqueness: 'there are more altars here than in all other parish churches, for it has fifty-one altars, all well provided and fully recognised; and they are fitted out not by princes or strangers but by the citizens of Ulm themselves.'

This system of allocating chapels and altars to individual families or to gilds and lay confraternities did much to extend an interest in the paintings and sculpture with which they were furnished. Patronage was not restricted to the clergy responsible for a particular church, but extended fairly widely into the community, from patricians to artisans. In some places gilds were made responsible for the upkeep of a church as a whole, its furnishing and alteration, and as gild officials commonly served on a rotating basis, this extended the number of individuals who would have to make a decision bearing on a work of art. Possibly public taste was educated by municipal commissions like the decoration of the Hall of the Great Council of Venice in 1480; that such commissions were sometimes open to public competition (the design of a façade for the Florentine cathedral in 1489 is an example) was another occasion for general comment and debate.

The rival workshops themselves, largely family concerns, but taking on youths from outside who wished to become painters or sculptors, acted as stimuli to keeping abreast with change. Moreover, though some works, portraits in the main, but an increasing number of other subjects, especially mythological ones, like Botticelli's Birth of Venus and Spring, were designed for private houses, this was still a time when works of art, however *avant garde*, were put at once before the general public, in churches, public buildings or in the courtyards of the quasi-public palaces of the rich. And the novelty of the style of an artist like Botticelli was never entirely kept exclusively for the eyes of collectors; all artists had work in the public domain as well. In a city the size of Florence the artists and their assistants were well known, their patrons familiar figures, the subject of political and personal gossip, and works of art were painted or eased into place for all to see. And a more positive point can be made. This was a time when woodcuts and engravings, especially from the presses of the Netherlands, Germany and Italy, were widely available to those who could not afford paintings of their own. Engravings could be expensive – some of Lucas van Leyden's large ones cost a gold florin apiece. Some prints were undoubtedly bought by fellow artists – thus Dürer's Apocalypse woodcuts influenced painters in France and Italy, even in Russia, and he in turn was influenced by the prints of Schongauer and Jacopo de Barbari. Some were no doubt nailed to the wall as icons, cheap substitutes for wooden crucifixes or carved saints, rather than as works of art, many, indeed, aspired to no more aesthetic an end. But prints were bought in large numbers, and they too could help keep the eye up to date and spread a familiarity with contemporary styles, as in the woodcuts reflecting the manner of Botticelli and Domenico Ghirlandaio which were produced in large numbers in Florence. Because they were for the most part produced outside the normal system of patronage they could represent the intentions of an artist in a free and personal way only surpassed (because they had to be saleable) by the drawing an artist did for its own sake, or to help him towards a painting. When all this has been said, however, and if we accept that there were known tastes for which artists catered – the love of violence for which woodcuts of carnage and monsters were produced, the pietism which Perugino for some years mechanically satisfied – it is likely that even in art centres like Florence, Antwerp or Vienna the number of men capable of being actually moved by a painting or other work of art for its own sake was far smaller than those who could be affected by music or the drama. On the other hand the degree of familiarity with what was going on meant that artists were dealing with a tolerant audience capable of taking stylistic change and personal eccentricity in its stride. The period 1480–1520 saw crucial changes in the painting, sculpture and architecture of Italy, France, Germany and the Netherlands, significant ones in England and Spain and at least isolated changes in Poland and Russia. But there was virtually no vandalism, no public outcry. It is not known what paintings (if any), drawings and prints perished in the Savonarolan bonfires of vanities. The protest was, in any case, against lascivious subject matter, not against any novelty of style.

The acceptance of works of art in public places was aided by their subject matter. Treatment changed, but the themes – saints and nativities in churches, political allegories and portraits in town halls – remained familiar. Scenes from ancient history and mythology were painted for the homes of individual enthusiasts. Though sarcophagi and other fragments of Roman statuary were to be seen in the towns of Italy and southern France, and though every pilgrim to Rome could see the collection of classical sculpture on the Capitol which Sixtus IV had opened to the public, the infrequency of prints and the absence of really clumsy paintings of classical subjects suggests that only the well-to-do chose to commission classical themes. Again, if there was little in the public domain to startle through its subject matter, there was also no significantly new demand made on the intellect. So far from playing down the symbolic content of medieval art, the increasing mastery of realism among the painters of the fifteenth century made the use of symbols even more exact and complex. No medieval work included so many symbolic objects as did Dürer's *Melancolia* engraving, nor so many allusions to layers of meaning as can be teased out of Leonardo's *Last Supper*. But because a realistic technique concealed symbol and allegory within an apparently naturalistic scene it was possible to enjoy the result without feeling that a challenge was being made to learning or ingenuity. Not that popular audiences were incapable of seeing more than the surface significance of a painting. Sermons frequently used the fourfold interpretation of scripture, literal, allegorical, moral and mystical. When noticing that Leonardo had divided the Apostles into four groups about Christ, not only the monks who ate in the refectory of the monastery of S. Maria delle Grazie where it was painted would have been reminded of the multiple significance of the words spoken by Christ as he referred to the bread and wine before him, but such a way of seeing the painting could have occurred to large numbers of their visitors. So pervasive was the doctrine that a man's health was determined by another four-fold formula, the balance of the humours, that many would have discerned another layer of significance; that the groups represented the choler, phlegm, sanguineness and melancholy that could only be perfectly reconciled in the perfect man.* On the other hand, the painting's chief impact must have been as an ennobled slice of life, the record of an event.

---

* I take these points from an article by Edgar Wind published in *The Listener* (May 8, 1952).

The youthful appearance of the Virgin in Michelangelo's Pietà would not have surprised those who went to worship in St. Peter's. Through sermons, tabernacles and earlier paintings, they were familiar with the telescoping of Christ's birth with the death and sacramental promise which was the whole point of God being made flesh at all. The Virgin's youth was merely a particularly poignant way of connecting the beginning and the end of the most oft-told of all stories. And in the nearby Sistine Chapel, Michelangelo's painting of the creation of Eve would have been seen not only as an 'event' but as a step in a process that inevitably led God to create a 'New Eve', the Virgin, who would enable God to re-enter his creation in person and give it the possibility of salvation. The notion that events in the New Testament had been prefigured, foreshadowed, by events in the Old was a commonplace of sermons and devotional literature and had been given wide circulation through such illustrated books as the so-called *Bible of the Poor* and the *Mirror of Human Salvation*. This is not to say that the average pilgrim would have caught the nature of Michelangelo's personal involvement or of the intellectual programme that helped him to give visual unity to the ceiling scheme as a whole. It is probable, however, that the mastery of naturalistic techniques combined with the continuing habit of assuming that everything could stand for something else either as a symbol (the rabbit for sensuality) or as a personification (David as courage powered by a sense of right) or as an allegory (the scarlet feather of the goldfinch clasped in the Christ child's hand an anticipation of the blood of the passion), led to a religious art more meaningful than any that had preceded it. The urge to identification through psychological and physical realism was catered for without alienating the mystical temperament that sought for deeper and deeper meanings under mere appearance.

Really esoteric art was largely restricted to Italy, was secular (the paintings of Bosch are a rare example of a minority, possibly 'secret' approach to religion finding visual expression) and outside the public domain. The humanist interest in rare texts and Hermetic and hieroglyphic *curiosa* led to a proliferation of images that could be understood only by the highly cultivated, by those who could spot the classical reference or see the appropriateness of an image to a specific individual. For the most part these works were medals, designed to be exchanged among friends and equals, or plaquettes. And even they sprang naturally, though in antique guise, from the heraldic habit of identifying the essence of an individual in a crest and a motto.

Such designs were not left to the sculptor or goldsmith. Indeed, with very few exceptions, such as technical exercises like the Medusa's head attributed by Vasari to Leonardo or the 'fake' antique cupid similarly attributed to the young Michelangelo, all paintings and works of sculpture were the result of direct commission. Monasteries, confraternities, gilds, city councils and individuals ordered works of art by contract unless the artist chosen happened to be in the permanent employ of the patron. This commonly specified the price, the materials to be used, the size of the work, the time by which it should be finished, and the subject. Sometimes the terms were vague, barely naming (say) the saints who were to be included in an altarpiece; occasionally, as in the contract for Ghirlandaio's frescoes in S. Maria Novella for the Tornabuoni family, the subject matter was spelled out more methodically. Very rarely there is a reference to a preparatory sketch which the finished work is to follow or to another painting which it is to resemble. What is particularly interesting about these contracts as a whole is that while they emphasise the economic dependence of the artist on the patron (an advance is often asked for the purchase of expensive colours, almost always for stone or marble) and his dependence on the patron's choice of subject, there is scarcely any stated limitation to the artist's freedom to adopt whatever style he wants. And at a time when an artist could change his style as abruptly as did Botticelli after his contact with Savonarola, or evolve through a series of styles as Raphael did in a prodigious spurt from a timid Peruginism through various phases of a grandly harmonious classicism to an anticipation of Mannerist distortion, the choice of a particular artist was not in itself a guarantee of a particular style. That patrons could accept the lowest bid among offers from painters with widely differing styles is another indication that style was considered less important than subject.

On the other hand too much must not be read into these contracts. Marriage settlements, after all, do not say anything about love. Julius II clung to Michelangelo at his most recalcitrant because he admired his particular approach to painting and sculpture, Isabella d'Este pursued the reluctant Giovanni Bellini because she liked the way he painted. And both men were pioneers, the nature of whose next work was to some extent incalculable. The Ghirlandaio brothers were kept busy because the Florentine particians liked the way they combined realistic portraiture with grave but somehow aristocratic grouping and setting. Jean Perréal and Jean Clouet were the portraitists favoured by the French court because they seemed to strike the right note between naturalism and decorum. The wealthy merchants of Augsburg supported Hans Burgkmair because his work had the Italian flavour which was then becoming fashionable. And in urban centres with an educated court or bourgeoisie the favour of patrons was likely to be given to those slightly ahead of stylistic tradition.

Modishness, no doubt, played a part in this. Men who went to great pains to procure the latest fashions in clothing and armour were likely to wish to be pace-setters in their artistic purchases as well. More important, however, was the fact that certain of the stylistic intentions that led to change were well suited to reflect attitudes that had been formed by the education and manner of life of wealthy and influential men. This was above all true of Italy. By the late fifteenth century painters and sculptors were in a position to draw together the threads of the experimental and sometimes quirkish generations that had preceded them: experiments in perspective, anatomy, emotional expressiveness, monumentality. During those same generations, under the influence of humanism (meaning, in this context, chiefly the ideas of Cicero and Quintilian and the *Lives* of Plutarch) and, to a lesser extent, of chivalry, the governing class had evolved a newly self-conscious image of itself. With due allowance for difference of place and function this image emphasised a glossing over of vocational preoccupations, a spacious hospitality to ideas, an imperturbable confidence in the face of adversity and a calculated ease of manner, a carrying lightly of varied accomplishments.

In the course of the late fifteenth and early sixteenth centuries the evolution of style in art led to a fairly close echoing of this style in life. There was a seeking for the broad, spatially coherent effect, an absence of fussiness, a concealment of the means whereby the overall impression had been gained, a portraiture that (master now of straightforward copying from nature) sought to reveal the working of the intellect; the human figure, supremely at ease whether in an architectural or a landscape setting, was ennobled and idealised. It was an approach through which patrons could find an enhancement of their own image of themselves and their relationship to the social world. The meeting of these two styles is symbolised by the friendship between Raphael and Castiglione (who had already drafted *The Courtier* before he met the painter), the 'perfect' painter and his counterpart the perfect gentleman. Raphael's art had the quickness of perception, the harmonious wholeness, the unpedantic dignity, the searching for the ideal, above all the sense of ease in accomplishment which Castiglione praised in the mind and behaviour of his courtier. This 'high Renaissance style' with its lofty harmoniousness, its tactful idealisation of man and the setting of his life did, doubtless, fit the feeling of a class about itself. But it also owed something to a deliberate return to the principles of an art produced in quite different social circumstances, to Giotto and Masaccio, carefully studied by Michelangelo and the only painters mentioned by Leonardo as being worthy of imitation. And so strong were the instincts of artists to evolve their own styles in terms of learning from and rejecting other styles that within twenty years of Dürer's learning from Leonardo, Pontormo was rejecting the 'high Renaissance style' with the aid of some of the more Gothic of Dürer's prints.

The patron was, however, still necessary to the artist. The time had not come when he could paint or sculpt to please himself in the hope that someone would buy his wares. Patrons could not give the impulse that made an artist radically change direction in the aims he was trying to achieve. But they could foster, give publicity to and encourage imitation of these changes, and give especially challenging opportunities or especially sympathetic support to individuals. Moreover, artist and patron were able to talk a shared language. Ideas like the dignity of man, his creative talent, the concept that there is a norm, an ideal beauty implicit in every face and object which the artist can aspire to see in his mind, that there are laws governing the beauty possible to a work of art which reflect the laws that determine the harmony of the cosmos: these were by now common property. It is likely that behind the bleak bones of a contract we should see conversations in which patron and artist, with or without the intervention of a learned go-between, would discuss not only the subject of a painting but to some extent the spirit in which it was to be executed.

Artists were literate men. In 1503 Leonardo possessed one hundred and sixteen books, an unusually large library for any private individual, and while most of these were concerned with conveying information, about medicine and mathematics, for example, he had books of poetry, including Pulci and Burchiello, and examples of the most popular form of contemporary escape literature, the chivalric romance. Though this was an exceptional case, the workshop, with its variety of occupations from coats of arms and trousseau chests to monuments and fresco cycles, was a lively environment, not far removed in mood from the printer's shop – to which, through engraving and woodcut it might, indeed, be linked. Personal rivalry among apprentices and inter-workshop rivalry gave an edge to an artist's training, an edge sharpened by the challenge of new techniques like painting in oil instead of tempera (still unusual in Italy in the 1480s) or drawing in chalks and by the desire for self-education beyond the training available in the workshop. The example in the middle of the fifteenth century of Leon Battista Alberti, who combined noble blood, humanist scholarship and executive brilliance as an architect and sculptor, had been of enduring importance. He had written treatises on painting, sculpture and architecture. He had shown that art could be learned and that learned men could, indeed should, take an interest in the arts. The result was to encourage the artist's increasing sense of the importance of his own personality and the intellectual value of his calling. Travel for the purpose of improving technique and absorbing the atmosphere of a more advanced milieu – the motives which took Dürer to Venice and Raphael from Urbino to Florence – became more frequent. But artists sought to cultivate their minds as well in the service of their art. Raphael was considered competent to draw up a report on the condition of the ancient monuments of Rome and make suggestions for their preservation. The aged Piero della Francesca wrote a treatise on perspective, Leonardo compiled material for a treatise on painting. Dürer published works on geometry and military engineering. The mathematician Luca Pacioli in his *De divina proportione* went out of his way to praise the ability with which painters like Giovanni Bellini, Melozzo da Forlì, Botticelli and Filippino Lippi applied their knowledge of mathematical theory to their art. Humanism's chief gift to art was the idea of the individual's creative power. From this followed a stress on originality, the ability to 'pour out new things which had never before been in the mind of any other man', as Dürer phrased it. By 1520 the artist had become so independent that Isabella d'Este could complain of 'these wayward masters' who 'either refuse to execute or else render inaccurately.'

Certainly the age of the artist as working for the eye of God, self-abnegatingly polishing details that would never be seen, or seen but dimly by the eye of man, was long past. A commission for a German tabernacle in 1493 contains such phrases as 'its base shall be worked out solidly but not expensively, since not much of it can be seen under the gallery...The main body...shall be made throughout with the finest and purest craftmanship, since it will be most fully exposed to the beholder's eye.' The rest, however, 'shall likewise be made well and solidly but yet not so subtly as the lower parts, for it will be placed higher up and not so clearly visible to the beholder.' And Dürer wrote with considerable sharpness to a patron who insisted that he should paint every one of a hundred figures in a picture with equally laborious detail. 'Whoever heard of making such a work for an altarpiece? No one could see it.'

He also made the point that, if he followed the patron's wishes, 'in my whole life time I should never finish it'. The remark not only illustrates the artist's vision of his career as a continual series of opportunities for self-improvement and experiment, but carries a characteristic note of independence. It was a common practice for painters to 'sign' their works, though as this was done in formal lettering on a scroll or on some architectural feature of the painting, the aim may have been to provide an advertisement for the artist's workshop rather than simply proclaim the work as his own. Another indication of increased self-confidence was the practice, particularly common in Italy, of including a self-portrait in a picture or fresco, or, more rarely, a small scale replica of one of the artist's own paintings. Dürer's preoccupation with himself and his progress was reflected in a series of independent self-portraits, beginning with a drawing at the age of thirteen, and in the consistency with which he dated his engravings.

By means of engravings and drawings, the travels of artists and the increasing traffic of diplomats and soldier-patrons to Italy after 1494, Italian ideas became diffused throughout the rest of Europe. The export of Italian paintings was not very important in this period; far more influential was the sending of Raphael's tapestry cartoons – supreme representations of the 'high' style – to Brussels, where the actual weaving was to be done. The atelier in which they were housed became for a while the Brancacci chapel of the north. But one of the reasons why Italian visual ideas were accepted was that they did *not* all represent this style. The degree of individual and regional difference in the peninsula – some due to the import of northern works and the employment of northern painters earlier in the fifteenth century – made it possible for artists to borrow from Italy according to their own needs.

The process of diffusion was slow and by no means uniform. In cities like Nuremberg, Munich and Cracow, for example, where a native tradition in sculpture was still evolving strongly according to its own rules, the Italian example was rejected. An Antwerp Italian painting failed to appeal to painters who were working out a novel manner of their own. Moreover there was a quite widespread move in the Netherlands to reinvigorate art by a return to the principles underlying *their* great masters of the early fifteenth century, Van Eyck, the Master of Flémalle and Petrus Christus. In Germany Grünewald, though unmistakably a painter of the early sixteenth century, drew his inspiration from looking back to the devotional art of the late fourteenth century rather than across to Italy. Indeed, the serenity which characterised the bulk of Italian religious art constituted a bar to the many painters and sculptors who wished to express strong devotional impulses of their own; the Gothic had two elements which could communicate intensity of religious feeling: a realistic, caricatural strain which could be applied to the human face and body, and a curvilinear decorative strain which could be forced into patterns of unease and anguish. Raphael, amid the classical remains of Rome, could dismiss Gothic as 'out of all reason' and lacking in 'grace', but to those who had grown up with it, it was still capable of development. Around 1500, from England to Poland and from the Baltic to the Straits of Gibraltar, Gothic was the truly international style, responding freely to local temperament and, largely because of the diffusion of Netherlandish (including Burgundian) influence, capable of containing a wealth of carefully observed detail. The prestige of Italian culture was higher among scholars than among artists. It was natural that French painters like the Master of Moulins, Jean Hay and Perréal himself (who had met Leonardo in Milan) should look first and foremost to their neighbour schools at Ghent and Bruges rather than to Venice or Rome. And in countries like Spain and Russia, where the subject matter of art was almost exclusively religious – especially in the former, where the crusading mood had been kept alive by the long wars against the Moors and, subsequently, missionary work in the New World – Italian influence penetrated very slowly. Without a knowledge of how Italian art had developed throughout the fifteenth century or of an acquaintance with the theory that underlay it, non-Italian artists took from it chiefly decorative details, the notion of the nude-for-its-own-sake, or lessons in how to portray mythological scenes for which a demand was growing outside Italy. The few attempts to imitate the overall manner of Italian painting – such as Mabuse's after his visit to Italy in 1508 – lacked any vitally imagined life of their own.

For want of a northern Vasari, little is known about the private lives of non-Italian artists. Wealth and social prestige was, as we have seen, possible. When Memling died in Bruges in 1494 he was among the city's richest men. That Jean Fouquet had painted – in enamel – his self-portrait, possibly indicates something like the personal self-consciousness so common in Italy. Perréal prided himself on being a poet and on having some knowledge of astronomy and philosophy; but he had what was possibly a unique personal acquaintance with artists in Italy. It is doubtful that among non-Italian artists as a whole there was either the desire for or the ability to take advantage of the educational process taken for granted in Italy. The fame that Fra Bartolommeo gained for himself and the workshop in the monastery of S. Marco in Florence which he directed, is in sharp contrast to the diagnosis offered by a fellow friar of Hugo van der Goes' attacks of pathological depression: 'since he was only human – as are all of us – the various honours, visits and accolades that came to him made him feel very important. Thus, since God did not want him to perish, He in His compassion sent him this humiliating disease which indeed made him very contrite.'

And if the educational atmosphere in which painters and sculptors worked outside Italy made it difficult for them to sympathise with the principles underlying Italian art, the difficulty was still greater for achitects. Outside Italy, architecture was largely in the hands of men trained as masons and serving their apprenticeship in the great cathedrals which were still being built in the Gothic style, Cologne and Tours among them, or in Gothic parish churches such as the one so praised by Felix Faber. Most of the influential Italian architects were, on the other hand, men who had never been trained to place one stone upon another. Bramante, Raphael, Michelangelo all were invited to turn to architecture after establishing themselves as painters. Fra Giocondo started as a scholar. Only Giuliano and Antonio da San Gallo appear to have been professional architects from an early age.

In Italy, therefore, architects inherited the theoretical interests considered appropriate to painters and the conditioning of painting itself by architectural settings which could afford to be pedantically classical because nobody but painted people had to live in them. In practice they looked chiefly to the sturdy regional architecture of the peninsula and to the Romanesque, which had adapted Roman architecture to Christian use, rather than to Rome itself, though they might rationalise space according to classical principles of harmony and add decorative detail modelled on ancient buildings. Bramante's St. Peter's or the Strozzi Palace in Florence were 'classical' in style, but they were by no means classical reconstructions. This meant that Italian architecture was particularly difficult to copy; its elements, though formally unified, were so disparate – extending, indeed, to Byzantine models as represented by S. Marco in Venice. To visit St. Peter's was not necessarily to grasp the point of its design.

Architecture, moreover, was necessarily the most conservative of the arts because it involved the greatest cash outlay and because it had to be suited to local climatic conditions and living habits. The arched colonnade, the steeply enclosed central courtyard: these features, among the first to reflect classical influence in Italy, were simply not suited to colder climates. Nor was the round church, favoured by Bramante and Giuliano da Sangallo, readily exportable: it depended on Italianate theory in that it attempted to reflect the mathematical perfection inherent in God the Father rather than the pathos and promise of the cross, and it harked back to an Italian medieval fashion for round detached baptisteries.

The part of Italy most visited by northern patrons was Milan: the first staging post in the numerous invasions of the peninsula. There 'classical' architecture was little more than the plastering of an exuberant wealth of antique detail on to a moderately adapted vernacular style of building. And this, in fact, was about as far as Italian influence in the north was to go. At the Château de Gaillon, as in Wolsey's Hampton Court, Italianate detail was applied to a native fabric. The same was true of Margaret of Austria's palace at Malines. As in painting and sculpture, strong and congenial native architectural traditions existed. The influence of Italy was shown in a rich man's library long before it seriously affected the building that housed it.

8

Secular Learning

The Appeal of Humanism

By origin the study of ancient texts, by extension an educational programme based on certain of them, particularly those concerned with history, moral philosophy and rhetoric: by the late fifteenth century it is possible to describe humanism as a state of mind. Alongside the discovery and editing of texts, and the use of them as educational tools, the outlines of a great civilisation had emerged, vast in extent and time. No doubt the rise and decline first of Athens and then of Rome had reflected the Christian God's will, but the Greeks and Romans had been unaware of it, and this enabled those who disinterred and read their narratives to see antiquity in its own terms. The present had come, as it were, to possess an *alter ego*. In addition to the inhabitants of the heavenly city of God, men could now imagine a society like their own, lacking only the compass, printing, gunpowder, the papacy and the Americas: a society which, thanks to time's winnowing of its more trivial sources and monuments, appeared to have been peopled by an intellectual and creative master-race. Whatever there was to do, in philosophical speculation, political action or cultural achievement appeared to have been done, and done with a supreme vigour and accomplishment, among a people whose history not only had the clarity of distance in time but the wholeness of a completed cycle, from obscurity through world empire to barbarian chaos.

Text by text, as the imaginative reconstruction of the ancient world proceeded, the relevance of this *alter ego* had become clearer. Their words no longer obscure, their personalities restored, replaced in the context of their own society, the appeal of the authors the Middle Ages had known, Plato, Aristotle, Virgil, Cicero and Ovid, became stronger than ever, and they had been joined by a host of others. The impact of so many minds on men who read them not merely with admiration for their knowledge or their particular expertise, but as models from whom to learn about statecraft, the waging of war, the creation of works of art and the more important art of bearing up under adversity: this impact had made humanism into a cultural force. It was not simply the perusal of neglected manuscripts but purposeful communication with a race of illustrious forbears. Machiavelli was not a professional humanist: he could not edit a Latin text (though in the *Discourses on Livy* he commented on one), he was not capable of teaching the humanities, but the tone of humanism sounds clearly enough in the most famous of his letters. Sore with political disappointments, he described his exile from affairs to his still busily employed friend, Francesco Vettori, in 1513. His days are spent hobnobbing with rustics, but 'when evening comes I return home and go into my study. On the threshold I strip off my muddy, sweaty, workaday clothes, and put on the robes of court and palace, and in this graver dress I enter the antique courts of the ancients and am welcomed by them, and there again I taste the food that alone is mine, and for which I was born. And there I make bold to speak to them and ask the motives of their actions, and they, in their humanity, reply to me. And for the space of four hours I forget the world, remember no vexation, fear poverty no more, tremble no more at death: I pass indeed into their world.'

Though the great period of textural discovery was over, humanism was still in a phase of pioneering enthusiasm. 'It is undoubtedly a golden age' Ficino wrote in 1492, 'which has restored to light the liberal arts that had almost been destroyed: grammar, eloquence, poetry, sculpture, music.' This secular millenarianism, this belief in the importance and the possibility of cultural regeneration was no longer a chiefly Italian phenomenon. Italy still attracted those who wished to learn from her, but their attitude, as we have seen, was one of growing independence. The Alps, besides, had never been a cultural boundary: ideas migrated at a pace determined not by nature but by the readiness of individuals and societies to accept them, and that readiness was quickened by the evidence of creative vigour in native vernacular culture as well as in classical scholarship. Florence was experiencing a 'golden age' because the Italian poetry of Lorenzo de' Medici, the sculpture of Verrochio and Benedetto da Maiano and the painting of Botticelli, Filippino Lippi and many others proved a breadth of vitality which could take advantage of the advice proffered from antiquity. Von Hutten, in a letter to Pirckheimer in 1518, referring to the Frenchmen Lefèvre and Budé and to the humanists of his own country, exclaimed 'Oh century! Oh letters! It is a joy to be alive! Studies thrive and minds flourish! Woe to you, Barbarians! Accept the noose, look forward to exile!' His optimism was buoyed up by Germany's greatest surge of creative vigour in literature and the arts before the eighteenth century. Educated in the Low Countries at a time when the church music of the Netherlands was an example to the rest of Europe, later a friend of Holbein, Erasmus, too, was expressing a hope that the humanities would refresh the quality of life at a time when the tide of creativity was running high; 'the world is coming to its senses as if awaking out of a deep sleep.'

For Erasmus and von Hutten humanism was a calling in of the wisdom of the old world to redress the values of the new. In northern Europe, the values that were felt most to need correction were those that concerned the religious life. Referring to the teaching of the New Testament, Erasmus emphasised that 'this sort of philosophy is rather a matter of disposition than of syllogisms, rather of life than of disputation... Moreover, though no one has taught this so absolutely and effectively as Christ, yet also in pagan books much may be found that is in accordance with it.' He was expressing what Ficino and Pico had written about more esoterically and Raphael – through the room in the Vatican where The Dispute about the Sacrament faced The School of Athens – had expressed in paint. It was primarily the Italian humanists' search for an accord between the teaching of the ancients and of Christ that enabled classical studies to be accepted as having a useful task to perform in countries which, by the late fifteenth century, had as yet made only a small contribution to the study of texts or the imaginative reconstruction of the ancient world: England, Spain, Portugal and Poland, countries where humanist studies were undertaken primarily because they were seen as relevant to the study of scripture.

One example will show the nature of the relevance that the achievements of antiquity were felt to have in other fields. The chapters on ancient art in Pliny's *Natural History* served not only as a statement of classical ideals but as an encouraging affirmation of tendencies that were already developing from the demands made on painters by their patrons and from their aesthetic and technical concern for their work. The strain of realism found ample backing from stories like Zeuxis' grapes, painted so realistically that birds tried to eat them, or Apelles' horse, at which real horses neighed. These examples, like all the others given by Pliny, had the greater force because they could not be checked; unlike statuary and architecture, ancient painting, apart from a few decorative fragments, was known only by verbal descriptions into which the artist could read what he wanted. Realism was being tempered by the notion of ideal beauty. Again, Zeuxis provided a model. Wishing to paint a perfect human figure for the temple of Hera at Girgenti, 'he held an inspection of maidens of the place paraded naked, and chose five, for the purpose of reproducing in the picture the most admirable points in the form of each.' Painters whose concern for perspective led them to value mathematics could read about Pamphilus, 'the first painter highly

educated in all branches of learning, especially arithmetic and geometry, without the aid of which he maintained art could not attain
perfection.' Artists who sought pictorial ideas, as Leonardo and Piero
di Cosimo did, from casual marks like the stains on a wall, were but
refining on the way in which painting, according to the Greeks, had
come to birth, for 'all agree that it began with tracing an outline
round a man's shadow.' Seeking an enhanced status for their craft,
painters were comforted to read that in the ancient world 'it has
always consistently had the honour of being practised by people of
free birth, and later on by persons of station, it having always been
forbidden that slaves should be instructed in it', and that Apelles was
so favoured by Alexander the Great that he handed over his mistress
Campaspe, with whom the artist had fallen in love when painting her
in the nude. And chiming harmoniously with the humanist emphasis
on man as creator, the importance of the artist's genius as well as the
finished product of his hand, was Pliny's statement that in antiquity
'the last works of artists and their unfinished pictures...are more
admired than those which they finished, because in them one sees the
preliminary drawings left visible and the artist's actual thoughts.'
Whether it was a defence of the nude, scorn for the use of expensive
pigments merely for ostentation, or the inclusion of a portrait of his
mistress in a sacred picture, the painter could find confirmation of
what he was already doing and an affirmation of the liberal status of
his profession. It is, of course, easier to show relevance than to
demonstrate effect but at least this example suggests the encouragement given by the popularisation of humanistic studies, an encouragement expressed in a very different context by Cortes' exhortation
to his little band of Spanish adventurers to imitate the heroic deeds of
the Romans; whereupon, his chronicler, Díaz, records, 'to a man we
all responded that we would do his orders, that the die was cast for
good fortune, as Caesar said at the Rubicon.'

The wide appeal of antiquity was dependent on parallels between
the nature of ancient and contemporary society. In war and
politics the parallel was (except for gunpowder) fairly close. It held
good for the rôle of the writer and orator, the lawyer and doctor, and
for certain occupations, particularly that of the farmer. That the
philosopher and the scientist had much to learn is obvious. More
difficult to estimate is the effect of noticing differences between the
two cultures. The ancient world depended on a substratum of slaves;
did this increase the scorn felt by humanist writers for the lowest
grades of their own society? It was anti-feminist: did this influence
the increasing subordination of the serious role of women in the
sixteenth century? A third difference was that the business techniques
of antiquity were inferior and had, in any case, left little evidence

behind them. Yet there was relevance here, too; not in the form of specific texts but of a general celebration of the active life, an ideal of playing a full and responsible part in the functioning of the community. It was an ideal that appealed especially to scholars, for it licensed their freedom from the cloistered associations of medieval learning. But the notion that virtue and learning thrive best in society, that love and wealth are not things to avoid but to use wisely, meant that humanistic ideas could find a welcome among merchants and bankers. Wealthy members of merchant families were, indeed, among the 'organisers' of humanism: patronising scholars, holding meetings for the discussion of classical literature and ancient history, investing their fellows with their own enthusiasm.

Such study groups, whether informal gatherings of friends or more self-consciously organised Academies like those associated with Ficino in Florence, Pontano in Naples, Pomponius Laetus in Rome or the German sodalities modelled on them, played an important part in giving a sense of structure to humanistic studies, especially where the official structure of education was dominated by theologically orientated universities. Linking these groups and aiding the sense of there being a commonwealth of humanist studies were a few men like Robert Gaguin in Paris, Abbot Trithemius, Konrad Peutinger and Cuspinian in Germany, Ficino in Florence and the peripatetic Erasmus, who carried on voluminous correspondences with other humanists and acted as sorting offices for their news and ideas. And this commonwealth was made visible, by the publication of its leaders' letters. By 1514, when the *doyen* of Spanish humanists, Marineo Siculo, printed his *Epistolarum familiarum*, this custom was sufficiently common to be used as a form of satire. In that year Reuchlin, under attack by the Dominican inquisitors for his defence of the study of Jewish religious writings, published by way of an open testimonial a collection of letters written in support of his views, the *Letters of Famous Men*. Two of his defenders, von Hutten and Crotus Rubeanus, were not content with this and in the following year published a pendant, the *Letters of Obscure Men*. This purported to be a selection of letters written to one of Reuchlin's chief adversaries, Ortvinus Gratius, a theologian at the University of Cologne, by his admirers. With considerable skill and great relish these 'admirers' made it clear that Ortvinus was an immoral and pettifogging ignoramus. They celebrated his sordid amours, praised his ability to determine such weighty matters as whether the eating of an egg containing an unhatched chick on a Friday were a venial or a mortal sin, and, above all, they impugned his learning. 'When I was in your study at Cologne' wrote one of them in mock respect, 'I could see well enough that you had a multitude of volumes, both great and small. Some were clad in wooden boards, and some in parchment bindings, some were covered all over with leather, red and green and black, while some were half bound. And there you sat, with a whisk in your hand, to flap away the dust from the bindings.'

This passive respect for authority attributed to Ortvinus and his like was in strong contrast to the use made of books by his assailants. The printing press was, indeed, crucial to the diffusion of humanist ideas. Governments were in general encouraging. John II of Portugal licensed book imports in 1483 'because it is good for the common-wealth to have many books circulating in our kingdom'. Louis XII referred to printing in an ordinance of 1513 as 'a divine rather than human invention'. The number of cities with presses of their own varied from country to country: in 1500 there were seventy-three such centres in Italy, fifty in Germany, forty-five in France and four in England. And the export of books was well organised. Printed texts enabled scholars in different countries to quote passages by page and chapter. By selecting with little discrimination what medieval works were to be put into circulation, printing had, in its first two genera-tions, 'fixed' the image of medieval culture. It thus played into the hands of the humanists who could represent it as an undifferentiated pile of superstition and frivolity which obscured a clear view of the ancient world. From the turn of the century their point of view gained ground. In Strasbourg, for instance, whereas up to 1500 only ten per cent of books dealt with the ancient world, between 1500 and 1520 thirty three per cent were editions of Latin and Greek authors or the writings of humanists. There, as elsewhere, the num-ber of copies printed of a particular edition varied from four or five hundred to between fifteen hundred and two thousand: one thousand would be a reasonable average to take for classical texts and would give 200,000 copies of Virgil published before 1500 and 72,000 of Erasmus' *Adagia* between 1500 and 1525.

These figures are a reminder that in spite of its relevance, the driving force behind the study of antiquity was still primarily schol-arly and literary. Humanism makes no sense unless we see at its core a purely intellectual excitement, the excitement of recovery, collation, publication, controversy: the unchanging scholarly enthusiasms. What was recovered most entirely was language. In the pages of men like Paolo Cortese and Pietro Bembo the language of Cicero was imitated as part of a movement to restore the writing of Latin to the purity of its outstanding model. After the 1520s, at least in Italy, Ciceronianism was to become an orthodoxy, and between the desire to write and the act of writing something of spontaneity and personal feeling was lost. Meanwhile, the controversy over style was a stimulus to wide and close reading; Greek, and more particularly

Latin authors were studied not only for their subject matter but in terms of how and why they wrote in the way they did. This interest in style involved an interest in form. This in turn influenced what was said by those who studied and imitated it. Thus not only the plan of a history but what was considered the subject matter appropriate to history was influenced by reading Tacitus, Livy or Thucidides. And in similar ways the poetry of Horace and Catullus suggested not only new forms of verse but new themes; the comedies of Plautus and Terence were both mould and stimulus to Machiavelli and Ariosto; the satire of Lucian pointed the wit and extended the fancy of More and Erasmus; the correspondence of antiquity, especially the letters of Cicero, broadened the range of what was thought to be the appropriate content of informal communication between friends.

Educational Reform

The intellectual excitement, the range of important human concerns which looked for illumination to what was in a deeper sense than were the Americas a 'New World' to the late fifteenth and early sixteen centuries, the popularisation of scholarship in the form of classical 'Christian' names, pageantry and decorative clichés: it is tempting to see humanism, by now a fashion as well as a syllabus, as the dominant theme in secular learning. To control this temptation we shall look at its contribution to religion, political thought and science, but there is a question that must be asked first: how pervasive, in fact, was humanism? What was its place within the educational system? Indeed, how many Europeans could be said to have been sufficiently educated to have had any intellectual life at all?

Only vague generalisations can be made about the extent of literacy. The clergy, secular and regular could all, in theory at least, read and write and had been trained to study. Episcopal visitations and reports on monasteries, however, suggest that especially in rural areas there were many priests and monks who were too ignorant to understand the services they read, too uncertainly literate to have their minds extended by reading. Among the labouring poor, the largest single element in the population, the ability to read was probably well under one per cent, the number of those able to write as well very small indeed. Peasants' sons who did go to school and showed promise there were likely to leave the country for the church or for town life. Men of substance in the country could commonly read and write and keep accounts. The proportion of those who could read and write in the towns was much higher; Thomas More thought that something like sixty per cent of Londoners could, and in a city like Florence the proportion may have been higher still. Both places were probably quite exceptional. However, men of middling social standing were able to write letters and keep diaries, and the statutes of many gilds postulated the ability to read and write as a condition of apprenticeship. But literacy in itself, whether it means as little as the ability to sign one's name or as much as to carry on a business correspondence, is little guide to the ability to learn from books, let alone derive ideas from them.

Though the number of schools increased, above all in the towns, the majority of them continued to use methods which were liable to dampen intellectual curiosity and the ability to proceed to self-educa-tion. Schooling was chiefly seen as a narrowly vocational process rather than as a general grounding from which a boy could move away from his father's occupation and intellectual standard. A mer-chant's son, for instance, would commonly leave school between twelve and fifteen to begin learning his father's business. A boy from a lower urban class would leave as soon as the minimum literacy required by a gild was achieved. For the small minority of those destined for the church, law or medicine there is little doubt that the teaching in many schools was thorough; if the child (usually a boy, there being far fewer schools for girls) stayed long enough he would be competent to read and write in his own tongue and in Latin. But the pace of advance and the variety of subject matter was restricted by the large size of classes and the high cost of books and writing materials. With a few notable exceptions the emphasis was on learning by rote from antiquated schoolbooks, some of them copied and printed unchanged from the twelfth and thirteenth cen-turies. Such books – Latin grammars for the most part – were read aloud and copied down sentence by sentence by the pupils, the metrical form into which many of them were cast emphasising the stress on mere memory training. Though the emphasis was on Latin as the chief subject to be studied as well as the chief medium of instruction, and in many schools boys were employed to spy on and report anyone caught speaking his own language in the schoolyard, these factors did much to cancel out the access a youth would other-wise have had to humanist literature. Rich men, and almost all of those who were of aristocratic birth, preferred to employ a tutor, and in this case the chances of mental curiosity being aroused were much greater unless the father had a prejudice against 'book-learning' as being something best left to poor men's sons who wanted to enter the church.

The great majority of schools were day schools, and this cut down the number of poor country boys who could attend unless they could stay for nothing with a relative – commonly a priest – in a large village or town which possessed one. On the other hand, it meant that the cost of a simple education was small; it was not uncommon for rural schoolmasters to accept fees in kind, in wood or farm produce. At universities, as well as the fees payable to the individual lecturers, money had to be found for board and lodging. Most universities had ways of aiding the poor students. They acted as servants in the households of doctors and masters or in the halls of residence, fees could be loaned, waived or reduced. The low proportion of students classified as 'poor', however (sixteen per cent at Cologne, only nine at Leipzig), suggests that many youths even in these circumstances were unable to go to a university. The course, commonly begun at the age of fourteen or fifteen, theoretically followed the traditional trivium – grammar, dialectic and rhetoric (all prepared for in elementary fashion at school) and quadrivium – arithmetic, geometry, astronomy and the theory of music. This was the essential preliminary to specialised doctoral work in theology, canon and civil law or medicine.

The days when one man could be master of many subjects was long past. Though universities were remarkably uniform in organisation, intense specialisation had resulted in their having a different tone and balance in the first degree curriculum and, still more, in their reputations at the doctoral level which it was essential for a youth seeking a professional career – including university teaching – or preferment in the church to reach. Thus Bologna and Ferrara were particularly identified with law, Oxford and Paris with theology, Padua with medicine. Then as now, the reputation of universities was subject to fluctuation. Cracow was at the height of its fame at the turn of the century while Salamanca, once the most revered of Spanish universities, was becoming overshadowed by the more liberal Alcalá de Henares, founded in 1508. In the same way, while the study of Aristotle continued to play a large part in the syllabuses of all universities, the method of approach could vary widely, from Paris, where he was taught in all faculties and in a thoroughly medieval way, to Padua, where the accent was mainly on his scientific writings and where these were taken as works to read as a whole rather than to snatch sentences for disputation from. Italian universities, in contrast to those in the north, played down theology or left it to specialised clerical institutions. Certain universities, Louvain being a conspicuous example, had the reputation of being especially 'safe' from a theological point of view, inhospitable to nominalist or pietist, let alone humanistic approaches to the subject.

This variety of tone, quality and specialisation meant that it was frequently necessary to travel far in order to obtain the most stimulating tuition, and this again probably weighted the scales against the poor student. In contrast, a well-to-do student, like Pico della Mirandola, could afford to move from canon law at Bologna to philosophy at Ferrara and Padua and to theology at Paris, supplementing his university courses with visits to Florence to meet Ficino and to Perugia, where there were Jews from whom he learned Hebrew.

Methods of instruction were reasonably similar in all universities. The lecture – not infrequently lasting as much as two hours – was the central feature. Another was the disputation on a set topic. Between them these occupied most of the day, leaving little time for the reading of whole texts, let alone for browsing outside the syllabus. Spontaneity in lectures was frowned upon; they were read. As at school, greater emphasis was laid on memory and argument than on originality or the development of critical ability. There was no more feeling in universities than in schools that the aim of education was a training of the mind which would be useful in a variety of avocations; they existed to turn out experts. Yet this is not to say that the universities lacked intellectual excitement. The considerable role played by students themselves in the running of university affairs; the encouragement of good teachers by the fact that they were frequently dependent on fees paid direct to them; the practice of itinerancy and the ease of enrolment in different universities; the possibility for independent and unorthodox teachers to set up shop, as it were, in university towns; inter-faculty rivalry, splits in individual faculties, as between the Realist and Nominalist wings of the arts faculties at Ingolstadt and Heidelberg: these were all factors that helped give life to a system unreformed in essentials for more than two centuries.

The point is worth stressing. Under the combative and highly readable onslaught of the humanists, it is easy to forget the vigour and subtlety that could be the product of the scholastic method – lecture and disputation, text books written in terms of questions, answers and qualifications. Under the widening shadow of Reform, it is tempting to dismiss the philosophy and theology of the universities as trivial and sterile. As a moral judgement this is probably fair, but though without the stimulus of thinkers of the originality and power of a William of Occam or an Aquinas, the intellectual standard of these faculties was, in the main, high. Again with Reform in mind, it is easy to agree with the most sweeping criticism of all those levelled against the universities of this period: that Nominalism (chiefly in the north) and a revived Aristotelianism (chiefly in Italy), by dismantling the Thomist harmony between faith and reason, had led to an emasculation of theology because the ordinary processes of argument could not 'prove' religious beliefs, and to a philosophy that had no bearing on a man's inner life. But this had little to do with the training of the mind. Before turning to the humanistic attack on the universities and the attitudes they stood for it is worth remembering that thinkers as creative as Pico and Ficino, More, Erasmus, Guicciardini and Lefèvre d'Étaples were all the products of orthodox higher education, and that while much of the tone of European society was set by artists, merchants, nobles and rulers who had not been to universities, the machines that ran church and state were largely controlled by men who had, and that the greater number of the reformers of the next generation were the product of a largely unreformed educational system.

Humanism itself had developed partly within and partly independently of the Italian universities. By the late fifteenth century, while individual students of antiquity ranged all the way from philologists every bit as crabbed and niggling as the pettiest of the schoolmen to original and systematic philosophers like Ficino, humanism as a movement had a clear plan for educational reform. At its core was a belief in self-improvement by taking thought and exercising the will. Expressed at its most mystical by Pico, who wrote that while a dog must always behave like a dog and an angel could not but behave angelically, man had the power so to shape his own development that he could become either bestialised or spiritualised, it led to a reappraisal of how, and about what, men should think. Without this mystical element, which was essentially private and contemplative, humanism would have lacked much of its intensity. Yet paradoxically this new concern with self-perfection enabled it to be seen for the first time as a reformist movement. Humanism could not have had its educational propagandists without its escapists.

From the belief that the individual can form his own nature as God gave form to the world itself, it was a short step to the belief that help could be given to others in forming theirs. One essential goal was to re-unite heart and mind – hence an attack on scholasticism. Another was to stress relevance. Not relevance in the sense of a career, a function perfectly well carried out by medieval universities except in the case of 'new' careers like that of professional diplomacy, but in the sense of a man's moral development. The child, and then the youth, should feel that all his studies were directed towards his moral stature as a man. A third goal was so far to reverse the notion that God had spoken only, and often unsearchably, through the mouths of His prophets and His son, as to claim that He had been scattering clues to His nature and His intentions through the writings of non-Jewish antiquity, so that, properly studied, the works of Plato could give spiritual, just as those of Cicero could give ethical, guidance. These last goals led to a re-appraisal of a few school and university syllabuses in the cause of harmonising the noblest messages from antiquity with the least riddling statements of scripture.

Humanism, then, had a mystical core, exemplified by such men as Pico, Colet and Lefèvre, a secondary circle of men like Erasmus and More whose leanings were predominantly moral, and an outer circle of popularisers whose inclination varied between the practical pedagogy of Linacre to the unconscious cynicism of Castiglione. All were sustained in their enthusiasm by a genuine love of the languages of antiquity, particularly Latin (for a mastery of Greek was still an uncommon accomplishment) and a desire to purify it in the teeth of the general run of teachers who, as Celtis put it, 'speak from their Chairs brokenly and crudely against all art and rule of speech like hissing geese or lowing oxen, pouring forth common, vile and corrupt words and whatever enters their mouths, pronouncing harshly and barbarously the smooth Latin tongue.'

The attack on teaching methods went closest to the heart of current practice. Throughout the trivium and quadrivium and to a lesser extent in doctoral studies, logic played so great a part that in the worst instances, at least, individual disciplines were exploited as fodder for the primary activity of debate and problem solving, ingenuity being put well above understanding, epitomes of quotations above the texts from which they were called. Against this practice the humanists emphasised the need to study texts as a whole, together with an analysis of their style and a knowledge of the times in which they were written. The purpose was to understand a writer in terms of why, how and when he wrote. In terms of the *trivium* this meant a playing down of grammar and dialectic and a radical up-grading of rhetoric – the study of literature and philosophy in order to understand what great men actually said and to be able to speak and write eloquently and pertinently oneself. For the great advantage of rhetoric in this new sense was that it combined an accession of knowledge with a growing mastery of self-expression. Individual humanists differed in their estimate of individual writers of the scholastic phase. Erasmus expressed considerable respect for Aquinas; Colet loathed him for putting his systematising zeal above the clear doctrine of Christ. Both Ficino and Pico admitted that the example of the best scholastics had exerted a steadying and unifying influence on their own thought – a point of view Pico defended with some vehemence against the reproaches of the great Venetian humanist Ermolao Barbaro, who wished humanism to start with a clean slate. The partial defence of scholastics on the one hand and whole-hearted onslaughts on the other depended in part on the stress individual humanists put on elegance of language as opposed to content, partly on religious zeal – as when Pirckheimer produced in 1520 a description of an 'operation' on Luther's adversary Eck designed to cut away his sophistries, syllogisms and corollaries. But all attacked the pre-eminence of logic over thought and feeling. In his *Pseudo-dialecticus* (1519) Juan Luis Vives explained his own attack on scholastic teaching methods, and – just as significantly – his doubts. 'Who could tolerate the painter occupying the whole of his life in preparing his brush and mixing his pigments...? If this expenditure of time would be intolerable over *good* logic, what language is adequate to designate that babbling which has corrupted every branch of knowledge?...I recognised I was changing the old for the new, what I had already required in the way of knowledge for what had yet to be won...The change was so odious to me that often I turned away from the thought of the better humanist studies to my old scholastic studies, so that I might persuade myself that I had not spent so many years at Paris to no good purpose.'

Another shared assumption was the need to return to the sources of moral, ethical and religious belief, rather than studying them through debased texts and medieval commentators. The cry 'back to the sources' was not a novel one. The desire to communicate as directly as possible with a fully realised personality in the ancient world had been expressed in Petrarch's feeling for Cicero. The editing of Latin and, to a lesser extent, Greek texts had been one of the chief preoccupations of humanists throughout the fifteenth century. In the deliberations of governments, besides, and in the fad for genealogy, a strong instinct to look back to origins was making itself felt: in many areas the intellectual drive of the period can be summed up in the phrase *reculer pour mieux sauter*. More revolutionary – for the scale on which the argument was pressed rather than for its originality – was the determination to get back past the scholastic theologians to the Bible itself and to the early fathers of the church, 'the old doctors who were nigh unto Christ and his apostles', as Erasmus put it.

In 1496 Colet's lectures at Oxford on St. Paul's Epistles to the Corinthians broke radically with the traditional methods of the divinity teacher. Instead of approaching his subject through medieval Latin commentaries, thus reminding his auditors that the church represented an accumulation of interpretations as well as of dogma, he used the Greek text directly. He explained how the form and language of the Epistles were conditioned by St. Paul's view of the men to whom it was directed. He placed Paul himself within the context of Roman civilisation and the early years of Christianity. And by locating him clearly in place and time Colet enabled Paul to speak almost as directly to the students of Oxford as he had spoken to the Corinthians – to bear witness from the beginnings of the church and to encourage personal reflection instead of being used as the excuse

for a display of erudition. Perhaps even more impressive as exempli-
fying the humanistic desire to return to the sources was the desire to
see the Bible in what was essentially the language of God and Christ,
Hebrew. Pico studied the language: Reuchlin formulated its rules so
that others could study it. But it is once more from Erasmus that we
see their motivation most clearly. 'No one ever understood any other
person's opinion without knowing the language in which that opinion was expressed,' he wrote in the *Adages*. 'And so what did St.
Jerome do, when he had decided to expound Holy Scripture? ... With
incalculable toil, he made himself master of the three tongues. He
who is ignorant of them', he added, with his usual capacity to annoy,
'is no theologian, but a violator of theology.' In 1508 Guillaume Budé
published a work on the *Pandects* of Justinian in which he urged that
this work, so crucial to the study of Roman law, should be read
entire, and not through the selections and interpretations of the
medieval glossators, and that the judgements and legal principles
contained in it should be read with close attention to the original
phraseology and against an understanding of the historical circumstances in which they were composed. In this work and in the *De
Asse*, Budé expressed very clearly the pioneering joy of cutting back
scholastic undergrowths to reveal the monuments of antiquity in their
pristine state. 'I am the first, I believe, to have undertaken to restore
this aspect of antiquity', he declared in the *De Asse*, but he also made
a remark which represents, in its critical detachment, the coming of
the age of humanism. *À propos* an error he had detected in Pliny's
monetary calculations, he wrote 'it seems to me an absurd obligation
to which most learned men of our age have bound themselves...
when they hold that the bare name of antiquity should be venerated
as a deity. I think that in fact the men of antiquity were men like
ourselves, who sometimes wrote of things about which they did not
know very much.'*

A last educational principle shared by humanists of widely differing interests was the most notorious, that of creating the 'all round
man'. 'In what branch of knowledge worthy of literary expression
was Plato deficient? How many generations' study did Aristotle
require to embrace not merely the whole range of philosophical and
rhetorical knowledge, but to investigate the nature of every beast and
plant? And yet they had to discover all these things which we only
have to learn. Antiquity has given us all these teachers and all these
patterns for our imitation, that there might be no greater happiness
conceivable than to be born in this age above all others, since all

---

*I owe these quotations to an unpublished paper on 'Le Roy and Budé' which Professor
James Stayer was kind enough to let me see.

previous ages have toiled that we might reap the fruit of their wisdom.' And again, the educated man 'should not confine his study to logic, but have a theoretical acquaintance with all the topics of philosophy... It is also desirable that he should not be ignorant of natural philosophy... nor, while he is acquainted with the divine order of nature, would I have him ignorant of human affairs. He should understand the civil law... he should also be acquainted with the history of events of past ages..., to be ignorant of what occurred before you were born is to remain always a child. For what is the worth of human life, unless it is woven into the life of our ancestors by the records of history?'

The significance of these passages is that they are taken respectively from Quintilian's and Cicero's treatises on oratory. That they *could* have been written in 1500 shows how firmly the humanistic ideal had seized on the classical notion that the rhetorician should be able to speak with knowledge, and in suitable terms, on a wide variety of subjects, broadening the narrowly conceived rhetoric of the *trivium* into a sort of container for education as a whole.

The fame of the concept of *l'uomo universale* owes much to its most famous exemplar, Leonardo da Vinci, and its most eloquent exponent, Castiglione. It was not a new idea. It was indeed in direct conflict with many humanists' own urge to study particular branches of learning in depth, acquiring laborious linguistic skills as they went. In study, in business, in administration, the drift of the period, indeed the urgent need of the period, was towards specialisation. For most men, anything even approaching universal knowledge was attainable only at the level of encylopedism or dilettantism, however attractively Castiglione glossed over the fact. Even at the level of dilettantism the ideal of universalism was attainable only by the leisured rich, and it was in this fact that much of universalism's appeal lay, because it distinguished the gentleman, who did not have to rely for an income on specialised knowledge or skills, from the scholar or craftsman who did.

The humanists' stress on understanding rather than memory, on texts rather than disputation and above all on making education fit the child rather than vice versa made some impact on schooling. The printing press enabled new teaching aids, particularly grammars and dictionaries, to speed up the crucial process of learning Latin. Restating an Erasmian principle, Marineo Siculo wrote of his own simplified Latin grammar that 'judging just these few things to be enough for beginners and the rest not necessary I leave it to others fruitlessly to weary the minds of their students. For if, after they have made acquaintance with the form of words, they will spend that time which others spend on the rules of grammar in hearing the authors from whom those same rules are taken, they will certainly advance more, and become not grammarians but Latinists. Thus boys are being taught in Italy, thus in Germany.' Lefèvre made the same point in France, and in the Netherlands, where the cautious humanism of the Brethren of the Common Life had already provided an example, teaching practice in a number of schools, most notably, perhaps, at Deventer, was revised still further on Erasmian lines. In England Magdalen College School was the pioneer in the early 1480s, and in 1508–9 Colet founded St. Paul's school in London in direct collaboration with Erasmus.

Universities, in the main, can be said to have accepted individual humanists as specialised teachers of Greek or Latin literature more willingly than they accepted humanistic proposals about syllabus reform. And if the tone of the *trivium* became more humanistic it was because such teachers, being free to select their own texts, were able to reach out into the other branches of the course and set in motion a benign infection of the arts course as a whole. The extent of this infection varied with the conservatism of the established faculties. Marineo was offered a chair of poetry and oratory at Salamanca, and Peter Martyr, as visiting lecturer there, reported that after a public lecture on Juvenal he 'was carried home like a victor from Olympia'. But the university itself remained stiffly traditional and the great scholar Elio de Nebrija found that his 'back to the sources' attitude to divinity was so unpopular with his colleagues that he was compelled to move on to the more sympathetic atmosphere of Alcalà. In spite of the presence of men of a humanistic stamp like Robert Gaguin the Sorbonne remained imperturbably under the influence of its conservative faculty of theology. Oxford and Cambridge were dominated by unyielding faculties of theology, and their resistance to change was made easier by the existence of the Inns of Court which drew off the sons of influential families who, with diplomatic or administrative careers in mind, wanted a more down to earth education.

Even though the chancellor of Cambridge from 1503 was John Fisher, a patron of Erasmus, the university only obtained one lecturer in Greek. At Oxford humanism made more progress, but here it was by means of a new college, Corpus Christi, grafted on to the university by Bishop Richard Fox in 1517. Though founded as a place where, as the statutes put it, 'scholars, like ingenious bees are by day and night to make wax to the honour of God, and honey, dropping sweetness, to the profit of themselves and of all Christians', all its twenty fellows were to be well versed in secular Latin literature. Even more important was the contribution Corpus was to make to the university through a Latin lecturer who was to deal with the poets, orators and historians of ancient Rome, a lecturer in Greek literature and a theology lecturer who was 'as far as possible to follow the ancient and holy doctors both Latin and Greek and especially Jerome, Augustine, Ambrose... and others of that sort, not Nicholas of Lyra, not Hugh of Vienne and the rest who, as in time so in learning are so far below them.'

Within a year opposition to the 'Greeks' of Corpus had reached such a point that they were set on in the streets by the 'Trojans' of the faculty of theology, and Thomas More was forced to come up from the court and rebuke the university authorities. He defended Fox's intentions by saying that unless theology were to involve a study of the early fathers and of Latin, Greek and Hebrew, it would fall back again into the sterile debates of the schoolmen – that is, continue in its present rut, and he made the point, familiar enough in humanistic literature but important nonetheless in that particular context, that not only was a knowledge of ancient wisdom no bar to the study of theology but it was of positive value to the men who went on to run the state and whose duties would involve as wide as possible a knowledge of human affairs.

Rulers were, indeed, appointing humanists as tutors for their children. Linacre was tutor to Henry's son Arthur. Peter Martyr was made head of the little palace school where Juan, crown prince of Castile, was educated together with a carefully selected group of noble youths. And if some of the topics endlessly discussed under humanist influence, such as whether the sword is mightier than the pen, were already hackneyed, they were at least more pertinent to life than the riddles of the theology faculties, such as 'whether we are bound by the law of love to deliver a neighbour, against his will, from oppression, infamy or death, when we cannot do so without hurt or danger to ourselves.' As Peter Martyr was to say of his warlike young charges, 'they are beginning to admit that letters are not a hindrance to soldiering, as they have been falsely trained to think, but even an active help.' It is probable, indeed, that such fashionable debating topics as arms *versus* letters, and proverbial and anecdotal collections such as Erasmus' immensely popular *Adagia* did more to spread interest in and respect for the pertinence of the ancient world than full editions of classical authors or the teaching by humanists in the universities.

The success of any attempt to introduce a new programme of learning and a new way of thinking is dependent on the extent to which it can be popularised. Rebuffed by, or but frailly established at the majority of formal institutions, the spread of humanistic attitudes depended on the tools available for self-education. These were still sparse. Few men, even of middling wealth, possessed more than twenty books. A few towns, among them Nuremberg, Leipzig and Frankfurt, had public libraries, but the great non-university libraries, like the Medici and Vatican collections, though open to the public, were in practice used only by scholars.

Above all, the great majority of books capable of prompting thought and suggesting comparisons and new ideas were still printed in Latin, and were thus inaccessible save to that proportion of the well-educated who had been taught not only to learn Latin but to go on reading it. Individual practice varied. Erasmus wrote only in Latin, Machiavelli only in Italian. Dürer sought advice from Latinists like Pirckheimer when he began to write his treatises in German, and by largely ignoring such advice helped shape German into a language which, as More said of English, 'is plenteous enough to express our minds in anything where of one man hath used to speak with another.' Yet More wrote *Utopia* in Latin. Yet again, it was Nebrija, a professional humanist who wrote in Latin and edited classical texts, who composed the first grammar of a modern European language and who justified it to Isabella with the famous and prophetic observation that 'language is the perfect instrument of Empire'. Nascent nationalism was indeed one of the factors making for the standardisation and increasing use of the vernacular, though, here again, it was a time of contradiction. Felix Faber energetically defended German as 'the noblest, most distinguished, most humane of tongues', but his defence was couched in Latin. From the point of view of self-education in humanist ideas, the common reader was to a certain extent a victim of this patriotism, because it led printers to publish national histories and national literature in the vernacular rather than popularise the works of contemporary humanists or translate classical texts. By 1520 the vernacular had still not gained general acceptance as a medium for expressing those aspects of humanism which could have given middle-class Europe something like a common culture, and for many who could read Latin but for whom it retained the artificial flavour of a second and unrelished tongue, the ancient world remained alien in its ideas as well as in time.

Christian Humanism

That humanists should combine one self-appointed role, the school-masters of secular Europe, with another as the re-educators of Christendom, was a foregone conclusion; it was a natural accompaniment of their desire to re-establish the original texts of the civilisation which had included not only Plato and Aristotle and Cicero but the establishment of the Christian church. And a natural consequence of their attack on the methods of scholasticism was an attack on the attitudes to religion the scholastic method inculcated and the type of pastor produced by the faculties of theology.

Because theology played a minor role in Italian universities it was above all north of the Alps that the efforts of humanists to get university posts for themselves and insert *bonae litterae* into the syllabus led to a close concern with the nature of the religious life. Attacking the neglect of sources, the learning by rote, the uncritical acceptance of bad authorities, the stress on form above substance, they became critics of a religion that underplayed the life and sayings of Christ himself, of observances like the 'worship' of saints and the automatic repetition of un-felt prayers, of prayers said for the dead by priests for a fee, of the cult of relics and pilgrimages undertaken by deputies. They saw that a theology that did not speak to the heart led to a religious life that consisted of tokens. And in reaching out from a criticism of teaching practice to one of religious practice they were sustained by the pre-existing movements of practical lay piety and mystical interiority in the north as well as by the Italian emphasis on the dignity of man and its corollary, an emphasis on the good life rather than the good death. As the Franciscans rather than the Benedictines of humanised Christianity they emphasised that while at the centre of Christianity was a mystery, the teaching of Christ was not itself mysterious.

This is the attitude to which the literary fervour of Petrarch, the philological acumen of Valla had led. Why then the Inquisition, why Luther, why Zwingli, why Calvin, why the censorship of books, why the tremendous reaffirmation of medieval doctrinal accretions by the Council of Trent?

The failure of this approach had little to do with the mild tincture of paganism which accompanied the study of antiquity. Though individual humanists differed in the extent to which they were prepared to bring classical authors into the Christian fold, as it were, without creating a disturbance there – Erasmus being more permissive than Lefèvre and Lefèvre than Colet, for instance – Erasmus spoke for the majority of his fellows when he remarked that 'surely the first place is due to holy scripture; but sometimes I find some things written by the ancients, by pagans and poets, so chaste, so holy, so divine, that I am persuaded a good genius enlightened them. Certainly there are many in the communion of saints who are not in our catalogue of saints.'

In a sense midway between playful and serious, certain humanists did see themselves as living in the context of ancient manners. Celtis commissioned Hans Burgkmair to anticipate his death in an engraving copied from a Roman tomb, where he lies in the sleep of death mourned by Apollo and Mercury. The tomb of two humanist doctors of medicine, Girolamo and Marcantonio della Torre went as far as to show them being ferried across the Styx towards the Elysian Fields. But classical iconography had become a fairly widespread fashion. The tomb of the two young children of Charles VIII and Anne of France bore scenes from the labours of Hercules in parallel with scenes from the life of Samson, and on Pollaiuolo's monument to Pope Sixtus IV Theology itself was portrayed in the guise of a nude Diana. In 1503 Paolo Cortese, secretary to Pope Alexander VI, published a *Compendium of Dogma* in which the Virgin was called the mother of the Gods, the souls of the dead were referred to as *manes*, Hell was provided with the rivers of the pagan Tartarus, and Aquinas was termed the Apollo of Christianity. When Leo X, patron of humanist learning and as great a collector of classical manuscripts as his fifteenth-century forbears, Cosimo *pater patriae* and Lorenzo the Magnificent, entered Rome, it was through arches decorated with classical quotations and statues of Apollo and Mercury, Venus and Bacchus. And Leo continued to cherish the art and literature of antiquity after he had published the decrees of his predecessor's Lateran Council which attacked an excessive concern with pagan learning.

More weakening to the sense of total conviction and surrender of the self which was needed for a widely shared regeneration of Christianity was the humanist emphasis on wisdom and ethics at the expense of the miraculous and of revelation. Pico and Pomponazzi were among the very few humanists who ran into charges of heresy. Most accepted the dogmas of the church. But they played them down. They took something of the terror from hell by teaching that the man whose ethical standards were considered and strict and whose moral self-scrutiny was honest, was justified in living more in the terms of here and now than in terms of coming death and judgement. Supported by Stoic and Epicurean strains common to much humanistic thought, man's special dignity was seen to reside in his ability, by taking thought and adding to his knowledge of ancient wisdom and Christ's teaching, to bring about an inner harmony pleasing to God. Thus there was less emphasis on the sacramental nature of Christianity. The essential optimism of this belief in self-perfectibility played down the dramatic role played by original sin in orthodox theology. The Garden of Eden and what happened there became an allegory of choice, a warning of the nature of the combat to be waged in the individual's nature, rather than the first step in a drama about real people that required the effusion of Christ's blood on the cross. And this demotion of the 'historical' drama of the forbidden fruit was sustained by the pseudo-historical belief in a Golden Age when man had lived for generations in a state of un-selfconscious bliss. Again, the humanists did not stress the saints as intercessors by virtue of the heaped treasury of their merits, rather, they urged man to use his own informed vigilance to nourish the seed of God-wardness implanted in him. All this was, of course, in the interest of personalising religion. The result, equally, inevitably, was to intellectualise it. Christianity became less readily visualisable. The words of Christ became more important than his miracles, even than his crucifixion. Devils, angels, vices, virtues, the cup of the communion held to the blood spurting from Christ's side, Judas hung by the neck, the torture of martyrs – the long heritage of art and drama was belittled by exhortations less to watch and pray than to study and think.

Leading the imagination still further from the liturgy and the subject matter of the pulpit was the surprising eclecticism, the wide variety of source material than humanists thought pertinent to the study of the religious life. One cause was strightforward scholarly curiosity. But there were others: emphasis on moral philosophy, which sought illustrations in poetry, history and rhetoric as well as in scripture; a concern for the very idea of Religion, the impulse to worship traceable in all creeds and at all times; the eclecticism already present in some of the basic humanist models, especially in Cicero.

The sympathetic study of other religions was no longer out of bounds. Each was held to reflect (though Christianity reflected it most directly) a single truth emanating from a single God; from the obelisks of Egypt to the Koran something relevant to God's purposes and man's inherent spirituality was to be found. The risk was that Christianity would not be buttressed but diluted. 'The rites and ceremonies of religion', wrote Cornelius Agrippa, 'are different on account of differences of time and regions; and each religion has something good, which is directed toward God Himself the Creator; and although God approves of the Christian religion alone, yet He does not entirely reject other cults practised for His sake; and He does not leave them wholly unrewarded, if not with eternal, then with a temporal reward; or at least He punishes them less.'

This syncretism was at its most diluting in its reflection of a tendency widely shared among humanists: to combine a refreshingly straightforward approach to the New Testament with an esoterically code-cracking one to the Old. Thus the Jewish Cabala was seen as a corpus of secret lore handed down orally from the time of Moses before being committed to writing, a tradition of wisdom which, if applied to the Bible (if necessary with an elucidation of the symbolic meaning of certain Hebrew letters) could supplement an understanding of the Old Testament. The fact that the wise men had been granted a fore-knowledge of the birth of Christ, and had come from the East, was taken as a pointer to the Christian scholar to look for earlier insights in the works (or pseudoworks) of the oriental sages whose ideas were believed to be incorporated in the writings of Pythagoras. Egypt, too, exerted a fascination because of a tradition reported in Herodotus and Plato that it had been the original home of religion. And this tradition appeared to have its practical side because of the existence of a body of writings attributed to Hermes Trismegistus, thought by Ficino (who translated them into Latin) and his successors to be the work of an ancient Egyptian sage, though in fact they were written in the third and fourth centuries A.D. An indication of the extent to which Hermes was welcomed into the troop of those who could throw light on the Old Testament is the inscription to a representation of him on the floor of the cathedral of Siena in 1488, where he is labelled as 'contemporary with Moses'. Ancient Egypt was also the home of hieroglyphs. These fascinated because of the possibility that they contained direct imprints of God's thoughts, which (under Platonic influence) were expected to be in the form of whole image-ideas until He gave Himself a human mouth at the incarnation. They figured increasingly in art and were, for instance, lavishly used by Dürer in the centrepiece of his vast Triumphal Arch. But hieroglyphs, and the code-breaking appetite as a whole, was a matter for specialists only. There could be no clear image of Christian humanism while its proponents sought at the same time combat with the theological establishment, simplicity for the masses and esoteric lore for themselves.

And if an emphasis on secular wisdom could lead to a playing down of revelation; if the search for God could lead to a neglect of Christ; if the breadth of this search could lead to a vague Pantheism – as it did with Celtis' affirmation that God could be worshipped as well in the countryside as in a church; then also the appeal to so many authorities could lead to a distrust of knowledge itself and thus undermine a central tenet of humanism: that by taking thought man could add to his spiritual stature. Burdened by the accumulation of knowledge since the days of Aquinas' reconciliation of reason with faith, oppressed by the number of approaches to the source of belief, it was tempting to pursue knowledge and let faith look after itself. It was tempting to become sceptical – as Pico's nephew Gian Francesco became sceptical – of reason, to see the Philosophy of Christ as essentially a self-contradictory phrase, and, indeed, a despairing one for the men who needed above all the sort of affirmation that only strikes deep enough to give comfort when it is the result of a lightning stroke on the road to Damascus. It was tempting, finally, for the hieroglyph to become confused with the symbols traced in the dust by the magician's staff, and for humanism to lead to man's attempt to ape rather than to seek God, a role into which Agrippa was led and in which he figures as one of the inspirers of Goethe's *Faust*.

Humanism inevitably became involved with religion. Equally inevitably it could act only as a very slow leaven within the spiritual life of Europe as a whole. The humanists wrote in Latin for a relatively, small, if important audience. A few, inside and outside the church, were self-supporting. Some were dependent on the fluctuations of patronage. Others were perched here and there and then not always securely, among universities and other educational institutions. They had no corps of preachers fired with their ideas. They were not involved with the patriotic feelings of any nation to any depth. Above all, perhaps, their message lacked humility and a sense of sin. And because it lacked a sense of sin it lacked the right note of hope. Luther's attitude to theology reflected something of the humanistic tinge which Erfurt university had acquired when he was studying there. In his early years he was an admirer of Erasmus. But one simple passage can explain the breach that developed between the two men and the greater penetrative force of the German's approach to religion. 'I believe,' he wrote, 'that I cannot of my own reason or strength believe on Jesus Christ my Lord, or come to him. But the Holy Ghost has called me by the gospel, enlightened me with his gifts, sanctified and kept me in the one true faith.'

Political Thought

Among those who stepped back to consider the nature of political society as a whole there was a wide range of mood. A considerable volume of sermons, pamphlets and treatises still continued the old-fashioned 'Mirror of Princes' theme: that if only a ruler would be a good Christian all would be well with his people. This strain was dominant in Erasmus' *Education of a Christian Prince*. A more moderate view was represented by Seyssel, whose *Monarchy of France* is founded on the idea that a ruler must base his actions first and foremost on his knowledge of his country, its institutions, the social composition and the needs of the people at large; he should rule, in fact, with his head rather than with his heart or conscience: once aware of the limitations on his freedom, his actions would be perspicacious and moderate. Machiavelli represents a similar approach but one used in the service of activism; knowledge of the facts about institutions and human nature enabled a ruler to release the potential dynamism in a political system. Lastly, at the opposite extreme to Erasmus' idealism was the view of Cornelius Agrippa, to whom the study of politics was a mere waste of time; monarchy, aristocracy, democracy – the working of any of them depended on the characters of the individuals concerned, so what was the point of discussing their merits as institutional forms?

Apart from this opting-out vein, there was a widely shared view among writers on politics that specific problems could be isolated, anlaysed and dealt with, whether it was social injustice (More) or apparently senseless international rivalries (Erasmus) or military weakness (Machiavelli). Just as historians were explaining history less in terms of a chess game played with human pieces between God and the devil and more in terms of individual ambition, greed and skill, political writers were aware that men's destinies were to some extent within their own control and that this control depended upon self-knowledge. It was useful to limber up by telling the familiar beads of Aristotle's best constitutions and their malign counterparts, but constructive thought could only begin when they were checked against reality. Thus Seyssel had added the pace-making officials, of whatever social background, to the aristocratic element in France's institutional life. Budé, in his very un-Erasmian *Education of a Prince*, pointed out that the nature of a country's economy was more relevant to the political planner than the character of its prince. And Savonarola, brought up on Aquinas' preference for monarchy as the nearest reflection both of God's single rule and that of nature (the queen bee), and anxious as a pastor for a constitution within which men could lead virtuous lives, praised the republican constitution of 1495 both in sermons and in his *Tractate on the Government of Florence* because it suited the temperament and rose naturally from the historical conditioning of a particular people.

This emphasis on the workable rather than the ideal was not solely the result of fresh observation. It was aided by medieval and ancient clichés. The body politic was subject to change as the individual body was; it needed the advice of the political diagnostician as the individual needed that of a doctor. Just as the individual was tied to a wheel bearing him from good to ill unless virtue applied the brake, so nations passed from one form of constitution to another, from prosperity to disaster, unless the pressure of knowledge were brought to bear. These metaphors of change had no significance in themselves. No political writer thought the world was slipping into senility, though some preachers and chroniclers did. Outside Italy there was little apprehension about one constitutional form giving way to another: hereditary kingship had been the rule for centuries. But they helped to communicate a sense of urgency and to give a sense of mission to writers. Budé, Seyssel and Machiavelli wrote in the vernacular in order to catch the eye of a specific ruler – in each case a new ruler, the young Francis I and the young Lorenzo de' Medici, grandson of Lorenzo the Magnificent. Matters are in a state of flux; this is how things stand at present; this is what you can do about it: for all their formal differences, this is the message common to their works.

Seyssel, a bishop, administrator and diplomat, referred to the heap of books written to advise princes from antiquity onwards with some disillusion: what practical effect had they had? Princes either did not need them or did not read them. Thanks, however, to the despatches and reports of the burgeoning number of long-term diplomats, the school-masterly confidence of humanist scholars, and the increasing trust in legally trained professional administrators, the role of the effective political adviser was easier to imagine than it had been in the past, and this gave him a new sense of the pertinence of what he said.

It was also easier to keep advice practical by making comparisons and drawing inferences from them; not so much from contemporary examples – Venice, the Empire, the Turks: these were chief among the few contemporary polities to be seen in terms of institutions rather than of rulers – but from antiquity. There was a record of actions and their consequences, institutions and their fates, which writers and readers had in common. Though Machiavelli laid ancient alongside modern situations with an unusually keen sense of their parallelism, and in the *Discourses* claimed to be blazing a new trail by stressing the relevance of ancient history to modern problems, the habit of invoking the history of the ancient world was almost universal. Working on very similar lines, but without knowledge of one another's works (though they had met in 1504), Seyssel and Machiavelli even used the same examples from ancient Rome with surprising frequency.

Political theorists of course took from the ancient world what supported their own interests. Those who were primarily interested in ethical values could ask themselves: what institutional environment would produce a nation of Christian Ciceros? Republicans could turn to Livy, monarchists to Suetonius, students of constitutional change to Polybius, idealists to Plato. In itself this plethora of models did not produce works of greater originality than those of the Middle Ages, let alone works that were more likely to influence those in power; it should, moreover, be remembered that some of what have in retrospect appeared to be key works were not printed until after this period, among them Francesco Guicciardini's *Logrogno Discourse* (1512, printed 1858), Machiavelli's *Prince* (1513, printed 1532) and Budé's *Education of the Prince* (1518 or

1519, printed 1547). But the more sharply classical institutions were seen in terms of their historical development the more apparent it became that all institutions had been made and could be altered by men, and that such alterations had to take into account the tone of society as a whole. The origins and much of the early development of contemporary nations were fogged with myth: those of Rome appeared to be clear. The lack of adequate contemporary reference or analytical books made it easier to see how the Romans had been governed than how the larger nations were at the moment, not always excluding a writer's own.

Outside the republics, it was the clarity with which Imperial Rome could be seen that most influenced writers on politics. In Germany, which actually had an emperor, but a weak one, political thought on a national scale remained aspirational rather than practical. In England the notion that the monarch was under the law and was there to protect as well as direct his people blunted the force of Roman analogy, as did the position of the *cortes* in Spain. In France, however, the scorn felt by nearly all those with a humanist education for the *plebs*, together with the growing effectiveness of the monarchy since the reign of Charles VII, led to the least inhibited citation of the Imperial Roman model.

For Budé, first and foremost a scholar by temperament, the power of the king was absolute. To prove that this was not only true in fact but ought to be true in terms of the nature of the ideal polity, he quoted (indeed amended to his purpose) examples from Roman history, he even went so far as to ignore the coronation ceremony, with its aura of responsibility to God and the church, because it had no analogy in the ancient world. The sole check on absolutism was the day-dream one of the ruler's conscience. Budé was using Roman history to abolish French history in order to free the king from the impediments of the national past.

In contrast, Seyssel, though sharing, at a more superficial level, Budé's knowledge of ancient Rome and agreeing with his desire for an enhancement of the king's authority, pointed out that this power could not in practice be absolute. The monarch was pledged not to act against the interest of religion. He was bound to take account of the law of the land as it was known to his judges. He was also bound by certain conventions which had come to have the status of fundamental laws, conventions governing succession to the throne, the inalienability of crown lands, the relationship of the crown to the papacy. In addition, Seyssel's analysis of the social composition of the nation revealed more 'brakes' (to use his own word) on the monarch's freedom of action, for his power would dissolve if he arbitrarily ignored the basic interests of any social group.

Thus while the availability of information about the ancient world helped to change the tone of political thought and added immensely to its range of illustrative material it did not determine its direction. It was used by prophets of absolutism like Budé and tacticians like Seyssel, enthusiasts for imitating the actions of the ancients, like Machiavelli, and sceptics, like Guicciardini, who looked on ancient history as a guide to thinking about, not to making history. The chief areas where the opinion of political writers was more or less unanimous was that of foreign policy and war. Feudal and clerical institutions had stained national political life so deeply with the sense of contract-keeping and Christian rectitude that most political theorists simply could not recommend an out-and-out amoralism when discussing the direction of internal affairs. In foreign affairs, however, the lessons of diplomatic and miltary chicanery that could be learned from the historians and writers on war of antiquity could be digested with hardly by qualm. When thinking in terms of Florence itself, Machiavelli was bound, and was delighted to be bound, by the traditions of its republican past; he thought in terms of social fairness, of mutual trust, the common good. But when he was thinking of the qualities needed in a leader who was bent on conquest or dealing with conquered territories or negotiating with potential enemies, he accepted the need to dissemble and lie. He expressed a distrust of human nature with more trenchancy than did most of his contemporaries, he pointed to the need for a divorce between private and political morality with more relish, but his views were not isolated. 'Because men are by nature corrupt', wrote Seyssel, 'commonly so ambitious and covetous of dominion . . . that one can put neither trust nor faith in them, it is most suitable and necessary that all princes responsible for the government of realms always keep a wary eye on their neighbours even in time of peace.' Budé sanctioned deceit, bribery and cunning in the national interest. It was not with Machiavelli in mind (of whom he had never heard) that Erasmus reminded his own ideal Christian prince that 'the ways of some princes have slipped back to such a point that the two ideas of "good man" and "prince" seem to be the very antithesis of one another. It is obviously considered foolish and ridiculous to mention a good man in speaking of a prince.'

This, the most 'realistic' aspect of contemporary political thought certainly owed much to the study of antiquity. It was not only that war as such played so prominent a part in the works of Roman historians that it was argued that war was *par excellence* the true subject matter of history, but that writers who paid taxes, knew wars to be expensive and were not born into a fighting caste sympathised with Vegetius' urging that almost any way of defeating an enemy was better than actually fighting him. The concept of Fortune was common to intellectuals. Vegetius, in his widely read *De re militari*, had drawn attention to the dominant role played by fortune on the battlefield. It was reasonable then to endorse the use of terror, deceit and subterfuge – sleights and policies anthologised by another widely read classical author, Frontinus. But it is doubtful whether this 'realist' strain would have been so explicit had it not been for the Old Testament's record of wiles and stratagems undertaken at the expense of the chosen people's enemies, or even for the less consistent teaching of the New; besides the classical examples cited by Seyssel in his chapters on diplomatic relations and war, he referred, *à propos* the wisdom of sowing dissension among one's enemies, to St. Paul who 'introduced a schism among the Jews, seeing that they unreasonably conspired together against him.'

It is doubtful, moreover whether this strain would have been so general were it not for the actual tone of international affairs and the fact that the most original political writers were either in a position to observe them – Budé in Paris – or had actually played a part in them as had Machiavelli, Guicciardini, Seyssel and More.

Science

No one was as yet called a scientist. 'Scientia' simply meant knowledge as a whole (or one of its parts), and those who studied or professed 'natural philosophy', that is, the nature of the physical world, put philosophy above investigation. Science in the modern sense was either the by-product of a professional interest in medicine, magic or alchemy, or a largely self-taught subject that had to fit in with another career. The man who was most recognisably a 'scientist' in this period (though his findings were not published till later), Copernicus, had studied medicine, canon law and philosophy as well as astronomy, became a canon of the cathedral of Frauenburg in Poland, and earned his money as secretary to the bishop and as a doctor. Though humanism affected the tone of most areas of secular study, it was inimical to the growth of a scientific approach except in one way: the passion for antiquity led to the publication of hitherto unavailable scientific texts. The humanists' opposition to scholasticism led them to ignore the scientific advances that had already been achieved in the natural philosophy taught in the medieval curriculum, while their predominant interest in human behaviour, as studied in relation to classical literature, led them away from the study of nature itself. In universities untouched, or scarcely influenced by humanism, science fared no better; the teaching of natural philosophy had become largely a matter of rote.

And if little was passed down from the universities that encouraged the scientific mood of observation-experiment-hypothesis-new experiment, little was passed up from the trial and error level of technology and craft. Just as there was no 'science' in the sense of a method of investigating natural phenomena which could be transferred, in however diluted a form, to other activities, there was no notion of 'technology' as implying the possibility of increased efficiency or the progressive control by man of his environment. Technological literature (how to paint, cast guns or distil liquors) contained hints that improved methods would enable the next generation to make further progress, but advances in particular arts and crafts did not blend into a general concept of technological progress; that was still inhibited by secrecy and craft exclusiveness. There were occupations where scholars with scientific interest co-operated with skilled and literate artisans. Painters learned anatomy with the aid of surgeons, medical literature benefited from the anatomical drawings and engravings provided by artists, surveyors and the makers of navigational instruments were assisted by mathematicians. Yet these contacts were too isolated and too rare to bring about any general cross-fertilisation between those who thought and those who did. Outside the arts, moreover, there was no welcoming place in contemporary social thought for the artisan with intellectual pretensions, and within the arts intellectual improvement, influenced by the desire to rise from craft status, led to some denigration of the manual element. Leonardo's scorn for the sweaty sculptor was paralleled by the university lecturers in medicine who left dissection to assistants plying the humble trade of surgeon. Hypothesis and experiment were lined up on either side of a canyon created by social as well as intellectual prejudice.

Many of the intellectual attitudes necessary for the achievement of a scientific outlook already existed. Curiosity led men to collect antiquities, keep zoos and to purchase freaks of nature. Though a German topographer could break off an eye-witness description of Ulm to remark that its foundation date was given by its name spelled backwards (MLV, or 1055), critical standards in much historical and most philological writings were high. The rigorous commonsense that led Leonardo to realise that the presence of fossil shells in the Apennines meant that the valleys there had once been filled by the sea was reflected, every day in courts of law. The coroner's report on the alleged suicide of Richard Hunne in the Lollard's Tower prison in 1515 is an excellent, and by no means unrepresentative, example of early sixteenth-century cause and effect reasoning.

All we of the inquest together went up into the said tower, where we found the body of the said Hun hanging upon a staple of iron in a girdle of silk, with fair countenance, his head fair combed, and his bonnet right sitting upon his head, with his eyes and mouth fair closed, without any staring, gaping, or frowning. Also, without any drivelling or spurging in any place of his body... The knot of the girdle that went about his neck stood under his left ear, which caused his head to lean toward his right shoulder. Notwithstanding, there came out of his nostrils two small streams of blood to the quantity of four drops, save only these four drops of blood, the face, lips, chin, doublet, collar, and shirt of the said Hun was clean from any blood. Also we find that the skin both of his neck and throat beneath the girdle of silk was fret and fased away, with that thing which the murderers had broken his neck withal. Also the hands of the said Hun were wrung in the wrists, whereby we perceived that his hands had been bound. Moreover, we find that within the said prison was no means whereby any man might hang himself, but only a stool, which stool stood upon a bolster of a bed, so tyckle that any man or beast might not touch it so little but it was ready to fall, whereby we perceived that it was not possible that Hun might hand himself the stool so standing... Also it was not possible that the soft silken girdle should break his neck or skin beneath the girdle. Also we find in a corner somewhat beyond the place where he did hang, a great persell of blood, also we find that upon the left side of Hun's jacket from the breast downward two great streams of blood. Also within the flap of the left side of his jacket we find a great cluster of blood, and the jacket folden down thereupon, which thing the said Hun could never fold nor do after he was hanged. Whereby it appeareth plainly to us all that the neck of Hun was broken, and the great plenty of blood was shed before he was hanged. Wherefore all we find by God and all our consciences that Richard Hun was murdered: also we acquit the said Richard Hun of his own death. Also an end of wax candle which as John Bellringer sayeth he left in the prison burning with Hun that same Sunday at night that Hun was murdered, which wax candle we found sticking upon the stocks fair put out, about seven or eight foot from the place where Hun was hanged, which candle after our opinion was never put out by him, for many likelihoods which we have perceived.*

That curiosity, critical judgement and commonsense did not unite to question received opinions about the nature of the universe is not surprising. The natural philosophers of the twelfth and thirteenth centuries had worked out a vision which embraced all creation from plants and stones to the outermost sphere of the fixed stars which was logical, beautiful and had the sanction of the church. It did not quite explain some of the movements of the heavenly bodies

* C. H. Williams, ed., *English historical documents*, vol. V, 1485–1558 (1967) 660–1.

noticed by astronomers. It left room for debate on, say, the nature of motion or the influence of the planets on human behaviour. But it was coherent, it made sense in terms of God's unique concern for man on his central still platform, the earth, and within it clustered smaller harmonies of explanation like the analogies to be found between temperaments, elements, qualities, winds, seasons, the time of day and the time of life; thus the sanguine temperament was associated with air, the qualities moist and warm, the wind Zephyr, with Spring, morning and youth. Invented by Jehovah, explained by Aristotle and Ptolemy and elaborated and confirmed by numberless medieval commentators, this venerable model was now taken for granted. Copernicus' counter-model, setting the earth rotating and swinging round the sun, challenged likelihood; the globe would be constantly swept by fiercely rushing winds, a stone would not fall in a straight line when it was dropped. It challenged Aristotle, for the natural place for the heaviest body in the universe was at its centre. It challenged the humanist and Christian emphasis on man by making the theatre of his life peripheral to a lifeless orb, the sun. It was presumably with this in mind that Copernicus delayed publication of his ideas, already well formed by 1512, until 1543. Even Pomponazzi, the most tough-minded and rational of contemporary philosophers, who denied that personal immortality could be proved, who mocked at miracles and doubted the efficacy of prayer, accepted the traditional model and locked man's destiny to the influence of the stars.

For a further aspect of the model that discouraged a disinterested reappraisal was the centuries of service it had given to the astrologer. Astrologers taught in universities and received pensions from princely courts. Henry VII supported an astrologer, as did Charles VIII and Louis XII. Condottieri like Bartolomeo Alviano and Paolo Vitelli consulted them. Governments took their advice (or at least asked for it) before sending an embassy, private individuals before laying the foundation stone of a house or before going on a journey. The alchemist needed advice on when to attempt a transmutation because of the relationship between metals and certain stars. The doctor picked his simples and administered them at astrologically determined times. Farmers planted, reaped and slaughtered with a copious cheap literature of prognostication in mind. To shift the earth from the centre of the universe would be to upset the calculations of all those who foretold the future or chose auspicious times of the day or month.

Belief in astrology was accompanied by a good deal of mockery. A king of France, so one story ran, went hunting in the expectation of enjoying the fine weather promised by his astrologer. Taking no notice of a miller who warned him that he knew from the horse-flies clustering round his donkey that it would rain, the king rode on into a drenching storm. The casting of horoscopes was actually forbidden by canon law because it denied the concept of free will, but by adopting the formula that the planets 'inclined without constraining' astrologers continued to ply their trade. The influence of humanism led on the whole to an enhanced respect for astrology. The attitude of Cicero was in doubt, but Virgil, Pliny and Ptolemy all appeared to have believed in the power of planetary and sidereal emanations, as did the Plato of the *Timaeus*.

Pico della Mirandola, the firmest opponent of astrology, believed that the planets were thought to be powerful simply because they bore the names of gods who had once been thought to influence men's lives. His attack ranged widely. After keeping a weather diary he found that astrological predictions were correct for only seven out of one hundred and thirty days. If astrology were a science, he asked, why could astrologers never agree among themselves? Astrologers relied on tables of heavenly movements, yet these were known to be erroneous. His key arguments, however, were not based on commonsense observations of this sort, but on his conviction that God had given man the ability to choose his own destiny. How could the planets, mere lumps of rock with pagan names, affect this choice offered to man's spirit? But Pico's attack stood alone because it was based on an intensely personal vision rather than on a chain of verifiable reasoning that reached all the way from keeping his weather diary to wishing to strip the stars of their occult powers. Even Ficino, his older associate, did not deny these powers, though he too pointed out the mistakes made by astrologers and the discrepancies between their forecasts. And significantly it was the Neapolitan humanist Pontano, who lacked the romantic and idealising vein of his Florentine colleagues, who argued most cogently in favour of astrology. Accepting the influence of heredity, education and environment, Pontano, by concentrating on man's psychology, found aberrancies that were at that time only explicable if (leaving out, as he did, the action of God in the soul) the influence of the stars were taken into account.

This range of philosophical argument, from the denial of Pico through Ficino's hesitant scepticism to Pontano's affirmation was, of course, irrelevant to the vast body of men who wanted a certainty about the future, guidance in their day-to-day affairs, and an explanation of character which only astrology could provide. And the astrological principles derived from the medieval cosmic model deflected criticism of that model in the interest of yet another deep-seated need – to exert an actual control over the future by spells and incantations. As the technology of the unskilled, the science of the non-numerate, the power of the unprivileged, magic was a necessity as well as a skill. The man who could not afford to irrigate his land could buy a piece of rigmarole which, if inscribed on a piece of previously unwritten-on paper and fed to a frog would produce rain as soon as the frog hopped back into a pond. A lodestone stroked along a piece of iron transferred its north-seeking property to the iron; so, logically, an extract of goat's testicle administered to an adored but cold woman would make her passionate. Gyves and bolts would melt if the starry influences that kept the metal rigid were interrupted by a well-chosen incantation. That magic had its forbidden, heretical side, involving a commerce with demons, and that there was debate as between the nature of true and false magic only made magic itself seem more a part of the order of things. Working within a framework of ideas that was intuitive where it was not traditional, magicians and astrologers were (outside the ranks of businessmen and government officials) the arch-calculators of the age. Pure science lay becalmed among the natural philosophy faculties of the universities. Applied science, the desire to use a knowledge of physical laws to change the environment and improve the quality of life for the individual, was more vigorous, but it was chiefly a matter of horoscopes and spells. As for experiment, it was chiefly amid the retorts and furnaces of the alchemist that inquiring men did not think it demeaning to pour acids and shovel fuel in order to break the secrets of nature.

Apart from a few men of genius, natural philosophy had long been looked upon as something to learn from a handful of near-sacred texts. Once absorbed, so great was the respect for written authorities that the knowledge gleaned became an end in itself, perhaps calling for comment but not prompting further inquiry. And by multiplying authorities humanism had intensified this attitude. Even Copernicus was more concerned to adjust Ptolemy to his theories than to make the ancient authorities obsolete. Moreover, buttressing this respect was a readiness to believe that something became true by being written down. Fostered by the rarity and value of manuscripts, this trait was transferred to the wide public who could now buy printed books. Printing, of course, extended scientific knowledge, but at the same time it spread errors and slowed speculation. By 1500 some three thousand different books dealing with scientific subjects had been published, bringing to the surface not only classical texts of fundamental importance, like Galen's anatomical work *On the Use of the Parts*, but the largely erroneous *Chirurgia* of Guy de Chauliac, thirteenth-century commentaries on Sacrobosco's *Sphere*, and numerous popular compilations purporting to distil all that needed to be known about, say, geometry or physiology in a few pages. Later in the sixteenth century, when the chaff had been winnowed out of this heap, printing would serve science by reporting up-to-date findings and, largely through the use of illustrations, by standardising the way in which these findings were discussed. For the moment, however, the need to absorb overwhelmed the desire to observe, speculate and attempt to prove by experiment.

Outside the alchemist's laboratory the desire to experiment (as opposed to the improvements sought in the metallurgical, printing and shipbuilding industries) was limited to the arts. The painter, anxious to make the basis if not the final effect of his work an accurate copy of nature, was forced to study appearances in nature and to ease his work in the studio by elaborating rules that would enable him to reproduce them without looking out of the window. And this rule-seeking was stimulated by the part an overall, mathematically-calculated perspective was now expected to play in the representation of space. 'Find out', Leonardo reminded himself in one of his notebooks, 'how much a man diminishes at a certain distance and what the length of that distance is; and then at twice that distance and at three times, and so make your general rule.' On the evidence of his drawings, Leonardo's visual sense was so phenomenal that he hardly needed formulae to convey a sense of distance, the effect of light on a solid body, or the spacing of leaves that distinguishes the branch of an old tree from that of a young one. But his desire to make his inner, reflective, rearranging vision as acute as the eye with which he regarded the physical world led him to utterances which convey the feeling later to become characteristic of science but then immensely rare: 'it seems to me that those sciences are vain and full of error which do not spring from experiment, the source of all certainty'; 'anyone who in an argument appeals to authority uses not his intelligence but his memory.' Leonardo's scientific desire to understand was rooted in his artistic impulse to copy. And this impulse cut through the usual contemporary way of considering a phenomenon, which involved seeing its allegorical or moral significance, or its relationship to phenomena quite different in kind.

To understand more fully what a human body looked like, to be able to portray it in violent motion or in combination with scores of others without having recourse to models, Leonardo dissected corpses and studied the function of muscles. 'Physicians', as Marineo Siculo wrote, 'should know more than merely to peer into the chamber-pot.' But what Marineo went on to say about them has nothing to do with the scalpel and is entirely characteristic of most of the scientific thought of the period: 'They should understand music, of course, and mathematical training, and whatever pertains to number and to measure, and the causes, motions, influence, nature and effect of the stars; for if a doctor is ignorant of these things he is able neither to diagnose nor to heal.' For the most part 'scientific' enquiry floated uneasily in the void between common-sense observation and an uncritically accepted cosmology.

Appendix

Europe *c.* 1500: a Political Gazetteer

Russia: population nine millions (very uncertain), hereditary grand duchy centred on Moscow and incorporating Novgorod, Vyatka, Tver and Ryazan. *Moldavia:* population uncertain, nominally an independent princedom but subject by turns to Turkish, Hungarian and Polish control. *Lithuania:* population uncertain, eastern border in dispute with Russia, a grand duchy ruled from and in conjunction with *Poland:* population nine millions, elective monarchy. *Hungary:* population uncertain, elective monarchy. *Bohemia:* population uncertain, elective monarchy. *Germany:* population twelve millions, as chief component of Holy Roman Empire under theoretical authority of the emperor-elect, Maximilian of Habsburg, hereditary ruler of the duchies of Austria, Styria, Carinthia and Carniola together with the county of Tyrol. In practice Germany was a congeries of independent units comprising some thirty principates (the most prominent being the Palatinate, Upper and Lower Bavaria, Württemberg, Saxony, Mecklenburg and Brandenburg), fifty ecclesiastical territories, about one hundred counties and sixty self-governing cities.* *Netherlands:* population about six millions, traditionally part of Holy Roman Empire, now ruled jointly with Luxembourg and Franche-Comté by Prince Philip of Habsburg, son of Maximilian. *Switzerland:* population about 750,000, federation of eleven cantons, part of Holy Roman Empire but in practice independent. *Denmark:* population uncertain, elective monarchy. *Sweden:* population about 800,000, elective monarchy. *Norway:* population unknown, hereditary monarchy. In theory, since the union of Kalmar (1397) the Scandinavian kingdoms were governed jointly; in practice Norway followed a course of her own as did Denmark, economically the strongest (controlling the Kattegat through its possession of Bohus, Halland and

---

* 'No-one ever succeeded in compiling a rational list of the number of sovereign units in Germany.' Gerald Strauss, *Historian in an age of crisis: the life and works of Johannes Aventinus 1477–1534* (Harvard U. P., 1963).

Scania), while Sweden was divided between an independence and a pro-Danish party. *Italy:* a term whose significance was chiefly geographical but which, in moments of political crisis or cultural debate could refer to a more-or-less common linguistic background and a sense of common origins in Roman antiquity shared by (to name the chief independent powers of the peninsula): *Venice:* population one and a half million, a republic and the only Italian state with an overseas empire, comprising part of Dalmatia, Corfu, Crete, Cyprus and some scattered colonies in southern Greece. *Milan:* population one and a quarter million, a duchy (in 1500, occupied and administered by the French). *Florence:* population three-quarters of a million, republic. *Papal States:* population two millions, elective ecclesiastical principality ruled by the pope. *Naples:* population two millions, hereditary monarchy. Among the smaller independent Italian states were the republics of *Genoa* (which had an uncertain control over Corsica), *Lucca* and *Siena,* the duchies of *Ferrara, Modena* and *Urbino* and the marquisate of *Mantua. Sicily:* population unknown, hereditary kingdom but dependent upon Aragon. *Spain:* comprising *Aragon,* population one million and *Castile,* population six and a half millions, both hereditary monarchies but ruled jointly by Ferdinand and Isabella, their respective sovereigns, since his succession in 1479. *Portugal:* population one million, hereditary monarchy. *Navarre:* population unknown, hereditary monarchy. *France:* population sixteen millions, hereditary monarchy. *England:* population three millions, hereditary monarchy. This does not exhaust the list of political entities which operated as independent states either by right, as in the case of the kingdom of *Scotland* and the duchy of *Savoy* or because their nominal superiors were unable to control them, as was the case with certain Baltic cities, like Lübeck and the area to the south of the Gulf of Finland controlled by the Teutonic Order of Knights – both nominally subject to the Holy Roman Emperor. Nor does it include a state which was not of, but was half in Europe, the empire of the *Ottoman Turks,* who by the death of Mohammed the Conqueror in 1481 ruled as much land west of the Dardanelles as they did in Asia and controlled a Balkan population south of the Danube amounting to some five and a half millions.

Note to the Second Edition: Population figures in this appendix have been brought into line with recent estimates in Hale's *Civilisation,* cit., p. 143 and Brady et al., *Handbook* cit., I, p. 13.

Maps

Map 1   Europe c.1500

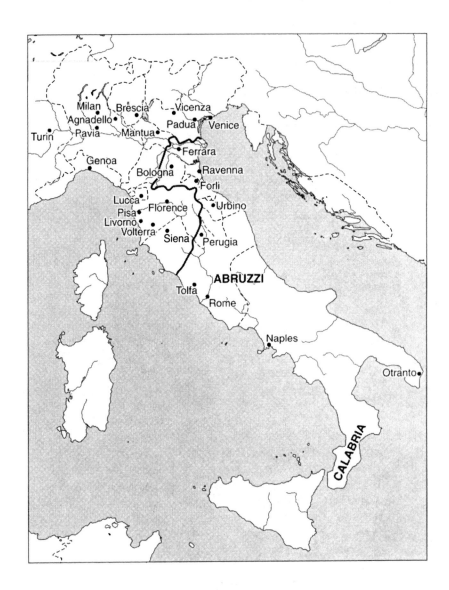

Map 2 Italy *c.*1500

Map 3   Germany *c.*1500

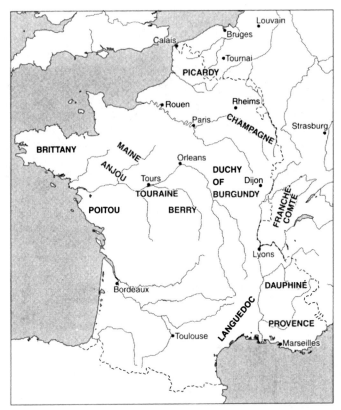

Map 4   France *c*.1500

Map 5   Spain *c*.1500

Bibliography

This bibliography is really a displaced dedication, for it is above all a record of my indebtedness. This fact, as well as its restriction to titles in English and French, maims it as a balanced introduction to the bibliography of the period. The best such introduction, to my knowledge, is the *Renaissance Bibliography* compiled by Gene A. Brucker for the use of history graduate students at the University of California, Berkeley.*

Many of the books and articles cited below illuminate more than one topic; they are placed under the heading to which they contributed most. Books were published in London unless another place is given.

(For additional bibliography provided for the second edition, sa below pp. 000–000.)

GENERAL WORKS

G. R. Potter, ed., *The new Cambridge modern history*, vol. i (Cambridge University Press, 1957); Myron P. Gilmore, *The World of humanism, 1453–1517* (N.Y., 1952); Roland Mousnier, *Les XVIe et XVIIe siècles* (Paris, 1961); H. Hauser and A. Renaudet, *Les débuts de l'âge moderne* (4th ed. Paris, 1956); Fernand Braudel, *Le Mediterranée et le monde Mediterranéen à l'époque de Philippe II* (revised ed., 2 vols., Paris, 1966); H. G. Koenigsberger and G. L. Mosse, *Europe in the sixteenth century* (1968); W. K. Ferguson, *Europe in transition, 1300–1520* (Boston, 1962); Denys Hay, *Europe in the fourteenth and fifteenth Centuries* (1966) and, as ed., *The age of the Renaissance* (1967); A. Chastel, *The age of humanism: Europe 1480–1530* (1963); R. van Marle, *Iconographie de l'art profane au moyen age et à la Renaissance* (2 vols., The Hague, 1931–2); Charles S. Singleton, *Art, science and history in the Renaissance* (Baltimore, 1967).

In the citation of contemporary opinions I have drawn especially on the following works (they are not listed elsewhere in this bibliography).

Beatis, Antonio de. *Die Reise des Kardinals Luigi d'Aragona (1517–1518)* ed. Ludwig Pastor (Freiburg im Breisgau, 1905). he text is in Italian. I quote from my forthcoming translation for the Hakluyt Society.

---

*Obtainable from Graduate Secretary, University of California, Berkeley, California, 94720, U.S.A.

Castiglione, Baldassare. *The book of the courtier*, tr. George Bull (1967).

Chêrot, M. La société au commencement du XVIe siècle (d'après les homélies de Josse Clichtove) 1472–1543, *Revue des Questions Historiques* (1895).

Coquillart, Guillaume. *Oeuvres* (2 vols., Paris, 1857).

Crotch, W. J. B., ed. *The prologues and epilogues of William Caxton* (1928).

La Borderie, A. de. *Oeuvres françaises d'Olivier Maillard: sermons et poésies* (Nantes, 1877).

Landucci, Luca. *A Florentine diary from 1450 to 1516*, tr. Alice de Rosen Jervis (1927).

Lynn, Caro. *A college professor of the Renaissance* [Marineo Siculo] (Chicago, 1937).

More, Sir Thomas. *Utopia*, in *The complete works of St. Thomas More*, vol. 4, ed. Edward Surtz and J. H. Hexter (Yale, 1965).

Nauert, Charles G. *Agrippa and the crisis of Renaissance thought* (University of Illinois, 1965).

Nève, Joseph. *Sermons choisis de Michel Menot, 1508–1518* (Paris, 1924).

Oulmont, Charles. *La poésie morale, politique et dramatique à le veille de la Renaissance: Pierre Gringore* (Paris, 1910).

Panofsky, Erwin. *The life and art of Albrecht Dürer* (Princeton, 1955).

Phillips, Margaret Mann. *The Adages of Erasmus* (Cambridge U.P., 1964).

Rojas, Fernando de, *The Spanish Bawd (La Celestina)*, tr. J. H. Cohen (1964).

Seyssel, Claude de. *La monarchie de France*, ed. J. Poujol (Paris, 1961).

Speroni, Charles. *Wit and wisdom of the Italian Renaissance* (U. of California, 1964).

Spitz, Lewis W. *Conrad Celtis, the German arch-humanist* (Harvard U.P., 1957).

Strauss, Gerald. *Sixteenth century Germany, its topography and topographers* (Madison, 1959).

Thompson, Craig R., ed. and tr. *The Colloquies of Erasmus* (U. of Chicago, 1965).

Williams, C. H., ed. *English Historical Documents 1485–1558* (1967).

TIME AND SPACE

Time: F. A. B. Ward, *Time Measurement* (1958); Carlo M. Cipolla, *Clocks and culture 1300–1700* (1967) republished with *Guns and sails...*(see below, this section) in *European culture and overseas expansion* (1970); J. Le Goff, Au moyen age. Temps de l'église et temps du marchand, *Annales* (1960) 417–33, and Le temps du travail dans la crise du XIVe siècle: du temps médiéval au temps moderne, *Le Moyen Age* (1963) 597–613; Edouard Jeanselme, *Traité de la syphilis*, vol. i (Paris, 1931); Creighton Gilbert, When did renaissance man grow old?, *Studies in the Renaissance* (1967) 7–32; Alberto Tenenti, *La vie et la mort à travers l'art du XVe siècle* (Paris, 1952); C. A. Beerli, *Le peintre poète Nicolas Manuel et l'évolution sociale de son temps* (Geneva) 1953); Erwin Panofsky, *Tomb Sculpture*, ed. W. W. Janson (1964); P. Burke, *The Renaissance sense of the past* (1970).

Space: E. H. Gombrich, *Meditations on a Hobbyhorse*, esp. Psycho-analysis and the History of Art (1963); A. Richard Turner, *The vision of landscape in Renaissance Italy* (Princeton U.P., 1966); M. Margaret Newett, *Canon Pietro Casola's pilgrimage to Jerusalem in the year 1494* (Manchester U.P., 1907); A. J. Mitchell, *Spring Voyage* (1964); E. G. R. Taylor, The Surveyor, *Economic History Review* (1947) 121–33. Exploration: J. H. Parry, *The Age of Reconnaissance* (1903); Boies Penrose, *Travel and discovery in the Renaissance* (Harvard U.P., 1952); J. R. Hale, *Renaissance exploration* (B.B.C., 1968); G. V. Scammell, The New Worlds and Europe in the sixteenth century, *The Historical Journal* (1969) 359–412; J. H. Elliott, *The old world and the new, 1492–1650* (Cambridge, 1970); Carlo M. Cipolla, *Guns and sails in the early phase of European expansion, 1400–1700* (1965); M. Mollat and P. Adam, eds., *Les aspects internationaux de la découverte océanique aux XVe et XVIe siècles* (Paris, 1966); V. Magalhaes-Godinho, *L'économie de l'empire portugais aux XVe et XVIe siècles* (Paris, 1970); C. R. Boxer, *The Portuguese seaborne empire, 1415–1825* (1969); C. O. Sauer, *The early Spanish Main* (U. of California, 1966); R. H. Major, tr. and ed., *Christopher Columbus, four voyages to the New World: letters and selected documents* (Reprint, N.Y., 1961); E. G. Ravenstein, ed., *The journal of the first voyage of Vasco da Gama, 1497–1499* (Hakluyt Soc., 1898); W. B. Greenlee, tr. and ed., *The voyage of Pedro Alvares Cabral to Brazil and India* (Hakluyt Soc., 1938); Lodovico di Varthema, *The Travels*, tr. J. W. Jones, ed. G. P. Badger (Hakluyt Soc., 1863).

POLITICAL EUROPE

General discussions: G. R. Potter, The beginnings of the modern state, *History* (1946) 73–84; Garrett Mattingly, Changing attitudes toward the state during the Renaissance, in *Facets of the Renaissance*, ed. W. H. Werkmeister (N.Y., 1959); Gerhardt Ritter, Origins of the modern state, and Federico Chabod, Was there a Renaissance State? in Heinz Lubasz, ed., *The development of the modern state* (N.Y., 1964). On propaganda: G. E. Waas, *The legendary character of the Kaiser Maximilian* (N.Y., 1914); J. Chartrou, *Les entrées solonelles et trionphales à la Renaissance 1484–1551* (Paris, 1928); Sydney Anglo, *Spectacle, pageantry and early Tudor policy* (Oxford, 1969); L. D. Ettlinger, *The Sistine Chapel before Michelangelo: religious imagery and papal primacy* (Oxford, 1965). Individual countries: George Vernadsky, *Russia at the dawn of the modern age* (Yale U.P., 1959); J. L. I. Fennell, *Ivan the Great of Moscow* (1961); Ian Grey, *Ivan III and the unification of Russia* (1964); J. H. Elliott, *Imperial Spain, 1469–1716* (1963); John Lynch, *Spain under the Habsburgs*, vol. i (Oxford, 1964); H. S. Offler, Aspects of government in the late medieval empire, in *Europe in the late Middle Ages*, ed. J. R. Hale, J. R. C. Highfield and B. Smalley (1965); Hans Baron, Imperial reform and the Habsburgs, 1486–1504: a new interpretation, *American Historical Review* (October, 1939) 293–303; H. J. Cohn, *The government of the Rhine Palatinate in the fifteenth century* (Oxford U.P., 1965); P. S. Lewis, *Later Medieval France* (1968); R. Mousnier, *Études sur la France de 1494 à 1559* (Cours de Sorbonne, Paris, n.d.); J.

Russell Major, *Representative institutions in Renaissance France* (Madison, 1960); Denys Hay, *The Italian Renaissance in its historical background* (Cambridge U.P., 1961); Nicolai Rubinstein, *The government of Florence under the Medici* (Oxford, 1966); D. M. de Mesquita, The Place of Despotism in Italian Politics in *Europe in the Late Middle Ages* (cit.); G. R. Elton, *England under the Tudors* (1955) and *The Tudor constitution* (Cambridge U.P., 1960); Paul L. Hughes and James F. Larkin, eds., *Tudor royal proclamations*, vol. i (Yale U.P., 1964); J. M. W. Bean, *The decline of English feudalism, 1215–1540* (U. of Manchester, 1968); *The Cambridge history of Poland*, vol. i (Cambridge U.P., 1950); P. Brock, *The political and social doctrines of the Unity of Czech Brethren* (The Hague, 1957); K. Gjerset, *History of the Norwegian people* (1927); Michael Roberts, *The early Vasas: a history of Sweden, 1523–1611* (Cambridge U.P., 1968); Garrett Mattingly, *Renaissance diplomacy* (1955).

INDIVIDUAL AND COMMUNITY

J. Huizinga, *The waning of the Middle Ages* (1924) retains to the full its attractiveness as an attempt to describe the tone of a society; more recently, and of more direct relevance for this period, there is Robert Mandrou, *Introduction à la France moderne, 1500–1640* (Paris, 1961). Demography: the chapter by Karl F. Helleiner in *Cambridge economic history of Europe*, iv. On family structure: Philippe Ariès, *Centuries of childhood: a social history of family life* (1962). Morality: C. Brunel, Opuscules provençaux du XVᵉ siècle sur la confession, *Annales du Midi* (1917) 174–224 and 355–409; J. de Pas, Moeurs rustiques aux XVᵉ, XVIᵉ et XVIIᵉ siècles dans les baillages de Saint-Omer et Aire, *Mémoires de la Société des Antiquaires de Morinie*, vol. xxxv, 329–78; G.-J. Witkowski, *L'art profane à l'église: ses licenses symboliques, satiriques et fantaisistes* (3 vols., Paris, 1908–12); H. C. Lea, *Materials toward a history of witchcraft*, ed. A. C. Howland (3 vols., reprint, 1957). Inter-nation feeling: C. A. J. Armstrong, The Language Question in the Low Countries, in *Europe in the Late Middle Ages*, cit.; G. Ascoli, *La Grande Bretagne devant l'opinion française depuis la Guerre de Cent Ans jusqu' à la fin du 16ᵉ siècle* (Paris, 1927); V. Ilardi, "Italianità" among some Italian intellectuals in the early sixteenth century, *Traditio* (1956), 339–67; R. Schwoebel, *The shadow of the crescent: The Renaissance image of the Turk, 1453–1517* (N.Y., 1967). Supra-national feeling: J. Ancel and Ö. de Törne, L'évolution de la notion de frontière, in *International Commission of Historical Sciences*, Bulletin, vol. v (Warsaw, 1933) 540–59; Denys Hay, *Europe: the emergence of an idea* (Edinburgh U.P., 1957); W. H. McNeill, *Europe's steppe frontier* (Chicago U.P., 1964); A. S. Atiya, *The crusade in the later Middle Ages* (1938). Life outside the Towns: Yvonne Bézard, *La vie rurale dans le sud de la région Parisienne de 1450 à 1550* (Paris, 1929); W. G. Hoskins, *Provincial England* (1963); and inside the towns: Gerald Strauss – a book I have drawn on heavily – *Nuremberg in the sixteenth century* (N.Y., 1966); Bartolomé Bennassar, *Valladolid au siècle d'or: une ville de Castille et sa campagne au XVIᵉ siècle* (Paris, 1967); J. B. Wadsworth, *Lyons 1473–1503, The beginnings of cosmopolitanism*

(Cambridge, Mass., 1962), and Lucien Romier, Lyons and cosmopolitanism at the beginning of the French Renaissance, in Werner L. Gundersheimer, ed., *French humanism 1470–1600* (1969); Miriam U. Chrisman, *Strasbourg and the reform: a study in the process of change* (Yale U.P., 1967); and Jacques Heers, *Genes au XVe siècle* (Paris, 1901).

ECONOMIC EUROPE

E. E. Rich and C. H. Wilson, eds., *The Cambridge economic history of Europe*, vol. iv (Cambridge U.P., 1967); Philippe Dollinger, *La Hanse, XIIe– XVIIe siècles* (Paris, 1964); Richard Ehrenberg, *Capital and finance in the age of the Renaissance*, tr. H. M. Lucas (1928); Raymond de Roover, *The rise and decline of the Medici Bank, 1397–1494* (Harvard U.P., 1963); Gertrude R. B. Richards, *Florentine merchants in the age of the Medici* (Harvard U.P., 1932); M. Bresnard, *Les foires de Lyon au XVe et XVIe siècles* (Paris, 1924); Jean-François Bergier, *Genève et l'économie Européenne de la Renaissance* (Paris, 1903); Jean Delumeau, *L'alun de Rome, XVe– XVIe siècles* (Paris, 1962); F. C. Lane, *Venetian ships and shipbuilders* (Baltimore, 1934) and *Venice and history: the collected papers of F.C. Lane* (Baltimore, 1966); Julius Klein, *The Mesta: a study in Spanish economic history* (Harvard U.P., 1920); Joan Thirsk, ed., *The agrarian history of England and Wales*, vol. iv (Cambridge U.P., 1967); Lawrence Stone, State control in sixteenth-century England, *Economic History Review* (1947) 103–20. And see *Class*, In the towns.

CLASS

General: R. Mohl, *The three estates in Medieval and Renaissance literature* (N.Y., 1933); Lawrence Stone, Social Mobility in England, 1500–1700, *Past and Present* (April, 1966) 16–55; Joan Simon, *Education and society in Tudor England* (Cambridge U.P., 1966). Two Italian models: D. L. Hicks, Sienese society in the Renaissance, *Comparative Studies in Society and History* (1960) 412–20; Paul Coles, The crisis of Renaissance society, Genoa 1488–1507, *Past and Present* (April, 1957) 17–47. Sumptuary laws: Henri Aragon, *Les lois somptuaires en France. La luxe sous les rois de France. Le XVe siècle et la Renaissance. Ordonnances et édits* (Perpignan, 1921); J. H. Vincent, *Costume and conduct in the laws of Basle, Berne and Zurich, 1370–1800* (Baltimore, 1935); M. M. Newett, The sumptuary laws of Venice in the fourteenth and fifteenth centuries, in *Historical Studies*, ed. T. F. Tout and James Tait (Manchester U.P., 1907). Lawyers: Lauro Martines, *Lawyers and statecraft in Renaissance Florence* (Princeton U.P., 1968); E. W. Ives, The reputation of the common lawyers in English society, 1450– 1550, *University of Birmingham Historical Journal* (1959–60) 130–61; Hans Thieme, Le role des *doctores legum* dans la société allemande du XVIe siècle, in *Individu et société à la Renaissance* (Paris, 1967). Other Groups: Pauline M. Smith, *The Anti-courtier trend in sixteenth century French literature* (Geneva, 1966); Fritz Redlich, *The German military enterpriser and his work force*, vol. i (Wiesbaden, 1964); Rudolf and Margot Wittkower, *Born under Saturn* (1963); R. Wittkower, Individualism in art and artists: a Renaissance problem, *Journal of the History of Ideas* (1961) 291–302; S. W. Baron, *A Social and religious history of the Jews*, vol. xiii (1969); Cecil Roth, *A history of the Jews of Italy* (Philadelphia, 1946). In the country: B. H. Slicher van Bath, *The agrarian history of Western Europe, 500–1550* (1963); Marc Bloch, *French rural history: an essay in its basic characteristics*, tr. Janet Sondheimer (1966); J. Blum, *Lord ana peasant in Russia from the ninth to the nineteenth Century* (Princeton U.P., 1961); Brian Tierney, *Medieval poor law* (Berkeley, 1959). Serfdom and slavery: J. Blum, The rise of serfdom in Eastern Europe, *American Historical Review* (1956–7) 807–36; Iris Origo, The domestic enemy: the eastern slaves in Tuscany in the 14th and 15th centuries, *Speculum* (1955) 321–66. In the towns: Jean V. Alter, *Les origines de la satire anti-Bourgeoise en France. Moyen age – XVIᵉ siècle* (Geneva, 1966); P. Boissonade, *Le socialisme d'état. L'industrie et les classes industrielles en France pendant les deux premiers siècles de l'ére moderne, 1453–1661* (Paris, 1927); L. Febvre, Types économiques et sociaux du XVIᵉ siècle: le marchand, *Revue des Cours et Conférences* (1921) 57–65, 143–57; Régine Pernoud, *Histoire de la bourgeoisie en France*, vol. i (Paris, 1960); Emile Coornaert, *Les corporations en France avant 1789* (Paris, 1941); Sylvia Thrupp, *The merchant class of medieval London, 1300–1500* (Chicago U.P., 1948); J. A. Goris, *Études sur les colonies marchands méridionales à Anvers, 1488–1567* (Louvain, 1925); J. H. Hexter, The education of the aristocracy in the Renaissance, in his *Reappraisals in history* (1961).

RELIGION

General: R. Aubenas and Ricard, *L'église et la Renaissance, 1449–1517* (Paris, 1951); Pierre Imbart de la Tour, *Les origines de la Réforme*, vol. i (Paris, 1905); Lucien Febvre, *Au coeur religieux du XVIᵉ siècle* (Paris, 1957); P. S. Allen, *The Age of Erasmus* (Oxford U.P., 1914); H. A. Enno van Gelder, *The two Reformations of the sixteenth century. A study of the religious aspects and consequences of the Renaissance and humanism* (The Hague, 1961); J. Toussaert, *Le sentiment religieux en Flandre à la fin du moyen-age* (Paris, 1960). Church and state: R. J. Knecht, The Concordat of 1516, *University of Birmingham Historical Journal* (1963) 16–32; Henry Kamen, *The Spanish Inquisition* (1965). Clerics: Ludwig Pastor, *The History of the Popes*, vols. iv–viii, tr. F. I. Antrobus (1894 *seq.*); M. E. Mallett, *The Borgias* (1969); D. S. Chambers, The economic predicament of Renaissance cardinals, in *Studies in Medieval and Renaissance History*, vol. iii (U. of Nebraska, 1966); David Knowles, *The religious orders in England*, vol. iii (Cambridge U.P., 1961); Margaret Bowker, *The secular clergy in the diocese of Lincoln, 1450–1520* (Cambridge U.P., 1968). Church and people: Emile Mâle, *L'art religieux de la fin du moyen âge en France* (Paris, 1925); Mirella Levi d'Ancona, *The iconography of the Immaculate Conception in the Middle Ages and early Renaissance* (College Art Association of America, 1957); D. Weinstein, Savonarola, Florence, and the millenarian tradition,

Church History (1958) 291–305 and *Savonarola and Florence* (Princeton U.P., 1970); G. R. Owst, *Literature and pulpit in Medieval England* (Cambridge U.P., 1933); J. W. Blench, *Preaching in England in the Late Fifteenth and Sixteenth Centuries* (Oxford, 1964). Learning: Margaret Aston, Books and belief in the later Middle Ages, in *Papers presented to the Past and Present conference on popular religion* (typescript, 1966); A. Renaudet, *Préréforme et humanisme à Paris pendant les premières guerres d'Italie, 1494–1517* (Paris, 1916); H. A. Oberman, Some Notes on the theology of nominalism with attention to its relation to the Renaissance, *Harvard Theological Review* (1960) 47–76; *Letters of Obscure Men*, reprinted as *On the Eve of the Reformation*, ed. Hajo Holborn (N.Y., 1964); Hajo Holborn, *Ulrich von Hutten and the German Reformation* (Yale U.P., 1937); Lewis W. Spitz, *The religious Renaissance of the German humanists* (Harvard U.P., 1963). Dissatisfactions: A. Hyma, *The Christian Renaissance: a history of the Devotio Moderna* (Hamden, Conn., 1965); H. R. Trevor-Roper, The European witch craze of the sixteenth and seventeenth centuries, in *Religion, the Reformation and social change* (1967); Auguste Jundt, *Histoire du panthéisme populaire au moyen age et au seizième siècle* (reprint, Frankfurt am Main, 1964); J. A. F. Thomson, *The Later Lollards, 1414–1520* (Oxford U.P., 1965); Myron P. Gilmore, Freedom and determinism in Renaissance historians, *Studies in the Renaissance* (1956), 49–60; Don Cameron Allen, *Doubt's boundless sea* (Baltimore, 1964) and *The star-crossed Renaissance* (Durham, U.S.A., 1941); Lewis W. Spitz, Occultism and despair of reason in Renaissance thought, *Journal of the History of Ideas* (1966), 464–69; D. P. Walker, *Spiritual and demonic magic from Ficino to Campanella* (1958); A. G. Dickens, *Reformation and Society in sixteenth century Europe* (1966).

ART

Music: Gustave Reese, *Music in the Renaissance* (rev. ed., N.Y., 1959); Dom Anselm Hughes and Gerald Abraham, *Ars nova and the Renaissance, 1300–1540* (Oxford U.P., 1960); Nanie Bridgman, *La vie musicale au quattrocento* (Paris, 1964); Edward Lowinsky, Music in the culture of the Renaissance, *Journal of the History of Ideas* (1954) 509–53. Drama: Gustave Cohen, *Le théâtre en France au moyen age* (2 vols. Paris, 1928, 1931), and *Histoire de la mise en scène dans le théâtre religieux français du moyen age* (Paris, 1926); Jean Jacquot, ed., *Le lieu théâtrale à la Renaissance* (Paris, 1964); H. G. Harvey, *Theatre of the Bazoche* (Harvard U.P., 1941); E. K. Chambers, *The medieval stage*, vol. ii (Oxford U.P., 1903); Glynne Wickham, *Early English Stages 1300 to 1600*, vol. I (1959); Douglas Radcliffe-Umsted, *The birth of modern comedy in Renaissance Italy* (Chicago University Press, 1969); G. R. Kernodle, *From art to theatre: form and convention in the Renaissance* (Chicago U.P., 1944). Fine Arts: Elizabeth G. Holt, ed., *A documentary history of art*, vol. i (N.Y., 1957); John White, *The birth and rebirth of pictorial space* (1957); E. H. Gombrich, The Renaissance theory of art and the rise of landscape, in his *Norm and Form* (1966); Anthony Blunt, *Artistic theory in Italy 1450–1600* (Oxford U.P., 1940); J. Jex-Blake and E. Sellers, *The Elder Pliny's chapter on the history of art* (1896); Otto Benesch,

The art of the Renaissance in Northern Europe (rev. ed., 1965); Charles de Tolnay, *Hieronymus Bosch* (1966; Charles Garside, *Zwingli and the arts* (Yale U.P., 1966); Wolfgang Stechow, *Northern Renaissance art 1400–1600* (Englewood Cliffs, N. J., 1966); Anthony Blunt, *Art and architecture in France 1500–1700* (1953); Albert Châtelet and Jacques Thuillier, *La peinture française du Fouquet à Poussin* (Geneva, 1963); Lawrence Stone, *Sculpture in Britain: The Middle Ages* (1955); André Chastel, *The Golden Age of the Renaissance: Italy 1460–1500*, tr. J. Griffin (1965), *The studios and styles of the Renaissance: Italy 1460–1500*, tr. J. Griffin (1966) and *Art et humanisme à Florence au temps de Laurent le Magnifique* (Paris, 1960); R. Klein and H. Zerner, *Italian Art 1500–1600* (Englewood Cliffs, N.J., 1960); Eve Borsook, *The mural painters of Tuscany* (1960); John Shearman, *Andrea del Sarto* (2 vols. Oxford U.P., 1965); Edgar Wind, *Bellini's Feast of the Gods* (Harvard U.P., 1948); John Pope-Hennessy, *The portrait in the Renaissance* (1967), *Italian Renaissance sculpture* (1958), and The Italian Plaquette, *Proceedings of the British Academy* (1964) 63–85.

SECULAR LEARNING

Humanism: R. R. Bolgar, *The classical inheritance* (Cambridge U.P., 1952); Robert Weiss, *The Renaissance discovery of classical antiquity* (Oxford, 1969); P. O. Kristeller, *The Classics and Renaissance thought* (Harvard U.P., 1955), The philosophy of man in the Italian Renaissance in F. L. Baumer, ed., *Intellectual movements in modern European history* (N.Y., 1965) and Humanism and scholasticism in the Italian Renaissance in his *Studies in Renaissance thought and letters* (Rome, 1956); Eugenio Garin, *Italian humanism: philosophy and civic life in the Renaissance*, tr. Peter Munz (Oxford, 1965); Ernst Cassirer, *The individual and the cosmos in Renaissance philosophy*, tr. Mario Domandi (Oxford, 1963); J. A. Mazzeo, *Renaissance and revolution: the remaking of European thought* (N.Y., 1965); Eugene Rice, *The Renaissance idea of wisdom* (Harvard U.P., 1958); E. Surtz, *The praise of pleasure* (Harvard U.P., 1957); K. H. Dannenfeld, Egypt and Egyptian antiquities in the Renaissance, *Studies in the Renaissance* (1959) 7–27; Werner L. Gundersheimer, ed. cit. Literacy and education: Lucien Febvre and H. J. Martin, *L'apparition du livre* (Paris, 1958); Elizabeth L. Eisenstein, Some conjectures about the impact of printing on Western society and thought: a preliminary report, *Journal of Modern History* (1968) 1–56, and The advent of printing and the problem of the Renaissance, *Past and Present* (November, 1969) 19–89; Albinia de la Mare, *Vespasiano and the Florentine book world* (forthcoming); R. Hirsch, *Printing, selling and reading, 1450–1550* (Wiesbaden, 1967); H. S. Bennett, *English books and readers 1475 to 1557* (Cambridge U.P., 1952); Henry F. Schulte, *The Spanish press, 1470–1966; print, power and politics* (U. of Illinois, 1968); Kenneth Charlton, *Education in Renaissance England* (1965); B. White, ed., *The Vulgaria of John Stanbridge and the Vulgaria of Robert Whittinton* (1932). Christian Humanism: J. Huizinga, *Erasmus of Rotterdam*, tr. F. Hopman (1952); P. Albert Duhamel, The Oxford lectures of John Colet, *Journal of the History of Ideas* (1953) 493–510; and see above, Religion: learning and dissatisfactions. Political thought: Felix Gilbert, Florentine political assumptions in the period of Savonarola and Soderini, *Journal of the Warburg and Courtauld Institutes* (1957) 187 seq., and *Machiavelli and Guicciardini* (Princeton U.P., 1965); R. E. Giesey, *The royal funeral ceremony in Renaissance France* (Geneva, 1960); Marc Bloch, *Les rois thaumaturges* (Paris, reprint 1961); Seyssel, *op. cit.*; Guillaume Budé, *L'institution du prince*, in C. Bontems, L.-P. Raybaud and J.-P. Brancourt, eds., *Le prince dans le France des XVIᵉ et XVIIᵉ siècles* (Paris, 1956); Erasmus, *The Education of a Christian Prince*, ed. L. K. Born (N.Y., reprint 1965); Philippe de Comines, *Mémoirs*, (Paris, 1925). Science: Edgar Zilsel, The genesis of the concept of scientific progress, in *Roots of scientific thought*, ed. P. P. Wiener and Aaron Noland (N.Y., 1957); Marie Boas, *The Scientific Renaissance*, 1450–1630 (1962); George Sarton, *Six Wings: men of science in the Renaissance* (1958); B. Gille, *Les ingénieurs de la Renaissance* (Paris, 1964); Margaret T. Hodgen, *Early anthropology in the sixteenth and seventeenth centuries* (U. of Pennsylvania, 1964); Giorgio de Santillana, The Role of art in the Scientific Renaissance, in *The Rise of Science in Relation to Society*, ed. L. M. Marsak (1964); Joan Gadol, The unity of the Renaissance: humanism, natural science and art, in *From the Renaissance to the Counter-Reformation: essays in honour of Garrett Mattingly*, ed. Charles H. Carter (1966).

Additional Bibliography
by Michael Mallett

What follows are very selective lists of books, published since 1971, which are relevant to the themes of this book. The choice has been governed in part by reference to the bibliography of Hale's *Civilisation*; this applies particularly to the section on the arts. The organisation of the original bibliography has been retained without any comments on the reading suggested.

General Works

R. Bonney, *The European Dynastic States, 1494–1660* (Oxford, 1991).

T. A. Brady, H. A. Oberman, and J. D. Tracy (eds), *Handbook of European History, 1400–1600*; I, *Structures and Assertions* (Leiden, 1994).

The New Cambridge Medieval History, VII, ed. C. Allmand (Cambridge, 1998).

D. Nicholas, *The Transformation of Europe, 1300–1600* (London, 1999).

S. Fletcher, *The Longman Companion to Renaissance Europe, 1330–1590* (1999).

J. R. Hale, *The Civilisation of Europe in the Renaissance* (London, 1993).

A. Brown, *The Renaissance* (London, 1988).

P. Burke, *The Renaissance* (Basingstoke, 1987).

R. Porter and M. Teich (eds), *The Renaissance in National Context* (Cambridge, 1992).

L. Jardine, *Worldly Goods: a New History of the Renaissance* (London, 1996).

Time and Space

F. Braudel, *The Mediterranean and the Mediterranean World in the Age of Philip II*, tr. Sian Reynolds (London, 1972).

A. Gurevich, *Categories of Medieval Culture*, tr. G. L. Campbell (London, 1985).

A. W. Crosby, *The Measure of Reality: Quantification and Western Society, 1200–1600* (Cambridge, 1996).

A. G. Debus, *Man and Nature in the Renaissance* (Cambridge, 1978).

K. Thomas, *Man and the Natural World: Changing Attitudes in England, 1500–1800* (Harmondsworth, 1984).

J-N. Biraben, *Les hommes et la peste en France et dans les pays européens et mediterranéens*, 2 vols (Paris, 1975–6).

C. Dyer, *Standards of Living in the Late Middle Ages: Social Change in England, c.1200–1520* (Cambridge, 1989).

F. Fernandez-Armesto, *Before Columbus: Exploration and Colonisation from the Mediterranean to the Atlantic, 1229–1492* (Basingstoke, 1987).

J. R. S. Phillips, *The Medieval Expansion of Europe* (Oxford, 1988).

G. V. Scammell, *The First Imperial Age: European Overseas Expansion, 1400–1715* (London, 1989).

A. Pagden, *European Encounters with the New World* (New Haven, 1992).

Political Europe

J. H. Shennan, *The Origins of the Modern European State, 1450–1725* (London, 1974).

J-P. Genet & M. L. Mené (eds), *Genèse de l'État moderne: prélèvement et redistribution* (Paris, 1987).

J. G. Russell, *Peacemaking in the Renaissance* (London, 1986).

A. Corvisier, *Armies and Societies in Europe, 1494–1789*, tr. A. T. Siddall (Bloomington, Ind., 1979).

N. G. Parker, *The Military Revolution: Military Innovation and the Rise of the West, 1500–1800* (Cambridge, 1988).

J. R. Hale, *War and Society in Renaissance Europe, 1450–1620* (Stroud, 1998).

D. Eltis, *The Military Revolution in Sixteenth-Century Europe* (London, 1995).

R. O. Crummey, *The Formation of Muscovy, 1304–1613* (London, 1987).

J. H. Elliott, *Spain and its World, 1500–1700* (New Haven, 1989).

J. N. Hillgarth, *The Spanish Kingdoms, 1250–1516: II, Castilian Hegemony, 1410–1516* (Oxford, 1978).

F. R. H. DuBoulay, *Germany in the Later Middle Ages* (London, 1983).

T. A. Brady, *Turning Swiss: Cities and Empires, 1450–1550* (Cambridge, 1985).

D. Potter, *The History of France, 1460–1560: the Emergence of a Nation State* (Basingstoke, 1995).

Y. Labande-Mailfert, *Charles VIII et son milieu: la jeunesse au pouvoir* (Paris, 1975).

R. J. Knecht, *Renaissance Warrior and Patron: the Reign of Francis I* (Cambridge, 1996).

J. Russell Major, *Representative Government in Early Modern France* (New Haven, 1980).

L. Martines, *Power and Imagination: City States in Renaissance Italy* (New York, 1980).

D. Hay and J. Law, *Italy in the Age of the Renaissance, 1380–1530* (London, 1989).

S. Anglo, *Images of Tudor Kingship* (London, 1992).

D. Loades, *Tudor Government* (Oxford, 1997).

D. Kirby, *Northern Europe in the Early Modern Period, 1492–1772* (Harlow, 1990).

N. Davies, *God's Playground: A History of Poland*, I (Oxford, 1981).

H. Inalcik, *The Ottoman Empire: the Classical Age, 1300–1600* (London, 1994).

Individual and Community

Accademia della Crusca, *The Fairest Flower: the Emergence of Linguistic National Consciousness in Renaissance Europe* (Florence, 1986).

P. Burke, *Popular Culture in Early Modern Europe* (Aldershut, 1988, 2 ed.).

N. Z. Davis, *Society and Culture in Early Modern France* (Stanford, 1975).

R. Muchembled, *Popular Culture and Elite Culture in France, 1400–1750*, tr. L. Cochrane (London, 1985).

R. W. Scribner, *Popular Culture and Popular Movements in Reformation Germany* (London, 1987).

J. Goody, *The Development of Family and Marriage in Europe* (Cambridge, 1983).

D. Herlihy & C. Klapisch, *Tuscans and their Families* (New Haven, 1985).

R. Bridenthal & C. Koonz (eds.), *Becoming Visible: Women in European History* (Boston, 1977).

I. MacLean, *The Renaissance Notion of Women* (Cambridge, 1980).

M. C. Howell, *Women, Production and Patriarchy in Late Medieval Cities* (Chicago, 1986).

M. L. King, *Women of the Renaissance* (Chicago, 1991).

J. C. Brown and R. C. Davis (eds), *Gender and Society in Renaissance Italy* (London, 1998).

Economic Europe

F. Braudel, *Civilisation and Capitalism*, tr. Sian Reynolds, 3 vols (London, 1981–4).

C. M. Cipolla (ed.), *The Fontana Economic History of Europe*, I and II (London, 1974).

C. M. Cipolla, *Before the Industrial Revolution: European Economy and Society, 1000–1700* (London, 1993).

H. A. Miskimin, *The Economy of Later Renaissance Europe, 1480–1600* (Cambridge, 1977).

P. Kriedte, *Peasants, Landlords and Merchant Capitalists: Europe and the World Economy, 1500–1800* (Leamington Spa, 1983).

R. S. Duplessis, *Transitions to Capitalism in Early Modern Europe* (Cambridge, 1997).

J. De Vries, *European Urbanisation, 1500–1800* (Cambridge, Mass., 1984).

J. D. Tracy (ed.), *The Rise of Merchant Empires: Long Distance Trade in the Early Modern World* (Cambridge, 1990).

I. Wallerstein, *The Modern World System: Capitalist Agriculture and the Origins of the European World Economy in the Sixteenth Century* (New York, 1974).

R. W. Scribner, *Germany: a New Social and Economic History, I, 1450–1630* (London, 1996).

Class

H. A. Kamen, *European Society, 1500–1700* (London, 1985).

T. H. Aston and C. H. E. Philpin (eds), *The Brenner Debate: Agrarian Class Structure and Economic Development in Pre-Industrial Europe* (Cambridge, 1985).

T. Scott (ed.), *The Peasantries of Europe from the Fourteenth to the Eighteenth Centuries* (London, 1998).

E. Le Roy Ladurie, *The French Peasantry, 1450–1660* (Aldershot, 1987).

M. L. Bush, *Rich Noble, Poor Noble* (Manchester, 1988).

J. Dewald, *The European Nobility, 1400–1800* (Cambridge, 1996).

C. Given-Wilson, *The English Nobility in the Late Middle Ages* (London, 1987).

R. Hellie, *Slavery in Russia, 1450–1725* (Chicago, 1982).

J. Edwards, *The Jews in Christian Europe, 1400–1700* (London, 1996).

Religion

S. E. Ozment, *The Age of Reform: an Intellectual and Religious History of Late Medieval and Reformation Europe* (New York, 1980).

J. Bossy, *Christianity in the West, 1400–1700* (Oxford, 1985).

M. Aston, *Faith and Fire* (London, 1985).

R. N. Swanson, *Church and society in Late Medieval England* (Oxford, 1989).

E. Duffy, *The Stripping of the Alters: Traditional Religion in England, 1400–1580* (New Haven, 1992).

J. A. F. Thomson, *Popes and Princes, 1477–1517: Politics and Polity in the Late Medieval Church* (London, 1980).

P. Partner, *Renaissance Rome, 1500–1559: Portrait of a Society* (Los Angeles, 1976).

P. Prodi, *The Papal Prince* (Cambridge, 1987).

D. Englander et al. (eds), *Culture and Belief in Europe, 1450–1600: an Anthology of Sources* (Oxford, 1990).

E. Cameron, *The Reformation of the Heretics: the Waldenses of the Alps, 1480–1580* (Oxford, 1984).

B. P. Levack, *The Witch-Hunt in Early Modern Europe* (London, 1987).

S. Clark, *Thinking with Demons: the Idea of Witchcraft in Early Modern Europe* (Oxford, 1997).

Art

A. Chastel, *The Renaissance: Essays in Interpretation* (London, 1982).

E. H. Gombrich, *The Heritage of Apelles: Studies in the Art of the Renaissance* (Oxford, 1976).

E. Wind, *Pagan Mysteries in the Renaissance* (Oxford, 1980).

L. Campbell, *Renaissance Portraits: European Portrait Painting in the Fourteenth, Fifteenth and Sixteenth Centuries* (New Haven, 1990).

A. G. Dickens (ed.), *The Courts of Europe: Politics, Patronage and Royalty, 1400–1800* (London, 1977).

R. Strong, *Art and Power: Renaissance Festivals, 1450–1650* (Woodbridge, 1984).

J. Stephens, *The Italian Renaissance: the Origins of Intellectual and Artistic Change before the Reformation* (London, 1990).

M. Baxandall, *Painting and Experience in Fifteenth-Century Italy: a Primer in the Social History of Pictorial Style* (Oxford, 1972).

F. W. Kent and P. Simons (eds), *Patronage, Art and Society in Renaissance Italy* (Oxford, 1987).

M. Kemp (ed.), *Leonardo on Painting* (New Haven, 1989).

R. J. M. Olsen, *Italian Renaissance Sculpture* (London, 1992).

R. Goldthwaite, *Wealth and the Demand for Art in Italy, 1300–1600* (Baltimore, 1993).

C. L. Stinger, *The Renaissance in Rome* (Bloomington, 1985).

M. Tafuri, *Venice and the Renaissance*, tr. J. Levine (Boston, 1989).

N. Pirotta, *Music and Culture in Italy from the Middle Ages to the Baroque* (Cambridge, Mass., 1984).

A. M. Cummings, *The Politicized Muse: Music for Medici Festivals, 1512–73* (Princeton, 1992).

Secular Learning

A. Rabil Jr. (ed.), *Renaissance Humanism: Foundations, Forms and Legacy*, 3 vols (Philadelphia, 1988).

A. Goodman and A. MacKay (eds), *The Impact of Humanism on Western Europe* (London 1990).

C. G. Nauert Jr., *Humanism and the Culture of Renaissance Europe* (Cambridge, 1995).

The Cambridge History of Renaissance Philosophy (Cambridge, 1988)

M. U. Chrisman, *Lay Culture, Learned Culture* (New Haven, 1982).

J. H. Overfield, *Humanism and Scholasticism in Late Medieval Germany* (Princeton, 1984).

H. A. Oberman and T. A. Brady (eds), *Itinerarium Italicum: the Profile of the Italian Renaissance in the Mirror of its European Transformation* (Leiden, 1975).

A. Grafton and L. Jardine (eds), *From Humanism to the Humanities: Education and the Liberal Arts in Fifteenth and Sixteenth-Century Europe* (Cambridge, Mass., 1986).

P. F. Grendler, *Schooling in Renaissance Italy: Literacy and Learning, 1300–1600* (Baltimore, 1989).

R. A. Houston, *Literacy in Early Modern Europe* (London, 1988).

E. Eisenstein, *The Printing Revolution in Early Modern Europe* (Cambridge, 1983).

M. J. C. Lowry, *The World of Aldus Manutius: Business and Scholarship in Renaissance Venice* (Oxford, 1979).

Q. Skinner, *The Foundations of Modern Political Thought*, I (Cambridge, 1978).

R. Mandrou, *From Humanism to Science, 1480–1700* (Harmondsworth, 1978).

D. Goodman and C. A. Russell, *The Rise of Scientific Europe, 1500–1800* (London, 1991).

Index

Page numbers in italics refer to maps